Hoo-Doo Cowboys and Bronze Buckaroos

HOO-DOO COWBOYS

AND

BRONZE BUCKAROOS

★ ★ ★ ★ ★ ★ ★ ★ ★ ★ ★ ★ ★ ★ ★

Conceptions of the African American West

Michael K. Johnson

UNIVERSITY PRESS OF MISSISSIPPI ★ JACKSON

Margaret Walker Series in African American Studies

www.upress.state.ms.us

Designed by Peter D. Halverson

The University Press of Mississippi is a member of the Association of American
University Presses.

First printing 2014
∞
Library of Congress Cataloging-in-Publication Data

Johnson, Michael K. (Michael Kyle), 1963–
Hoo-doo cowboys and bronze buckaroos : conceptions of the African American
West / Michael K. Johnson.
pages cm. — (Margaret Walker Alexander series in African American studies)
Includes bibliographical references and index.
ISBN 978-1-61703-928-7 (hardback) — ISBN 978-1-61703-929-4 (ebook)
1. American literature—African American authors—History and criticism.
2. American literature—West (U.S.)—History and criticism. 3. African Americans
in popular culture. 4. African Americans—West (U.S.)—Intellectual life. 5. African
Americans—West (U.S.)—History. 6. Frontier and pioneer life in literature. I.
Title.
PS153.N5J645 2014
810.9'896073—dc23   2013025422

British Library Cataloging-in-Publication Data available

Contents

Acknowledgments

Writing a book is hardly a solitary experience. As many hours as I may have logged sitting in front of my laptop, just as important to the composition of *Hoo-Doo Cowboys and Bronze Buckaroos* were the multiple conversations about the African American West and about the genre Western that I have enjoyed over the past few years.

Many of the chapters here started as conference papers, presented at conferences held by the Western Literature Association, the American Literature Association, and the Science Fiction Research Association. My colleagues at the WLA, especially Neil Campbell and Christine Bold, have contributed in multiple ways—through conversations, through their writing about the American West—to my thinking on the African American West. Past WLA president Sara Spurgeon gets a nod of thanks for her enthusiasm and encouragement in all things Whedonesque. Thanks go as well to Sabine Barcatta, Melody Graulich, and Nicolas Witschi, who helped guide to their initial publications a couple of the pieces expanded into chapters here. Likewise, thanks go to Charles Braithwaite, Wheeler Dixon, and Joycelyn Moody, for their editorial insights and assistance and to Walter Biggins at the University Press of Mississippi for guiding the book through the editorial process.

I also thank the many scholars who have taken part in conference panels on the African American West over the years and whose work has greatly influenced and helped shape my own: Bertram D. Ashe, Carolyn Dekker, Hollis Robbins, Kimberly N. Ruffin, and Joshua Damu Smith; Cynthia Miller, with whom I have presented on several occasions and with whom I share interests in the African American West, Oscar Micheaux, B movies, and science fiction and horror films; and especially Eric Gardner, Kalenda Eaton, and Emily Lutenski, who have joined me on panels at both the ALA and WLA.

Thanks go as well to Craig Jacobson, who organized a Science Fiction Research Association conference on science fiction and the Western that provided a venue for trying out my ideas on the African American sci-fi Western and that informed much of my thinking on the relationship between the two genres. And thanks to Karen Hellekson for leading me down the path to the SFRA.

I thank as well several of my colleagues at the University of Maine at Farmington who offered encouragement, insight, and good conversations about both literature and popular culture: Eric Brown, Dan Gunn, Sabine Klein, and especially Steven Pane, whose enthusiastic advocacy of sound studies contributed to my attention here to the role of sound and music in the depiction the African American West.

The Montana Historical Society in Helena holds the Emmanuel Taylor Gordon Manuscript Collection. Over the years, I have had many excellent conversations with Jodie Foley about Taylor and Rose Gordon.

Several chapters here are revised and expanded versions of articles originally published elsewhere:

"'This Strange White World': Race and Place in Era Bell Thompson's *American Daughter*." *Great Plains Quarterly* 24.2 (Spring 2004): 101–11.

"'Try to Refrain from That Desire': Self-Control and Violent Passion in Oscar Micheaux's African American Western." *African American Review* 38.3 (Fall 2004): 361–77.

"Cowboys, Cooks, and Comics: African American Characters in Westerns of the 1930s." *Quarterly Review of Film and Video* 22.3 (2005): 225–35.

"Looking for the Big Picture: Percival Everett's Western Fiction." *Western American Literature* 42.1 (Spring 2007): 26–53.

"African American Literature and Culture and the American West." *A Companion to the Literature and Culture of the American West*. Ed. Nicolas Witschi. Oxford: Wiley-Blackwell, 2011. 161–76.

Hoo-Doo Cowboys and Bronze Buckaroos

Introduction

In a column published in the 25 May 1955 *Meagher County News* under the title "My Mother Was a Slave," White Sulphur Springs, Montana, resident Rose Gordon narrates the story of a remarkable African American western pioneer, her mother. "In the year of 1881," Gordon writes, "a brown-skinned colored woman who bore the name of Mrs. Annie Gordon stood at the boat landing at Cairo, Illinois where the Ohio flows into the mighty Mississippi. Tears rolled down her cheeks and were falling on her baby boy whom she held in her arms. Her friends had gathered to bid her farewell. Her baggage and trunks had been loaded on the river steamer called the Katie. She sailed up the Mississippi River to Saint Louis and from there she began her journey up the Missouri River" (2). After three months of river travel, Annie joined her husband, John Francis Gordon, in Montana Territory. The Gordons made their way to a mining camp in Barker, where John was employed as a cook and where Rose was born in 1883. A lifelong resident of Montana, Rose Gordon grew up in White Sulphur Springs, where she assisted with her mother's catering business and eventually owned and operated a restaurant. Throughout her life, Gordon regularly submitted letters as well as articles of local history and biographical items to the *Meagher County News*, to which she eventually contributed a regular column, "Rose's Recollections."

Drawn by jobs made available by a mining boom, Annie and John Gordon were just two of the many emancipated slaves who traveled from the former slave states of Kentucky or Missouri up the river into Montana Territory and beyond. From a territory-wide population of 346 African American individuals in 1880, continuing migration brought the total African American population in Montana to 1,523 by 1900 (Taylor 135). These African American pioneers settled in Butte, Great Falls, and Helena as well as in smaller communities such as White Sulphur Springs. Irwin Smith, a talented blacksmith, preceded Annie Gordon on the journey from a former slave state to seek greater freedom and prosperity in the newly opened western territory. Arriving in White Sulphur Springs in 1880, he operated a forge in the town for twenty years. "Buggies, wagons, riding plows, etc., crowd the way in front of Irwin Smith's blacksmith shop," reports the *Rocky Mountain Husbandman* in a one-sentence item published on 11 April 1889, "while steady rings the hammer of the stalwart smith within." A pioneer settler in the Springs, the "stalwart smith" quite literally helped build the town into a prosperous turn-of-the-century resort.

From the earliest incursions into the Americas by Spanish explorers to the California Gold Rush and the Oklahoma land rush, African Americans have been present at every frontier and have been active participants in transforming those frontier settlements into thriving communities. Montana as well as all of the other western mountain states and territories (and the Plains states and the Pacific Coast) saw rising black populations after the Civil War, with those numbers increasing "thirteen fold" in Idaho, Wyoming, Colorado, New Mexico, Arizona, Utah, and Nevada between 1870 and 1920 (Katz 183).

That the stories of such vibrant and even larger-than-life historical figures as Annie and Rose Gordon and Irwin Smith remain largely invisible and untold may seem surprising, but the dominant mythologies surrounding western migration and settlement have until recently dampened investigation of the black West. However, as Peggy Riley observes, "The history of African Americans in the West, long marginalized, is emerging as a dynamic field . . . in part because of a growing recognition that blacks were active participants in the westward movement" (123). Recent books such as Quintard Taylor's *In Search of the Racial Frontier: African Americans in the American West, 1528–1990* (1998), Matthew Whitaker's *Race Work: The Rise of Civil Rights in the Urban West* (2005), Art Burton's *Black Gun, Silver Star: The Life and Legend of Frontier Marshal Bass Reeves* (2007), Douglas Flamming's *African Americans in the West* (2009), and the anthologies *African American Women Confront the West*, edited by Quintard Taylor and Shirley Ann Wilson Moore (2003), and *Buffalo Soldiers in the West: A Black Soldiers Anthology*, edited by Bruce A. Glasrud and Michael Searles (2007), provide evidence for Riley's claim that specialists in African American history are reinvigorating the study of the historical development of the American West.

If the history of African Americans in the West has become an emergent field of study, literary history is still lagging far behind. Even in the context of a spate of such publications as Noreen Groover Lape's *West of the Border: The Multicultural Literature of the Western American Frontiers* (2000) and Nathaniel Lewis's *Unsettling the Literary West:*

Authenticity and Authorship (2003) that have worked to revise and expand the canon of western American literature to include the work of minority writers, anthologies of western literary criticism contain, as Eric Gardner observes, "at best, a radically limited sense of the black West" (Introduction xxvii). Individual articles on African American western writers have appeared in journals and anthologies, but only three book-length studies of the African American literary West have been published: Michael K. Johnson's *Black Masculinity and the Frontier Myth in American Literature* (2002), Blake Allmendinger's *Imagining the African American West* (2005), and Eric Gardner's *Unexpected Places: Relocating Nineteenth-Century African American Literature* (2009). Indeed, the lack of literary criticism related to the black West leads Gardner to comment, "The first step in this process may simply be recognizing that there *was* a black literary West, one that reached back well into the nineteenth century, and one that most scholars have ignored" (Introduction xxvi).[1]

This paucity of critical literary and cultural studies work on the black West stands in direct contrast to the richness of the field of available texts depicting and imagining African American western experience, which includes such traditionally defined literary documents as memoirs and novels as well as other forms of literature such as letters, newspaper columns, and periodical writing in general. To the available field of documents, we might add depictions of African American western experience in such mediums as music, film, and television. Beginning the task of understanding the African American West requires that we let go of the paradigms that limit our ability to strike out into new territory as well as to revise and expand the ways literary history has conceptualized the West as a field of study. Most important, it requires us to reconsider a restricted notion of the literary text and be more open to the discovery of the full richness of the ways the African American West has been experienced, imagined, written, represented, and performed. *Hoo-Doo Cowboys and Bronze Buckaroos* moves us further in that direction by exploring the available textual material and by suggesting several interpretive frameworks for understanding these representations of the African American West.

★

In both memoirs and fiction, writers have documented the experiences of black western pioneers. The earliest account may be *The Life and Adventures of James P. Beckwourth* (1856), an as-told-to biography of the life of the famed trader, scout, and the discoverer of Beckwourth Pass through the Sierra Nevada mountains. Thomas Detter's *Nellie Brown; or, The Jealous Wife, with Other Sketches* (1871) was, as Dan Moos points out, "the first book published by an African American in the American West" (*Outside* 90). Although the title story is set in Virginia, Detter's autobiographical sketches describe his experiences (and encounters with racism) living in Idaho. Mifflin Wistar Gibbs's *Shadow and Light* (1902) describes his journey to seek out "hidden opportunities in a new country" in gold-rush California, where he arrived in 1850 (37). *The New Man* (1895) is Henry Clay Bruce's account of his escape from Missouri slavery to freedom in Kansas. In *Black Frontiersman: The Memoirs of Henry O. Flipper, First Black Graduate of West Point* (1916), Flipper narrates his experiences with the Tenth Cavalry while stationed in Oklahoma and Texas. Nat Love's *The Life and Adventures of Nat Love, Better Known in the Cattle Country as "Deadwood Dick"* (1907) is probably the best known and definitely one of the most written-about narratives of the African American western experience. Love's photograph, posed with a saddle and rifle and wearing his cowboy clothes, has become the iconic image of the black cowboy. Oscar Micheaux features less gunslinging and more farming in his autobiographical novels, *The Conquest: The Story of a Negro Pioneer* (1913) and *The Homesteader* (1917), which focus on his experiences homesteading in South Dakota. Rose Gordon's brother, Taylor Gordon, wrote in his autobiography, *Born to Be* (1929), of his childhood in turn-of-the-century Montana before turning to the story of his rise to fame as a spirituals singer in the 1920s. Robert Ball Anderson's *From Slavery to Affluence: Memoirs of Robert Anderson, Ex-Slave* (1927) is a memoir of homesteading in Nebraska. Era Bell Thompson focuses similarly on homesteading experiences (in North Dakota) in her autobiography, *American Daughter* (1946).

Although memoir and autobiography have been the primary forms of African American western writing, fiction (particularly for contemporary writers) has also been an important mode for depicting black western experience. Sutton Griggs's *Imperium in Imperio* (1899) reimagines Texas as an all-black state within the larger United States. Pauline Hopkins's *Winona: A Tale of Negro Life in the South and the Southwest* (1902) adapts the tradition of the dime-novel Western to tell a story of conflict between slavery and antislavery forces set on the Kansas-Missouri border. In addition, numerous contemporary African American writers have depicted black experience in the historical West. Several of Anita Scott Coleman's short stories from the 1920s and 1930s are set either in the American Southwest or in California, drawing on the author's experiences living in Silver City, New Mexico, and in Los Angeles.² Pearl Cleage's play, *Flyin' West* (1995), takes place in turn-of-the-century Nicodemus, Kansas, one of the all-black towns established by the Exodusters. Toni Morrison's novel *Paradise* (1998) focuses on an all-black town in Oklahoma. Percival Everett, who in novels such as *Watershed* (1996) and *Wounded* (2005) often writes about contemporary black western experience, visits the Old West in his satirical novel, *God's Country* (1994), a parody Western that follows in the footsteps of Ishmael Reed's story of the Loop Garoo Kid (the "Hoo-Doo cowboy") in *Yellow Back Radio Broke-Down* (1969). David Anthony Durham's *Gabriel's Story* (2001) is a more serious take on the Western genre, a violent coming-of-age story centered on title character Gabriel. Bruce Glasrud and Laurie Champion's *The African American West: A Century of Short Stories* (2000) collects a range of short fiction. We might observe as well recent fiction by white writers such as Paulette Jiles, who bases the story of one of the characters in her novel, *The Color of Lightning* (2009), on her archival research into the life of Britt Johnson, a free black man who lived in Texas near the end of the Civil War.

The richness of this material as well as other African American writing about the West leads to the question of why the African American contribution to the literary West remains mostly undiscovered territory. Some of the issues that have long plagued western history have also been problematic for literary history. As Matthew Whitaker writes in *Race Work: The Rise of Civil Rights in the Urban West* (2005), his biography of Lincoln and Eleanor Ragsdale and their civil rights activism in Phoenix, Arizona, the dominant story of the West (influenced by historian Frederick Jackson Turner) has "posited that rugged Anglo American pioneers, fighting to subdue an ever-expanding western frontier, ushered in the taming of the wilderness, civilization, and a process of self-definition" (9). A vision of western history that has opposed "chivalrous white men" and "barbaric Indians" has had literally no place for African Americans: As neither conquerors nor indigenous inhabitants of the West, they fall outside the established categories (9). African American authors have faced the challenge of finding a way to write their specific experiences of race and place into an existing narrative that has no vocabulary for articulating those experiences.

In "My Mother Was a Slave," for example, Rose Gordon's description of her own birth demonstrates the difficulty of articulating her identity as a black westerner through the dominant conventions of frontier narratives: "I was born in this mining camp and claim the distinction of being the first white child born there. All the rest of the babies were Indian babies. I was delivered by an Indian woman." The story of Rose's individual life begins here, with the conventional "I was born" opening of the slave narrative, a connection to African American tradition and identity that is subsequently erased by her claim to being "the first white child born there," seeming to mean the first non-Indian born in what was formerly Indian territory. Born to a black former slave, delivered by an Indian midwife, and destined to grow up in a predominantly white community, Rose's sense of identity is more complicated than the vocabulary made available for her by existing narratives of western experience. She thus falls back on the traditional racialized white/Indian opposition in her attempt to describe her place in the story of western settlement.

The Life and Adventures of James P. Beckwourth suggests another reason that such experience has gone relatively unnoticed. Biographer Thomas Bonner makes no mention of Beckwourth's race. Such erasures, intended perhaps to make the stories of black western heroes acceptable to white audiences, contribute to a dominant vision of the American West "as a region with few if any African Americans and virtually no black history" (Whitaker 9). We see similar erasures taking place in other fields. In folk song collector John Lomax's typology of American ballads, he separates "cowboy" songs from "negro" songs and describes the archetypal cowboy in distinctly white racial terms as a descendant of "King Arthur" (quoted in Cantwell 71). In the collection *Cowboy Songs and Other Frontier Ballads* (1910), John and Alan Lomax write that the cowboy "brought the gallantry, the grace, and the song heritage of their English ancestors" (quoted in Cantwell 70). However, as Robert Cantwell points out, "Lomax collected his most famous song, 'Home on the Range,' not from a golden-haired prairie Galahad but from a black cook, who once worked a chuck wagon on a Texas cattle trail, in a 'low drinking dive' of San Antonio" (72). "Delivering the cowboy songs retroactively into the hands of an imaginary cowboy Galahad, even as it anglicized a racially and ethnically hybridized subculture," histories of "cowboy songs" by Lomax and others "consistently obscured black collaboration" in the creation of the culture of American folk songs (72). That collaboration, Cantwell argues, "was not a 'contribution' or a 'corruption' but a full participation in the vernacular culture that the black and white working classes" had created and shared beginning in the nineteenth century (72).

Percival Everett's contemporary novel, *God's Country*, ostensibly tells the story of Bubba, a black cowboy and expert scout and tracker. *God's Country* reads at times like a parody of *The Life and Adventures of Nat Love* and at other times as a commentary on the genre of the as-told-to biography to which *The Life and Adventures of James P. Beckwourth* belongs. Like Nat Love, Bubba is a heroic black cowboy who accomplishes seemingly impossible feats of daring with his fists and his gun. Like *The Life and Adventures of James P. Beckwourth*, the story of this particular African American scout is told by a white narrator, but while Bonner conceals his authorial voice, Everett creates a white narrator, Curt Marder, whose consciousness—and whose conscious prejudice—stand at the forefront of the story. Through Marder's narration, Everett comments on the way that white-authored histories of the American West have erased or obscured black collaboration in western experience. The novel begins when Marder's house is burned down and his wife kidnapped by white outlaws. Marder hires the African American Bubba to find the woman; Bubba agrees to do so for the price of half of Marder's homestead. Immediately after making the agreement, however, Marder loses the whole homestead in a card game, a fact that he never shares with Bubba and that says much about Marder's character or lack of it. The only thing Marder has going for him is his whiteness, and the only time that whiteness is much of an asset is when Bubba does something useful or heroic, for which Marder takes the credit.

Bubba fixes the broken wagon wheel on the stranded stagecoach, Bubba knocks General Custer cold with one punch, and Bubba guns down the fastest gunfighter in the West, but Marder mistakenly thinks he's telling his own story rather than Bubba's. The filtering consciousness of Marder's narration produces a disjunction between his response and Bubba's actions that contributes both to the humor of the tale and to its implicit critique of white narratives of westward migration. As we often have to look to the margins of historical accounts of the West to see the real presence of African Americans, so do we have to look to the margins of the story Marder tells to find out about Bubba.

Even for those African Americans who have told their stories without the filter of a white biographer (or the obscuring frame of a white folk song collector), erasure of race is one of the dominant tropes of black western writing, and it is a troubling one that has contributed to the relative absence of consideration of the black West not only in dominant culture accounts of the American West but also in African American literary history. As Houston A. Baker Jr. observes, "Tales of pioneers enduring the hardship of the West for the promise of immense wealth are not the tales of black America," even though such tales of enduring frontier hardship for the promise of wealth (or at least a good steady income) are indeed the tales of African American individuals such as Oscar Micheaux, Nat Love, and Robert Ball Anderson (2). The mythic western narrative is a story of opportunity and conquest, of obstacles overcome, of rebirth and transformation. Those works by African American writers that follow those conventions sometimes do so at a cost—the erasure or at least the understated depiction of racial identity and difference. Such erasures (or seeming erasures) have also contributed to negative critical assessments of these books, which have often focused on their incorrect or inaccurate portrayals of racial relations. The "tales of pioneers" and the "tales of black America" are inevitably opposed to one another, and the individual narrative must fall on one side or the other of that opposition.

Thus, as the title of Joseph Young's *Black Novelist as White Racist: The Myth of Black Inferiority in the Novels of Oscar Micheaux* (1989) suggests, there is no potential for complexity in Micheaux's negotiation of early twentieth-century racial discourse. He is a black man who has completely accepted white dominant culture views of black identity, so much so that he has become a (black) "white racist." However, in considering the African American West, we will discover that oppositions of all sorts are difficult to maintain, and the work of African American western writers often contains complex (and even contradictory) representations of racial experience—even if criticism about that work has not always recognized that complexity. Between "the tales of pioneers" and the "tales of black America" is an unexplored textual space still in need of explication. Following deconstructive reading practices, we might regard race as being placed under erasure, *sous rature*, in these texts, bracketed but not eradicated. Much work needs to be done to understand the strategies (and we might consider erasure not as a betrayal or a failure but as a representational strategy) that African American writers have used to adapt unfriendly and even hostile cultural narratives to articulate their own experiences.[3]

The Life and Adventures of Nat Love, which follows the mythic story line of opportunity, conquest, rebirth, and transformation in telling Love's life history, provides a good example of the strategy of erasure. A former slave, Love leaves Tennessee in 1869 for Kansas, where he begins a career as a cowboy and becomes part of an integrated group of predominantly white cowboys, "as jolly a set of fellows as on[e] could find" (41). After proving he knows how to ride a wild horse with the best of them, Love is accepted as an equal in the group. His membership becomes further cemented by a fight with a group of Indians, during which "I unlimbered my artillery and after the first shot I lost all fear and fought like a veteran" (42). Love presents his experiences as a model of perfect assimilation into white society. Within a vision of western history that has opposed "chivalrous white men" and "barbaric Indians," Love aligns himself with the "chivalrous white men," his own otherness seemingly erased by violent action against "barbaric Indians."

The Life and Adventures also tells the type of story that Quintard Taylor has referred to as the new myth of African American life in the West (replacing the "old myth" of a West in which blacks were absent), the "stereotype of the black westerner as a solitary figure loosened from moorings of family, home, and community" (22). The solitary black westerner is such a popular stereotype that he has been a staple character in Western films from the silents and early sound films to contemporary movies. The black westerner transcends race in part by separating himself from the black (eastern) community to become a member of a white (western) society. However, even a book that follows this "new myth" as neatly as Love's narrative does can at the same time undermine it. For the frontispiece of the book, Love has chosen a photograph of himself posing with his wife and daughter. The photograph tells a different story (of Love's continuing connection to African American community, of the importance of family and home) than the narrative. The photograph suggests silently that Love's life history tells another story about African American western experience, one that is not narrated but that he nonetheless chose to represent visually. Rather than a complete erasure of race, Love's identity in *Life and Adventures* exists between the textual absence of verbal racial markers and the photographic presence of the same.[4]

If some nineteenth- and early twentieth-century writers have adapted erasure as a strategy, other writers have taken the opposite approach, using their experiences of continuing racial prejudice in the American West to critique and contest the myth of an egalitarian and exceptional West. For example, in *Shadow and Light*, Mifflin Wistar Gibbs goes to California seeking "hidden opportunities in a new country" (37). He finds not opportunity but another set of limitations on black achievement. While life in California might be better for African Americans than in other parts of the country, "from every other point of view they were ostracized, assaulted without redress, disfranchised and denied their oath in a court of justice" (46). Life in the West, it turns out, can be very much like life in the East.

Thus, we might make two observations about African American narratives of western experience. They often repeat the dominant myths of western history and tell stories of an exceptional West where the limitations of race can be transcended and the African American individual can find prosperity and equality. They also often tell the opposite story—of hopes for a new life crushed by the existence of unexceptional western prejudice. The first type of narrative follows white western conventions to the degree that it no longer seems to fit within the category of African American literature, especially in terms of the element of "social protest" against inequality that has been central to African American writing from fugitive slave narratives to the contemporary novels of Alice Walker and Toni Morrison. The second type of narrative calls into question the myth of western exceptionalism and thus has been marginalized as "unrepresentative" of western experience. Which story of African American experience in the West is true?

That is perhaps the wrong question to ask, as it assumes an opposition that is not supported by the available textual evidence, which suggests that African American western experience is sometimes paradoxical and that both the myth of western exceptionalism and the revisionist critique of that myth contain elements of truth. As Blake Allmendinger observes, "African Americans disagree about whether or not the West is a place of promise," so we may find that the West of Oscar Micheaux and Nat Love is not the same West as that of Henry O. Flipper (*Imagining* xvii). The whole picture that emerges of African American life in the West is a complicated one, suggesting the existence of both prejudice and opportunity.

In *Imagining the African American West*, Allmendinger writes, "I came to realize that there is no such thing as a 'representative' African American western experience" (xvi). Rather, "there are many different impressions of place, just as there are many different types of racial experience," an observation that is borne out by the diverse and often complicated responses to western experience found in the work of black writers and in the many different mediums and forms through which the African American West has been imagined (xvi). The variety of historical experience, combined with the variety of primary materials, much of which does not fit neatly within traditional paradigms, requires us as scholars to be open-minded and to continue to develop flexible methods for understanding and interpreting this expanded archive of the African American West.

★

Hoo-Doo Cowboys and Bronze Buckaroos undertakes an interdisciplinary exploration of the African American West. The title of the book comes from two sources, Reed's *Yellow Back Radio Broke-Down* and Herb Jeffries's film, *The Bronze Buckaroo* (1938), and is indicative of the book's twin examinations of written and audiovisual narratives. Reed's hero, the Loop Garoo Kid, is described as a Hoo-Doo cowboy. The Kid wanders the wild frontier of the American West, but he is also a priest and practitioner of Vodun, Voo-Doo, or Hoo-Doo, which Reed describes as an American version of ancient African religion. The portrayal of the shape-shifting Loop Garoo Kid also draws on tales of African and African American tricksters. Jeffries's singing cowboy films, from *Harlem on the Prairie* (1937) to *The Bronze Buckaroo*, likewise incorporate elements of African American culture—including trickster tales—into their western stories and settings. One of the threads the book follows is the character type of the African American westerner as trickster as that figure appears across a variety of media texts.

The backbone for my exploration of these disparate texts involves not only an interest in the trickster archetype but also two key conceptual ideas, erasure (as described earlier) and twoness. The exploration of what W. E. B. Du Bois calls "double-consciousness" has long been considered a central element of African American writing, and it is thus not surprising to discover twoness in representations of the African American West. Chapter 2 looks at twoness in Micheaux's *The Homesteader,* a novel that tells the story of Jean Baptiste, whose success depends on his willingness to leave the black East and become part of a community of white homesteaders in South Dakota. The novel's primary tension derives from Baptiste's efforts to both operate his farm and maintain his connection to Chicago's black community. In *American Daughter,* which I examine in chapter 3, Thompson finds herself similarly torn between her allegiance to the beautiful North Dakota prairie that she comes to love and the "land of my people" back east, "the world of colored girls and boys as well as white, of colored stores and churches, of big city lights" (159). One of the clever ways that both Micheaux and Thompson adapt western conventions to better reflect African American experience is to revise the Western's traditional West/East opposition to illustrate double-consciousness. Torn between the opportunities available in the predominantly white society in the West and the sense of belonging to African American community back east, black western writers sometimes externalize their internal division through narratives that emphasize movement from one place to another. This projection of the internal experience of twoness onto the external landscape is a central feature of representations of the African American West that cuts across various media. Chapter 5, "Oscar Micheaux, *The Exile*, and the Black Western Race Film," continues the discussion of double-consciousness in Micheaux's work by shifting from his novels to his films, specifically the silent era *The Symbol of the Unconquered* and the early sound era *The Exile*. The chapter also examines the influence on later black-audience filmmakers of Micheaux's cinematic representations of the frontier and of twoness.

Because the texts that I examine reference more than a century of African American experience (from the descriptions of touring minstrel bands in the 1890s to the work of contemporary novelist Percival Everett), the tropes of double-consciousness and erasure will be articulated differently not only according to the geographies of the places where the narratives occur but also depending on the specific historical context. Thus, Micheaux's American West is not the same as the West of the civil rights era. As the photographs that accompany Nat Love's written autobiography suggest, narratives that employ different types of storytelling media may use the available tracks to tell contrasting stories. In the case of film and television, the different tracks of sound and image may be employed—in a similar way that word and image function in Love's *Narrative*—to accomplish the double move of erasure and reinscription that is an important component of African American western texts. Therefore, my analysis takes into account both the varying geographies of place and the different strategies of depiction, erasure, and reinscription put in play at different historical moments and through the particular formal elements of various types of media.

Rather than attempting a comprehensive or complete overview of African American western texts, I emphasize close readings of select texts from a variety of media with a primary focus on literature, film, and television. This approach allows for both an in-depth analysis of individual texts and a discussion of material often left out of or underrepresented in studies focused only on traditional literary material: heretofore unexamined writing by Rose Gordon, who wrote for local western publications rather than for a national audience and whose writing I examine in chapter 3; memoirs and letters of musicians, performers, and singers (W. C. Handy, P. G. Lowery, Taylor Gordon) who lived in or wrote about touring the American West, the topic of chapter 1; black-audience films, including those of Micheaux and the series of black-cast *Harlem* Westerns starring Jeffries, topics discussed in chapters 4 and 5. The book's final three chapters examine contemporary texts. Chapter 6, "Sammy Davis Jr., Woody Strode, and the Black Westerner of the Civil Rights Era," looks at a group of largely unappreciated and unexamined episodes from the golden age of Western television (from the late 1950s into the 1970s) that feature African American actors, using Davis and Strode as the primary lenses; this chapter also briefly discusses a group of blaxploitation-influenced Westerns starring Fred Williamson. Chapter 7 examines Percival Everett's short stories and novels addressing contemporary black western experience. Chapter 8 looks at film and television Westerns that use science fiction settings to imagine a postracial or "post-soul" frontier, focusing primarily on the Hughes Brothers' film *The Book of Eli* and the Joss Whedon television series *Firefly*. A short conclusion briefly addresses 2012's *Django Unchained*, directed by Quentin Tarantino and starring Jamie Foxx in the title role.

As Quintard Taylor writes, despite recent interest, "we still know woefully little about large areas of the African American past in" the West (23). In addition we still know woefully little about how the African American past in the West has been depicted in a full range of imaginative forms. *Hoo-Doo Cowboys and Bronze Buckaroos* takes us another step further in the journey of discovering how the African American West has been experienced, imagined, and performed.

Performing (in) the African American West

*Minstrel Shows, Brass Bands, Hoo-Doo Cowboys, and
Other Musical Tricksters*

In his autobiography, *Father of the Blues* (1941), W. C. Handy remembers being on tour with the Mahara's Minstrels troupe in 1896 and visiting the "10th U.S. Cavalry at Fort Missoula, Montana, and marvel[ing] at the spic and span cavalry band on horseback—all Negroes except the English bandmaster. Horses maneuvered at the sound of the bugle, instruments flashed in the sun, stirring music echoed and re-echoed across the plain. The pageantry of the scene won me. I wanted to join up then and there, but yielded to persuasion and remained with the show" (65). Although we might associate Handy most closely with places made famous by his songs, such as Memphis or Beale Street, the first third of his autobiography narrates in detail his travels in the American West. In those travels, Handy interacted with and was indeed inspired by the African American western communities that he encountered. Through travel, Handy claims national space as his own, inhabiting and experiencing many American localities, all of which, the autobiography suggests, directly and indirectly influenced his later musical compositions. Proclaiming himself the Father of the Blues and thereby the father of America's most American music, he constructs a national identity that is based in musical performance. His description of the Tenth Cavalry band suggests the importance of his western experiences to that construction—an assertion of national identity through a performance made all the more majestic by the Montana plains that serve as a stage.

Like Handy and the members of the Tenth Cavalry band, other African American professionals and amateurs in the West used musical performance as a strategy for making visible and audible their participation in local and national communities. In the context of limited access to

American public space, taking possession of the stage (or the city streets through which brass bands often marched) became a means of claiming a place in the public sphere. This chapter places Handy's autobiography in the context of other African American writing related to musical performance in the West: Montana-born singer Taylor Gordon's autobiography, *Born to Be* (1929); newspaper items about cornet player and bandleader P. G. Lowery from his hometown, Eureka, Kansas; correspondence from other traveling minstrel shows and bands published in the *Indianapolis Freeman* (an African American weekly newspaper with a national circulation), including columns written by "The Smart Set" headliner Salem Tutt Whitney.[1] Within the pages of these memoirs and newspapers, whether they are narratives of travel or stories of settlement, we have extensive documentation of African Americans making homes for themselves— and making themselves at home—in the American West through performance.

In telling their stories and in constructing their personas as narrators and as performers, these writers also draw on African and African American culture's rich history of trickster tales. Contemporary African American writers who have set stories in the American West, such as Ishmael Reed and Toni Morrison, explicitly allude to both African and African American folklore, including the trickster tradition. Handy, Gordon, and Whitney similarly evoke that tradition, although they do so more covertly. The allusions to black folklore in these earlier texts suggest the existence of a continuing tradition of shared imagery and themes in African American literature of the American West that stretches from the late nineteenth-century to the present.

These writers/performers also reveal the complex effect of the legacy of minstrelsy on African American experience, identity, and history. At the same time that minstrel performance (with or without blackface) provided employment opportunities and freedom of mobility (at a time when both were sharply restricted) for black performers, conforming to minstrel tropes also created limitations against which performers struggled. The endurance of those tropes and stereotypes—and whites' expectations that black performers (and black people in general) would play out those roles—would affect black performance well into the twentieth century.[2]

Although associated primarily with the American South, minstrel troupes performed throughout the American West in the latter half of the nineteenth century and into the twentieth. Groups traveling via railroad and performing beneath portable canvas tents or inside established theaters followed routes that took them through Texas and into the Indian territory of Oklahoma and beyond or through the upper western states—Nebraska, the Dakotas, Colorado, Wyoming, Montana, and so forth. As a correspondent for the Famous Georgia Minstrels wrote in a piece published in the *Indianapolis Freeman* on 26 July 1902, "We are at last in Montana. . . . The show meets a hearty welcome all through this country, but it should as it has been living in the West straight along for several years and a visitor to the West for nearly thirty years. Hence it is very clear why the Georgias can always meet with success in the West." In addition to groups of traveling African American performers, amateur minstrel companies sprang up throughout the West, with local white performers blacking up for the occasion.[3] But not all amateur minstrel performance in the West involved white performers. In some places, local African American performers took to the stage in their western towns and cities, performing their own version of minstrelsy or entertaining their fellow citizens by forming "colored" brass bands or groups of "Jubilee" singers. Whether they were travelers or settlers, African Americans used performance as a strategy for making themselves at home in the American West.

Black musical performance, whether in the form of African American brass bands or minstrel shows (traveling or local), was a fact of late-nineteenth- and early twentieth-century western American culture. In spite of the limitations it created and the stereotypes it promoted, minstrelsy was an important element of African American western experience and of the representation of black westernness in multiple forms—performance (theatrical and musical), film, television, and written texts.[4] African Americans who migrated west at the end of the nineteenth century used musical performance strategically, as a rallying point for the black community and as a means of creating visibility for that community in the public sphere. Handy's *Father of the Blues* can best be understood in the context of other African American experiences with musical performance in the West, as turn-of-the-century black westerners made themselves at home through these performances. By juxtaposing stories of black performance in specific black communities located in particular western places with narratives of traveling black professional performance groups, this chapter demonstrates the development—on both the local and national levels—of African Americans' shared strategy of using musical performance to claim civic public space.

Born in Topeka, Kansas, in 1869, Perry George Lowery grew up in the Flint Hills community of Eureka, Kansas, in Greenwood County, just east of Wichita. He became the first black man to graduate from the Boston Conservatory of Music and went on to enjoy a long career as the "World's Greatest Colored Cornet Soloist" and as bandleader for numerous groups, ranging from the Fashion Plate Minstrels to sideshow bands for such major circuses as the Hagenbeck-Wallace Shows and the Ringling Brothers.[5] As Clifford Edward Watkins observes in *Showman*, Lowery was also a barrier-breaking black performer. As late as 1913, the refusal of his Fashion Plate Minstrels to perform in blackface "remained noteworthy" (91). Lowery assertively resisted both blackface conventions and segregation practices in the performing world. After beginning his twelve-year tenure with the Ringling Brothers in 1919, Lowery quickly broke the long-standing circus tradition that segregated black performers in the sideshow tents: "On April 17 [1920], the *Freeman* noted that Lowery's group had become the 'first Colored band to play a feature number in any big show'" (114).

Lowery's family arrived in Kansas as part of a wave of postbellum African American settlement in the state. Preceding the more modest black migration to Montana and other mountain states but similarly drawing migrants from former slave states who passed through St. Louis as the gateway west, a decade of African American movement to Kansas culminated in the Kansas Fever Exodus of 1879, the first major mass African American migration westward. Kansas's black population increased from 16,250 in 1870 to 43,110 in 1880 (Painter 146). Kansas drew migrants because of its combination of "ample homesteading lands and abundant crops" and its reputation as "the quintessential Free State, the land of John Brown" (Painter 158–59). In addition, Nell Irvin Painter writes, "old abolitionist, temperance Republicans ruled the state, and they held out precisely the same welcome to Black settlers as to white. This even-handed sense of fair play amounted to an open-armed welcome, in comparison to much of the rest of the country at the time" (159). Like other western states, Kansas was no paradise of racial equality, but those western places seemed to offer black settlers more opportunity than did the states they left behind. And at a time when there was a rapidly spreading epidemic of lynching in the South, they certainly found a greater sense of safety.

Greenwood County also had a history of opposing slavery. By 1880, the census indicated eight black families in the county, and items in the county newspaper, the *Eureka Herald*, suggest several forms of African American civic involvement, including attending Republican political conventions, the enrollment of children in the local school, and participation in the community's musical culture (C. E. Watkins 5). As Clifford

Edward Watkins notes, "Brass bands were quite the rage at the end of the Civil War, and the Lowery family band apparently met with great success in the Eureka area" (7). In March 1875, the *Herald* printed a challenge from the "Star of the West Brass Band of Eureka" (the Lowery family band) to the Eureka Brass Band for a "trial of skill" (7). The *Herald* reported later that year of a "great parade and celebration" on 4 July with a procession that included "fifty wagons" as well as "two cornet bands and a martial band" ("Century"). One of those cornet bands was likely the Star of the West, marching with its rivals in a conjoined celebration of national belonging.

Eureka was not the only western town with a participatory black performance culture that ultimately produced a performer with a national reputation. Taylor Gordon was born in 1893 in White Sulphur Springs, Montana, at the time a thriving resort town located on the stage route between the Missouri River town of Fort Benton to the east and Helena to the west. Gordon, with partner J. Rosamond Johnson, enjoyed a period of fame in the 1920s as a singer of spirituals and as author of the autobiography *Born to Be*. Like many African Americans migrating to Montana, the Gordon family followed a path from Cairo, Illinois, to St. Louis and then traveled up the Missouri River by steamboat to Fort Benton. In the 1890s, when Handy was touring through Montana, White Sulphur Springs had a small but significant African American community—thirty to forty individuals in a town of a few thousand residents.

The visibility of this black community, especially as reported in the local white-owned newspapers, makes White Sulphur Springs an unusual western town, a trait that the Springs shared with Greenwood County, Kansas.[6] As early as 1889, the *Rocky Mountain Husbandman* reports on the formation of a "colored cornet band." From 1889 through 1893, the *Rocky Mountain Husbandman* and the *Meagher County News* (the two papers printed and published in White Sulphur Springs) recorded a flourishing of such performance groups. The members of the cornet band joined other African American residents of Meagher County to form the Home Colored Minstrel company, which put together a full-length minstrel show for the community. On 8 April 1892, the *Meagher County News* printed,

> the programme of the Home Colored Minstrel company, which will give their first performance at O'Marr's hall, on Thursday evening, April 14, 1892. It will be an evening of mirth, and those who fail to attend this concert will

miss a treat. The quick change artist, Bob Langhorn, will make complete changes in costume in three seconds, and is without peer in this line. When Mrs. Mason comes on the stage "Jess unloose yo vest."

Following is the programme:

PART FIRST

OPENING CHORUS . . . . By Company

OVERTURE, Minstrel; bones, Mason; Tambourine, Langhorn; interlocutor, M. Organ.

PART SECOND

JUBILEE SONG, "Put on Your Old Shoes," by Company.

SONG, "Kathleen," . . . . Mrs. Wellman

QUARTETTE, "Where Have You Been So Long?" John Smith, Robert Langhorn, Mrs. Mason, George Mason

PART THIRD

OLD PLANTATION ACT, "Picking Cotton," by Company

TAMBOURINE SOLO . . . . by Langhorn.

PART FOURTH

JUBILEE SONG, "One More River to Cross," by Company

SONG, "Old Black Joe," Laura Howard, Maud Smith, Robert Langhorn, Robert Gordon

QUICK CHANGE ARTIST . . . . . Robert Langhorn

FINALE "Breakdown" . . . . Company

Admission, 50c.; reserved chairs, 75c.

Drummers George Mason and Irvin Smith (performing here under the stage name of M. Organ) and cornet player Robert Langhorn were members of the cornet band, while Robert Gordon was Taylor Gordon's older brother. A talented multi-instrumentalist who specialized in the violin, Robert became a mainstay of turn-of-the-century White Sulphur Springs musical and performance culture. Minstrelsy, with its reliance on stereotyped images of African American people, is certainly a form of participation in the public sphere that has its limitations. However, the program suggests that the Home Colored Minstrels took the opportunity to offer a less tendentious version of minstrelsy than that performed by white minstrels. The song titles include no references to chickens or razors (to note just two stereotyped tropes of blackface minstrelsy) and very little of the fractured dialect associated with minstrelsy. The program does not suggest that the audience will see an "authentic" portrayal of plantation life, as was standard in minstrel shows. Rather, the emphasis is on the unusual and unique skills of the performers, especially Bob Langhorn's abilities as quick-change artist and tambourine soloist.

But the performances by members of the African American community in White Sulphur Springs were also intended as something more than mere entertainment. The Home Colored Minstrels saw their performances as a contribution to the civic life of the community that they indeed called "Home." On 21 April 1892, the *Rocky Mountain Husbandman* published a letter "To the People of White Sulphur Springs":

> Through the kindness of the publishers of this paper we take this opportunity of explaining our position and extending thanks. In the first place we wish to say that we have not engaged in the entertainment business for the purpose of making money for ourselves individually. This we are abundantly able to do at hard labor—at the flaming forge and other honorable vocations—but, having incurred a considerable debt in equipping a cornet band with instruments, uniform and band wagon, which is a public enterprise, and designed as such, we thought it would not be out of place to ask the people of the town and valley to assist us by patronizing an entertainment gotten up among our people for the purpose of paying off our indebtedness. We gave the entertainment, you turned out en mass, and the desired end has been accomplished; our band has been freed from all encumbrances and we desire to express to you our sincere thanks and gratitude for your generosity. Now we wish to state further as an evidence of the appreciation of what you have done for us in this matter that we propose to give an entertainment, or series of entertainments, the net proceeds of which we will apply towards the erection of the proposed town hall. Again thanking you for your most generous patronage, and hoping to further assist in enterprizes designed for the good of our town, as well as furnish you an occasional pleasant evening, we remain sincerely yours,
>
> THE COLORED JUBILEE SINGERS.

Independent and self-sufficient, supported through their own hard labor in "honorable vocations," the members of the company and of the cornet band considered their performances "a public enterprise, and designed as such"—a contribution by the black citizens of the town to the betterment of the whole. This remarkable letter suggests that the African American citizens saw White Sulphur Springs as "our town" and saw themselves in partnership with the town's white majority in the public enterprise of civic improvement.[7]

At a minimum, the letter demonstrates a rhetorical move on the part of the writers, an assertion of belonging and equality voiced in the public sphere through the newspaper. Just how much their fellow citizens were willing to allow the African Americans to participate in the public enterprise of town building is another question. The newspaper record in White Sulphur Springs suggests a greater openness among the white majority than we might expect. Smith, for example, successfully operated his blacksmith business in the Springs for over twenty years. His advertisements in the local newspapers provided a steady and consistent income stream for those publications, and his activity at the smithy quite literally helped build White Sulphur Springs from a frontier town into a thriving turn-of-the-century resort.[8]

Both Taylor Gordon and P. G. Lowery ultimately left home to forge their careers, but both had relatives who stayed in their hometowns and maintained connections to their western homes through periodic letters to the local newspapers and by making sure that their tours passed through those towns. In so doing, they continued to make black performance an important element of the public lives of those communities, keeping black citizenship a visible element of civic life in those western places. As Clifford Edward Watkins writes, newspapers "provided Lowery with a constant connection to his home. His letters to the publications became news reports, which in turn became a source of pride for the citizens of the Eureka, Kansas, area" (20). When Lowery returned in 1896 with his stepbrother and fellow musician, E. O. Green, as part of a tour with the Nashville Students, the *Eureka Herald* reported that the "two Greenwood boys" were "prime favorites with our people, having spent much of their life in this county, and the fine attendance on both occasions was largely due to the regard of our people for them. [Lowery and Green] expect to be at home, Spring Creek township, in a couple of weeks for the summer" (quoted in C. E. Watkins 27). In the early part of his career, Lowery frequently returned "home," even spending the whole winter season in 1902 in Reece, Kansas, "where he directed the town's band and gave private music lessons" (Berresford 35).

The African American citizens of White Sulphur Springs and Greenwood County used musical performance as a means of making a home in those western communities. Newspaper accounts of those performances suggest an American West that was more amenable to African American participation in American citizenship than other parts of the country, at least between 1890 and 1910. These newspaper accounts suggest that minstrelsy (and musical performance more generally) represented a widespread turn-of-the-century African American strategy for claiming space in the public sphere. However, such performances constituted a complicated and sometimes compromised means of asserting African American community and national belonging, as Handy's *Father of the Blues* reveals.[9]

W. C. Handy was born in Florence, Alabama, in 1873, son of a Methodist pastor who strongly disapproved of musicians. "I'd rather follow you to the graveyard than to hear that you had become a musician," he at one point told his son (*Father* 11). However, Handy was undeterred by parental disapproval: "If, as my father often said, 'You are trotting down to Hell on a fast horse in a porcupine saddle,' I rode with a song on my lips and its echo in my heart" (303). Handy's entertaining memoir, *Father of the Blues*, is a narrative explanation of how he came to be associated with blues music and how he came to write two specifically regional songs, "The Memphis Blues" and "The St. Louis Blues," that earned him a national (and international) reputation. Handy did not invent the blues, but his compositions helped popularize the folk music form that became known as the blues. *Father of the Blues* is simultaneously the story of the birth of the blues as a popular form and a story of Handy's musical education. And despite the title, Handy's role as he describes it in the memoir is at various times mother, father, and midwife to the blues.

"With all their differences," Handy observes, "most of my forebears had one thing in common: if they had any musical talent, it remained buried" (*Father* 5). Handy's skill as a musician and, more important, the songs that he composed result from experience, not heredity. In particular, *Father of the Blues* suggests that his experiences as a young traveling musician provided the basis for his later blues compositions. Even the birdsongs of his childhood contributed to his musical understanding of the world. *Father of the Blues* is in some ways an autobiography comprised of sounds as Handy travels through an America that is itself a nation of distinctive sounds: a snatch of a lament women sing while the broke and homeless Handy tries to sleep on a cobblestone levee in St. Louis; the whistle of riverboats on the Tennessee River; the bellow of bulls in a field; the scrape of "a twenty penny nail across the teeth of the jawbone of a horse" (14); the rat-a-tat-tat machine-gun-like noise made on drums by stones thrown by rowdy white boys at a black marching band; the "strange, tortured sound" that escaped from the lips of fellow musician William Malone when he slept (67); the "weirdest music" played by "a lean, loose-jointed Negro [who] had commenced plunking a guitar beside me" at a train station (74); the "haunting" sounds made by three men playing battered instruments at a Mississippi dance (77).

Published in 1929, Taylor Gordon's memoir, *Born to Be*, preceded Handy's autobiography by more than a decade, even though Handy was the older of the two men and was already famous by the time Gordon made his first appearances singing spirituals with J. Rosamond Johnson in 1925. The two men knew each other (Handy and Johnson were friends), and various elements of *Father of the Blues* suggest that Gordon's memoir influenced Handy's narrative. Both begin their stories with pastoral childhood scenes that suggest that their musical interests were inspired by the sounds of nature. Both titles suggest the importance of generation and creation to the men's life stories. Gordon was "born to be," he asserts, and his memoir is the story of that becoming. Handy's story is in some ways an Oedipal narrative, as suggested by the conflict with his father that begins the story and by the details of his ascendancy to the status of not just father but *the* Father. Rather than organizing his memoir through a series of conflicts with other men (as Handy does), Gordon, whose father died in a train accident before he was born, structures his story as a search for a father (or a father figure), with multiple individuals filling that role: Montana ranch owner B. H. Sherman, who "adopts" Gordon and teaches him how to be a cowboy; circus impresario John Ringling, who aids Gordon in setting out on his life adventures by hiring him as a personal porter for his private railway car; Johnson, Gordon's teacher and performing partner; and Carl Van Vechten, a friend who supported Gordon financially at various times (and who provided the foreword for *Born to Be*).

The railway played an important part in both Handy's and Gordon's lives, and much of the early part of Handy's narrative details his travels by rail throughout the country. Similarly, a significant section of *Born to Be* describes Gordon's adventures as the porter in Ringling's private railway car, a position that enabled Gordon to see much of the country. Rail travel provided both men with a means to greater mobility, physical and financial. Train travel also inspired Handy's songwriting, especially his "Yellow Dog Blues," and Gordon's big break came when composer Will Marion Cook heard Taylor singing from inside Ringling's railcar as he was walking past. Although Gordon was not yet a professional performer, the circus followed similar routes to the traveling bands, and Gordon's train travels in the 1910s took him through some of the same places as Handy, Lowery, and Whitney.

The most significant connection between the two books is in their representation of the American West in general and, specifically of Texas and Montana. For both Gordon and Handy, Montana functions as an ideal place, a refuge from the prejudice in the rest of the country. Helena is the site of Handy's first recording experience, the place where Mahara's Minstrels recorded several songs for a local Edison outlet. Helena is also the site of the memoir's only observation of an interracial couple, an African American lawyer and his white wife. Montana was the location of Fort Missoula and the location of the Tenth Cavalry, an important symbol of national belonging in *Father of the Blues*. Gordon depicts Montana as the place where his exuberant personality was allowed to flourish but portrays southwestern places such as Texas and Oklahoma as just the opposite. In Houston with the circus, Gordon dresses up—a "new Jack Johnson plaid suit, patent leather shoes, hotcap"—to see the town (116). He is immediately collared by "a man dressed in a gray civilian suit, slouch Stetson hat, with a big star, nearly six inches across, on his left breast" (116). The Texas lawman informs Gordon that he "can't come in here with those clothes on" (116). Gordon returns to the railcar and changes back into his porter's red cap and uniform.

For Gordon, Texas is just another southern place, the Stetson hat of the lawman just a bit of western window-dressing, but Handy represents Texas more ambivalently—as a crossroads of sorts on the frontier between the South and the West and as such a mixture of both. That portrayal is consistent with the picture of Texas that emerges in the *Indianapolis Freeman*. To understand both the actual historical experience of minstrel bands traveling in the South and West and the rhetorical functions those places serve in minstrel accounts, it is important to look at the representation of Texas as a crossroads place that serves multiple purposes in minstrel narratives and in *Father of the Blues*.

★

A key experience in Handy's development was his time with Mahara's Minstrels. He traveled with the troupe of musicians and performers from 1895 to 1903, and his account of his experiences serves in some ways as a defense of minstrelsy, at least as performed by African Americans: "The minstrel show at that time was one of the greatest outlets for talented musicians and artists. Some of them were paying for education of brothers and sisters, some taking care of aged parents, others supporting their own families, but all contributing to a greater degree of happiness in the entertainment world" (Handy, *Father* 62). As Lynn Abbott and Doug Seroff write in *Ragged but Right: Black Traveling Shows, "Coon Songs," and the Dark Pathway to Blues and Jazz*, "Minstrelsy has become another 'forbidden' subject, lately reduced to a metaphor for historical racism in popular culture" (7). However, they argue against the confusion of blackface minstrelsy performed by white actors with the performances of "African American minstrel companies of the ragtime and blues era" (7). These black companies "stole the audience away from the pale imitators, thus opening a pathway of employment for hundreds of musicians, performers, and entrepreneurs" (7).

As Adam Gussow observes, "A central paradox of *Father of the Blues*" and perhaps a central paradox of minstrelsy in general lies in the performer's "willingness as minstrel, songwriter, and bandleader to wear the mask of the 'reliable,' the submissive and trustworthy Negro . . . while simultaneously engaging in overt and coded racial revolt against the 'hard conditions' southern life imposed on him" (68).[10] The particular double-consciousness of the turn-of-the-century black performer is documented quite clearly in *Father of the Blues*. The necessity of "wearing the mask," of sometimes strategically adopting the minstrel role, is one example of the twoness that existence in American society forced African Americans to adopt. As Karen Sotiropoulos writes in *Staging Race: Black Performers in Turn of the Century America*, "Du Bois did not have stage artists in mind when he so eloquently described black America's psyche in *Souls of Black Folk*," but "work on the popular stage made African American performers hyper-conscious of the veil, of that 'peculiar sensation' that Du Bois had described . . . of 'always looking at one's self through the eyes of others'" (2). We see Handy and other performers in *Father of the Blues* engaged in various levels of masking and racial role playing, onstage and off, as they negotiate the complex interracial politics of an unequal social system in which wealth and power were concentrated in white hands. Wearing the mask could be figurative or literal (as in the case of blacking up to play the minstrel role onstage), but whatever the case, such masking was a strategic move—in keeping with African and African American trickster traditions—that aided black survival in dangerous circumstances. In addition, by taking advantage of white expectations about black people (that they are entertaining performers), minstrelsy and black musical performance in general provided an avenue for asserting a black presence in a community's public space and consciousness.

Adopting the minstrel mask also enabled African American performers to engage critically with stereotyped representations of blackness as "they manipulated the stage mask in innovative ways that helped them forge a space for dialogue with their black audiences—dialogue that included both assertions of black nationhood and critique of the racism that perpetuated stereotyped imagery" (Sotiropoulos 2).[11] Continues Sotiropoulos, "Black entertainers consciously used racist stereotypes in their performances in part to distance themselves from these images, since it was abundantly clear (at least to themselves and their black audiences) that they were *performing* these roles, not embracing them as representative behavior" (9). In contrast to the white minstrels who preceded them, black entertainers promoted their shows "as entertainment rather than ethnology," as "performance rather than as a depiction of authentic African American life" (Sotiropoulos 36–37). Performers used various strategies to draw attention to this role playing *as* playing. A singer might perform both classical opera and "coon songs" (comic dialect songs) as part of the same program. Within a skit (and sometimes within a song), performers might shift back and forth between dialect and standard English. Publicity materials (especially those used in the black press) often included "portraits of the actors offstage and in formal wear, rather than onstage and in makeup" (Sotiropoulos 99).[12]

When the Home Colored Minstrel company performed in White Sulphur Springs, a similar strategy was employed. Turn-of-the-century African American performers—amateur and professional—considered minstrelsy a public enterprise. When representing themselves in the public forum of the newspaper, they adopted various roles as part of a strategy of self-presentation that was situational. In White Sulphur Springs newspapers, the performers represented themselves quite differently in the two published documents. In the minstrel program, they speak as entertainers. In the letter "To the People of White Sulphur Springs," they speak as fellow citizens engaged in the joint enterprise of progressive civic uplift. The letter underscores that the show was an entertaining performance. The performance itself served a larger civic purpose, and once completed, the performers returned to their other community roles "at the flaming forge and other honorable vocations." The letter to the newspaper not only thanked the people of the Springs for their attendance at the "entertainment" but reminded them of the fictional nature of that performance. Although the Home Colored Minstrel company was a decidedly local group of amateur performers, we see them here employing strategies similar to those of national performers, suggesting that with regard to asserting civil rights, a creative interchange was taking place between the local and national, with local groups of African Americans influenced by (and perhaps, in turn, influencing) civil rights activism at the national level.

Newspaper accounts of P. G. Lowery's travels and performances similarly emphasize the public enterprise of a working musician, but the weakness of newspaper accounts in general as a source of historical information is that they only seldom take us beyond the surface of the public face. As an autobiography, *Father of the Blues* not only describes the activity of the entertainer but also takes us into the consciousness of the performer, showing us what is going on beneath the mask of a public enterprise. However, Handy's strategic and adept deployment of masking may have prevented many readers from seeing beyond that surface and may have contributed to the lack of critical interest his book has received. As Gussow writes, "The apparent lack of overt protest in *Father of the Blues* may well be one reason for its near total neglect by critics of African American autobiography," an observation that could be applied equally to Gordon's *Born to Be* (71). That "lack," however, is only "apparent," as social protest in *Father of the Blues* sometimes appears in covert form, the protest elements subordinated to Handy's dominant story of achievement and success—a story that, in Houston A. Baker Jr.'s critique of the autobiography, is "a simplistic detailing of a *progress*, describing, as it were, the elevation of a 'primitive' folk ditty to the status of 'art' in America" (*Blues* 4). As Gussow argues, however, "Handy's detailing of his entrepreneurial ascent is shadowed always by his uneasiness at the continuing threat posed by white violence, a threat that he both evokes and resists and that renders *Father of the Blues* anything but a simplistic uplift narrative" (69).

What also renders *Father of the Blues* as something other than a "simplistic uplift narrative" or even just another rags-to-riches self-made-man memoir is Handy's emphasis on drawing from multiple generic forms in his composition. He is as eclectic in his use of literary tropes as he is in his collecting and listing of American sounds. Handy deftly brings together the African American folklore tradition of the trickster tale with the literary traditions of social protest and that of the Western. His stories of his travels and travails with Mahara's Minstrels juxtaposes descriptions of antiblack violence and racial protest with a narrative of Wild West adventure. Doing so enables Handy to articulate his particular version of social protest through the conventions of the Western, which offer a structure that enables both a critical depiction of white violence and a justification for violent self-defense. The strength and weakness of social protest literature is in its vivid portrayal of victimization. The Western provides Handy with a form that allows him to combine a critique of white racism and its effects on black people with an equally vivid narrative of black resistance. Those Western elements, however, may also have contributed to the critical neglect of *Father of the Blues*, placing the autobiography outside the dominant paradigms of African American studies and perhaps concealing too effectively the book's protest elements. A careful reading of the Mahara's Minstrels section of the memoir, however, brings those elements to the forefront and reveals Handy's clever braiding of disparate narrative threads and generic conventions.

When "prairie rowdies" threaten to bust up the show one night in Texas, a cowboy-hero steps out of the pages of a dime novel. A single Texas Ranger, Handy writes, shows up to protect the company: "One of them could, and sometimes did, rout a hundred bullies at a time" (*Father* 44). Even the company's managers, the Irish Mahara brothers, contribute to the sense that we have stepped into an Old West adventure. Jack Mahara, Handy writes, "won his spurs in the days of the Dalton gang. He was riding with other passengers on a Texas train when the outlaws came aboard and ordered everyone to his knees. Jack obeyed, along with the others, but he stayed down only long enough to whip out his gun and open fire" (44). Handy similarly cowboys up, putting together a "private collection of arms, a Winchester 44, a Smith and Wesson and a Colt revolver" (48). During a band rehearsal in Montana, another performer leaps from the stage to threaten Handy's friend, Jim Turner, and Handy goes "directly for my gun. During the remainder of the rehearsal I kept it plainly exposed" (57). Handy observes, "A legend promptly went abroad in minstrel circles, a legend to the effect that I always laid my gun on the desk during Mahara's band rehearsals. This, obviously, was something of an exaggeration" (57). He is rarely described with weapons in other parts of the memoir and never again so dramatically as in the western sections of the narrative. With his Winchester rifle and Colt revolver, each of which has been popularly known as the "gun that won the West," Handy claims as his own a place in western history (and western myth). However, in contrast to Nat Love's cowboy adventures, playing the western role for Handy does not mean a concomitant erasure of racial identity.

As we might expect in a Western, Handy encounters "outlaws" and "prairie rowdies," but he joins the Western convention of the "outlaw" with that of social protest by revealing that these particular Wild West rowdies are motivated by racial prejudice. When traveling by train through the Texas town of Orange, the minstrels learned "to extinguish the lights and lie quietly on the floor" of their car, as the "conception of wild, he-man fun" for the "home town mob" was "to riddle our car with bullets as it sped through their town" (44). In another Texas town, while playing "a cornet solo in the public square during the noon concert," Handy observes "a rifle pointed at my eye. . . . A few moments later, the drums rumbling as we began to march back to the theatre, a gang of cowboys appeared and began roping our walking gents with their lassos" (43).[13] The rhetorical thrust of Handy's social protest comes via his use of ironic contrast. Here, Western conventions are reversed, the "gang of cowboys" represented as the villains rather than the heroes.

Although, from a contemporary perspective, we might not immediately think of a minstrel band's parade as a radical act, Handy demonstrates that in certain communities, the public space of the square, the street, and the stage was contested space and that claiming that space was a potentially deadly action. As Gussow observes, "The black minstrels were projecting themselves across the South as a glorious, enviable spectacle during a decade when white racist reaction was concerned with restricting black freedom of movement through public space" (88). Parading through the streets, the band members seated on a spectacularly outfitted wagon, "the minstrels transformed their bodies, not to mention their mobile accommodations, into spectacular emblems of black uplift—inspiring to black audiences, potentially infuriating to local whites" (88). The danger to traveling black musicians, whether those travels took them through the South, the Southwest, or the Far West, was such that Frank Mahara installed a "bear-wallow" or "get-away," a secret compartment in the floor of the railcar that at times held food reserves, weapons, and even Handy himself after an incident in Tennessee brought a town sheriff in search of him (*Father* 45–47). Other accounts by traveling musicians similarly demonstrate the potential danger of performing in public.

Mahara's Minstrels were not the only group that had problems in Texas. Similar incidents appear with some frequency in "The Stage," the section of the *Indianapolis Freeman* devoted to letters and reports from traveling musicians. In the 30 September 1899 edition of the *Freeman*, the correspondent for Melroy, Chandler, and Company's Real Negro

Minstrels reports, "While our business far exceeded expectations in the Lone Star State, everybody was glad enough to say good-by to Texas at Whitesboro last Wednesday night, and the majority of the members of the company declare it their last visit to Texas—'You aint nothing but a nigger no how in Texas' so they say." The correspondent for Allen's New Orleans Minstrels reported in the 5 January 1901 *Freeman* about a Christmas Day show in San Angelo, Texas: "The parade left the cars at 11:45 and when we reached the square the porches were crowded with men and boys, who had bundles of fire crackers, and as the parade passed, fire crackers fell in showers, but the boys gave them no attention and marched ahead. The intention was to break up the parade, but they were unsuccessful. Mr. Viccas, one of the oldest, quietest and best liked members of this company, had his left eye injured by the bursting of a cannon cracker" (quoted in Abbott and Seroff 219). Handy's account of the band's parade being followed by "a gang of cowboys" shows a similar pattern. In addition to the men, "a swarm of rowdy boys joined in the fun and threw rocks down the bell of the big bass horn. Then the kids turned on the drums. They pelted our drums so vigorously the noise sounded like the rat-a-tat-tat of a machine gun" (*Father* 43–44). In both incidents, the attack on the minstrels also takes acoustic form, with the attackers attempting to make louder or competing noises (the sound of firecrackers, the pelting of the drums with rocks) as a way of disrupting the performance and ultimately as a way of controlling sonic as well as physical space. In both cases, the bands answer noise with pointed silence, refusing to entertain but steadfastly keeping to their parade. Handy writes, "I was furious and stoutly refused to play a note during the parade. We marched faster than usual," but like the New Orleans Minstrels, Handy's troupe "kept our ranks" (44). Such strategic retreats appear at various places in *Father of the Blues* and in other accounts of minstrel performances. The protest here is a covert one, a notable silence that speaks, a refusal to play the role of entertaining and subservient black as well as a refusal to allow the gathering mob the pleasure of completely disrupting the band. In both incidents, we also see a calmness in the face of potential calamity—"We kept our ranks," the "boys gave them no attention and marched ahead"—an ordered retreat that both subverts the mob's intention (to break up the parade) and protests the crowd's bad behavior (stoutly refusing to play).

In Handy's narrative, Texas "cowboys" perform dual roles as both heroes and villains, Texas Rangers protecting performers from "local badmen [who] boasted that they would break up our show" as well as a "gang" that disrupted the march by "roping our walking gents with their lassos" (44, 43). That duality appears in other ways as well, as Texas emerges in several minstrel accounts as a crossroads space, both southern and western, sullied by the restrictions and potential antiblack violence associated with the Deep South but also reflective of the "opportunity" asserted to be available less ambivalently in other western states. Large black populations in Dallas and other urban areas made parts of Texas particularly friendly as well as profitable. A correspondent from the Famous Billy Kersands Minstrels observes in the 28 October 1905 *Indianapolis Freeman*, "The weather has been more than favorable and the business phenominal all through this section of the country (Texas) is nothing but a continuous seal of praise from press and public. We have furnished a week of the greatest business ever done by the company. We play San Antonio, Houston, Galveston, Waco, Temple and Beaumont, the big cities of the State in the same week." However, when traveling in areas *without* friendly black populations, Texas could be a challenge. Augustus Stevens, with the New Orleans Minstrels, reports in the 16 November 1901 *Freeman* that "we have been in anti Negro towns for about three weeks. Some of them where colored people have not been seen for seventeen years." Given that trying three weeks, the letter continues, "you know how glad the boys were to get to Ft. Worth. After the show there was a grand ball given for the boys."

Another traveling company, the Smart Set, also had Texas troubles. During the 1909 season, its members "bounced around Texas for . . . two months," where headliner Salem Tutt Whitney found "the hospitality of the Texans [to be] unbounded"—at least in the state's black communities (quoted in Abbott and Seroff 111). Outside of those black communities, however, "a different reality prevailed," especially for a company that had not hired a private railway car for travel and thus had to rely on public transportation and housing (112). A 13 November 1909 letter from the company observed, "In some towns they were unable to obtain anything to eat or a place to lodge. . . . At one place the men had to make a guard line around the women to keep the white men from assaulting them" (quoted in Abbott and Seroff 112).

As these comments suggest, the concerns of traveling minstrel companies converged with those of all African Americans living in a segregated society that prohibited their participation in American public space—access to public transportation, finding a place "to eat or a place to lodge," protection from assault. In the early twentieth century, the theater itself became a staging ground for black activism against a specific form of segregation. Discussion of segregated seating in theaters (where African Americans were often relegated to the balcony) appears frequently in the *Freeman*. As Sotiropoulos writes, calls in the black press for "a war on segregated seating" demonstrate "how much black performers, critics, and audiences had established the performing world as a sphere for struggle" (74). In his periodic column in the *Freeman*, Whitney often touched on the subject. In the 20 March 1915 issue, he relates,

> In Mexia, Texas, the balcony of the new opera house seats about 450 persons. This was reserved for colored people during our engagement there. The lower floor was held for the whites. Long before time for the performance the colored people had packed the balcony and more than 300 were clamoring for entrance at the doors. The lower floor contained not more than 200 whites, leaving room for 400 more persons. A white stage hand, looking through the peephole in the curtain, expressed the sentiments of all when he said "It's a d—— shame to turn all those colored people away." . . . The local manager was fearful that [allowing the African Americans seats downstairs would start] a race riot. I remarked to the stage manager that I was certain if the house manager would let me go before the audience and explain that this was an attraction especially given for the colored people, that it was their one opportunity in a year to see their own people perform. . . . If he could give me the chance to say this to the white audience I was certain they would give up a portion of the downstairs to the colored. . . . Any one familiar with conditions of the south will realize that it was a ticklish occasion. I stepped before the footlights, claimed their attention and proceeded. I hardly remember what I said, but I first appealed to their sense of fairplay, then to their humor, then to their reason, with the result that every white person in the audience applauded my remarks; all moved forward and allowed the colored people to sit on the same floor with them without any rope or canvass being stretched to mark the line of distinction.

Slipping back through the curtain, Whitney discovers "several members of the company backed up against the emergency exits, all claimed they anticipated a fire alarm," indicating by their action that they had less confidence in their company leader's ability to win over a white audience than he did. Whitney's comments here and elsewhere are indicative of the way the state of Texas appears in the pages of both the *Freeman* and Handy's memoir—that is, as an ambivalent place in the early twentieth-century battle over public space. In some accounts, white Texans violently opposed black incursions in public space; in other cases, they were surprisingly accommodating, "allow[ing] the colored people to sit on the same floor with them without any rope or canvass being stretched to mark the line of distinction." If not completely erased, the color line here is made decidedly less visible. The account also suggests the adeptness with which performers such as Whitney, Handy, and others negotiated such "ticklish occasion[s]." "I hardly remember what I said," Whitney writes, "but I first appealed to their sense of fairplay, *then to their humor*, then to their reason, with the result that every white person in the audience applauded my remarks." Using multiple rhetorical strategies (fair play, humor, reason), Whitney wins over the audience, apparently deploying his minstrel skills (appealing to the audience's "humor") when necessary but also stepping outside that role.[14] In so doing, Whitney manages the desegregation (if only temporarily and partially) of this particular public space, using his position as an entertainer to expand the public access rights for several hundred African Americans.

Whitney closes this anecdote by commenting, "I mention this circumstance because we have been unable to obtain like conditions in some theaters in northern cities." As Sotiropoulos observes, for black performers and audiences, gaining equal access to the stage and the theater were not side issues but were a central part of a "broader political trend of challenging segregation and exclusion in larger society" (74). The rhetorical thrust of Whitney's account is to use the reasonableness of the Texas audience to comment on the unreasonableness of segregated seating in other parts of the country, in effect nationalizing this local incident.

For some performers, the best part about Texas (or at least the second-best part, after the moneymaking opportunities) was leaving it. As the correspondent for Allen's New Orleans Minstrels reported a week after the firecracker assault, "The boys are wearing smiles on their faces because they heard that 10 more days puts us out of Texas. It is true that we broke the record for business in Texas this season, but we want some other country for awhile" (quoted in Abbott and Seroff 219). In *Father of the Blues*, Handy likewise registers his ambivalence about Texas, finding in some places a freedom and opportunity quite different from his descriptions of traveling elsewhere in the South. However, Texas is also the site of the most dangerous incident that Mahara's Minstrels experienced, one that almost resulted in the deaths of the entire group.

In *Yellow Back Radio Broke-Down*, Ishmael Reed explicitly draws on African and African American trickster traditions in constructing his Western hero, the Loop Garoo Kid. The Kid wanders the Wild West like many a cowboy-hero, but, unlike, say, Roy Rogers, Reed's character is also a priest and practitioner of Vodun, or Voo-Doo, or Hoo-Doo, which is, Reed writes, "an American version of the Ju-Ju religion that originated in Africa" (152). If the practice of Vodun connects the Kid to his African roots, his membership in a traveling circus performing across the frontier connects him as well to this specific element of African American western history. Like Handy and Whitney, the Kid's first experience of the American West is as a traveling performer.

With Jake the Barker, the Juggler, the Dancing Bear, Zozo Labrique ("charter member of the American Hoo-Doo Church"), and Loop Garoo riding broncos, bulls, and performing amazing lariat tricks, the circus's "fame spread throughout the frontier and bouquets of flowers greeted them in every town until they moved into that city which seemed a section of Hell chipped off and shipped upstairs, Yellow Back Radio" (10). Other elements of the story similarly suggest a connection to the history of traveling black performance groups. The Kid's flamboyant cowboy outfit, with its "pink fringed black buckskin," suggests the costume of a stage performer, as does Zozo's "corncob pipe," a prop used in minstrelsy to suggest the rural south (117, 12). With "a full skirt and a bandana on her head," Zozo's clothing similarly suggests minstrel costuming (12).

As they approach Yellow Back Radio, the traveling performers discover that the children of the town, tired of forced labor and learning "facts by rote," have rebelled against the adults, kicked them out of town, and "decided to create our own fiction" (16). White ranch owner, villain, and occasional cross-dresser Drag Gibson has his own plans—to distract the children with the circus and take back the town. After a fabulous and entertaining performance, "the children reveled and danced around," bedding down with the troupe "beneath warm buffalo robes" (25). Loop Garoo awakens "to find horsemen surrounding the circle," children screaming and burning from torches tossed by the men (26). Before she dies, Zozo tells Loop Garoo, "Don't forget the gris gris, the mojo, the wangols old Zozo taught you" (26). Barely escaping the ensuing slaughter, the Kid vows to take vengeance: "Never again will they burn carnivals and murder children" (62). Loop Garoo indeed employs Zozo's lessons to create a "tailor made micro-Hoo-Doo-mass" that is the first step in his counterattack on Drag Gibson, the Pope, and their various cronies (63).

Reed's fanciful tale of Hoo-Doo, traveling circuses, rebellious children, and the nefarious collusion of a cross-dressing ranch owner and the Pope has its uncanny parallels in stories told by actual black performers touring the West, both in its depiction of the dangers faced by those performers and in its story of a defiant trickster evading those dangers.

Trickster tales, especially those coming out of an American context, "were among the most popular and commonly expressed varieties of slave folklore, and outside of physical resistance and rebellion, probably represented the most aggressive and cynical view of white America expressed by slaves" (Mel Watkins 70). Although often based on African tales or using variations on African characters (such as the West African Elegba or the Ashanti spider trickster Ananse, who often appears in African American tales as Aunt Nancy), the African American trickster stories coming out of the period of enslavement were adapted to those circumstances, their meanings sometimes concealed through the allegorical medium of animal stories or sometimes rendered more directly in, for example, the stories of John (sometimes Jack) the slave who (almost) always outwits "Ol' Massa." Animal stories, such as the Brer Rabbit stories collected in Joel Chandler Harris's Uncle Remus tales, often "depict the triumph of physical weakness, hypocrisy, mischievousness, trickery, and cunning over brute strength and guilelessness" (M. Watkins 72). "It is now generally accepted," Mel Watkins writes, "that Harris's tales were based on black American stories firmly based in the West African tradition of storytelling—one in which fables and tall tales provided entertainment but were also used for moral instruction and protest" (72). Whether the enslaved John or the animal Brer Rabbit was at the center of these stories, a consistent theme was the weaker character overcoming the stronger one, often through a combination of fast thinking and fast talking.

★

At first glance, Taylor Gordon's connection to either African or African American tradition may be difficult to see as a consequence of his primary rhetorical strategy, which involves representing himself as a Montana-born westerner raised outside the influence of social notions of race or racial identity. Robert Hemenway observes in his introduction to the 1975 edition of *Born to Be* that Gordon invents "an ingenious strategy for protesting prejudice, one of the frequent themes of Black autobiography" (x). Knowing that white America might consider a black writer's exposure of racism as "proof that one's personality has been distorted by it" (xxiii), Gordon claims for himself a persona formed outside of society, "the role of the romantic child of nature" (xi). "What a lucky bird I am," writes Gordon, "to have been laid on top of the Rocky Mountains, hatched out by the Broiling Sun, a suckling of Honey Bluebacks and educated by the Grizzly Bear, with all the beauty and fresh air Nature can provide for her children" (234). Gordon's persona as a "raceless innocent," as a "lucky bird . . . educated by the Grizzly Bear" rather than by experience in a racially stratified society, enables him to position himself as an ironic observer of life in the segregated southern and eastern areas of the United States.

What we see here is again the strategy of erasure. We will also see Gordon employ the counterpoint to erasure, the reinsertion of black difference through other means. By using his Montana innocence as a springboard for protesting the racial restrictions he finds elsewhere in the country and by covertly introducing African influences and trickster elements into a narrative that on the surface seems to fall outside the main currents of black autobiography, Gordon returns to the narrative those central elements of African American memoir (social protest, depiction of black culture) that are seemingly erased. Gordon's pose as "raceless innocent" is also undermined at various moments when he reveals himself to be very much aware of his race—even when he is surrounded by the beauty of the Rocky Mountains. One of his earliest jobs in White Sulphur Springs is working for the brothels that line one of the side streets. He delivers messages for prostitutes, whose customers "were not all miners and bachelors. I fitted right in the network perfectly on account of the pigment of my skin. I was accepted both high and low, never questioned why or what I was doing in conspicuous places" (17). In White Sulphur Springs, Gordon asserts, "my face was a passport stamped in full" (17). As Hemenway notes, Gordon "understood at an early age white assumptions about a Black man's place" (xxvii). His "passport" is not so much his "face" as his awareness of white beliefs about what activities represent appropriate black behavior. That is, Gordon, from early childhood on, knows very well how to wear and manipulate the minstrel mask that is his—and other early twentieth-century African Americans'—"passport" through the dominant white culture.

Gordon also indicates a belief (consistent with African cosmology) that ancestral spirits visit and influence the living. Those spirits, in the form of disembodied voices, aid him throughout the autobiography. One key element of African culture that Gordon evokes is the belief in "many African societies" that the "dead return to the living world either in body or in spirit" (Higgins 29). The dead fall into two categories: "Ancestral and non-ancestral spirits," and these spirits "both protect and potentially harm" (30). At least in his early life, Gordon seems to associate "the dead" primarily with the potential to harm, which makes him the easy target of ribbing and practical jokes from the older men in White Sulphur Springs. Rancher C. H. Sherman teases Gordon "about being afraid of the dead" and tries to convince him to visit a grave site at night (45). Gordon comments, "My brothers had told me so much about ghosts and Mother was so superstitious I wouldn't go," even though he was offered "ten head of young heifers and a bull" if he would (45). Oddly, Gordon then comments, "What I know about the dead now! It makes me sigh to think of that deal" (45). This statement stands out because Gordon does not explain it. What indeed does he now "know about the dead"?

What Gordon "knows" remains implicit, although he hints at various points that supernatural forces have intervened to come to his aid. Again and again throughout the book, he uses the phrase "something told me," the repetition of which suggests a reference to African cultural beliefs in protective spirits that he weaves into his autobiography primarily as a subtext. What is this "something" that seems to speak in Gordon's ear, especially at moments of stress or potential danger? Refused service in a St. Paul, Minnesota, restaurant, Gordon writes, "I can't describe the lonely feeling that came over me. I have never felt like it since. It seemed as though everyone whom I knew had died at once" (68). After this reference to death, he comments, "Something told me that if I didn't move, I would have a fight" (68). After offending a white man in Florida by not using *mister* when addressing him, Gordon comments, "Some thing told me then that I shouldn't go down South too many times" (110). At a moment of potential danger, Gordon receives a warning from an unknown source—either his own unconscious or, interpreted from the perspective of African cultural beliefs, a thing that has Gordon's best interests in mind. The printing of the word *something* as two words, as *some thing*, might lead us to ask what the "thing" that speaks is. As these examples demonstrate, Gordon sometimes uses the phrase "something told me" as a substitute for "my intuition told me" or "common sense told me." However, at other times, this voice of intuition provides Gordon with information that seems to originate from somewhere outside his own mind.[15]

In one of the many scenes in which he adopts the role of trickster, Gordon plays a trick on a fellow Ringling employee, Fred Loomis, with whom he has a running feud. John Ringling loves German pilsner beer, which he keeps in an icebox and which is off-limits to anyone else. Loomis likewise has a fondness for the German beer and claims that he has Ringling's permission to drink it, which Gordon doubts. Gordon observes, "My mind was working overtime. I was trying to think how I could trick that guy. He set the empty bottle and glass nearly in the center of the dining-room table. . . . Something told me John Ringling would be in town on the six A.M. train. Leave that bottle and glass right there, and see what he'd say when he saw it. I did" (135). The voice here provides Gordon with very specific information—"something told me John Ringling would be in town on the six A.M. train"—that goes well beyond the sort of common sense advice he sometimes receives. Maybe the "something [that] told me" here is Gordon's unconscious reminding him of information that he knew but had forgotten or that had become newly relevant, but the sentence is not written that way. Having informed Gordon of Ringling's train schedule, something then speaks to him in the form of a command ("Leave that bottle and glass right there") and thus provides him with the bait for his trap. Ringling indeed arrives on the early train, sees the empty bottle, and asks about it; Gordon responds, "Oh, the private secretary had it. He said you didn't care." As Gordon notes, "When we left Atlanta, old Sec was not with us. And the rest of the summer I spent in peace" (136).

Gordon's consistent portrayal of himself as a trickster suggests his knowledge of African American folklore. Gordon's persona also draws on the African folktale tradition associated with Elegba (or Legba), a West African trickster deity who often mediates between opposing realms (heaven and earth, God and human).[16] Connected to transitional spaces such as crossroads, doorways, and windows, Elegba is associated with change and movement. Most important, Elegba is the deity associated with music and musicians, and Gordon's descriptions of his performances as a singer evoke Elegba's role as a mediator between heaven and earth, for he experiences singing spirituals as an act that brings together the living and the dead. Elegba's association with music, with change and movement, also makes him an important figure in the context of the other trickster/musicians.

Gordon's descriptions of his public performances clearly indicate a belief in the return and intervention of ancestral spirits. That Gordon takes on the role of mediator between the living and the dead during those performances further suggests a specific knowledge of Legba as a source of his persona in the narrative. A divine trickster, Legba won his position as chief of the seven lesser gods, or *vodun*, by winning a contest set by the creator God Mawu-Lisa. Of the *vodun* beneath the Creator, only Legba was able simultaneously to play four instruments (a gong, a bell, a drum, and a flute) and dance to the music he made. "Since Legba was the first to master the art of music," Thomas F. Marvin comments, "all human musicians may be considered his 'children'" (588). According to Marvin, African American singers in particular may be considered "followers" of Legba "because they are liminal figures who stand at the crossroads where cultures meet, connecting their listeners with the spirits of the ancestors and the lessons of history" (587).

Gordon's descriptions of his performances provide the narrative's clearest indication of supernatural occurrences: "I have had some peculiar things happen while singing" (193). As Legba is described as having "one foot in the visible world and the other in the realm of spirits" (Marvin 587), Gordon's performances similarly place him at the crossroads of the visible and the invisible. At one performance, he called his mother forth from the grave to join him: "It was on a Sunday afternoon, December the 22nd, when we sang spirituals on the Brown's Theatre stage in Louisville, not far from my mother's birthplace. I called her out of the grave to sing the songs for the people that once held her in bondage. A queer electric halo seemed to hover over the audience, as they listened to dead slaves, whose forms seep through walls, ceilings, and windows—a thousand-fold—to sing the Christian fables to their pagan melodies and rhymes. After the concert they waved their webby forms back to their bones to rest in the grave, until they are needed again" (221). Gordon performs the role of a child of Legba here, connecting his listeners both "with the spirits of the ancestors and the lessons of history." Through his performance, Gordon "opens the barrier" between heaven and earth and brings forth the dead to aid his performance. A "thousandfold," the dead testify to the living through the singing of songs that connect Gordon to his ancestors and that represent a particular connection his mother.

These allusions to African spiritual beliefs suggest that Gordon's story, which is strongly rooted in his Montana childhood, also has roots in African folklore. He is a child of the Rocky Mountains as well as a child of Legba. Forty years or more before Reed's Loop Garoo Kid appeared in print, Taylor Gordon was already representing himself as a Hoo-Doo cowboy.

And Gordon is not the only precursor to Loop Garoo, not the only black performer to draw on trickster tradition to describe his western experience. In *Father of the Blues*, multiple scenes illustrate Handy's ability to use his wits to get out of trouble. When Handy depicts the dangers of antiblack violence, he also demonstrates performers' ability to adapt to difficult circumstances and at times, especially when traveling in the West, to out-cowboy the cowboys. Handy observes that the troupe's interlocutor, George Moxley, was particularly adept at outwitting his audiences whether he was on stage or off: "We had been traveling through the Black Hills by stagecoach and had seen cowboys occasionally ride up to a bar and recklessly buy drinks for the house. By the time we reached Billings [Montana], Moxley was ready to show the natives something. . . . Empty of pocket and on his wits as usual, he set up the house, and told Wild West stories. His poise had never been more magnificent. The crowd responded gleefully, and presently everybody was royally tight" (38). What we see here is a familiar black trickster figure, "empty of pocket and on his wits as usual," gone west; he follows cowboy fashion by buying drinks for the house but then talks his way out of paying for them.

The *Freeman* reported on 10 December 1910 that the Southern Smart Set had managed to "thread its way through Texas 'without one whit of trouble, though at times trouble seemed unavoidable' (quoted in Abbott and Seroff 114). According to Abbott and Seroff, "A commentator half joked that, in order to maintain a low public profile during their Texas sojourn, the women of the company dressed as 'ordinary cotton pickers' and 'wash women,' and the men except for [Homer] Tutt, who maintained his dudish look and therefore was adjudged the boss of the gang, dressed as 'jobmen' and 'compress hands.' The star player took a different tact [*sic*]: 'Determined not to put on any open air dancing stunts, Mr. Whitney generally appeared as a Texas ranger of the frontier type . . . ready to round up a herd of Texas steers'" (114).[17] In response to western violence, the players use subterfuge, pretending to be of lower status than they actually were, "ordinary" workers rather than (relatively) prosperous performers, with only headliners Tutt (in his usual "dudish" dress) and Whitney dressing to impress. Like George Moxley in Montana, Whitney here decides to out-cowboy the cowboys. If the West did not offer freedom from racism, it did seem to offer more options for responding to racist threats.

Dressing as "ordinary cotton pickers" and "jobmen" suggests a type of "masking," a pretense of subservience put on as a survival strategy. However, Whitney's appearance as "a Texas ranger of the frontier type" suggests a more aggressive style of trickery. In these stories of minstrel players performing (offstage) Western roles, we have the first Hoo-Doo cowboys. As will be the case with Reed's Loop Garoo and his "pink-fringed" cowboy shirt, these performers play the cowboy role with distinct (and flamboyant) style. Combining trickster tradition with western costuming (or, in

Moxley's case, telling Western stories with the "magnificent" "poise" of his stage persona), Moxley and Whitney are cowboys who play the role with a black difference. In contrast to Nat Love's cowboy stories, the strategy here is not erasure but a more aggressive assertion of black western belonging.

In *Father of the Blues*, Handy describes another incident that similarly involves a combination of trickery, role playing, and aggression on the part of the performers to escape from a sticky situation. The most serious and potentially deadly incident Mahara's Minstrels experience occurs in Tyler, Texas, where a local doctor diagnoses one of the performers, Cricket Smith, with smallpox. The band's performance in a public square is disrupted by the doctor, who rushes onto the scene, shouting, "Stop this damn music. . . . [T]hese niggers have got the smallpox. If they don't get out town—and that right quick—we'll lynch them all" (47). Although initially stunned, the performers "quickly regained our wits well enough to fall into step with the rat-a-tat-tat of George Reeves' snare drum and commence a double-quick to the [railroad] car" (47). They quickly get an engine hitched to the car, which is taken to a siding on the outskirts of town. Unfortunately, their escape is stopped there, as county officials inform them "that the appearance of one more case of smallpox among [them] would be the signal . . . to burn the car and carry out the doctor's lynching threat with the rest of us, men and women" (48).

The tense situation lasts several days, during which fourteen men develop smallpox, but the group conceals this fact. Although provided with "no food, water or sanitary arrangements," the performers are saved by their own advance planning—they have packed tanks of water and "food reserves in the 'bear-wallow'" (48). In addition, the bear-wallow contains weapons, and "something told me," Handy writes, "to brush up on my shooting" (48). As the encampment becomes surrounded by guards, the group "began to be disturbed by the lack of privacy. We requested the guards to allow our women to walk the tracks down to the nearby woods" (48). Denied this courtesy, Handy's "blood boiled" (48). He and another performer "grimly raided the arsenal, took positions and calmly instructed the women to take their walk. We invited the guards to oppose us, if they dared. They didn't" (48–49). No matter where this incident took place, the performers might have taken the same measures and achieved the same results. But it is also possible that the western location gave them greater leeway of response—taking up arms—than they would have dared in the Deep South. When endangered in Tennessee, Handy hides himself in the "get-away" rather than using it as a source for the weaponry to fight back.

As the smallpox spreads through the band, the group takes further action, devising a plan to spirit away the sick men before their illness is discovered: "During the afternoons I got the band together and played a concert behind our barricade. The townsfolk, as usual, swarmed around like flies drawn to a molasses drop. In the midst of the musical program big Gordon Collins came on with a stunt that left the folks limp from laughing. Two hundred and eighty pounds of brown meat, Gordon would leap high into the air, thrust his legs before him and come down with a whosh on his mighty buttocks. He was well-cushioned by nature, and no calamity resulted for the big boy. Moreover, the spectators thought it was tremendous. He would follow his leaping act with humorous songs" (*Father* 49–50). As enjoyable as the crowd found the minstrel performance, "entertainment was not our underlying aim on these occasions. Gordon was not bruising his bottom just for fun" (50). While the guards "were holding their sides as they laughed at Gordon," the fourteen men, disguised in women's clothing and "provided with sufficient money to get [them] out of Texas," snuck off down the tracks into the woods and escaped (50). About an earlier incident, Handy writes, "Many times I have had to use such native wit or suffer for the lack of it" (47). Like Moxley, "empty of pocket [or out of options] and on his wits as usual," Handy and his fellows use subterfuge to outwit the well-armed and more powerful white men who threaten them. Gordon's buffoonery, his willingness to abuse his body for the sake of a laugh, serves a greater purpose than entertainment. With the infected band members gone, the rest of the performers can demonstrate their good health and make their getaway.

★

Father of the Blues depicts the West as an alternate space, not completely devoid of southern prejudice but suggestive of possible freedoms available nowhere else. *Born to Be* similarly represents the West—and Montana in particular—as a haven from American racism. Gordon's story is also a trickster tale in the guise of a memoir. Like Handy, Gordon unveils a black trickster figure who is both adept at wearing the dissembling mask of the subordinate and capable of demonstrating a more assertive trickery. Handy's stories of "native wit" recall the aggressive humor of folklore developed under slavery, and while *Born to Be* contains an element of that type of trickster tale, Gordon's stories are more suggestive than Handy's of a familiarity with African folklore tradition. By drawing on both his western and his African roots, Gordon constructs himself as a Hoo-Doo cowboy. Handy's descriptions of Moxley buying drinks and spinning western tales in a Montana saloon (and talking his way out of paying the resulting bar tab) and newspaper accounts of Whitney as a "Texas ranger" similarly suggest that the Hoo-Doo cowboy is an archetype, one that Ishmael Reed does not invent but one that he reimagines and revises in his creation of the Loop Garoo Kid. The continuities between these texts suggest a shared set of images, experiences, strategies, and conventions—in other words, elements of a tradition—specific to the representation of the African American West.

Through travel, Handy claims national space as his own, inhabiting and experiencing many American localities. The story of those travels told in *Father of the Blues* represents a remapping of the United States in a way that makes the black presence visible. Through his travels with Ringling as well as his later adventures as a singer, Gordon places himself in every section of the country. The tales of minstrel bands and other African American performers crisscrossing the country published in the *Indianapolis Freeman* similarly represent a claiming of the public space of America as African American space. An ancillary (but complementary) strategy to that used by African Americans who settled in a particular place, both groups (stationary and traveling) used musical performance to make themselves at home. To borrow Eric Gardner's term, these performers quite literally locate themselves in "unexpected places," and Handy's memoir, Gordon's autobiography, and the myriad reports published in the *Freeman* document that placement.[18] If, as Gardner asserts, "black struggles for identity formation were carried out in specific locations" and those locations "have often fallen off of our maps of early black culture," then it is because we have lost the maps, not because black writers did not clearly map out their presence in American public space and across the nation (13).

That mapping is particularly important in *Father of the Blues*, where Handy suggests that his travels and experiences—the sounds he hears, the things he sees—have all directly and indirectly influenced his later musical compositions, with "The St. Louis Blues" appearing in the text as the culmination of his experiences as an American and an African American.[19] The astounding popularity of the song, he suggests, results from its condensation and amalgamation of multiple American experiences and musical influences.[20] As a song, the lyrics of "The St. Louis Blues" are open to multiple possibilities for interpretation. I close out this chapter by considering "The St. Louis Blues" in a western context—as a song that, among the other things it does and means, specifically alludes to African American western experience both by playing on conventional western tropes and by alluding to specific moments in African American western migration.[21]

It is important to remember St. Louis as a border town between not just the East and the West but also between the South and everywhere else. Many African Americans passed through St. Louis on their way to the Northwest, particularly Montana and other Rocky Mountain states, in the late nineteenth century. St. Louis was the central transition point during the Kansas Fever Exodus, as hundreds of African Americans made their way by steamboat up the river and out of the South. Handy follows a similar trajectory (although hopping a train rather than a steamboat) in *Father of the Blues*, leaving behind hard times in Birmingham, Alabama, with the goal of reaching Chicago for the World's Fair. Ultimately, however, he winds up in St. Louis, which he describes as both central to the development of black popular music ("the cradle of ragtime") and symbolic of social and economic mobility (26). Handy describes a St. Louis that also suggests a wide-open frontier city: "I don't think I'd want to forget the high-roller Stetson hats of the men or the diamonds the girls wore in their ears" (28).

St. Louis is popularly known as the Gateway to the West, but in *Father of the Blues*, the West is also the gateway to "The St. Louis Blues." When Handy arrived in the midst of the Panic of 1893, he was reduced to sleeping "on the cobblestones of the levee of the Mississippi" (27). As Handy observes, "I always imagined that a good bit of that hardship went into the making of the *St. Louis Blues* when, much later, that whole song seemed to spring so easily out of nowhere, the work of a single evening at the piano. I like to think that that song reflects a life filled with hard times as well as good times" (28–29). As important as the hardship was, his response to it—not to give up and head back to Alabama but to continue on, to keep moving, reaching Chicago to join Mahara's Minstrels and, via his travels with the group, heading out West (28). "When I left St. Louis," Handy writes, "My luck changed suddenly" (30). St. Louis is indeed the gateway through which Handy passes on his way to Mahara's Minstrels. And his travels with the troupe and his experience of black music in western places contribute to the accumulation of sounds and experiences that produce "The St. Louis Blues."

"The St. Louis Blues" famously begins with the line, "I hate to see de ev'-nin' sun go down" (Handy, *Blues* 71). That is, "The St. Louis Blues" begins where the Western usually ends—with the sun setting in the West. But rather than the cowboy-hero riding triumphantly into the sunset at the end of his adventure, the song's speaker remains in place, lamenting that fact that "ma baby, he done lef' dis town" (72). The speaker may hate to see the sun go down because it reminds her of the direction her baby went when he left her town. However, St. Louis and the West play a double role in the song. On the one hand, St. Louis is the source of the speaker's blues—the place that has taken her baby from her. On the other hand, St. Louis is the place and west is the direction that represent a possible cure for those blues. In a verse that is rarely performed now in recorded versions of the song, the speaker visits a Gypsy who tells her to go to St. Louis because she can win her baby back if she does. The singer vows to "pack ma trunk and make my get away" (72). In the final verse, the speaker sings,

> Help me to Cairo, make St. Louis by ma self.
> Git to Cairo, find my old friend Jeff.
> Gwine to pin ma self close to his side.
> If I flag his train I sho' can ride. (72–73)

The song tells two stories, the lament of the woman left behind and the story of her own leave-taking. St. Louis is not only the location of the nefarious woman with the diamond rings and "store bought hair" (73) who stole the speaker's baby but also a symbol of the freedom that might be available if, like her baby, she heads west as well.

Coincidentally, "The St. Louis Blues" describes a path similar to that followed by Taylor Gordon's mother and father. Like the speaker of the song, they made their way to Cairo, Illinois, and from there west to St. Louis. Whereas the speaker of "The St. Louis Blues" imagines St. Louis as the endpoint of her journey, for the Gordons, St. Louis was truly a gateway to further western migration. This later verse of the song also suggests a St. Louis that is not so much a source of the blues as a place where the speaker can indeed "make ma get away," where tomorrow might be better than today. The sense of western possibility that we find in the narrative of *Father of the Blues* reemerges in this second verse of "The St. Louis Blues." By the end of the song, the speaker imagines herself on the move, aided by her friend, Jeff, and riding toward the sunset, contemplating the new possibilities the sunset now symbolizes.

The complexity of "The St. Louis Blues" lies in its mixture of despair and hope for the future. The evening sun going down emerges as a particularly layered symbol—not only of loneliness but also of improved prospects for the future. As Gussow observes, the opening lyric also recalls the "Don't let the sun go down on you here" signs that Handy encounters outside some southern towns. Gussow suggests that the missing lover, "the 'disappeared' black man" of "The St. Louis Blues" and of other "black women's blues [songs] was, among other things, blues song's way of mourning the men killed by white lynchers and race rioters, or arrested on vagrancy charges, prison-farmed, convict-leased, thrown in jail" (13). With the opening reference to the sun going down, Handy introduces the specter of southern violence as a possible cause for the blues. "The St. Louis Blues," Gussow argues, "may be read, in other words, as racial protest resonating within a narrative of lost love, a black man's lament, recast in the voice of his lover, at white southern violence and the dislocations it imposes" (70).

Gussow also points out the uncanny return of Handy's minstrel experiences through the repetition of the phrase *get away* in the song's lyrics. Observing that Handy had his own "get-away" (the secret compartment on the Mahara's Minstrels train car in which he hid himself to escape death in Tennessee), Gussow suggests that Handy "finds a way of converting his own near-lynching as a minstrel into the central trope-of-flight animating" the song (12). If we follow Gussow and interpret *get away* as a reference to Handy's minstrel's days, the reference also alludes to his western travels—to the prosperity and mobility he enjoyed with Mahara's Minstrels, the group that indeed helped him make his own getaway from both the American South and his impoverished circumstances. Like other elements of the song, *getaway* suggests a double meaning, the danger of racial violence and the possibility of escaping to a better tomorrow.

By specifically naming this song "The St. Louis Blues," Handy evokes a series of conflicted associations about this particular place in the American and African American imaginaries. Not only do the lyrics of the song suggest autobiographical readings (connections to Handy's personal history), but those lyrics call on a long history of St. Louis in reality and myth. As Gardner observes, St. Louis in antebellum writing emerges as "a complex nexus of American conceptions of the frontier and civilization" (*Unexpected* 15). In the genre of the slave narrative, St. Louis by the middle of the nineteenth century represented "a locus of the evils of the slave system" (22). William Wells Brown's 1847 *Narrative* helped establish and popularize this image of the city in abolitionist circles, with Brown cleverly playing on the city's mythologized and heavily promoted reputation as a gateway to western freedom and prosperity to contrast with the reality of the violent enslavement he describes therein. As Gardner notes, Brown's "conception of St. Louis as a 'gateway' to the heart of slavery [was] clearly designed to challenge the depictions of St. Louis as the gateway to the West (and thus to America's future) that dominated white texts from guidebooks and city directories to early St. Louis newspapers" (*Unexpected* 25). In Brown's St. Louis, "blacks were viciously 'moved' (often to Deep South deaths) amid the white westward mobility that supposedly held the promise of the nation" (24).[22]

For many postbellum African Americans, St. Louis symbolized just the opposite. During the Kansas Fever Exodus, "the most remarkable migration in the United States after the Civil War," St. Louis was the gathering point for African Americans seeking escape from the South (Painter 184). Some estimates suggest that "20,000 Exodusters reached the city in 1879–80," with more than 6,000 of them arriving in March and April 1879 (184). As Painter writes, "St. Louis occupied a pivotal position in the mythology of the Exodus. It linked the two parts of the idea, negative and positive, slavery and freedom. The first step, and the most decisive, took Exodusters out of the South, beyond the grasp of re-enslavement" (195). "The crucial point," Painter continues, "was St. Louis. When Exodusters reached that city they were out of danger" (195). St. Louis was the Red Sea that would part to allow the Exodusters passage to the Promised Land (see Painter 195). The hard part was getting to St. Louis. In some ways, "The St. Louis Blues" retells the story of the Exodusters, with Cairo occupying the crucial pivot point and St. Louis itself rather than Kansas the final destination. If she can get help to make it to Cairo, the speaker states, she can get to St. Louis by herself (or with a little help from Jeff). The Exodusters' primary mode of travel was steamship rather than train, but they similarly needed a little help from a friend, especially as "flagging" a steamship became increasingly difficult as southerners sought ways to stop the Exodus.[23] In late-nineteenth- and early twentieth-century America, restrictions on black mobility and public travel made having a friend—whether on a train or a riverboat—a useful commodity in general.

When Handy wrote "The St. Louis Blues" one night in 1914, the concepts of St. Louis as both gateway to slavery and gateway to western freedom would have been part of generational memory. Whether the association between St. Louis and the idea of western freedom is used to underscore ironic contrast (as in the slave narrative) or to create a concrete symbol of postbellum African Americans' desires for a better tomorrow, both St. Louis's roles are articulated through "The St. Louis Blues." The song's paradoxical portrayal of the city as both the source and the possible cure for the singer's blues plays on this divided vision of St. Louis in African American history. In choosing St. Louis as the key location for this particular blues song, Handy alludes to a wide range of African American history and experience and draws on a discourse about St. Louis that has consistently played on that city's role in myth and reality in westward expansion. In that sense, "The St. Louis Blues" is as much a western song as it is a blues song.

"Try to Refrain from That Desire"

Self-Control and Violent Passion in Oscar Micheaux's African American Western

---

Jean Baptiste, the protagonist of Oscar Micheaux's novel, *The Home-steader* (1917), first appears in the narrative struggling against a howling blizzard on the plains of frontier South Dakota.[1] Micheaux's depiction of this storm, which transforms the plains into "one endless, unbroken sheet of white frost and ice," is both a realistic winter landscape description and an allegorical representation of Baptiste's social situation—a black individual who has left behind African American communities in the East to seek economic opportunity in a predominantly white western frontier settlement (38). As Baptiste observes, there were "Germans from Germany" and "Swedes from Sweden" as well as Danes, Norwegians, "Poles, and Finns and Lithuanians and Russians," all homesteading in the area surrounding Gregory, South Dakota, "but of his race he was the only one" (64). This opening sequence of a solitary heroic black man advancing "resolutely forward" through the snow, sometimes "directly against" the "fine grainy missiles that cut the face," effectively condenses into a single naturalistic image much of the action that follows as Baptiste struggles to succeed in an America dominated by white people (21).

This image may also figure Micheaux's situation as a black writer working within a genre—the Western—associated with white writers. The Western, the fictional story of life on the American frontier, with its "imperial plot of valorizing white men," seems a particularly alien genre for the African American writer (Ammons 216). How then does Oscar Micheaux negotiate the difficult task he has set for himself—to tell a story of specifically African American experience through a genre associated with advancing an ideology of white superiority and imperialism?[2]

On the one hand, Micheaux writes a Western that is perfectly in keeping with the ideology of the genre. In *West of Everything* (1992), Jane

Tompkins points out that in the Western, the "West functions as a symbol of freedom, and of the opportunity for conquest" (4).³ *The Homesteader* is just such a story of conquest, of transforming wild and savage land into civilized productive farmland. "Jean Baptiste had come West," Micheaux writes, "and staked his lot and future there, doing his part toward the building of that little empire out there in the hollow of God's hand" (107). In American myth, the West is the place of transformation and self-making, or, as Micheaux renders it, "the place for young manhood," where with "indefatigable will," a "firm determination," and a "great desire to make good," the unknown man who "had no heritage" except for his "French name" could find a level playing field "with its virgin soil and undeveloped resources" and the opportunity to "work out his own destiny" and build his own little empire (*Homesteader* 24).⁴ As in many white-authored frontier adventures, the story also justifies and celebrates the taking and redistribution of Native American lands and territories, activities that are necessary precursors to the building of empire and the bringing of civilization to a "savage" land. In *The Homesteader*, Micheaux neither condemns nor critiques the dominant culture myth of Manifest Destiny but rather claims a share of the spoils for the enterprising black man.

On the other hand, *The Homesteader* carefully revises the Western as Micheaux filters the elements of the genre through his own experience as an African American, through his understanding and response to the cultural beliefs of his day, through his reading of African American literature generally, and through his specific knowledge of the writing and philosophies of W. E. B. Du Bois and Booker T. Washington. Micheaux dedicated his first book, *The Conquest*, a thinly veiled autobiography that provides a blueprint for *The Homesteader*, to Washington. As Pearl Bowser and Louise Spence note, Micheaux believed in "Booker T. Washington's ideal of pulling oneself up by one's own bootstraps" and shared Washington's belief that the majority of African Americans "needed models, heroes, to mold public opinion and for the elevation of public sentiment" (19–21). One such hero is Jean Baptiste, whose comments on the cause of racial uplift reveal that he shares his creator's beliefs: "If I could actually succeed, it would mean so much to the credit of a multitude of others.—Others who need the example" (109).⁵ Micheaux's admiration for Washington and belief in the goal of racial uplift inform and guide his revision of the Western.

The Homesteader is divided into four "epochs." Epoch 1 follows one year in Baptiste's life, from winter through spring planting to the fall harvest, where we see Baptiste reap a successful crop and declare his love for Agnes Stewart, the (presumably) white woman who saves him from freezing to death in the novel's opening sequence. Epoch 2 begins with Baptiste's decision to "sacrifice" his love for Agnes in the name of race loyalty. "Examples they needed," ruminates Baptiste, "and such he was glad he had become; but if he married now the one he loved, the example was lost" (147). Already in possession of 320 acres of land, Baptiste makes purchases to expanding his holdings: "If he or any other man of the black race could acquire one thousand acres of such land it would stand out with more credit to the Negro race than all the protestations of a world of agitators in so far as the individual was concerned" (132). To reach that number, he needs an African American fiancée on whose behalf he can make a claim. The story of Baptiste's courtship of and troubled marriage to Orlean McCarthy follows. This epoch ends with the death at birth of their first child, a coinciding drought that threatens to destroy Baptiste economically, and with Orlean returning to Chicago with her father (the Reverend Newton Justine McCarthy) as Baptiste watches helplessly.[6]

Epoch 3 describes Baptiste's fall from grace, his descent into bitterness and anger at his father-in-law's manipulative efforts to destroy his marriage. Nearly ruined financially and emotionally, he pulls himself up by his bootstraps in epoch 4 and writes the story of his life, which he publishes, sells, and distributes himself. The resulting return to economic health restores him emotionally as well. He eventually triumphs over the McCarthy family, and the distraught Orlean murders her father and then kills herself, clearing the way for Baptiste to marry the woman he has loved from the beginning, Agnes, who (as the reader has long suspected) is revealed to be of African descent, thus dissolving the barrier between them. Some four hundred pages after his "sacrifice," Baptiste triumphs. At the novel's end, he brings in a successful harvest, pulls himself out of debt, and both marries the woman he loves and remains the example his race needs.

Adam Gussow's comments about W. C. Handy's memoir are applicable here: His "detailing of his entrepreneurial ascent is shadowed always by his uneasiness at the continuing threat posed by white violence, a threat that he both evokes and resists and that renders *Father of the Blues* anything but a simplistic uplift narrative" (69). Micheaux's Jean Baptiste is likewise "shadowed," but the threat is not so much that of white violence but the project of uplift itself. Baptiste's difficulties in the central sections of the book seem to comment on Micheaux's troubles as a writer, trying to create a fiction that adapts dominant culture mythology to African American experience. Baptiste's racial uplift goals in fact undermine his efforts to become a successful homesteader. The promises of freedom, conquest, empire, and transformation offered by the Western seem available to the black man only if he assimilates thoroughly and abandons any sense of responsibility to others of his race. Dan Moos argues that Micheaux does just that by choosing a "pioneer over [a] racial identity" and by "subordinat[ing] almost all issues of race to those of a progressive and civilizing frontier" (*Outside* 358, 360). However, the novel is "anything but a simplistic uplift narrative" because *The Homesteader* registers a great deal of ambivalence over that choice; rather than subordinating racial issues, Micheaux foregrounds the conflict engendered by Baptiste's efforts to be both an African American hero and a Western one. What at first glance may seem like an act of erasure (choosing a "pioneer over [a] racial identity") ultimately appears as something else, as Micheaux's attention to racial issues forms a central element of the narrative.

The Homesteader is a generic hybrid, part Western, part racial uplift saga, filled with contradictions, doubles, and doppelgangers. Micheaux adapts the central structuring opposition of the Western—the essential difference between the civilized East and the Wild West—to articulate Baptiste's sense of double-consciousness, his conflicting desires both to maintain and to erase his racial identity, to remain connected to the African American East and at the same time to strike out on his own into the white world of the western frontier. At times, the novel seems to pull itself apart as Micheaux tries to bring both plots—of frontier conquest, of racial uplift—to successful completion. Only the melodramatic concluding events (the murder-suicide, the "surprise" revelation of racial ancestry) enable Baptiste's happy ending. This generic twoness is reflected by other incidents of doubling throughout the novel. For example, the virtues and behaviors the book celebrates (practicality, determination, property ownership) and those it condemns (weakness, frivolity, vice) are personified through opposing characters. Micheaux uses contemporaneous notions of gender as a way of naturalizing positive and negative character qualities as manly or unmanly, womanly or unwomanly. The West is "the place for young manhood," while the East is the home of Baptiste's other and opposite, Rev. McCarthy, with his "womanish smile" (268).

Father of the Blues becomes a "western" book through Handy's detailing of his journeys through various western places from Texas to Montana. *The Homesteader* is a Western in terms of genre (especially as that genre was formed through turn-of-the-century novels such as Owen Wister's *The Virginian*) and because of Micheaux's placement of his story in a specific western place, frontier South Dakota. Whereas Handy makes a "home" for himself in the American West (and America in general) through travel, Micheaux's is a story of a settler rather than a traveler—or, at least, it is a story of an attempt to settle, for Baptiste to indeed become the homesteader of the title. In his own way, Micheaux illustrates the difficult task the black migrant faced in making a "home" in American West. Although Baptiste is not a musician, he is nonetheless a performer. In *The Homesteader*, it is by acting and through action that Baptiste constitutes his identity as a westerner. The opening scene of *The Homesteader*, in which Baptiste struggles across "one endless, unbroken sheet of white frost and ice," is a depiction of a heroic performance, taking advantage of the dramatic setting of the cold Dakota plains as the stage for that action. Baptiste's performance is an assertion of national identity and national belonging that is amplified by being staged against the backdrop of that majestic and dangerous landscape. By telling the story of a heroic black man fighting for survival in an "endless" white western world, Micheaux also stages a performance that is specifically a story of the African American West.

In the Western, Tompkins writes, the West is the symbolic place of freedom that offers "escape from the conditions of life in modern industrial society: from a mechanized existence, economic dead ends, social entanglements, unhappy personal relations, political injustice" (4). In the myth of the West, freed from the constraints of civilization, the individual returns to an Edenic state of existence—to natural ways of being and behaving. For the black pioneer, the West symbolizes escape from those "conditions of life" specific to African American existence in the East and the South (segregation, antiblack violence, Jim Crow laws). Baptiste's western freedom involves being a "man like any other man" unencumbered by race restrictions or class distinctions. The West offers the African American man the possibility of full participation in a social system where individual qualities will be recognized and rewarded.

The developing romance between Agnes Stewart and Jean Baptiste symbolizes the possibilities of freedom on the frontier once individuals have escaped from the arbitrary restrictions of civilization. Epoch 1 concludes as we expect a Western should—with the savage land conquered and transformed into productive farmland that yields a successful crop and with hero and heroine declaring their love for each other amid the

Edenic beauty of an "enchanted garden" where "harvest birds twittered" and where Baptiste's "lips found hers, and all else was forgotten" (139). In the West, where nature rules over custom, "He was as a man toward the maid now" (138). A new Eden, however, is not so easily attained by the African American pioneer. Agnes's "halfwitted brothers" return from the fields and recall the two lovers to social reality: "It was only then that they seemed to realize what had transpired and upon realization they silently disembraced. What had passed was the most natural thing in the world, true; and to them it had come because it was in them to assert themselves, but now before him rose the Custom of the Country, and its law" (145). Although "custom" and "law" governing interracial romantic relations may indeed be as "halfwitted" as the two brothers that personify them, they remain a strong influence on behavior, even in the Wild West. The primary deterrent, however, is not the pressure of custom and law (which can be defied) but Baptiste's sense of social responsibility—the fact that "he liked his people" (147). The black Western hero has concerns that his white counterparts do not, and thus Micheaux adapts the genre's conventions to address those concerns.

The blizzard that begins the novel is a variation on the classic Western scene of the heroic individual struggling against the savage environment, but Baptiste's immersion in the whiteness of the storm also represents his social situation as the lone African American "in this land where others than those of the race to which he belonged were the sole inhabitants" (*Homesteader* 68). This sequence, which involves Baptiste driving two wagons loaded with coal through the storm, concisely establishes several points. We learn much about Baptiste's character. He is "just passed twenty-two—and vigorous, strong, healthy and courageous," possessed of "indefatigable will" and "firm determination" (22–24). The story is also a Washingtonian parable of gaining the acceptance and respect of one's white neighbors through "useful work." For delivering the coal, Baptiste earns not only a profit for himself but also accolades from his white neighbors: "That coal to everybody was a godsend, yet think of the risk you took" (65). As another townsman observes, "That Baptiste is *some* fellow" (52).[7]

The Homesteader makes an argument generally in line with early twentieth-century racial uplift ideology. Rather than protesting against or attempting to change the social environment, racial uplift advocates believed that African Americans should change themselves—should imitate the manners, values, and civilized behaviors of white middle-class America. As Kevin Gaines remarks, "Black elites hoped their support for the spread of civilization and the interests of the American nation would topple racial barriers and bolster their claims to citizenship and respectability" (345). For Micheaux, Baptiste's actions provide evidence that blacks can contribute to the spread of civilization and in so doing accomplish more for the credit of "the Negro race than all the protestations of a world of agitators" (*Homesteader* 132). His character qualities—his strong will and self-control, his practicality and work ethic—mark his civilized status according to the middle-class mores of the era. Although Micheaux notes the occasional racist incident on the frontier, Baptiste's neighbors for the most part indicate their willingness to accept him into the American family once he has proven that he is worthy—that he is indeed "*some* fellow."

The quality of Baptiste's character counters white stereotypes of black behavior. However, *The Homesteader* (like much of Micheaux's work) also employs those same stereotypes in the representation of African American characters other than Baptiste. As Bowser and Spence observe, "Part of the means by which [Micheaux] built the appearance of success included singling out those of the Race whom he characterized as immoral, or without ambition and perseverance, and censuring them for impeding the progress of the Race, and therefore holding *him* back" (25). Baptiste observes that his race seemed "to progress rather slowly. He had not yet come fully to appreciate and understand why they remained always so poor" (*Homesteader* 107). As a race, "their standard of morals were not so high as it should be" and they were "possessed with certain weaknesses" and "were given still to lustful, undependable habits" (160–61).[8] The hardworking Baptiste observes "that the most difficult task he had ever encountered was" not transforming the wild prairie into farmland but rather "convinc[ing] the average colored man that the Negro race could ever be anything" (107). For Baptiste, other African Americans are like his homestead—full of potential but wild, savage, primitive, and in need of development into a productive and civilized state. "His race needed examples," a contemplative Baptiste thinks to himself, "they needed instances of successes to overcome the effect of ignorance and an animal viciousness that was prevalent among them" (109). The novel's drama or melodrama involves in part the tug-of-war between Baptiste and "the average colored man," as his efforts to increase the speed at which the race progresses are stymied by recalcitrant refusals to be uplifted. Rather than lifting up the race, Baptiste by the middle of the novel finds himself in danger of succumbing to the weaknesses, vices, and "undependable habits" he otherwise condemns.

Typical of the Western, Micheaux uses two primary settings to create an opposition between the West and the East that reflects the values and qualities the novel celebrates or condemns: South Dakota/Chicago; white people/black people; freedom and opportunity/vice and poverty; integration/segregation; practicality/frivolity; Jean Baptiste/the McCarthy family; Agnes Stewart/Orlean McCarthy; manly and womanly behavior/ unmanliness and unwomanliness. For Baptiste, the West symbolizes escape not only from prejudice in the East but also from the qualities of "animal viciousness" he associates with "the average colored man." Micheaux writes that Baptiste "had virtually run away from those parts wherein he had first seen the light of day, to escape the effect of dull indolence; the penurious evil that seemed to have gripped the populace, especially a great portion of his race. In the years Jean Baptiste had spent in the West, he had been able to follow, unhampered, his convictions" (*Homesteader* 269). Baptiste, the assimilated and successful African American, is nonetheless unwilling to sever his connection to black America. If we return to the opening scene of the novel, to the image of Baptiste struggling through the white storm with two wagons "loaded with coal, which towered above his head and shoulders," we might argue that the coal represents the burden of blackness—the "towering" weight of racist attitudes against which he must struggle (21). The coal also represents the burden of racial uplift—the collective weight of those African Americans whose "ignorance" and "animal viciousness" prevent Baptiste's full integration into American society. The struggle of dragging these twin burdens through the surrounding world nearly kills him.

In perhaps his most significant revision, Micheaux adapts the central trope of the Western and of frontier literature—the essential difference between the East and West—to represent geographically what Du Bois describes as "double-consciousness." The African American, writes Du Bois, "ever feels his two-ness,—an American, a Negro; two souls, two thoughts, two unreconciled strivings" (5).[9] At the same time that Micheaux sees and advocates the opportunities afforded by migration and assimilation, his hero maintains a sense of "race loyalty," an unwillingness to submerge himself completely in the white world that nearly drags him under in the novel's opening scene. Thus, he condemns the example of a black man who "had taken a white wife" and "decided to claim himself as otherwise than he was," as someone of "Mexican" rather than African descent (*Homesteader* 146). "Even to merely claim being something else," Micheaux writes, "was a sort of compromise" that Baptiste was unwilling to make (146). Baptiste would not (to quote Du Bois) "Africanize America" or "bleach his Negro soul in a flood of white Americanism" (Du Bois 5). He simply wishes, as Du Bois writes, "to make it possible for a man to be both a Negro and an American" (5). For Baptiste, though, merging these identities becomes increasingly difficult.

Gerald Early comments that Du Bois "saw blacks as being caught, Hamlet-like, between the issue of" living as "an assimilated American" or "an unassimilated Negro" (xx). Micheaux uses the novel's two primary settings, South Dakota and Chicago, to symbolize these two states of being. South Dakota is the place of the assimilated American, Chicago of the unassimilated Negro—of "Darktown proper," the very "center of the Negro life" (*Homesteader* 147–48). The physical movements in *The Homesteader* illustrate Baptiste's efforts to overcome his sense of twoness as he travels back and forth between South Dakota and Chicago, between a sense of racial isolation in the West and a contrasting sense of racial belonging in the East. His marriage to a Chicago-born African American woman, Orlean McCarthy, represents both a joining of West and East and a resolution to double-consciousness. Baptiste desires not to abandon the members of his race but to bring them with him, morally and (if necessary) physically. His transportation of Orlean to South Dakota represents his effort to remake the race, as Orlean's frontier transformation signifies that a beneficial change in geography can improve the character of even the least likely of candidates. Torn between a need to succeed in terms of the white narrative of frontier conquest and empire building and a sense of racial solidarity and responsibility, Baptiste finds himself spread too thin by the effort expended in pursuit of both goals. Bowser and Spence observe that Micheaux "challenged white definitions of race without actually changing the terms [or] demanding new definitions of Race from within Black America" (26). For Baptiste, resolving double-consciousness means remaking those others who represent his sense of identity as an unassimilated black man. Perhaps the difficulties in which Baptiste finds himself result from his inability or unwillingness to see his fellows from a perspective that does not cast them as Others who must be changed.

In *Manliness and Civilization*, Gail Bederman notes the connection in late-nineteenth and early twentieth-century America between theories of white superiority and beliefs about gender roles—notions of true manhood and true womanhood that developed from the Victorian concept of separate spheres (domestic and private for women, public and workplace-oriented for men). True womanhood emphasized the qualities of piety, purity, maternity, submissiveness, virtue, and domesticity. True manhood involved having a strong manly character exemplified by self-control and self-restraint. All men, turn-of-the-century Americans believed, possessed passionate and potentially violent natures that had to be kept in check. The strength of character—manliness—capable of controlling those urges was a racial trait specific to white men. Black men and women (according to this racist turn-of-the-century discourse) lacked the civilized qualities of self-restraint, virtue, and chastity that constituted true manliness and womanliness.[10] Claudia Tate points out that early twentieth-century African American writers felt that repudiating accusations of unmanly and unwomanly sexual behavior "was crucial to black people's changing their subjugated social status" (10). Thus, black writers of the period often use dominant concepts of masculinity and femininity as evidence that African Americans were indeed men and women deserving of the same political and civil rights as white men and women. Baptiste's sacrifice of his love for Agnes Stewart is just one example of his civilized self-control, his ability to contain and transcend his own passionate impulses.

In *The Conquest*, Micheaux highlights the exceptional qualities of autobiographical protagonist Oscar Devereaux (a precursor to Jean Baptiste) by "creating a contrast between his hero's 'manly' behavior and the 'unmanly' behavior of other black men" (Johnson 238). In both *The Conquest* and *The Homesteader*, the character who exemplifies the unmanliness that impedes the progress of the race is the protagonist's father-in-law, named McCraline in the earlier book and McCarthy in the later one.[11] The Reverend N. J. McCarthy is described as "the rock of unreason," as a man who was "by disposition, environment and cultivation, narrow, impractical, hypocritical, envious and spiteful" (*Homesteader* 209, 228). A domineering figure, a despot in his own household, he requires that those around him reinforce his sense of self-importance: Says Orlean, "If you would get along with papa, then praise him—you understand, flatter him a little. Make him think he's a king" (210).[12] "Not only was he the father of two illegitimate children," Baptiste discovers, "but he had taken another man's wife to become so—and all this while he was one of the most influential men in the church" (311). McCarthy's inability to control his passions—his temper, his sexual desires, his need for dominance—denotes his unmanliness.

The women in the McCarthy family allegorically represent undesirable feminine traits. Ethel, the older sister, is a "disagreeable person, ostentatious, pompous, and hard to get along with" (*Homesteader* 175). Like her father, Ethel has an "evil temper" (176). She dominates her husband and refuses to perform such wifely tasks as preparing his dinner. She is condemned not because she is a woman with masculine traits but rather because the excessiveness of those qualities indicates her lack of self-control. As Ethel is too masculine, Orlean, like her mother, is too feminine—timid, obedient, and subservient. "Orlean *isn't* a woman," laments Baptiste, "and that is what I've been trying to make her. She has never been a woman—wasn't reared so to be" (297). She lacks "the force of will that he desired," but at least "she was not wicked" (182). Like Baptiste's land, Orlean is undeveloped but not without potential. Removed from the deforming influences of Chicago and her father, Orlean indeed begins to flourish: "Since her marriage her health on the whole had improved wonderfully. The petty aches and pains of which she complained formerly had gradually disappeared, and the western air had brought health and vigor to her" (259–60).

The difficult task of making a woman of Orlean is exacerbated "by a stream of letters from Chicago, giving volumes of advice" (*Homesteader* 227). Letters from her sister Ethel, filled with the unwomanly "condemnation of motherhood," encourage Orlean to try (but fail) to abort her unborn child (229). Rev. McCarthy arrives in person to throw her into a quandary over "subservience to her father, who insisted upon it, and obedience and loyalty to her husband who had a right and naturally expected it" (242). This polluting stream of advice leaves her "perceptibly weak" (248). Via the bond of matrimony, Baptiste enters into a relationship with McCarthy as much as with Orlean. Rather than uplifting his fellow, Baptiste finds that his bond with the reverend provides a means by which the bad qualities of eastern life flow westward to corrupt him: "Dull indolence . . . penurious evil . . . the Reverend's presence seemed to have brought all this back" (269). That corruption is symbolized by Baptiste's increasing inability to curb his temper. The civilized virtue that proves the manliness of his character, his self-control, erodes in the face of McCarthy's exacerbating presence.

A surrealistic dreamlike sequence early in the novel foreshadows the relationship that will develop between hero and villain. At the first mention of the name of Orlean's father, Baptiste's head begins "throbbing" as his brain "struggl[es] with something that happened a long time before" (*Homesteader* 163). For the superbly controlled Baptiste, this symptomatic headache foreshadows the return of repressed memory as he drags back to consciousness a childhood incident with McCarthy. This incident, involving a conflict between an adult male and a child over the attention of an adult woman, has clear Oedipal overtones and foreshadows the nature of the relations that will develop between Baptiste, his wife, and his father-in-law.[13] The five-year-old Baptiste, "his mother's baby boy," first encounters McCarthy in his parents' home in Illinois as they host a dinner for a group of male preachers and female teachers (163). Baptiste cannot recall "how many preachers there were, except that there were many," and they "were all large and tall and stout" (165).

Forbidden from the dinner table until the adults have finished eating, the young Baptiste watches through a window as the preachers "eat, and eat, and eat. He saw the quail the boys shot disappear one after another into the mouths of the big preachers" (*Homesteader* 165). The big preachers have big uncontrolled appetites that symbolize their unmanliness. Miss Self, one of the teachers, is particularly kind and attentive to Baptiste, and he recalls "how beautiful and sweet he had thought she was" (165). The teacher lifts the boy onto her lap and treats him to half her quail, and Baptiste "fell to eating, feeding his mouth with both hands for he was never before so hungry" (166). Feeling McCarthy's "angry eyes" on him, the child realizes that "his crawling upon the teacher's lap had spoiled" the reverend's flirtation with her (166–67). Responding to McCarthy's remark that the boy is impudent and deserves to be spanked, the child "extended his little face forward, close to the preacher's, as he poured" out an enraged diatribe: "Now you goin' eat it all and leave me none when I'm hungry. You're mean man and you make me mad" (167–68).

McCarthy's victory over the child consists of making him lose control. The boy becomes so "strangely angry" that his mother punishes him for the outburst (167). As she whips "him longer than she had ever done before," he falls "into a slumber while the blows continued," only to wake up later, his body "sore all over," with his teacher commenting, "And to be punished so severely because he wanted to eat is a shame" (168). The child wants to satisfy his desire, his hunger, but is prevented from doing so by the overindulgence of the other men. This incident, placed in the narrative almost immediately after Baptiste sacrifices his love for Agnes, comments as much on that frustrated desire as on the child's hunger for dinner. His position on the teacher's lap and McCarthy's flirtation link eating and hunger with sexuality and sexual desire. The return of this memory may express Baptiste's suppressed rage over the necessity of his sacrifice. As the child observes, "He had done nothing wrong, yet had been severely punished" (169).

Angry at this treatment, the child slips out of the house and ventures "deep into the forest" (*Homesteader* 169). As he walked, the "forest grew deeper, the trees larger, and the underbrush more tangled" (170). Confronted with a log bridge over "muddy waters whirling below," the boy "closed his eyes, and thought of the whipping he had received and the preacher he hated, opened them, and with calm determination born of anger, crossed safely to the other side" (170). There is a deep, deep anger inside of Baptiste—an anger perhaps at the restrictions placed on him by the "halfwitted" customs and laws of white society but that he displaces onto the figure of Rev. McCarthy, his African American Other whose uncontrolled and unnatural appetite prevents the boy from satisfying his natural hungers. Ironically, that repressed anger is part of what drives Baptiste, feeding his will, courage, and determination to succeed.

Deep in the woods, Baptiste remembers stories of "something evil in the forests," a catamount that has been attacking and destroying livestock (*Homesteader* 171). Hearing a terrible cry, he "crouched in a hole he had found where only his shoulders and head were exposed" (171). From the hole, he can "see the eyes plainly" of the beast that stalks him, "red eyes" that "shone like coals of fire" (172). The beast springs, and the boy strikes it with a large stick: "Again and again he struck until the head was like a bag of bones. When his strength was gone, and all was quiet, he became conscious of drowsiness. He sank down and laid his head upon the body of the dead animal, and fell into a deep sleep" (172). The description of the catamount's eyes reminds us of the dinner table scene, when "the eyes of the other were upon him, and they were angry eyes," connecting the beast in the forest with McCarthy's "animal viciousness" (166). Through the attack on the animal, Baptiste enacts the revenge against the reverend that he otherwise cannot obtain. Baptiste's fury can only be safely released in the wilderness against a savage beast that serves as a substitute for the object of his hatred. The threatening existence of this beast enables—in fact necessitates—the release of his suppressed anger and rage. In the context of the novel as a whole, Baptiste's relationship with McCarthy reveals the younger man's anger at the burden he must assume for the sake of racial uplift. Only in a wilderness space can he indulge the rage that he must otherwise suppress because of his sense of social responsibility.

Baptiste responds to his attack on the animal in the same way he responds to being beaten by his mother—by falling into a deep sleep. Once the anger that has propelled him through the forest has been released, the boy collapses. Rather than directly substituting for McCarthy, the beast may represent Baptiste's wrath, which he must subdue and control. Does the "something evil" encountered in the woods exist without or within? Is the attack in the wilderness a release of anger directed against another, or does it represent in symbolic form a method of regaining mastery over an anger that has been dangerously set loose? If so, that method is ironic and contradictory—controlling anger through a violent attack that unleashes rather than contains passion. Such a momentary passionate outburst of violence, while typical of the Western, is so contrary to the novel's philosophy that Micheaux must return to and rewrite this scene later in the narrative. Although he repeats the scenario of stalking and being stalked by the beast (McCarthy) in the wilderness (the streets of Chicago), he must find a way of defeating the beast without the passionate outburst that for Micheaux signifies unmanly rather than manly behavior.

In *Westerns: Making the Man in Fiction and Film* (1996), Lee Clark Mitchell argues that as familiar to the Western as the climactic gunfight are scenes in which the male hero is severely beaten. Westerns reveal an "almost obsessive recurrence of scenes of men being beaten—or knifed and whipped, propped up, knocked down, kicked in the side, punched in the face, or otherwise lacerated, clubbed, battered, and tortured into unconsciousness" (169). As a spectacle, the Western employs scenes of men being beaten primarily "so that we can *see* men recover, regaining their strength and resources in the process of once again making themselves into men" (174). The hero's recovery from a beating symbolizes his superior masculinity—his ability to rise up from the most severe punishments. In *The Virginian*, Wister introduces a scenario that eventually becomes as conventional to the Western as the shootout. Molly Wood discovers the Virginian, wounded in an Indian attack, unconscious in the wilderness. Following this discovery, the narrative focuses on the long process of the Virginian's convalescence as Molly nurses him back to health. Mitchell argues that such a "feminine presence" is a necessary "catalyst" for the man's recovery, for the "restorative female 'gaze' at the male body" acts as a civilizing influence that ensures that the hero will recover both physical health and manly self-control (178–79).

Few characters in Westerns are beaten as often as Jean Baptiste. In epoch 1, he is rendered unconscious twice, first by the storm and second by a kick in the head from a horse. In both cases, Agnes Stewart's "feminine presence" ensures the return of manly control. In the flashback to childhood, Baptiste is so severely beaten by his mother that he likewise lapses into unconsciousness. In the absence of a civilizing feminine presence (his mother, after all, is the one who beats him), he responds by delving deeper into savagery—into the wilderness where "something evil" lives. Although McCarthy's removal of Orlean from South Dakota does not involve a physical assault, Baptiste's response indicates that he has received an emotional beating that affects both his body and his mind. With the bond of matrimony severed (and resolution to double-consciousness undone) by Orlean's return to the East, Baptiste is consumed by the fear that he will "lose his mental balance unless he journey[s] to Chicago and see[s] his wife" (287). Micheaux writes that "in the days that followed the real Jean Baptiste died and another came to live in his place. And that one was a hollow-cheeked, unhappy, nervous, apprehensive creature" (316). In Chicago, unable to find a way through the barrier McCarthy has erected around Orlean, "all the manhood in him crept out" (347). Baptiste soon engages in the behaviors he earlier condemned: "stud[ying] the various forms of vice about," listening to "ragtime music," and drinking too much (348). In the absence of a civilizing feminine presence, Baptiste becomes more unbalanced and his actions increasingly unmanly. If heterosexual marriage symbolizes a harmonious rather than conflicted sense of twoness, the dissolution of that marriage means that Baptiste must find another way to resolve the opposing demands of his "unreconciled strivings." Narrative events create the expectation that he will resolve inner and outer conflict in time-honored Western fashion—through violent action.

Perhaps the defining characteristic of the Western is the climactic showdown, usually a gunfight. "The most salient fact about the Western," Tompkins comments, is that "it is a narrative of male violence" (28). The Western often consists of a story that not only justifies the hero's violent actions but also insists that such actions are necessary—that the only way for a man to remain a man is through an act of murder. Early Westerns address a growing turn-of-the-century fear that white American men had become too civilized, that too many years of manly restraint had caused the atrophy of male passion and resulted in the feminization of white manhood. White-authored Westerns from the early part of the twentieth century (among them Wister's *The Virginian*) emphasize the importance of a "balanced" masculinity. "A man," the Virginian comments, "any full-sized man, ought to own a big lot of temper. And like all his valuable possessions, he'd ought to keep it and not lose any" (188). If being a man means controlling one's temper, the book also asserts that manhood turns on knowing when to let one's passions explode. In Wister's world, unmanliness appears in two opposing figures, the man who cannot control his passions and the man whose life of civilized restraint has so buried those passions that he has become effeminate. The Virginian stands between these two extremes, filled with male passion which he can release when needed but otherwise always carefully in control of himself. At one point, another character, Balaam, savagely beats a horse, provoking a strong, angry response from the Virginian: "Then vengeance like a blast struck Balaam. The Virginian hurled him to the ground, lifted and hurled him again, lifted him and beat his face and struck his jaw" (264). Certain circumstances (defending the defenseless from truly savage behavior) justify the exercise of male passion. Justice—the defense of his manly honor against Trampas, the villain who has slandered his name—ultimately demands that the Virginian gun down his enemy.

In the Western, passionate masculinity erupts in the form of violent actions, gun battles, fistfights, and so forth, but murder and manliness cannot be reconciled as easily for Micheaux as they are for Wister. As Baptiste reflects, for any man, "the sight of one who has wronged him might cause him for a moment to forget all his good intentions and manly resolutions," and that loss of hard-earned manliness is the one thing that Baptiste cannot afford (312). To murder would be to enact black manhood as white society conceives it, would be to destroy the goal of racial uplift by becoming like a member of that class of blacks above which he supposedly has risen. When the conventions of the Western conflict with the goals of the racial uplift saga, Micheaux departs from the formula. That departure is signaled by a change in place, the shift from South Dakota to Chicago, which becomes the dominant setting for the last half of the book. In the Western, the white hero must prove his manhood through a justifiable—indeed, necessary—act of violence. For Micheaux, the black hero must prove his manhood through precisely the opposite action—by demonstrating his ability to refrain from a savage act of violence, no matter how tempting or justifiable that act might be.

Despite this change in the location, *The Homesteader* still evokes the expectation of a climactic showdown. In language that recalls the killing of the catamount, Baptiste wanders through the streets of Chicago thinking to himself that "the only justifiable action would be to follow the beast to his lair and kill him upon sight" (312). "I feel as if it would do me good," Baptiste comments, "to get drunk tonight and kill somebody" (313). As he contemplates the wrongs done to him, "wrath became his.

. . . He wanted to go forth and slay the beast" (352). As Baptiste as a child killed the catamount, we suspect that Baptiste the man will indeed "slay the beast" that is McCarthy. During his unmanly descent into the under-world of urban vice, he even visits a prostitute, who tells him, "I can just see that some one has done you a terrible wrong, and that when you rose now you would have gone forth and killed him. . . . But try to refrain from that desire" (352). On the verge of succumbing to the "animal viciousness" against which he has fought, Baptiste finds in the most unlikely of places a womanly woman who helps restore his manly self-control just when he needs it.

The novel's final (and most explicitly violent) beating scene counters the expectations otherwise evoked by the narrative. Baptiste does not face McCarthy in a man-to-man showdown that settles their conflict. Rather, the emotional climax of the novel occurs in a scene that repeats the key elements of Baptiste's flashback to childhood. Baptiste loses his temper while speaking to McCarthy over the phone, and Orlean (like Baptiste's mother in the earlier scene) responds by furiously beating him. Baptiste grasps the telephone and pushes Orlean "roughly aside," and we hear "his loud voice screaming over the 'phone" as he cries "savagely" at his enemy on the other end of the line (382). The equally enraged Orlean begins to strike him: "He made no effort to protect himself. He allowed her to strike him at will and with a strength, born of excitement, she struck him in his face, in his eyes, she scratched him, she abused him so furiously until gradually he began to sink. . . . As he lay with eyes closed and a slight groan escaping from his lips at her feet, she suddenly raised her foot and kicked him viciously full in the face. This seemed, then, to make her more vicious, and thereupon she started to jump upon him with her feet" (383). As in the childhood dinner table scene, Baptiste becomes "strangely angry" and is subsequently punished so severely for his outburst that he loses consciousness: "How long he lay there he did not know" (383).

The primary threat represented by McCarthy is his ability, even over the phone, to provoke in Baptiste an uncontrollable rage and in so doing to unman him. The point of *The Homesteader* is not simply that good and bad behaviors exist but that the existence of unmanliness threatens the achievements of civilized African Americans such as Baptiste, whose success derives from his strong will and self-control. Baptiste, the exemplary figure of racial uplift, becomes his own double, slipping into the behaviors that place him among "the others who need the example," his downfall brought about by the others whom he had hoped to uplift. Even worse, the child Baptiste responds to his mother's example by savagely attacking the catamount, and Orlean—the project he was supposed to develop into a woman—similarly responds to his unmanly example with unusual and uncharacteristic viciousness. Rather than lifting her up, he has provoked her to worse behavior. All Baptiste's efforts—manly self-control, romance, homesteading, and racial uplift—collapse in conjunction with his passionate outburst and his subsequent beating at the hands of his estranged wife. As Mitchell notes, however, the Western employs beating scenes to indulge in the drama of the hero's recovery—so that we can admire the superior masculinity that enables him to rise from the physical (as well as in Baptiste's case moral) low to which he has fallen.

For Micheaux, masculine and feminine represent complementary rather than opposing qualities. Adherence to traditional gender roles appears primarily in terms of work assignments, housekeeping, cooking, and raising children for women, working in the fields for men. The qualities he most admires (self-control, strong will, practicality) exist equally in both sexes. Agnes Stewart, one of the novel's examples of admired womanhood, is adventurous (she rides alone out into the blizzard, where she discovers the fallen Baptiste) as well as compassionate. The novel's opening scenario—Agnes's rescue of Baptiste—illustrates what Micheaux sees as the proper relation of the sexes. When the forces outside of the individual's control that are arrayed against him (the burden he must carry, the surrounding whiteness against which he must struggle, the forces of nature within and without) become too much, the woman rescues him, lifts him up and through proper feminine behavior (tender care, nursing) restores him to health and manhood. Agnes's adventurous spirit places her so that she can save Baptiste, but her womanly care returns him to himself. In the other beating scenes, unwomanly behavior—both Orlean and Baptiste's mother physically attack him—contributes to the hero's loss of self-control.

Brought low by his own unmanly behavior (and by Orlean's response to it), Baptiste fortunately encounters a series of womanly women, beginning with Mrs. Merley, who had tried to reunite husband and wife and who "bathed his wounds . . . and bandaged his face carefully" in the wake of his beating (386). In southern Illinois, he visits a young woman, Jessie, and finds that "her kind sympathy" serves "to revive in a measure his usual composure, and when he left a few days later, he was much stronger emotionally [and] determined to try to regain his fortunes" (396–97). He decides to publish and sell his autobiography: "He secured orders for fifteen hundred copies of his book in two weeks . . . and in sixty days . . . had deposited twenty-five hundred dollars to the credit of the book in the banks" (410). This money enables Baptiste to stall his creditors and delay foreclosure proceedings. While traveling the country selling the book, he contacts Irene Grey, a marriage prospect earlier in the novel before circumstances led to his proposal to Orlean. He discovers that Irene is "the kind of girl" and the Greys "the kind of family his race needed" (422). Unlike McCarthy, who wants to be treated like a king, Irene's father, Junius N. Grey, is one—the "Negro Potato King," owner and operator of a vast and successful farm (426). Through the Greys, Baptiste comes into contact with uplifting examples who inspire him to renew his "great desire to make good" (24).

When news arrives that Orlean has sold her claim for a pittance, Baptiste realizes that "the *turning point* in his life had come. At last his manhood had returned, *and he was ready to fight*" (438). Although in *The Virginian*, Wister asserts that "it is only the great mediocrity that goes to law in these personal matters," Micheaux relocates the Western showdown from the wild streets of the frontier town to a Chicago courtroom (399). His decision to seek justice in the court rather than the street signals Baptiste's victory over his passionate impulses. The trial places Orlean in the position of saving her father by "falsifying to the court," an action that frees McCarthy but ultimately unhinges Orlean (486). Despite McCarthy's legal success, "in the minds of every man and woman in the crowded court room, N. J. McCarthy stood a guilty man," resulting in a public relations victory for Baptiste (488). When Baptiste is falsely accused of causing the violent deaths at the McCarthy household, Agnes Stewart reenters the narrative to rescue Baptiste once again. She hires a Pinkerton detective, who establishes Baptiste's innocence in court. Coinciding with Baptiste's release, Agnes discovers an old letter from her mother that reveals her African ancestry. The story ends with Jean and Agnes happily married on their own homestead and with the news that Baptiste had sold his crops "at a price so high that he had sufficient to redeem at last the land he was about to lose and money left for future development in the bargain" (529).

Although Baptiste triumphs, what is the cost of that victory? Gerald Early writes that for Du Bois, "to be an assimilated American and to be an unassimilated Negro were both real and, more importantly, equally or near equally appealing choices" (xx). In the Western, life in the West is always better than in the East. Unwilling or unable to overturn this opposition, Micheaux represents double-consciousness not as a choice between equally appealing options but as a choice of superior (assimilated western American) and inferior (unassimilated eastern Negro) ways of life. At the end of the court proceedings, Baptiste reflects, "It seemed that a great burden had been lifted from his mind, and he closed his eyes as if shutting out the past now forever. He was free. Never would the instance that had brought turmoil and strife into his life trouble him again. Always before there had seemed to be a peculiar bond between him and the woman he had taken as wife. Always he seemed to have a claim upon her in spite of all and she upon him" (490). Freed of the "peculiar bond," Baptiste puts an end to the "turmoil and strife" of twoness by declaring himself free from the mutual "claims" of husband and wife as well as free from the bond between the individual and the larger collective that their marriage symbolized. As a resolution to the problem of double-consciousness posed by the novel, the conclusion seems unsatisfactory. Those characters who represent an unassimilated cultural identity conveniently kill themselves off, and although Baptiste keeps his vow to marry within the race, he chooses a woman of African ancestry who has lived her entire life as a member of the dominant culture. "One ever feels his two-ness," Du Bois writes, "two unreconciled strivings; two warring ideals in one dark body, whose dogged strength alone keeps it from being torn asunder" (5). The difficulty of joining West and East, assimilated and unassimilated, of reconciling "two warring ideals," seems too much, and Baptiste abandons the effort.

McCarthy, Baptiste's double, the inferior Other who cannot remain part of his consciousness, must be defeated and driven out of the story before the hero can enjoy the happy ending promised by the Western. As Bowser and Spence observe concerning Micheaux's work in general, "By setting himself up as a model of one who had risen above the prevalent notion of the Negro as 'inferior,' he was inadvertently reinforcing the very attitude he imagined he was overcoming—the idea that the morality, ambition, and abilities of the Negro was 'the problem'" (25). Instead of explicitly addressing how racial bigotry (white "law" and "custom") might have affected Baptiste's troubles or how racial prejudice has limited African American success in general, Micheaux redirects our attention to "behavioral problems" within the black community. What prevents Baptiste from succeeding is not racial bigotry but the unjust actions of another black man—his father-in-law, Rev. McCarthy, whose characterization repeats dominant culture stereotypes regarding "the morality, ambition,

and abilities" of black people. Such problematic elements—the use of stereotypes, the absence of explicit protest against bigotry—have no doubt
contributed to the relative lack of critical attention Micheaux's written
work has received.

The developing body of scholarship devoted primarily to Micheaux's
films is much more extensive than criticism devoted to his literary work.
In the cinema, Micheaux is pioneer in a way that he is not in the field of
literature, a fact that may explain to a large degree the critical attention
his films have received. Moreover, his films demonstrate a greater willingness to address the problem of white racist attitudes and actions. For example, the controversial *Within Our Gates* (1920) is sharply critical in its
depiction of a white lynch mob; in *The Symbol of the Unconquered* (1920),
a story of the frontier that takes several plot points from *The Homesteader*, the role of the villain is filled primarily by the Ku Klux Klan. A
poster advertising the film emphasizes the spectacle of the "MURDEROUS
NIGHT RIDE" of the Klan as they try "to drive a BLACK BOY off of Valuable Oil Lands" (reproduced in Bowser and Spence 158). In some ways,
The Homesteader can be regarded as a transitional work in Micheaux's
development as an artist. The elements of racial protest that Micheaux
will foreground in his films may already be present, in submerged form,
in *The Homesteader*—in, for example, the naturalistic image of the black
hero struggling to survive in the cold, violent, white world of the blizzard. Not yet willing to indict directly white actions (such as vigilante
violence) that impede African American success and survival, Micheaux
encodes social critique in descriptions of the natural phenomena. As Gussow comments, Handy's memoir "detailing of his entrepreneurial ascent
is shadowed always by his uneasiness at the continuing threat posed by
white violence" (69). Though Micheaux's films more prominently feature
the "threat posed by white violence," it is not necessarily absent from his
novels but is merely present primarily in displaced or coded form.

Numerous parallels exist between Micheaux's films and his novels. According to Bowser and Spence, Micheaux constantly re-created an image
of self, a "biographical legend" that "was neither sole nor unitary. Perhaps
Micheaux himself was searching for a unifying vision of his life through
narratives of achievement" (xix). Although both *The Conquest* and *The
Homesteader* are based on events in Micheaux's life, the two heroes of
these books are clearly different characters created to achieve particular
effects. Oscar Devereaux in *The Conquest* is a tenderfoot unprepared for
life on the frontier, and Micheaux traces Devereaux's gradual development

of the character and skills necessary to his success. The opening scene of *The Homesteader* reveals a key difference in the fictional hero Baptiste and the more autobiographical persona of Devereaux. Baptiste is no tenderfoot. He has already learned the ropes and is presented to us as a heroic rather than as a necessarily realistic or autobiographical figure.

Both *The Conquest* and *The Homesteader* are stories of settlement, of transforming a wilderness frontier into home. The novel ends with Baptiste having just raised and sold a successful wheat crop. And here the story of Jean Baptiste departs sharply from the story of Oscar Micheaux. As Patrick McGilligan observes, the same week in 1913 when Micheaux announced the publication of *The Conquest* in the *Gregory Times Advocate*, "local newspapers posted an official foreclosure notice on Micheaux's original homestead near Gregory. . . . Except for the site farmed by his sister Olive, whose husband helped save it from creditors, all of Micheaux's land would eventually be foreclosed" (93–94). From this point on, Micheaux's story more closely resembled that of Handy and other traveling performers, as Micheaux took to the road rather than the homestead to make his way in the world. He initially sold copies of *The Conquest* door-to-door and worked to establish a distribution network for future projects. In *The Homesteader*, Baptiste is described huddled in his sod house working on the manuscript of *The Conquest*. In contrast, *The Homesteader* was written in Sioux City, Iowa, where Micheaux had moved to incorporate a publishing company, Western Book Supply. Micheaux's talent, it seems, was not so much farming as marketing and salesmanship, with himself and his writing as his primary product. The distribution network he established and the practices he developed served him well when he changed the company's name to Western Book and Film Supply and began making and distributing films, starting with a silent film version of *The Homesteader*.

Micheaux's key idea for the film, the way he planned to create a stir with it, was to present it as "a 'road show,' accompanied by tasteful 'live' attractions" (McGilligan 115). Micheaux's version of film distribution involved making *The Homesteader* part of a "traveling extravaganza," a marketing approach that recalls the traveling minstrel shows of Handy's era (115). Filmed mostly in a Chicago studio, with some exteriors filmed near Sioux City and on location in South Dakota, and completed in late 1918, the film premiered on 20 February 1919 and was billed as "the first full-length, 'all-colored' motion picture" (129). The occasion was indeed "the kind of road show-style gala Micheaux had envisioned," complete with an orchestra playing music composed by jazz band leader Dave Peyton (129). The film was a great success and was immediately banned. Micheaux's father-in-law, the Reverend Newton J. McCracken, and "two other ministers filed a complaint with the Chicago censorship board, accusing Micheaux of vilifying preachers" (130). Micheaux appealed the ban, which was overturned. The surrounding publicity "improved the advertising" and pretty much guaranteed that when the film was relaunched "in the new 1,300-seat Vendome Theatre, the most commodious and prestigious of all Black Belt venues," lines began forming in the morning for the evening screenings, and by the end of the day, "5,700 people had seen the once-banned film" (131). As McGilligan notes, "Making films was only half of Micheaux's genius. The other half was his P. T. Barnum–like salesmanship," especially his ability to exploit controversy and setbacks for greater publicity (131).

In May 1920, Micheaux took the film on a six-week tour of the South and the Midwest: "*The Homesteader* had its second premiere in Kansas City, Missouri, followed by a tour to Wichita and Topeka, Kansas; Omaha, Nebraska; Florence, Sheffield, Decatur, Mobile, Montgomery, Birmingham, and Bessemer, Alabama; Chattanooga, Memphis, and Nashville, Tennessee; Shreveport, New Orleans, Alexandria, Monroe, and Baton Rouge, Louisiana; Spartanburg and Columbia, South Carolina; and Reidsville, North Carolina" (McGilligan 132–33). Following a route that would have been familiar to Mahara's Minstrels or the Smart Set, Micheaux set out to take black America by storm and, in the process, to greatly upset white America, especially as represented by local censorship boards. Traveling prints of films were expensive, and only four of them were struck for *The Homesteader*. The film's eight reels were then steadily trimmed down by edits demanded by multiple local censor boards. The film is no longer extant, in large part because its popularity caused much wear and tear on the prints, and censorship boards sometimes cut out offending segments and did not return the excised footage to the filmmaker. *The Homesteader* disappeared, almost literally, as a result of its own popularity and notoriety.

In terms of Micheaux's later life, what is most significant about the final chapter of *The Homesteader* is not the revelation of a successful crop and the redemption of Baptiste's foreclosed land but where the scene passing along this information takes place. Baptiste "sat alone at this moment in a stateroom aboard a great continental limited, just out of Omaha and speeding westward to the Pacific coast" (529). Soon joined in his stateroom by Agnes, his new wife, Baptiste enjoys a quintessentially Western moment—riding off into the sunset. Micheaux himself, newly successful as an author, already starting to formulate plans for a film, must likewise have felt at the moment of writing this chapter that he too was "speeding westward," symbolically if not literally. Paradoxically, Baptiste, the homesteader, enjoys his greatest moment of satisfaction not at home but on the move; in so doing, he foreshadows the fate of his creator, Micheaux, who spent the next phase of his life moving from one place to another, making himself at home and making his livelihood and his name, if not his fortune, through performance.

3

"This Strange White World"

Race and Place in Era Bell Thompson's American Daughter *and Rose Gordon's Newspaper Writing*

Aboard a train heading out of Minneapolis toward frontier North Dakota, Era Bell Thompson describes a landscape that grows steadily bleaker with each mile further west: "Suddenly there was snow—miles and miles of dull, white snow, stretching out to meet the heavy, gray sky; deep banks of snow drifted against wooden snow fences. . . . All day long we rode through the silent fields of snow, a cold depression spreading over us" (*American* 26–27). Like Oscar Micheaux in *The Homesteader*, Thompson uses realistic winter landscape descriptions in her autobiography, *American Daughter* (1946), allegorically to represent the social situation of herself and her family. The phrase "this strange white world," which she uses to describe the view from the train window, refers to both natural and social environments (27). "Aren't there any colored people here?" her mother asks. "Lord, no!," responds her father, who has preceded the family to North Dakota (27). As the only black child in her school, Thompson soon discovers the difficulty of her situation in this strange white world: "When they . . . called me 'black' and 'nigger' . . . I was alone in my exile, differentiated by the color of my skin, and I longed to be home with the comfort of my family; but even with them I would not share my hurt. I was ashamed that others should find me distasteful" (83–84).

In *American Daughter*, the changed appearance of the physical world signals the crossing of the border from such settled and urban areas as Minneapolis to a frontier space recently opened for homesteading and from a sense of belonging to an African American community to a sense of "exile" in a predominantly white western settlement. Richard Slotkin argues in *Gunfighter Nation: The Myth of the Frontier in Twentieth-Century*

America that frontier narratives emphasize an opposition between "the frontier" and "civilization," or the "wilderness" and the "metropolis," that often falls along a geographical divide between the wild unsettled American West and the urban East. Like Micheaux, Thompson revises this traditional opposition of frontier literature—the essential difference between the wilderness and the metropolis—to symbolize what W. E. B. Du Bois describes as double-consciousness, the psychological tension and turmoil the African American individual experiences as he or she attempts to maintain a sense of belonging to two worlds, one black, one white. In *American Daughter*, the metropolis represents the black world, the place of African American community and culture. Moving west to the frontier means assimilating into mainstream society, separating from the black community, and becoming part of a strange white world. Like Micheaux's *The Homesteader, American Daughter* describes a sense of restless movement reflecting the difficulty of that choice, with Thompson sometimes shuttling back and forth between her frontier home and urban black communities as her race-based and place-based senses of self repeatedly diverge, conflict, and intersect. Although Thompson shares with Micheaux an understanding that descriptions of place can serve an allegorical purpose (as indicated by her use of the wilderness/metropolis opposition as a metaphor for double-consciousness), she balances that allegorical approach with naturalistic and poetic descriptions of a prairie landscape that she observes closely and comes to appreciate for its variety and beauty.

Although not a celebrity like her brother, Taylor Gordon, Rose Beatris Gordon was a remarkable individual in her own right, a pioneer settler whose long residence in Montana began when the state was still a territory. Like Era Bell Thompson, Rose Gordon grew up in a predominantly white frontier community. In contrast to Thompson, who eventually moved to Chicago, Gordon spent her entire life in "the strange white world" of White Sulphur Springs, Montana, where she found a way to both become part of the small-town community and create connections to the rest of the state's scattered African American community. Writing for her local newspaper, Gordon maintained an awareness of her predominantly white readership that led her to make specific choices in terms of subject matter and voice. By comparing her published articles and unpublished writings (such as personal letters), this chapter examines how Gordon carefully crafted a public persona that helped her gain access to the public sphere and how she used that persona to transform "the strange white world" of Montana into home.[1]

As in chapter 1, I juxtapose here different accounts of black western experience—in this case, the writings of two African American women. Gordon's writing reflects her strategies for making home in one particular place—a story of settlement that converges and diverges with accounts of black western travel.[2] Thompson's autobiography tells a story of making home in a particular place and, like W. C. Handy's memoir, describes movement and travel across the West and the United States as a strategy for mapping out African American belonging in both region and nation. For Thompson, home involves her specific sense of connection to the North Dakota landscape, especially in the earlier parts of the memoir; her ability to make herself at home in different places evolves as the memoir progresses and as she develops a series of strategies for adapting to the natural and social environments that she encounters.

Thompson ends up in North Dakota after her father, concerned about his sons' futures, observes, "We'd better take the boys to Dakota. . . . They need to grow and develop, live where there's less prejudice and more opportunity" (*American* 21). The Dakota frontier represents for Tony Thompson an opportunity unavailable in the civilized East, with its system of legal and social segregation. "Nothin' for colored boys to get in this town," Tony states, "but porter work, washin' spittoons" (21). Inspired by his half-brother, John, who writes to him praising "the boundless prairies" as a "new land of plenty where a man's fortune was measured by the number of his sons, and a farm could be had even without money," Tony strikes out "for far-off North Dakota to find a new home in the wide open spaces, where there was freedom and equal opportunity for a man with three sons. Three sons and a daughter" (18, 22). As "a daughter," Era Bell Thompson is barely an afterthought in her father's plans of freedom and equal opportunity and is certainly inadequate as a measure of his success. For the first third of the story, she almost seems an afterthought in her own narrative, downplaying her actions in favor of reporting the successes and failures of her father and brothers, Tom, Dick, and Harry. Her witness-participant persona, however, enables an objective and often ironic commentary on the men's wilderness-taming efforts. Although *American Daughter* at certain moments feels like a parody, specifically of *The Homesteader*, it is more likely that Thompson is parodying the same traditions of African American literature and western writing on which Micheaux draws.

The Thompsons eventually sign a tenant lease on the "Old Hansmeyer place," a homestead that comes with a house, barn, land, and a pair of horses, which have been let loose on the prairie. Those horses immediately capturc hcr fathcr's imagination: "Thcm's the wildest tame horses I ever see. But ain't no horse livin' I can't handle. No, sirree. Ain't no horse livin'" (*American* 39–40). As Tony is seduced by the sight of the wild horses, he is also taken in by Hansmeyers' sales pitch about the "hidden possibilities of the soil (hidden two feet under the snow)" (39). When the snow melts, the family discovers beneath the snow not possibilities but "rocks, millions of rocks pimpling the drab prairie: large blue-gray boulders . . . long, narrow slits of rocks surfacing the soil like huge cetacean monsters" (41). The horses prove as troublesome as the rocky ground. After the spring thaw, the men (with much effort) lure the animals into the barn. While Tom follows them inside, the no longer boastful Tony takes "a safe position outside the barn window—club in hand" (42). From inside the barn "came a high shrill whinny, the thudding sound of bodies, splintering stalls. The old barn moved ominously" (43). Eventually, with the help of a neighbor, Gus, a Norwegian immigrant bachelor with a fondness for whiskey, Tom gets the horses hitched to a wagon. Leaping forward from the barn, "the horses made a new gate through the yard fence and tore down the muddy road on a dead gallop, as Gus sat waving his bottle and yelling in Norwegian" (43). Two hours later, Tom guides the exhausted horses home: "The buggy was a shambles, Gus was stone sober, but we had a team" (43). Tom's taming of the horses proves only temporary, as Tony continues to have trouble with them. Although he drives the team into town one day without mishap, the horses return an hour later "on a dead run, heads up, heels flying, a picture of rhythmic beauty. Turning in the gate on two wheels, they stopped only when the buggy lodged in the barn door. Pop and one seat were missing" (44).

As her brothers take to the tasks of taming the horses, plowing the fields, and "dodging the rocks," the nine-year-old Era enviously watches "the shining shares slide along beneath the stubborn sod, turning over long rows of damp, blackish earth like unending dusky curls" (*American* 46–47). Excluded by age and gender from plowing, Thompson begins to develop a different relationship with the prairie than her father and brothers do. Once the initial shock of the North Dakota winter passes, Thompson indicates a growing sense of appreciation for the natural world around her: "As fall drew near, the intense heat subsided. There were quiet, silent days when the grainfields were hills of whispering gold, undulating ever so softly in the bated breeze. So warm, so tranquil was the spell that one stretched out on the brown, dry earth, whose dead, tufted prairie grasses made the lying hard, but put even the breeze above you. The sun alone stood between you and the blue sky of God" (58). If bleak winter landscape descriptions reflect Thompson's sense of "exile, differentiated by the color of my skin," she nonetheless establishes a sense of belonging to this world. She makes the land into home not by trying to transform it (like her father and brothers) but rather by reshaping her vision of her self in relation to the world. She does not dominate the land as much as place herself within it, "stretched out on the brown, dry earth." According to Joanne M. Braxton, Thompson achieves a sense of "perceptual unity with nature" (162). In Thompson's landscapes, prairie, sun, sky, and individual exist in close relation to the other.

Thompson's perspective on landscape can be compared to that of Micheaux, who similarly tells of an early twentieth-century African American pioneer trying to establish a prairie farm. In *The Homesteader*, Micheaux writes that his protagonist, Jean Baptiste, came to South Dakota "because he felt it was the place for young manhood," and because "here with the unbroken prairie all about him; with its virgin soil and undeveloped resources . . . here could a young man work out his own destiny" (24). Writing in the social context of early twentieth-century prejudice, Micheaux uses Baptiste's transformation of a wild place into a profitable enterprise to symbolize what African Americans in general can accomplish in a world of equal opportunity. His landscape descriptions are shaped by that purpose, so much so that he shows little interest in the prairie's natural beauty. Rather, he emphasizes storms, fires, droughts—natural obstacles to success that Baptiste overcomes through the quality of his character and his admirable work ethic. Whereas Thompson comes to appreciate the prairie in and of itself, Micheaux's Jean Baptiste most appreciates a prairie transformed: "He gazed out over a stretch of land which two years before, had been a mass of unbroken prairie, but was now a world of shocked grain" (131). In Baptiste's eyes, "no crops are like the crop on new land," and the land itself "seemed to appreciate the change, and the countless shocks before him were evidence to the fact" (24, 131). Baptiste does not stretch "out on the brown, dry earth" but rather "gaze[s] over" it, establishing himself in a position of visual dominance rather than perceptual unity.

Thompson's descriptions often take the form of a catalog of the flora and fauna of the prairie that emphasizes a naturalist's eye for detail and a poet's sensibility. "The tumbling tumbleweeds," writes Thompson, "heralded the coming of winter. Huge Russian thistles, ugly and brittle now, free of their moorings, rolled across the prairie like silent, gray ghosts, catching in fence corners, piling up in low places, herded and driven mercilessly by the cold wind that whistled down from the far North" (*American* 66). Like Micheaux, Thompson is attentive to planted fields as well as undisturbed prairie, but her descriptions emphasize beauty over bounty. If "a world of shocked grain" represents financial success for Micheaux, Thompson finds that there is "something clean and sweet about the harvest," discovers that there is "an art in shocking grain" (58–59). Even her descriptions of crop failure recognize the beauty in a natural process that begins with the transformation of a "stubbornly" green "twenty-acre strip of flax" into a "whole field burst into delicate blue flowers, miniature stars against the yellow mustard blooms," and ends when "the blue flowers disappeared as quickly as they had come, and tiny bulbs of seed began to form in their place, to brown and ripen too quickly in the searing wind" (50).

As Annette Kolodny suggests, male writers who describe the American landscape often use the figure of "virgin" terrain that "apparently invites sexual assertion and awaits impregnation" (67). Through references to the prairie's "virgin soil and undeveloped resources" and to the "virgin soil [that] had been opened to the settler" (to name just two examples), Micheaux follows this pattern by implicitly sexualizing the landscape (*Homesteader* 24, 109). Other male writers indulge in a more explicitly sexual relationship through descriptions of physically merging with or penetrating the land. Although sensual, Thompson's landscape descriptions are not allegorical representations of the earth as a female body to be taken, opened, possessed, penetrated, or dominated. Although she may animate her landscapes (they "whisper" and "undulate"), she does not overtly sexualize them, nor does she penetrate or physically merge with the environment. Though "stretched out on the brown, dry earth," she observes that the "prairie grasses made the lying hard," a description that emphasizes both close proximity and distinct physical separation of the individual and the environment (58). Returning from delivering a load of grain, she observes, "Sometimes I sat silently on the high seat or stood down in the bottom of the deep wagon . . . watching gold-streaked heavens turn blue with approaching night" (101). Thompson's landscape descriptions pointedly include her presence as part of the depicted scene. Although she does not establish a dominating gaze that inscribes a hierarchical relationship between observer and observed, she nonetheless maintains a distinct sense of boundaries between Self and Other. By describing her position within the scene as the observer "on the high seat" or "in the bottom" of the wagon, she implies both perceptual unity with and physical separation from the scene under observation.

Although her landscapes do not explicitly connote the female body, she does connect the prairie to her mother. That connection is emotional rather than physical, for she increasingly turns to the prairie for the sort of comfort—especially in terms of salving a consciousness wounded by prejudice—and restored sense of wholeness that her mother provides earlier in the autobiography. During her first day at the Driscoll school, she is subjected to the intrusive curiosity of the other children: "One of Sue's friends put her arm around me and felt of my hair; Tillie stared at the white palms of my hands, and I closed my fists tight until they hurt. For the first time I began to wonder about that and about the soles of my feet" (*American* 33). When she returns home, she discovers her mother waiting. She "clasped me in her arms, hugging me as though she had never expected to see me again, and I soon forgot about the soles of my feet and the palms of my hands" (33). Later in the narrative, she turns for such forgetfulness to the natural world or loses herself in the rhythm of farm chores: "With my dog and my pony I was happy beyond the realm of people, for I had found a friendship among animals that wavered not, that asked so little and gave so much of loyalty and trust, irrespective of color" (84). "The coming-home on a load of hay in the warm silence of twilight," Thompson writes, "had a sacredness about it that filled us with the inner happiness that comes of a day's work well done" (52). The prairie becomes a place of peace and healing that supplements or substitutes for her family. Repeated throughout her landscape descriptions are references not only to beauty, tranquillity, silence, and peace but also to solitude and loneliness. Alone with a horse and wagon, Thompson describes the experience of hauling grain to the elevator: "I loved the long, solitary ride through the golden autumn sunshine . . . when the days stood still and the warm silence was unbearable in its poignant beauty" (100). Although the prairie represents healing, her moments of experiencing a sense of wholeness are most often achieved at the cost of separation from the social world. "Of all the family, I alone was happy on our land, content to call it home," Thompson writes, but that happiness in solitude mirrors the sense of social isolation she often feels in her predominantly white community (111). Thompson's landscape descriptions encode a seemingly contradictory sense of both isolation from and unity with her surroundings that points to the central question of the narrative: How does one establish a sense of natural wholeness and unity as part of a social world divided by race?

For Du Bois, the question of how to achieve a sense of whole self in an America divided by the color line is the central dilemma of African

American experience.[3] Like Micheaux, Thompson contributes both to the literature of the frontier and to African American literature through her clever joining of the central oppositions of each body of literature by using frontier literature's wilderness/metropolis opposition as a metaphor for double-consciousness. The metropolis for Thompson represents African American culture and identity, and the wilderness/prairie represents assimilation into the predominantly white world of the American mainstream. Although Thompson ultimately tries to overcome these oppositions, others in the book try to resolve their sense of double-consciousness by severing their connection to the black East. In response to her mother's curiosity about other black people in the area, Thompson's uncle, John, states, "What'd you want with colored folks, Mary? Didn't you come up here to get away from 'em? Me, I could do without 'em for the rest of my days" (27–28). In the mythology of the frontier, life on the frontier is always better than in "civilization," and for John, assimilation in the frontier community is preferable to an unassimilated life among black people in the metropolis. To a certain extent, Uncle John reflects a Baptiste-like point of view, although he lacks the counterweight of race loyalty that both balances and helps to undo Micheaux's hero.

Others indicate less certainty than John does, and many of the characters in *American Daughter* address the difficulty of that choice. Ed Smith, an African American man with whom Tony Thompson rooms while working in Bismarck, exemplifies this dilemma. In Bismarck, he operates a successful pawn shop, but he acknowledges his wife's loneliness: "She hasn't got anybody to associate with but white folks. Oh, they're nice enough, treat us fine and all that, but they're not colored, see" (80). With the birth of their son, the Smiths find themselves divided. They "don't want to bring the kid up ignorant about his own people," but at the same time they "don't want him learn how to run from white folks" (80). As Ed states, "I was bred and born in the South, lived there most of my life, but I don't want my son to be brought up there either" (80).

Thompson's brother, Dick, who abandons the farming enterprise early in the story, makes a different choice and migrates eastward to the city as soon as he's old enough to leave the family. In a letter, he asks, "How . . . can you folks stay out there in that Godforsaken country away from civilization and our people?" (*American* 113). Dick also sends a copy of the *Chicago Defender*, "the first Negro newspaper I had ever seen" (113). While the newspaper represents part of Thompson's education in African American culture, a story on lynching and a photograph of a hanging remind her of the problems blacks face back in "civilization." "The life-less body dangling from the tree," writes Thompson, "became a symbol of the South" and of "Dick's civilization," a place where "black and white Americans fought each other and died" (113). Through the stories of in-dividual family members and neighbors, Thompson describes the differ-ent responses and psychological adjustments of these pioneers who have left behind black communities to become part of a strange white frontier world, which offers greater opportunity for landownership, less (but not a complete lack of) racism, a degree of safety from the antiblack violence erupting throughout much of early twentieth-century America, and es-cape from the corrupt Jim Crow culture of segregation and second-class citizenship. That escape, however, comes at the cost of separation from African American culture and community. Is it preferable to remain iso-lated from "our people" in the relative safety of the frontier or to risk the dangers of antiblack violence in the civilized metropolis?

Just before Christmas, the Thompson family members experience their first blizzard, and Thompson describes the storm closing in and "forming a blurry whiteness" (*American* 69). Even within the whiteness of the storm, a sense of belonging to the black world left behind is re-created when several African American families get together to celebrate Christmas: "Now there were fifteen of us, four percent of the state's entire Negro population. Out there in the middle of nowhere, laughing and talk-ing and thanking God for this new world of freedom and opportunity, there was a feeling of brotherhood, of race consciousness, and of family solidarity. For the last time in my life, I was part of a whole family, and my family was a large part of a little colored world, and for a while no one else existed" (74). The physical distance between the urban black world and the predominantly white frontier community exaggerates the dilemma of double-consciousness, but the Thompson family finds "a little colored world" within the surrounding blurry whiteness and maintains a feeling of "race consciousness" and a sense of solidarity with black friends and family that contributes to their ability to transform this new world into home. Although many frontier narratives maintain an essential difference between civilization and wilderness, *American Daughter* undermines that distinction by re-creating a sense of the urban black community on the Dakota frontier.

Transforming North Dakota from a strange white world into home involves not only adjusting to the new natural environment but also con-necting with other families—white and black—to create an integrated community. At the Christmas celebration, "two white families stopped by to extend their greetings. The spell of color was broken, but not the spirit of Christmas, for the way Mack greeted them and their own warm response erased any feeling we may have had of intrusion" (*American* 74). Thompson complicates her initial image of the "white world" by acknowledging that her frontier community is multiethnic if not multiracial. The establishment of an integrated community involves friendships established between the Thompsons and other neighbors, primarily European and Scandinavian immigrants. Seeing that the Thompsons are in desperate straits, a German neighbor buys them sacks of food: "Nein, nein! I no vant money. Ven you git it you pay me, if you vant. I got money, I your neighbor, I help you. Dot iss all" (55). Integration for Thompson does not mean assimilation—losing one's black identity by merging completely with the surrounding white world—but involves rather a mixing of cultural elements, as symbolized by her brothers development of their own patois, "Negrowegian" (82). Although Driscoll, North Dakota, is no utopian space free from racial prejudice, Thompson consistently (if temporarily) locates here and elsewhere the possibility of integrated communities that represent her vision of what America should be.

Feelings of being at home are fleeting, however, and the wholeness of the "little colored world" enjoyed at Christmas fragments with the death of Thompson's mother the following February. The family begins to break apart as Era Bell's brothers one by one abandon the farm, leaving only her and her father, who walked around "in a halo of grief, whistling or humming the old hymns" (*American* 97). Braxton observes that Mary Thompson symbolizes Era Bell's "connection with the primary source of [her] black and female identity" (146). Her mother's death begins a process whereby Thompson becomes more and more alienated from the black world of which she feels so much a part at Christmas. Although the prairie landscape to which she turns for comfort may substitute as a source of maternal and female identity, the land does not provide that same sense of connection to black identity. The loss of her mother and the connection to black identity she symbolizes initiates a search both for self and for a lost home, a physical and psychological space representative of wholeness rather than twoness. The prairie that Thompson loves, with its "white clouds of peace and clean, blue heavens," cannot overcome the pull she feels to learn more about the black world of the East (*American* 113).

After his wife's death and his sons' departure, Tony abandons farming to move further west to Mandan, North Dakota, where the mountain time zone and "the real West" begin (*American* 145). At this midpoint in her autobiography, Thompson's story becomes a narrative of education and of discovery of a voice, as symbolized by her developing career as a writer. As her father moves west, she travels in the opposite direction, seeking the "land of my people," where she secures a summer job in St. Paul and begins to explore "the world of colored girls and boys . . . of colored stores and churches" (159). Her people, resentful that an outsider has taken one of the few available white-collar jobs for African Americans, do not accept her with open arms, and by summer's end, "I was glad to leave . . . glad to get away from grocery stores and restaurants and rows of colored houses and colored people's gates—gates where I was still a stranger—and colored boys and girls who did not want me" (164). Thompson's effort to resolve her sense of double-consciousness is reflected after her mother's death by the narrative's restless movements back and forth. "I wondered what it was I had sought to escape," Thompson writes, "running back and forth from prairie to city" (198). In each move, she finds herself located in either white or black worlds or uneasily negotiating the space between the two. At the same time that she loves the silence of the prairie, she also loves the voice that she discovers in her journeys to the city. To be on the prairie is to be comforted and healed, but it is also to be silent and alone.

Rejected by St. Paul's black community, she turns her attention to another strange white world, becoming one of the few African American students at the University of North Dakota. Thompson inherits the ability to survive in this and other environments from her father, who flourishes when asked to bring together black and white social worlds. After taking over a furniture store in Mandan, he and Era Bell set up in a new house that is separated from their neighbors, the Harmons, by "a high fence" through which "four little boys fretted" and "tried to make friends through the cracks. Mrs. Harmon didn't approve of Negroes for neighbors" and spent her day "watching from behind her starched curtains" (*American* 137). Thompson writes, "Pop was irked by the constant watching, and he felt sorry for the little boys jailed in behind the fence, so gradually he began to break the lady down. Every morning he'd come outside by the kitchen window and bow politely to the starched curtains and say good morning to the kids. His whistling about the yard and garden drew them to the fence like a magnet. He talked to them as he worked, apparently unmindful of the woman's watching eyes. Little by little the curtains began to part, slowly Mrs. Harmon began to nod, then smile. It wasn't long before she came out on her back porch to sit and listen to what Pop said to her boys, before the little boys were slipping over the fence and into our yard" (138). Not all walls that separate black and white are so easily breached, and the book offers plenty of examples of people whose prejudice withstands even the considerable Thompson charm. Nonetheless, Thompson's father provides her with strategies for surviving in the white world that she must negotiate to earn her college degree. His daughter will develop the same sort of talent for creating friendships across ethnic and racial boundaries.

Following her mother's death, Thompson establishes a series of relationships with girls and young women of different ethnic groups, and these friendships help her begin to reestablish a sense of female identity and community. After her father abandons the farm, the two live in several North Dakota towns, where Thompson finds a wider sampling of ethnicities than in the farming community of Driscoll. Her new community includes Russian-German friends who live in neighborhoods where "English was seldom spoken" as well as her Sioux friend, Priscilla Running Horse, whose non-English-speaking mother, Thompson observes, was likewise "Old Country," except that "it wasn't Old Country: it was this country" (*American* 145–47). In Bismarck, she befriends a Jewish girl, Sarah Cohn, and the two "became inseparable" (127). Together, they wander "into enemy territory, neighborhoods where the kids called us names; but if they called me a coon, they called her a kike, and when I was with her there was none of the embarrassment I felt when I was with my other friends" (128). As a student at the University of North Dakota, she takes up residence with the adventurous Opal Block in the Jewish section of Grand Rapids, where she adds Yiddish to her "strange vocabulary" of Norwegian, German, and English and where she develops "a taste for lokshen and kosher fleish" (174). Through female friendships, Thompson creates a multiethnic social community whose members transgress the official and physical boundaries that segregate groups of people within distinct areas of space—the German neighborhood, the Jewish section, the Indian school.

She begins to experience through these social relations a sense of unity and comfort similar to that found earlier in her solitary sojourns on the prairie, but her task remains to find a way to bring together her experiences of the social and natural worlds and to connect both to an African American community that seems increasingly distant. Although Thompson enjoys a degree of social mobility as an individual, that mobility does not exist for the majority of African Americans who remain confined by the physical patterns of segregation. Her task becomes more difficult with the death of her father, which also symbolizes the severing of the final familial connection to the western landscape: "Between two deaths I stood at prairie eventide; the last symbol of family lay lifeless at my feet. Gone, too, were the bonds and obligations, and in their stead a bereftness, a desolate freedom. My life was my own choosing, and there could be no more coming home" (201). After her father's death, her explorations take her further east, and the narrative emphasis turns to a search for a place in the world of the metropolis.

Thompson eventually finds a place in the home of a white family, the Rileys, who help sponsor her attendance at Morningside College in Iowa. Although she is happy and comfortable within both the Riley family and the Morningside College community, after graduation Thompson moves to Chicago "seeking work and a home among my people" (*American* 249). Although her "new home was ideal," her African American landlord and landlady "didn't like white people," and when she brings her white friend, Silver, to visit, "we were met with a cold, hostile silence" (267). Individual efforts to create an integrated society of close friends are made difficult by the larger divisions of the social world, and rather than resolving her sense of double-consciousness, her Chicago experience leaves her "feeling that I was fighting the world alone, standing in a broad chasm between the two races, belonging to neither one" (268). In segregated Chicago, she also finds herself under tighter economic and social restrictions than she had experienced while under the protective care of white friends in North Dakota and Iowa. When the Rileys come to visit, "for a while I was back in the boundless white world, where all gates were open, all the fences down. . . . It was a temptation to go home with the Rileys, but I chose to stay in my new black world, feeling that somewhere I would find a happy side, that between the white and the black there must be a common ground" (255).

That wished-for common ground is sometimes found. When visited by her white friend, Gwyn, Thompson takes her to a "shady knoll in Washington Park, where we could sit on the cool grass and talk, where, under the pure blue sky and the whispering trees, no shadow of race would come between us" (268). Natural space operates as both the figurative opposite of the urban metropolis and as a possible point of mediation between the black and white social worlds that split Thompson's allegiance. Thompson occasionally finds in such natural spaces as the park momentary integrated homes that exist in contrast to the segregated social spaces we see in the book. As Braxton observes, "Chicago's 'pure blue sky' brings back Era Bell's childhood sense of wholeness symbolized by her perceptual unity with nature and the blue skies of her North Dakota girlhood" (174). In contrast to those earlier moments of unity with nature, Thompson shares this moment with another. If Thompson figures double-consciousness through her twin desires to find a sense of unity in both the natural world of the prairie and the social world of the metropolis, the park, which exists within urban Chicago, represents the interrelationship of both those worlds. The "whispering trees" recall the whispering grain fields of the prairie. That the same "pure blue sky" exists above both Chicago and North Dakota posits the two not as opposing terms but rather as part of the same continuum of experience. Thompson realizes that she must rethink the separation of natural space from social space, must overturn the frontier narrative's metropolis/wilderness opposition to create for herself places of healing, comfort, and integration—to create home in other environments.

In the final chapter, Thompson narrates a trip by bus across America. As with Handy's descriptions of his minstrel journeys, Thompson claims a place in all parts of America through her travels, linking different regions (North, South, East, West) and seemingly opposed social worlds. Thompson resists seeing the city and the frontier as essential markers of difference, as inferior and superior places. She also does not lift one social world, black or white, over the other, calling both regions and both communities home. Still, she realizes that she alone cannot close the social gap, that the resolution to twoness ultimately involves social forces larger than the self. She concludes with the comment, "The chasm is growing narrower. When it closes, my feet will rest on a united America" (*American* 296). Although *American Daughter* registers a pattern of location and dislocation, of finding home, of being in exile, Thompson never abandons her effort to resolve double-consciousness by establishing, even tenuously, a sense of home and of belonging in both the city and the prairie, in both the black and the white worlds.

A lifelong resident of Montana who was born in the rough-and-tumble mining town of Barker, Montana Territory, in 1883, Rose Beatris Gordon lived in the small town of White Sulphur Springs from 1885 until her death in 1968. At a time when black women in America were consistently denied a public role or a public voice, Gordon both established her economic independence and made a place for herself in the public sphere of White Sulphur Springs. Although she began training in Helena in 1905 for a career as a practical nurse, she returned to the Springs to help her ailing mother operate Gordon's Delicatessen and Notions Store.[4] Gordon's became Rose's Café in the 1920s and moved onto Main Street, where Rose operated the business into the 1940s, when she completely changed directions and enrolled in a Swedish massage course; for the last twenty or so years of her life, she enjoyed a successful career as a physiotherapist and served as an officer in both business and religious organizations, attended state and national physiotherapy conventions, and served as secretary for the White Sulphur Springs branch of the Episcopal Churchwomen.

With a degree in journalism from Morningside College, Era Bell Thompson used her education and training (after a long period when the only work she could find was as a housekeeper) to win a fellowship that enabled her to write *American Daughter*. That manuscript in turn resulted in a position at Johnson Publishing in Chicago, where she worked on several of the company's publications, including *Negro Digest*, and finally with *Ebony* magazine. Working in a company devoted to publications intended for an African American audience, Thompson became a well-respected journalist and activist during the civil rights era. Holding various editorial positions, she wrote for and influenced the content of *Ebony* for more than forty years. Although Gordon and Thompson shared the experience of growing up in western frontier towns, their paths diverged quite sharply after they became adults, with Gordon remaining in her predominantly white Montana town and Thompson becoming a central figure at an important popular black magazine in a big city, a position that enabled her to visit and write about Africa (see Thompson, *Africa*) and provided her with a platform for active participation in the civil rights movement. Although similarities exist between the experiences of these two women, Gordon remained in the "strange white world" of Montana and sought publication opportunities not in black-audience periodicals but in her local newspaper. Those key differences shaped both the content and the style of Gordon's writing about her life.

Glenda Riley comments that western African American women have "suffered near-invisibility in western history" in part because many "archivists [have] neglected to collect these women's source materials, and most historians [have] disregarded their stories" (22). Because of Taylor Gordon's celebrity status in the 1920s, however, an extensive archive related to Rose Gordon's life and career has been preserved. In the segregated America of the twentieth century, Rose Gordon negotiated the color line and established herself as an important community voice, the "village historian" of White Sulphur Springs. At some point in the 1930s, she started work on a book, "Gone Are the Days," a combination of memoir and Montana history, with White Sulphur Springs as its focus. Although the book was never published, it provided a source for the shorter articles she began publishing in the *Meagher County News* in the 1940s, where she continued to publish her writing until her death in 1968.

Gordon's newspaper contributions fall into three categories: memorial tributes to recently deceased members of the community, which varied in length from a few lines to several columns; historical writing published as "Rose Gordon's Recollections" or "Centennial Notes," both of which contained a mixture of autobiography, biography, and local history; and general letters to the editor, which sometimes commented on local events and activities (such as weddings attended) or offered her take on items published earlier, sometimes with direct comments on current politics and social issues. Gordon published hundreds of items in the *Meagher County News*—some only a few sentences long, others taking up several newspaper columns, and longest her 1955 tribute to Annie Gordon, "My Mother Was a Slave," to my knowledge the only published first-person narrative of nineteenth-century African American migration to Montana.

As the title of "My Mother Was a Slave" suggests, Gordon's writing is both consistent with other depictions of the black West and offers something new. In this as-told-to biography of Annie Gordon within the larger framework of Rose's autobiography, Gordon, like Nat Love, tells a story in which western migration is a means of leaving behind an identity as a slave to experience a more fully realized humanity. Such self-realization is made possible by becoming an accepted member of a predominantly white western community (the band of cowboys for Nat Love, the community of White Sulphur Springs for Annie Gordon). However, the fact that Rose's story centers on a black female pioneer (and is narrated by that woman's daughter) makes "My Mother Was a Slave" quite a departure from the better-known black western memoirs such as Love's. From the moment when Annie Gordon is described with tears "roll[ing] down her cheeks" and "falling on her baby boy whom she held in her arms," Rose signals that she is telling a very different sort of western story than that of the "solitary figure loosened from moorings of family, home, and community." "My Mother Was a Slave" is first and foremost a story of family and of an African American family making a home in a seemingly unlikely place—the pioneer town of White Sulphur Springs.

"My Mother Was a Slave" is also part of a genre of writing that became Gordon's particular specialty, the memorial tribute, examples of which appeared frequently in the *Meagher County News*, sometimes at the request of the editor or of family members of the deceased. The tributes were a genre of writing well suited to her strengths as a writer, allowing her to combine her interest in local history with her talent for personal narrative, as most of the tributes involve an overview of the individual's contribution to the Springs community as well as Gordon's narration of her personal memories of the deceased. She was also democratic in her choice of subjects, writing memorials for the town's prominent as well as lesser-known citizens. Even with the town's notable citizens, she includes anecdotes of everyday life. In her tribute to Bide Edwards published in the *Meagher County News* on 20 January 1965, for example, she acknowledges his public role as "county commissioner and mayor of the city for many years" but places greater emphasis on more homely public service: "Our winters were bitter cold years ago and Mr. Edwards always did his best to see that all had coal and would leave a little extra in his wagon in case of emergency at night so people could get coal."

A typical example appeared in *News* on 15 February 1950:

> I want to pay tribute to Mrs. Lavina Bandel.
>
> I well remember the first time I met her. She was a charming young lady, full of life and very pleasant. She possessed stability and inner poise. Everything she did was done well. She often spoke of her childhood days, saying she was taught to be obedient, and above all to finish every duty she took part in. She married Mr. Eugene Bandel many years ago; she was a wonderful wife and real helpmate.
>
> I will miss her very much. She was a kind neighbor. When I was planting my front yard, she gave me lilac bushes, golden glow and many other plants. They will be living memories of her. She was a great lover of nature.
>
> Her son Theodore lives in California. He will always hold fond memories of his wonderful mother and may her memory lead him in the path of destination she had always dreamed of for him.

Rose's memorials almost always begin with some variation of the phrase "I want to pay tribute to." Although similar to an obituary in content, the recitation of key moments in the individual's public life is a much smaller part of the tribute, leading to Gordon's comments on a character trait or traits that she particularly admired. Gordon most often mentions service to others, whether to family members or the community as a whole, especially in terms of little kindnesses that are easily forgotten. Most of all, Gordon celebrates the mundane, doing so through personal anecdotes that reveal something about the personality of the deceased. Gordon often mentions how the life of the individual has cleared a path for others to follow, and her admiration for pioneers of all sorts, especially the "grand old timers" of the West, is clear in all her tributes.

Gordon's tributes to women in particular also emphasize the importance of making a home, and the personal connection to the deceased often touches on that individual's contribution to Gordon's homemaking. In a tribute to Luella Watson preserved in a scrapbook, Gordon writes, "I had the pleasure of calling at her home several years ago and found her to be a most charming hostess. She possessed the western hospitality which is fast fading from the old west." Gordon's tribute takes us to a place seldom visited in an obituary, into the intimate space of the home, a space that suddenly opens outward to represent the whole of the West, as Gordon claims a certain type of hospitality as an essential quality of westernness. As is often the case in writing about the West, Gordon's tone is elegiac, not only because the topic is a memorial to the deceased but also because that individual death is reflective of a larger sense of cultural loss. Rather than a Turnerian lamentation on the closing of the frontier, Gordon mourns the loss of "hospitality," the quality that for her defines westernness. Throughout her tributes, the mourning for the lost individual consistently reflects this greater sense of loss—of the particular qualities that define westernness for Gordon or of the people and places that represent western ideals.

On 25 January 1950, Gordon writes, "I want to pay tribute to the late Herbert Harris," whose "passing brought back memories of the Red Brick school house which was demolished by earthquake several years ago, but nevertheless that spot is cherished by us who attended the school." Her tribute to Harris thus becomes simultaneously a memorial to the White Sulphur Springs of her childhood, since his death reminds her of other important childhood symbols that have passed on. In paying tribute to Harris, Gordon pays tribute as well to such important markers of her childhood as the schoolhouse and the Methodist church that both she and the Harris family attended. Like the school building, Gordon writes, the Methodist church "has been reduced to a few scattered bricks here and there, but its walls once echoed with song and prayer." Although like Era Bell Thompson, Gordon praises the beauty of the western landscape, her focus in her writing is less flora and fauna and more people and places. Rather than the "perceptual unity with nature" that restores a sense of wholeness and belonging to the "exiled" Thompson, Gordon finds unifying wholeness in her connection to particular places—especially buildings associated with her childhood, the school and the church, the home that her father bought in the mid-1880s and in which she lived until her death. For Gordon, home is the place of "cherished" spots, and her memorials pay tribute to those spots as much as to people.

The longer tributes often take several turns, beginning with a memorial to a particular individual but sometimes ending in completely different places. Born in South Dakota, Harris "came to White Sulphur Springs, Montana when he was six months old in the days of the covered wagon." After observing Harris's success in life as a farmer and cattle rancher, the tribute turns to other members of the Harris family and more specifically to Rose's connection to them. We also return to the redbrick school, as the tribute turns from Herbert to his sister, Lottie A. Harris: "I was one of her pupils, a nervous pupil, but she was grand to us all." Miss Harris "made us walk the chalk line and I am glad she did," Gordon remembers, and her mother reinforced that firm discipline: "If we would go home and tell mamma that the teacher was cross today, mamma would say, 'Well, you were not obedient or she would not have been cross.' So we were on our own." Gordon continues, "I had to help mamma so much, and would get behind with my arithmetic. [Miss Harris] always helped me. My success in later years was due to her patience. One day I was really hard at work on problems and all at once I sneezed. Miss Harris said, 'Rose, you must not sneeze so loud.' I said, 'Miss Harris, I did not know it was going to be so loud.' I can still see the smile creep on her face." Although Rose turns the story into a joke, she also incorporates into the telling some of the hardship her family faced after the death of her father left her mother the family's sole support. Gordon periodically missed school to help her mother do the laundry she took in. The tribute form, especially as Gordon developed it, allowed shifts in subject matter that enabled her to incorporate her personal connections to the deceased and that created opportunities to continue one of Gordon's central concerns as a writer—telling the story of her remarkable mother.

Gordon's newspaper writing, scattered over thirty years of letters and columns, provides a vivid picture of life in the Springs during its heyday. Her writing also reveals something about herself. As with "My Mother Was a Slave," Gordon defers her story to the stories of others, but she often appears in the margins—babysitting for a "grand old timer," serving this prominent lawyer at her café on Main Street, or chatting with circus king John Ringling about his love of good cooking and his disdain for fine dining. Gordon's memorials first and foremost pay tribute to her friends and neighbors, but they also serve several strategic purposes. They provide a way for her to enjoy seeing her writing published, especially after years of failing to find a publisher for her book manuscript. They also represent an unconventional strategy for autobiographical writing: Spread across several decades of issues of the *Meagher County News* is the story of Rose Gordon's life. Finally, through her memorial tributes, Gordon comments covertly—and sometimes overtly—on race relations in White Sulphur Springs in the 1950s and 1960s.

In *American Daughter*, Thompson directly addresses the uncomfortable experience of being one of the few African American students in her rural school. Imagining the point of view of her befuddled teacher, Miss Breen, Thompson writes, "Now, suddenly, without warning, here were two studies in brown [Thompson and her brother, Harry], not quite like the pictures in the geography or funny papers, but near enough to be identified. They were the first bona fide Negro children she or the pupils had ever seen" (32). If Gordon addresses her own experiences as an unusual sight for her fellow students, she does so obliquely, as when she observes in her tribute to Miss Harris, "I was one of her pupils, a nervous pupil, but she was grand to us all." Rose underscores her difference—among the pupils, she was the "nervous" one—but says little about what might have made her uncomfortable about her situation in the school. Without directly stating that Miss Harris was notable for her equality of approach to both white and black students, Gordon nonetheless suggests it: "She was grand to us all."

Like her brother, Taylor Gordon, in *Born to Be*, Rose Gordon asserts the unusual equality of treatment in White Sulphur Springs. "I knew I was black and different in appearance from most of the kids I played with," Taylor writes, "but my being so never changed the values of the game we might be playing. I got a chance to pitch or bat at the time my merits won for me either of the positions" (233). Rose similarly emphasizes the lack of prejudice in her life in the Springs. "Never once when I was a child," Rose writes in "Gone Are the Days," "was I treated as if I were any color except white" (15). It is certainly possible that Rose felt that her life as a child was untouched by racism. John Francis Gordon's standing in the community as a family man and dependable wage earner may have earned a respectable status for him and his family, a hedge against the prejudice evident in other communities. Likewise, Annie Gordon, well practiced in negotiating unequal social relations after having grown up under slavery, may have been very effective at protecting her children from any surrounding prejudice. But perhaps the key thing to note about Rose's comment in "Gone Are the Days" is the phrase "Never once when I was a child," which suggests that there might be a different story to tell about Rose's adult life.

In his introduction to the 1975 edition of *Born to Be*, Robert Hemenway observes that "the normal initiation motif of the Black autobiography" involves the representation of a defining moment "where innocence is shattered" by an awareness of racial prejudice—a moment that would presumably not occur where prejudice did not exist (xxxi). In *The Souls of Black Folk* (1903), W. E. B. Du Bois vividly writes of his own first encounter with prejudice when in the "wee wooden schoolhouse" of his childhood, the students decided to exchange "visiting-cards" (4). "The exchange was merry," Du Bois writes, "till one girl, a tall newcomer, refused my card,—refused it peremptorily, with a glance. Then it dawned upon me with a certain suddenness that I was different from the others; or like, mayhap, in heart and life and longing, but shut out from their world by a vast veil" (4).

Like Du Bois, Thompson places this moment of sudden awareness of difference in the schoolhouse. For her, it is the curious and uncomfortably personal attention she receives from her classmates, who touch her hair and stare at "the white palms of my hands" (*American* 33). "For the first time," Thompson writes, "I began to wonder about that and about the soles of my feet" (33). For Du Bois, this moment signals the initiation of double-consciousness, the first moment of "looking at one's self through the eyes of others" (5). Thompson's account revises Du Bois by concluding this story with her return to her home and to the comforting arms of her mother. Home provides Thompson with a refuge from double-consciousness.

Hemenway is undoubtedly correct in pointing out the centrality of the initiation motif in African American literature, but Taylor and Rose Gordon, in a move typical of their writing styles and of their relationship to African American literary tradition, both evoke that tradition and sharply depart from it. In "My Mother Was a Slave," Rose writes, "In a land seared by death, battle and poverty, yellow fever and smallpox, the Negro race had to fight something as bad as slavery: prejudice. . . . It was so hard for Mamma to tell us that we were colored children and that we would always have trouble because we were. But thank God, the grand old timers never let us know we were black and they were southern people, eastern people and western people and by the time we grew up we had it all figured out.

We would say to ourselves, they just don't know the world is made up of all races, colors and creeds." In contrast to Du Bois and Thompson, Rose's awareness of prejudice comes not from a member of the dominant race but from her mother, who gently breaks the news and who seems to have more emotional difficulty with it ("It was so hard for Mamma to tell us") than Rose does. In a sense, Rose conflates into one moment the two key moments from Thompson's account: the incident that makes the narrator aware of difference, the comforting mother love that salves the wound of double-consciousness.

In "My Mother Was a Slave," Gordon writes that her mother revealed "that we were colored children and that we would always have trouble because we were," but in the double-movement that is typical of Rose's aesthetic, her introduction of her awareness of racial difference is subsequently erased by the next sentence: "But thank God, the grand old timers never let us know we were black." What follows that statement, however, is the reintroduction of awareness of difference: "By the time we grew up we had it all figured out." Perhaps it is not that the "trouble" never comes but that it comes later—"by the time we grew up"—than her mother expects. We might consider Rose's depiction of a prejudice-free White Sulphur Springs childhood as being as much a rhetorical strategy as a realistic portrayal—as a means of setting up a silent contrast between the White Sulphur Springs of the past and of the present.

Comparing "My Mother Was a Slave" to the unpublished version of the story in "Gone Are the Days" enables us to see just what Gordon chose to erase from her comments on race and racial prejudice in Montana as she prepared her story for publication in the *Meagher County News*. In "Gone Are the Days," Gordon observes, "I want to pay tribute to those grand people of my childhood days. They did not allow prejudice to creep into the archives of their brains" (15). However, she follows that tribute with a more negative comment that suggests her explicit awareness of contemporary racial prejudice and indicates her defiant attitude toward that prejudice: "*Now* as I sometimes see people that do not like my brown face, it does not affect me in the least" (15; emphasis added). In public forums such as the newspaper, Gordon adopts a strategy for addressing the existence of prejudice in her home town by portraying the "grand old timers" consistently, if implicitly, as a point of comparison and contrast to another group that is never directly indicated as it is in the draft of "Gone Are the Days." Her attitude toward those "people that do not like my brown face" is also more trenchantly expressed in manuscript form: "I may make the remark that they are vulgarians" (15). "Gone Are the Days" makes clear that the praise of the "grand old timers" in her tributes is there, in part, to draw a contrast between past and present. If that contrast is drawn quietly in her published writing, we can nonetheless make it more audible by comparing Gordon's public and private writing.

Gordon's personal letters and other unpublished writings, including "Gone Are the Days," reveal the existence of contemporary prejudice that vexed her periodically throughout the twentieth century. The unpublished writings also demonstrate a fiery side to Rose's personality that does not always make it into her public writing. In an undated personal letter, Gordon writes,

> I have just heard the latest gossip that Mrs. Winters is being asked to resign from her Lodge for keeping my company.
>
> Mrs. Ashford can you prove that my company is such that one would be damaged by my association?
>
> I know my skin is black [which] I can't help, you might have been born black would that necessarily have to corrupt your character?
>
> Mrs. Ashford I pity you as a mother would pity a child, and each night as you pray ask God to teach you to understand that each race is [his] own and that you are not to abuse and wound their feelings.
>
> Mrs. Winters came into my life in one of the greatest sorrows that comes to a human being who loves home, the loss of my Mother, and if being kind to the sad and suffering is against the rules of your order, may God send an angel to teach them the right way.
>
> I am sorry for Mrs. Winters. Her pleasures are limited but you know some even envy us of them. May [God] Help you and Bless you.[5]

Although clearly offended, Gordon emphasizes the offense to Mrs. Winters. At the same time, kindhearted though Gordon was, she is also clearly willing to take to task those who are deserving of such a reprimand. Despite her anger, she still stresses Christian charity and concern for a lost soul who has strayed from God's "right way." At the same time, telling someone they need this much help can hardly be considered complimentary. In her closing, Gordon inadvertently leaves out the word *God*, an elision that may suggest her frustration and anger. This letter offers a glimpse of a private fire that does not often make it into public discourse and that suggests the careful work that went into crafting Gordon's public persona.

The private anger that Gordon so effectively masks at times finds its way into her public writing, sometimes directly, other times more obliquely. Gordon's scrapbook contains an undated memorial tribute to her neighbor, Fanny Gushart, Gordon remembers, "One day I was having a little unpleasantness, and she said, 'Rose, you are black, but I love you.'" Although Gordon does not explain the nature of the "little unpleasantness," Gushart's comment seems to be a response to something that Gordon has told her and to suggest that the "unpleasantness" was racial in nature. The tribute goes on to praise Gushart for being "untainted by the foul breath of prejudice." Without directly accusing in print any of her neighbors of prejudice, Gordon quietly suggests just that by emphasizing the unusual quality of another neighbor's lack of prejudice.

The members of the White Sulphur Springs Home Colored Minstrel company (chapter 1) were friends and neighbors of the Gordons when Rose was growing up, and she would have attended their 1892 performance if for no other reason than because her older brother, Robert, was one of the performers. Rose was a talented pianist and singer who frequently contributed to the Springs's performance culture. Her letters to the newspaper were no less public performances. Like the Home Colored Minstrel performers who composed a letter to the "Citizens of White Sulphur Springs," Rose Gordon is very much aware that her tributes, her letters to the editor, her memories of White Sulphur Springs history, constitute a "a public enterprise," and her writing is "designed as such," a carefully crafted and strategic entry into the public sphere of the community. Part of that strategy was a careful approach to describing racial relations in the Springs, and we can see Gordon in her writing performing a balancing act between praising the western "hospitality" of her white neighbors who befriended her and who supported her restaurant (and thus her livelihood) and protesting the moments of inhospitable behavior that disturbed her.

In 1951, Gordon decided to run for mayor of White Sulphur Springs. Marcella Sherfy suggests that she did so because she was "frustrated by slow attention to community problems" (557). Quixotic as her election campaign may have been—she was a political neophyte running against an experienced incumbent—her attempt brought out prejudice in the community that at other times might have remained less visible. At one point, she received a letter signed "Annonomus" threatening that even if she won the election, "I doubt very much if, any of the incumbent councilmen . . . would even accept their office, with you as mayor." To make sure that Gordon does not miss the implications, the writer clarifies, "This Miss Gordon is due to your color." The letter closes, "I suggest that, you withdraw your name from the ballot for no one will serve with you."[6] Gordon lost the election to Elmer Schye by a 207–58 vote, a good showing for an inexperienced candidate who was also an African American woman running for mayor in a rural town that had only two registered black voters (Rose and Robert Gordon).

In the 1940s and 1950s, Gordon was actively involved with the Montana Federation of Colored Women's Clubs, attending meetings at the Great Falls chapter with her friend and frequent correspondent, Elizabeth Hill, and attending the federation's annual convention in 1947 and 1951. In addition, she participated in several letter-writing campaigns organized by the federation—a late-1930s effort to pass a state civil rights bill as well as a later effort to repeal an antimiscegenation law. Like Thompson and her family in North Dakota, Gordon sought out the companionship of other African Americans in Montana, creating at times a "little colored world" within the surrounding white world. Her active involvement with the Montana Federation of Colored Women's Clubs may have contributed to a more assertive stance on her part, as indicated by her willingness to run for mayor. That assertiveness also may have been sparked by an increasing number of racial incidents that revealed the "foul breath of prejudice" in the Springs.

After the election, Gordon published a letter in the 11 April 1951 issue of the *Meagher County News* explaining her decision to run for mayor:

> I was born in Meagher county and have always had a deep regard for White Sulphur Springs. I filed for office because any one regardless of race, color or creed has a right to file for office. We vote for whom ever we wish to. I was in business for many years on Main street. They came into my place of business from the smallest county office in town to the governors of the state and the senators who were elected to congress to get me to do what I could for them. . . .
>
> My hobby has always been people. I love to study them and watch their reactions.

Whatever originally motivated Gordon to run for office, this letter suggests that she shared a civil rights agenda with African Americans across the country, that she "filed for office" as way of exercising her right, "regardless of race, color or creed," to do so. That agenda may have developed after the fact, as Gordon's comments seem to speak as well to the anonymous letter she received. She, like her brother, Taylor, understood the advantages of performing to racial expectations. Her writing is sprinkled here and there with bits of minstrel humor, indicating her ability and willingness to occasionally slip on the minstrel mask to make her stories more appealing to her audience—the readers of the White Sulphur Springs newspapers or the larger, presumably white, reading audience that was the intended target of her memoir. However, her letter explaining her intentions in filing for office also indicates that Rose Gordon was willing and able to take a more assertive stance when the situation called for it.

In one of her final letters to the *Meagher County News*, published on 9 May 1968, she commented explicitly on what she called the "Battle of the Pigment," which had been brought to the foreground in the 1960s by the civil rights movement and by the assassination of Dr. Martin Luther King Jr. just over a month earlier: "On a beautiful summer day when you take a ride and gaze upon the beautiful hills, valleys and running streams and all the different colors of nature, it is difficult to think the Great Creator made this all for people of one color. . . . It is our different colors that makes this world such a wonderful place in which to live. If everything was one color we would soon go mad. . . . It is a great adventure to be born with dark skin. While traveling about, you meet many people who do not like the idea. This is what puts you to the test." In "My Mother was a Slave," Gordon writes of her birth in Barker, Montana Territory, "I was born in this mining camp and claim the distinction of being the first white child born there." In "Battle of the Pigment," Gordon provides an alternate description of her birth: "It is a great adventure to be born with dark skin." That statement suggests an awareness of racial identity initiated at birth, a seemingly opposite assertion of identity to "being the first white child born there." In the distance between these two contradictory statements developed Rose Gordon's complex identity. For Micheaux and Thompson, double-consciousness is represented by the East/West, metropolis/wilderness opposition. For Gordon, whose lack of movement between places contrasts with these other writers, the key split is between past and present, between the White Sulphur Springs of the "grand old timers" and the Springs of the mid-twentieth century. In Gordon's writing about the past, she seeks a sense of belonging, of being at home, that has been difficult to maintain in the present. In the 1960s, with Montana celebrating the centennial of its statehood, Gordon used her writing to remind her fellow citizens of a continuing African American presence in the state and in her hometown. Gordon's memorial tributes, her "recollections" and other writing, may work to create a sense of home in two ways—by returning her through writing to the remembered home of the past and by providing her with a means of participating in the community's present. In the partially true, partially imagined home in the White Sulphur Springs past, Gordon sought refuge from double-consciousness. In telling her own and her mother's stories of making a home in Montana, she asserted her right to belong there. Being born in black skin may indeed have "put her to the test" at times, but in writing about the past, she asserted her right to belong—her right to call Montana home—in the present.

4

Cowboys, Cooks, and Comics

African American Characters in Westerns of the 1930s

Combining action, humor, and musical performance, a series of black-cast Westerns filmed in the late 1930s and starring singer Herb Jeffries places African Americans at the center of their stories of life on the American frontier. By so doing, such films as *Harlem on the Prairie* (1937), *Two-Gun Man from Harlem* (1938), *The Bronze Buckaroo* (1938), and *Harlem Rides the Range* (1939) provide a vision that counters the way most Hollywood Westerns marginalize or ignore the role blacks played in settling the West. Although produced for African American audiences, these Westerns have been accused of repeating many of the same stereotypical images of blacks found in films of the same era addressed to white audiences. Daniel J. Leab points to *Harlem Rides the Range* in particular for its "standard unflattering caricatures of blacks" and for using minstrel show humor as the source of the movie's comedic types (174).

Mark Reid observes in *Redefining Black Film* that black-oriented comic films often involve a type of "hybrid minstrelsy" that borrows "aural and visual qualities" and caricatures "from white-oriented minstrel humor," even though such films replace the white actors in blackface of the minstrel shows with African American actors (23). In her discussion of Oscar Micheaux's silent film, *Within Our Gates* (1920), Michele Wallace suggests that film studies critics need to "reconceptualize stereotypes or 'types' as something of greater importance, ambiguity, and theoretical sophistication" than have the "most prominent conceptions of black stereotypes in cinema studies," which tend to "define such representations too narrowly" (54). While acknowledging the problematic elements of these black-cast Westerns, I believe that we can better appreciate what the Herb Jeffries films accomplish by placing them in the context of the genre that they imitate and in some ways, revise—the Hollywood Western. As Julia

Leyda suggests, we should also place these films in the context of other "black-audience movies" of the 1930s. Any interpretation of the Jeffries films should be aware of the "movies' reception by their intended viewers," who would have experienced the films as members of a predominantly African American audience in one of the "430 'all-Negro' theaters" operating in the United States in the late 1930s (48). Combining Wallace's and Leyda's observations, an awareness of a film's audience may alter the way we interpret the purpose and effect of comic characters, especially when we consider the addressee of a film's humor to be an African American audience member.

This chapter examines the *Harlem* films and places them in two contexts: mainstream Western cinema of the era and its portrayal of the black westerner, and the specific context of "race films" or "black-audience films." Although continuities exist between the portrayals of the black westerner in these two cinematic traditions, the fact that these films addressed different audiences requires a strategy of double reading when attending to the *Harlem* series. That is, we must be conscious that the films both draw from the mainstream Western and revise the genre to appeal to a specifically African American audience. Chapter 5 continues to explore this practice of double reading but focuses specifically on the films of Oscar Micheaux. Chapter 5 also considers the Jeffries films, especially *Two-Gun Man from Harlem*, as a response to both mainstream Western cinema generally and to Micheaux's vision of the African American West specifically.

Although contemporary filmgoers struggle to think of an African American Western character other than Cleavon Little's Sheriff Bart in *Blazing Saddles*, African American actors and characters appear in Western films throughout the twentieth century, with certain periods (especially the 1960s and 1970s) demonstrating a particular emphasis on including black westerners, even if the roles they play are often limited. Black characters appear with some frequency in Westerns of the early sound era, in such A and B films of the 1930s as *Cimarron* (1930), *Wild Horse* (1931), *Haunted Gold* (1933), *Riders of the Black Hills* (1938), *Drums along the Mohawk* (1939), *Destry Rides Again* (1939), *Jesse James* (1939), and *The Return of Frank James* (1940).[1] In Westerns of the era, black actors sometimes appear as entertainers, as in a brief appearance by a young man who dances for change in a bar scene in Gene Autry's *Man of the Frontier* (1936), but more commonly these characters are associated with domestic spaces or duties, appearing as cooks, maids, servants, and/or as messengers, and they most often function in comic roles. In *Drums along the Mohawk*, starring Henry Fonda and Claudette Colbert, Beulah Hall Jones plays Daisy, a maid who is consistently seen within the frame doing various chores; she seldom speaks, although, in a nod to minstrelsy, she is frightened in one scene by a jack-o'-lantern carried on a stick by holiday revelers. Stepin Fetchit plays a servant in *Wild Horse*, but while star Hoot Gibson tames and rides the wild horse of the title, Stepin Fetchit is stuck playing out an old gag with a stubborn mule—when he isn't being knocked over by a horse at a rodeo or accidentally gluing an advertising poster to his own back.

What Reid calls hybrid minstrelsy replaces white actors with African Americans without changing the "inherently racist and tendentious nature" of the humor, "which reflects its minstrel sources"; this hybrid minstrelsy is particularly prevalent in mainstream films that use black actors in comic roles (41). In his analysis of the structure of the minstrel joke, Reid draws on Freud's argument in *Jokes and Their Relation to the Unconscious* that "tendentious" jokes "make possible the satisfaction of an instinct (whether lustful or hostile)" (119–20). A tendentious joke, Freud writes, "calls for three people: in the addition to the one who makes the joke, there must be a second who is taken as the object of the hostile or sexual aggressiveness, and a third in whom the joke's aim of producing pleasure is fulfilled" (118). Reid observes that the structural elements of blackface minstrelsy ("an addresser, an imaginary 'black' object of ridicule, and an interested spectator") echo the "textual construction" of the tendentious joke (20). In terms of film, we have an addresser (those involved in making the film), an object of ridicule (the African American actor performing the comic role), and "a viewer-listener," the member of the moviegoing audience—presumably (in terms of the original audience for these 1930s films) a white viewer for whose pleasure the black figure is ridiculed (Reid 20). Not only does the comic black figure perform for the pleasure of the audience in the theater, he or she also often performs for an audience within the mise-en-scène, and the laughter of the characters on-screen in part veils the hostility of the joke.

In *Destry Rides Again*, starring Marlene Dietrich as bar owner Frenchy and Jimmy Stewart as new sheriff, Destry, the primary black character is Frenchy's maid, Clara, played by Lillian Yarbo, who first appears on-screen bent over and holding pillows against her ears because she is frightened by the sound of gunshots. Her raised butt proves an irresistible target for Frenchy's foot. "I was just trying to shut out the boomin' and bangin' of them there popguns. . . . I 'spect I is just gonna remain a mass of quivering flesh," Clara explains. Clara's reaction evokes the minstrel tradition of presenting the black person as "a mass of quivering flesh," even if the source of fear in this case is not a ghost but the sound of shoot-ing. Frenchy plays a double role in the structure of this joke. She makes the joke—by kicking Clara, an action that is funny only because of long-standing minstrel tradition, and the hostile aggressiveness of this joke is clear. She also serves as the third person in the joke, as an on-screen "viewer-listener" who is amused (and annoyed) both by Clara's response to the kick and by her fear of gunfire. Her amused reaction mirrors—and encourages—a similar response from the audience.

As indicated by Clara's frightened response to gunfire (a banal occur-rence in a Western), the idea that African Americans are out of place in the Wild West is a repeated source of gags. In the film *Cimarron*, which won the Best Picture Oscar in 1930, the out-of-place black character is Isaiah, played by Eugene Jackson, a young boy who stows away on the wagon of Yancey and Sabra Cravat (Richard Dix and Irene Dunne) as they leave behind the civilized world of Wichita, Kansas, to establish a news-paper in a frontier town in Oklahoma territory. Wichita is depicted as a transplanted piece of the Old South, and the presence of African Ameri-can servants is just another indication of Wichita's civilized decadence. Even though most of these films are set after the Civil War, the black character's position is often ambiguous—more in keeping with that of the stereotype of the favored and favorite contented slave than that of an employee. The film opens at the Wichita home of Yancey's in-laws as they are eating dinner and conversing with heavily inflected southern accents. We first see Isaiah perched above the table, fanning the air to provide the diners with a cool breeze. In the film's first pratfall, he becomes so excited by Yancey's speech praising life on the frontier that he falls onto the table.

When Isaiah is discovered rolled up in a carpet packed in their wagon, he begs to join the Cravats in Oklahoma, and Yancey comments, "There's loyalty that money can't buy." Again, Isaiah's status is ambiguous. Is he a servant? A slave? An adopted son? There is no mention of a mother and father who might object to Cravat's adoption/abduction of the boy. Despite his desire to head into the Wild West, the film cannot resist using his presence on the frontier for a joke. In one scene, we follow the Cravats on their way to a church meeting, where Yancey has agreed to deliver the sermon. Their walk is interrupted by the sound of loud laughter. They turn to look, and we see Isaiah marching proudly toward them (to the raucous accompaniment of the town's laughter) in his "Sunday clothes," Yancey's castoffs, a too-big cowboy hat, oversized boots, and a too-large gun belt with empty holster. Isaiah is a distorted and imperfect copy of the film's real hero, Dix as Yancey. Even though, as historian Quintard Taylor notes, ten thousand African Americans were among the Sooners who staked claims in the Oklahoma territory, the Hollywood film cannot imagine the black character as a legitimate actor in the film's Western plot—those clothes do not fit (158). It is particularly important that Yancey, our hero, laughs at Isaiah; otherwise, the over-the-top response by the other townspeople reveals rather than veils the joke's hostility. If Dix laughs at the black character's antics, then we can, too. The hostility is further veiled through a kindhearted (but patronizing) speech that Yancey makes to Isaiah.

The Hollywood Western also feminizes or desexualizes the African American male character by associating him with a domesticity that precludes him from participating fully in the masculine adventures of the white male characters. For example, the character Pinky (Ernest Whitman) from *Jesse James* and *The Return of Frank James* is both farmhand and cook, but he appears primarily in domestic spaces—making and serving dinner, washing dishes, and sometimes even wearing an apron. Peter Stanfield goes so far as to describe this character as "an Uncle Tom and Mammy rolled into one" (217). Pinky's role in *Jesse James* is relatively minor, and his dialogue consists primarily of repeating "Yessuh." His role in *The Return of Frank James* is much larger, and his importance to the film is underscored by his introduction in the opening scene. After the events of *Jesse James*, Frank is living in hiding under the name Ben Woodson. In the opening scene, Frank is plowing and Pinky is working to remove a stump. When Pinky calls him "Mr. Frank," Frank chastises him for failing to use his new name.

> *Pinky*: Seems I've been calling you Mr. Frank ever since you was knee-high to nothing. Ain't no harm calling you Mr. Frank when there ain't nobody around, is there?
> *Frank*: Except one day you're gonna forget and bawl out Mr. Frank when folks is around. Pinky, Frank James isn't hiding in the hills. He's dead.
> *Pinky* (eyes widening): Dead! Wa . . . Wa . . . You ain't dead!
> *Frank*: You calling me a liar?
> *Pinky*: No, sir, no sirree, but—
> *Frank*: Ain't no buts about it, Pinky, Frank James is dead and buried and underground.

Pinky: Sho, sho, he's dead and buried and under the ground and rotted.
Frank: Now, remember!
Pinky: Yessuh, I'll remember, Mr. Frank.

The camera remains on Frank as Pinky walks away. Frank puts his hands on his hips in a gesture of frustration, but then he breaks into a smile as he shakes his head in amusement. The joke continues to play out as the film progresses. While serving dinner, Pinky comments, "Dinner's ready. Sit down, Mr. Frank. I mean Mr. Ben. Mr. Frank is dead, so I mean Mr. Ben." Again, the hero functions as the audience's surrogate, his amusement mirroring the expected audience response to Pinky's dimwittedness.

The tendentious humor here, which is mild in comparison to what appears in some of the other films, establishes Pinky as a "lovable darky" type to set up Frank James's dilemma later in the movie. On a mission to kill Bob Ford and avenge Jesse James's murder, Frank is halted by a newspaper report: "Negro Farmhand Convicted as Accomplice in Express Office Murder. 'Pinky' Washington receives death sentence as aide to Frank James." Even at this serious moment, the film cannot resist a minstrel joke, as Frank comments, "Pinky never so much as even stole a chicken in his whole life." At the moment when Pinky becomes an important element in the film's plot, he disappears completely from the screen and never returns. His fate is important only as Frank's reaction to that fate reveals something about the white hero. As the cause of Frank's dilemma, Pinky is linked to the traditional woman's role in the Western—as the obstacle to male vengeance, which Frank must forgo to testify on Pinky's behalf.

In 1933's *Haunted Gold*, John Wayne (as the advertising poster for the film puts it) "grapples with ferocious phantoms and devilish desperadoes in a ghost-ridden gold mine!" Of interest here is Wayne's sidekick, Clarence, played by African American actor Blue Washington. Typically, Clarence is a ranch cook, but he is also identifiably a black cowboy who dresses the part, rides a horse, and knows how to use his guns (which he even draws at one point to save Wayne from the "devilish desperadoes"). However, his distinguishing characteristic in the movie is his superstitious and exaggerated fear of ghosts, a carryover from minstrel stereotypes. Washington's performance style, with an emphasis on hyperbolic gestures, particularly facial movements (most of which involve widening his eyes to contrast them to his dark skin), differs notably from the more realistic performances of the other actors. Washington's dialogue, which is written in the exaggerated dialect of minstrel speech, also contrasts with the colloquial movie-Western dialogue used by the other characters. For example, at one point in the film, to scare the villains, Washington throws a black cloth over his head to masquerade as a ghost. When he speaks ("I is da phantom"), he gives himself away. As one villain responds, "He ain't no phantom with that watermelon accent." We might compare the colloquial *ain't* to the dialect *I is* to show the difference. Clarence is a type, "pure watermelon," as one of the characters describes him, whose exaggerated racialized characteristics stick out against the generally realistic settings and performance styles, a point that the villains repeatedly notice and comment on.

The appearance of a minstrel character, even when played by a black actor, is oddly disturbing to the Western's mise-en-scène, not only in terms of performance style but also in terms of the character's ability to absorb kicks, falls, and other violence that would damage the body of a white character. In minstrelsy, the black character is the object and butt of the joke, with a literal kick in the butt often serving as the punch line. Physical abuse of the black body—whether caused by his own actions, by other black characters, or by whites—is a central element of the minstrel gag and an obvious indication of the way the joke encodes hostile impulses. Although *Haunted Gold* contains plenty of action, plenty of depictions of bodies subjected to what in real life would be painful physical experiences, only with the character of Clarence is that physical abuse played for laughs. Instructed to bunk down for the night in an abandoned house, the fearful Clarence enters, gets caught up in a spider web, spins around, and backs violently into a protruding piece of furniture that provides the minstrel gag's kick in the butt (and the film treats us to a close-up of Clarence getting it in the rear). Clarence's exaggerated fear sparks all the physical humor, and the scene ends when he runs out the door, through a fence (which he simply knocks over as he runs), and to the main house, where Wayne talks with the heroine, Sheila Terry. After hearing Clarence describe all the "ghostly" abuses visited upon his body, Wayne comments, "Ah, Clarence, you're just seeing things." Clarence replies, "Yessuh, seeing them, hearing them, *and* feeling them." This sequence builds to the punch line—"*and* feeling them"—and Wayne laughs good-naturedly, gives Clarence a comradely slap on the shoulder, and sends him to wait in the hall. Again, the white hero serves as the audience's on-screen surrogate, and his good-humored response (even if patronizing) veils the hostility of the joke.

In a later scene, the terrified Clarence rides past a graveyard, where he is accosted and robbed by the villains. Following the robbery, the villains are shown discussing and laughing at his antics, their amusement based primarily on Clarence's embodiment of the minstrel type: "The black boy sure was scared," says one. Another responds: "Did you see those eyes?" Clarence performs for heroes and villains alike. The villain's comments, however, could push the audience to an uncomfortable place. They openly express the hostility the film otherwise attempts to veil. Should we be laughing *with* the villains? United as a romantic couple at last, Wayne and Terry are about to enjoy a movie-ending kiss when Clarence enters the scene, stumbles, falls flat, and comments, "Is my face red." The film ends with Wayne and Terry guffawing loudly at this pratfall and at the embarrassed Clarence's lack of awareness at the irony of describing the red color of his black face. Whatever questions might have been introduced by the villainous laughter at Clarence are foreclosed by the final scene's return to an on-screen depiction of the hero and heroine as the audience's surrogate, the viewer-listeners who receive pleasure from the comic's actions.

Mel Watkins notes in *On the Real Side* that "there is a crucial distinction between purposeful jest or wit (the creative telling of a joke or knowing assumption of a comic posture) and naive comic expression (unwittingly saying or doing something that others find funny)" (29). Watkins goes on to observe that "the introduction of minstrelsy" codified the mainstream view of blacks as "naive humorists" (29). Neither Pinky nor Clarence realizes that he is being funny. For a brief moment, we might interpret Isaiah's proud strut down the Osage main street as a satirical comment on Yancey Cravat's prideful stride, but such an interpretation of "purposeful wit" is undercut by Isaiah's dialogue and by Yancey's flattered amusement at what he sees as the boy's sincere attempt at worshipful imitation. Black characters in the Western are consistently portrayed as naive humorists. They do not realize that they are doing or saying something funny, although the audience and other characters on-screen do.

Although many of the gags in the *Harlem* series certainly point to the minstrel stage as a source, the films also significantly alter the conventions both of minstrelsy and of the genre Western. The films portray their comic figures not only as naive humorists but also as witty ones—as clever jokesters and tricksters who knowingly adopt a comic posture. We might attribute this change in part to the involvement of African Americans in many different areas of the production, not just as actors and performers (although the production company was white-owned and members of the production crew were likely white). In addition to playing the lead role as the series' heroic "singing cowboy," Bob Blake, Herb Jeffries (credited in the films as Herbert Jeffrey) was instrumental in creating that character and in finding financial backing for producing the films.[2]

On tour in 1934 as a singer in the Earl Hines Band, Jeffries observed an incident that he claims as the inspiration for the series: "There was a bunch of children running down the street. A little black boy was with them, crying" because he'd been excluded from playing cowboy with his white friends, who had never heard of a black cowboy (Dempsey 24). Prior to that incident, a tour through the American South brought Jeffries his first encounter with segregated theaters: "I noticed a thousand little tin-roofed theaters, created because of discrimination . . . and they were all playing white cowboy pictures. So it came to me that this was an opportunity to make something good out of something bad" (Berry 46–47). Duly inspired by these two incidents, Jeffries became the driving force behind (and singing cowboy star of) the *Harlem* series of black-cast Westerns. No remaining prints exist of *Harlem on the Prairie*. The films might not have been produced had Jeffries not been so persistent in pitching the idea, spending a year trying to raise money before finally interesting producer Jed Buell.[3]

S. Torriano Berry writes that the success of *Harlem on the Prairie* attracted the attention of Richard C. Khan, a white man who owned Sack Amusements and who "approached Jeffrey about continuing the saga of the black cowboy" (45). The original character played by Jeffries was named Jeff Kincaid, and since Buell owned the rights to that character, Jeffries and Khan "created the character of Bob Blake and introduced his trusty horse Stardusk," which Jeffries purchased and used in all three of the later films (45). Although the credits of the three extant films list Kahn as the director and writer, Jeffries was involved developing the character and in casting the films, and according to Dempsey, Jeffries also "convinced Spencer Williams . . . to write a script and sign on as the film's co-star" (24). Thomas Cripps likewise observes that Williams not only contributed to the scripts but also "directed a bit" (130). In addition to starring in the movie (and performing his own stunts), Jeffries "wrote and sang the music and edited the film," although the films are inconsistent in crediting him for his musical contributions and make no mention of his involvement in the editing (Dempsey 24).[4]

The films present fairly conventional plots. The bad guy commits a murder and frames Blake for the crime (*The Two-Gun Man from Harlem*), or the villain attempts to steal the rights to either a radium mine (*Harlem Rides the Range*) or a homestead on which gold has been discovered (*The Bronze Buckaroo*) from a beautiful young heroine and her father (*Range*) or younger brother (*Buckaroo*). Each movie provides Blake with a love interest to romance, a villain to defeat, and plenty of opportunities to demonstrate his abilities to both fight and sing. The plots primarily take us from one musical interlude or comedy routine to another. Part of the way the Bob Blake movies create a bridge between the Hollywood Western and the black filmgoers who would have been the primary audience is by incorporating such elements of African American culture as contemporary slang and references (verbal and musical) to jazz and blues music.[5]

Two-Gun Man from Harlem opens with Jeffries and the band the Four Tones performing "I'm a Happy Cowboy," which Jeffries wrote as the theme song for the series. A comic interlude involving Jeffries as Bob Blake and Mantan Moreland as ranch cook Bill follows. Although this scene introduces yet another comic cook, there are several key differences from the Hollywood Western. First, the on-screen audience for the comic figure's antics is composed of other black characters, and he performs for their pleasure, not that of a white observer. Bill's speech is colloquial but not as exaggeratedly so as Clarence's dialect. The humor in this scene involves Bill's lack of musical skill and is physical but not hostile—that is, the joke does not turn on the black body on-screen suffering physical injury and pain. At the end of "I'm a Happy Cowboy," Bill, who has been listening and watching the performance, comments, "Boys, that was all right, but let me see what I can do with this musical houseboat," his name for the upright bass, which he mistakenly believes he can play, and his singing might be worse than his bass playing.

> *Bob*: Your singing reminds me of a penguin.
> *Bill*: A penguin?
> *Bob*: Didn't you ever hear a penguin singing as it flew through the clouds?
> *Bill*: You is crazy. A penguin can't fly.
> *Bob*: And you can't sing.
> *Bill* (after Bob and the Four Tones laugh): Maybe not, but I can cook musical. . . . When I cook a steak, they just as tender as a mother's lullaby. Why, when I bear down on a pot of chili beans, why it's just the same as a swing tune coming from Cab Calloway's band.
> *Bob and Band* (in unison): How's that, Bill?
> *Bill*: Red hot, boys, red hot.

The key difference in the representation of this African American comic cook is that as the routine progresses, the structure of the joke shifts. Initially, all the participants of the tendentious joke are on-screen:

an addresser (Bob Blake), a "'black' object of ridicule" (Bill), and an interested spectator (the Four Tones). Although initially the object of Bob Blake's joke (a penguin can't fly and you can't sing), Bill becomes the maker of the joke and displays his verbal skill by turning a joke on him into a statement about his culinary abilities. The on-screen shift in addresser changes the textual construction of the joke as well as the positioning of the addressee. Although positioned by Bob Blake's insult as the third participant in the structure of the tendentious joke, the Four Tones (the movie audience's on-screen surrogate) shift from laughing at to laughing with Bill. Rather than expressing ridicule, the laughter expresses appreciation for his clever turning of the joke. Although initially a naive humorist—he does not know that his bad singing and playing are funny—he becomes a witty humorist. These black-cast Westerns make a move that does not occur in mainstream Westerns with black characters: depicting a shift in the portrayal of the comic black figure from the object to the agent of humor. That shift represents a move away from the tendentious humor of the Hollywood Western.

Although the comedy in the Jeffries films is often conventional humor, there are moments in which the films incorporate what Mel Watkins calls "authentic black humor" into the story. "Black humor," Watkins writes, "most often satirizes the demeaning views of non-blacks, celebrates the unique attributes of black community life, or focuses on outwitting the oppressor—as it were, 'getting over'" (29). Black humor also often draws on the long tradition of African and African American folklore and oral storytelling traditions—and storytelling styles. "Black American humor," Watkins comments, "is nearly as dependent on a delivery that incorporates black America's generally more expressive and flamboyant style as it is on wit or verbal dexterity" (41). In *Two-Gun Man from Harlem*, Bill is more than a comic cook—he also provides the most consistent means of including the style of African American humor in the film. His use of black vernacular English and slang contrasts with and complements Blake's speaking style, which punctuates more polished standard English usage with occasional bits of "western" dialect and African American slang.

The loose plots of the *Harlem* films leave plenty of room for improvisational humor and joking asides. In one example from *Two-Gun Man*, Bill takes center stage to tell a story that draws on African American storytelling tradition in both its delivery and content. Disguised as "the Deacon" to investigate a murder, Blake infiltrates a gang of desperadoes lead by

Butch (Spencer Williams). Sending Butch off on an errand, Bob in his preacher persona shouts after him, "And don't look back. Remember what happened to Lot's wife." Back at the cabin, a puzzled Butch asks Bill, "Hey, what happened to Lot's wife?" Bill sits down at the table with Butch and, while peeling potatoes, tells him a story:

> Lot's wife? Oh, you mean the lady in the Bible. Uh . . . She done turned to salt. You see, she lived in the town of Soda, and she married a fellow by the name of Lot. Now why they called him Lot, was because he had a lot of dough and a lot of sheep and everything. She started tramping around with a fellow from Sonora, that's where Salt Lake is now. She started tramping around with him, and the neighbors started to scandalize. You know how they do, see? She was on her way home, and just as she started out, one of the neighbors said, "Honey, say, your husband is looking for you," so she got scared . . . and she started running, and she started to running down the street, and just as she got two blocks away from where she was, it started raining, and the rain started pouring down. It rained forty days and forty nights. Oh, man, it was cold! She kept on running and looking back. Till she got tired. . . . She got to a place to sit down and rest, and, you know, she couldn't move. She sat right there and couldn't move. She hadn't turned to stone. She had done turn to salt. The waters kept on getting up on her, and kept on getting up on her, and kept on melting her, and melting her, melting her, and she kept getting low, and it washed her away. And when the water washed her away, that's how come the lake is salty.

Bill's story is a variation of the "how it happened tale." As Mel Watkins explains, "etiologic or 'how it happened tales' . . . display the narrator's cleverness at embellishing or concocting stories about the origins of various things, including heaven, hell, and the world, as well as specific animals and races" (452). Bill invents a new version of the biblical story of Lot's wife, a "how it happened tale" that creates its humor from our awareness of the original story and of the way Bill embellishes and alters that story, combining it at one point with the story of Noah's flood. The seeming malapropisms of Soda and Sonora for Sodom and Gomorrah are intentional renamings in the larger context of Bill's clever changes to the story. Retelling stories from the Bible, embellished with contemporary references and with the familiar characters speaking in vernacular style ("the neighbors started to scandalize"), has been an element of African American storytelling since the days of slavery. Bill finishes the story with a western twist—using the story of Lot's wife as an explanation for the origin of a particular feature of the American West, the Great Salt Lake.

Moreland's delivery of the story also suggests the sort of improvisation that would take place in a storytelling context. The repetition of phrases sometimes suggests a storyteller filling in space as he makes the story up on the spot. Although my transcription of the story does not convey all the elements of performance (gestures, vocal emphasis), the repetition also contributes to the rhythm of the storytelling, particularly as Bill approaches the end of the story and picks up the pace as he nears the climax. In Moreland's delivery, repetition of phrases such as "melting her, and melting her, and melting her," combined with his hand gestures, which suggest her steady diminishment, do not add to the story's content but rather contribute to the tension and help increase the tale's pace. Similarly, interjected elements such as "You know how they do, see?" and "Oh, man, it was cold!" have more to do with Bill's individual style as a storyteller and with conveying the oral context for the storytelling, tossing in short improvised comments that directly address his listener—Spencer Williams's Butch, who makes an excellent straight man in this scene, maintaining a noncommittal but interested expression throughout, seemingly absorbing Bill's story as if it were the Gospel itself. However, the scene comes to an end when "the Deacon" enters and comments, "Brother, you better take another look at your Bible."

Leyda writes, "Manthia Diawara points out [that the] race-specific pleasure in Hollywood cinema is often created by representing African American characters as nonthreatening, usually 'deterritorialized from a Black milieu and transferred to a predominantly White world.' It follows from Diawara's thesis that, because black-audience westerns enact a reterritorialization of African American characters into a predominantly black milieu, they at least attempt to sidestep this major hallmark of Hollywood cinematic representation" (50; internal citation omitted). Building on Diawara's discussion of the "deterritorialization" of black characters in white cinema, Leyda argues that the Jeffries films symbolically "reterritorialize" a black presence in the American West through the creation of a "predominantly black milieu" within the setting of the Western film (50). "Furthermore," she argues, "this reterritorialization often took place within a physically and geographically reterritorialized theater setting" where most audience members were African American (50). Mel Watkins observes that in a joke-telling situation in which "the listeners were all black, the comic referents understood, and the satire unsullied by the intrusion of an outside viewpoint," black-oriented humor that might be considered tendentious in "integrated gatherings" might take on a different cast (36–37). "In the privacy of my own living room," he writes, "the antics of Kingfish or Calhoun did not seem 'slanderous.' They were simply funny characters, cartoonishly unreal" (37). The black-cast film's assumption of a black spectator is echoed within the mise-en-scène by the inclusion of a specifically black audience for the comic figure's antics. This difference from the Hollywood Western in both the on-screen and the in-the-theater audience alters (at least, potentially) the tendentious nature of the humor, even when the basic structure of the joke telling (an addresser, an object of ridicule, an interested spectator) remains the same.

Reterritorialization is a particularly important concept for understanding the black-cast film's representation of what in the Western are two important settings symbolic of a larger public sphere—the saloon and the bunkhouse, which in the Hollywood Western are decidedly segregated spaces where African Americans are seldom allowed. R. Philip Loy observes that while "white sidekicks went wherever the hero went" in the Hollywood Western and were considered "buddies and social equals," that was not the case when (as in *Haunted Gold*) the sidekick was African American, as the black character "did not eat or sleep (unless it was outdoors around a campfire) with the hero" (193). The *Harlem* series returns the black sidekick to the cowboy's side, portraying him as a social equal who shares the same public space and who eats, drinks, and sleeps alongside the hero. The presence of African American characters in what is usually segregated space in the Western also transforms those settings into hospitable spaces that we might regard as on-screen representations of the social space of the black-audience theater. In the "private" space of the saloon, the bunkhouse, and the black-audience theater, black entertainers can perform (and African American listener-viewers can be entertained) without being concerned about "the intrusive presence of white evaluation" (M. Watkins 36).

In *Cimarron*, the church meeting that Yancey and Sabra are going to attend when they are interrupted by Isaiah's comic masquerade takes place in the town's saloon, which has been converted for Yancey's sermon. The saloon is the Western's symbol of the public sphere, and the demographics of the people gathered there suggest the film's ideological vision of American society. Although the sermon is attended by the film's other ethnic figure, the Jewish character, Sol Levy, as well as the rest of the town, including the film's villains and the women (prostitutes and churchgoing ladies alike), Isaiah is pointedly excluded from the public space. As Stanfield observes, "This exclusion is crucial to the film's ideological project of offering what appears to be an 'open door' policy to the American democratic promise but which is, in actuality, exclusive. By first excluding Isaiah from the community and then later having him killed trying to protect Yancey's child, the film represses the presence of blacks within America" and effectively erases from the film's version of history the real and continuing presence of African Americans in Oklahoma (210).

On the rare occasions when Westerns allow African Americans into the saloon, they are not full participants in the public sphere but entertainers whose presence and actions are sharply circumscribed. In Gene Autry's *Man of the Frontier*, Eugene Jackson (who played Isaiah in *Cimarron*) finally makes it into the saloon, but only so that he can dance for the gathered clientele. His dance (which takes him from the raised platform that serves as the saloon's stage, across tables, around the roulette wheel, and over the bar) ends with a split that leaves him seated on the stage. The audience applauds and tosses coins to him—or, rather, at him, as most of the coins bounce off his body and several strike him in the head as he scrambles to pick up the money. The coin tossing seems more contemptuous than appreciative, and after the performance, Jackson quickly disappears from the scene. Autry's performance (of the song "Red River Valley") a few scenes later on the same stage is presented very differently. The camera is positioned so that we see the stage as if we were seated in the audience. Rather than raucous and inattentive saloon patrons (the games of roulette and checkers continue throughout Jackson's dance), these cowboys sit with their backs to the camera attentively watching Autry's performance. After receiving loud applause, he graciously makes way for his comic sidekick, Smiley Burnette, whose humorous song receives a standing ovation; several audience members step forward to shake Burnette's hand while Autry pats him on the back. No one tosses coins at either of the white performers. As Autry and Burnette leave the saloon, everyone stands and applauds, and individuals reach out either for a handshake or to give the performers an appreciative slap on the back. The view of the cowboy and his sidekick walking through the crowded bar making friendly physical contact with the bodies of their fellows effectively demonstrates their sense of belonging in the America the saloon symbolizes, while the final shot of Jackson nearly prone on the stage as he is pelted with coins just as clearly demonstrates his exclusion.

Only in the Bob Blake films are African Americans at home in the saloon and, by extension, in the public sphere the saloon symbolizes. In *The Bronze Buckaroo*, following the performance of a song, the film's two comic sidekicks, Slim (F. E. Miller) and Dusty (Lucius Brooks), have an encounter with the villainous trickster Pete (Spencer Williams), whom they have just seen shoot a man for cheating at cards. Although initially pleased when Williams offers him four cigars, Dusty's pleasure turns to dismay when he realizes that Williams intends for him to smoke all the cigars at the same time and when he is told that he will be shot if he drops a single bit of ash. The humor in this scene turns on the ridiculous sight of Dusty fearfully puffing on four cigars that barely fit in his mouth. Although Dusty may represent a variation on the "coon character" of minstrelsy, the black milieu that is established within the mise-en-scène of the saloon setting contributes to a sense of privacy that would have enabled the original African American audience for this film to enjoy the humor of Dusty's predicament (and of Lucius Brooks's performance).

The scene also draws directly on the African American trickster tradition discussed in chapter 1. *Two-Gun Man from Harlem*, which features Bob Blake slipping into the disguise and persona of "the Deacon," involves the most extensive reinvention of the trickster tale. However, in *Bronze Buckaroo*, many of the scenes involving Dusty and Slim involve playing tricks of one sort or another (including an encounter with a "talking" mule). In some cases, either Dusty or Slim plays a trick on the other man; in other instances, including the scene in the bar, both characters come up against another trickster character. This particular scenario also provides an example of the "trickster-outtricked" folktale. Pete gets the better of Dusty and Slim, but he does not notice Bob Blake slipping in behind him.

As with the byplay between Bob Blake and Bill the cook in *Two-Gun Man from Harlem*, the rigid distinction between the agent and the object of humor that the Hollywood Western maintains is destabilized as the *Bronze Buckaroo* sequence progresses. We initially see on-screen the three participants associated with the hostile joke—the one who makes the joke (Williams), an object (Dusty), and an "interested spectator," Slim, who laughs with great pleasure. That structure changes when Williams forces Slim (now the object of the joke rather than the spectator) to drink four glasses of whiskey at the same time "without dropping one drop." Blake's entry into the scene again shifts the structure of the joke, as he takes Williams's gun and positions him as the new object. Gun in hand, Bob feeds Dusty a straight line: "Having a little trouble, Dusty?" Dusty responds, "'Bob, that gentleman is just carrying hospitality too far." Although initially the object of the joke, Dusty (like Bill the cook) gets the last laugh.

Prior to this interlude, *The Bronze Buckaroo* stages a saloon performance that contrasts sharply with the saloon scenes from *Man of the Frontier*. The scene begins when Dusty and Slim enter the saloon through swinging doors. Much to their surprise, the crowd of drinking and card-playing men break into the song "Almost Time for Round-Up." The song, with plenty of references to "hitting the trail," "saddling broncs," and herding "dogies," sets conventional Western lyrics in an arrangement that recalls a particular African American musical form. Rather than being performed by a single individual, the song uses a call-and-response pattern (common in African American musical forms such as spirituals) to break down any distinction between performer and audience as individuals take turns singing out a line of lyric and are in turn answered by the whole group repeating the words of the title as the chorus. The humor of the scene derives from the juxtaposition of such different elements— in particular, the contrast between the aural (a hymnlike song) and the visual (a setting far from a church). As the cowboys sing about life on a cattle drive, they also continue with their drinking and gambling—and with cheating at cards. When Pete shoots a card cheat, the action stops the song, but only momentarily, giving the rest of the cowboys time to gather their breath for one more "almost time for round-up." There is no distinction between black performer and white audience here, and in this particular representation of the public sphere, no hierarchical distinctions exist between the members of the collectivity—all are equal participants (as long as they follow the rules and do not cheat).

A later bunkhouse scene in *The Bronze Buckaroo* follows a similar pattern. Cowboy Bob Blake, sidekick Dusty, and the other black ranch hands equally inhabit this space from which the Western generally excludes them. Although the scene centers on Jeffries's performance of the song "Payday Blues," almost everyone in the bunkhouse participates in the performance, either as part of the band or by humming the melody in the background. At one point, a cowboy who had been sitting quietly to the side on a bunk gets up, moves to the center of the room, and begins tap dancing. Although his routine resembles the dance Jackson performed in *Man of the Frontier*, in the context of a friendly black milieu, the dancer's performance marks him as part of the group rather than as excluded from it.

The reterritorialization in these films, the creation of a black milieu, also results from references and allusions throughout the films to contemporary black culture. In *Two-Gun Man from Harlem*'s opening rendition of "I'm a Happy Cowboy," the presence of the Four Tones results in a slightly different version of the song than that played over the title credits (as is the case with later films).[6] With lyrics praising the joys of the cowboy life and performed in the style of a pop Western ballad, the tempo of the song reflects a sense of loping along in the saddle. However, in *Two-Gun Man from Harlem*, Jeffries steps briefly aside and lets the band take over. The song shifts from cowboy ballad briefly toward a jazz arrangement when the Four Tones launch into an up-tempo interlude of vocal and instrumental improvisation before returning to the loping-along tempo for the final verse. At the end of the song, when ranch cook Bill describes his cooking as being as "red hot" as "a swing tune coming from Cab Calloway's band," he introduces into the setting of the Old West a contemporary point of reference. This particular technique is repeated throughout the film series. In *The Bronze Buckaroo*, Jeffries's performance of a "Payday Blues" (which he wrote) turns the conventional bunkhouse scene into a musical number, linking the cowboy life to a traditional blues theme—lack of money—and doing so through a genre (the blues) that, like the reference to Calloway, is as anachronistic to the Old West as it is relevant to African American culture. The tap-dancing cowboy in this scene is also cheerfully anachronistic, his performance of a contemporary dance routine another example of the way the films incorporate African American expressive culture into the Western mise-en-scène as way of transforming that setting into a friendly black milieu.

The use of music to adapt a Hollywood production to a black milieu may have started in the silent film era. Mary Carbine, in an article on audience and exhibition practices in Chicago's segregated theaters of the time, argues that "As recorded in oral histories and contemporary black periodicals, the voices of this era reveal a number of ways that blacks exercised tactical consumption, incorporating motion pictures into specifically African American cultural practices" (237). In the silent film era, "live performances by black acts, including vaudeville blues, and jazz, featured prominently and even predominantly in community venues," altering the reception and consumption of even "mainstream white movies" by placing those movies in the context of black musical and theatrical performance (237). "Black cultural presence" in these urban theaters was asserted "not through the entertainment on the screen but by the performance on stage" (245). Orchestras with exclusively African American musicians performed the scores for silent films, and mainstream white movies were often screened as part of a longer program of theatrical entertainments, vaudeville and variety acts, blues singers such as Ma Rainey and Ethel Waters, spirituals performers, and jazz bands. In Carbine's words, "A performance context was layered over the film reception context, and the thematics and content of Hollywood movies were set against specifically African-American practices, which addressed the experiences of the black community" (248).

In addition to these live performances onstage before and after film screenings, African American musicians "did not simply share the entertainment district with movies; they participated directly in motion picture exhibition through the pit orchestra," accompanying the silent films screened in the segregated theaters (but not always following the Hollywood score) (Carbine 248–49). A pit orchestra filled out with jazz musicians, for example, did not simply "offer conventional piano or symphonic accompaniment for silent films. Rather, they played in quintessential jazz bands—featuring saxophones, trumpets, banjo, tuba, and snare drum, or jazz instrumentation mixed with strings—and were led by popular figures such as Erskine Tate, Jamie Bell, Sammy Stewart, Clarence Black, and Clarence Jones," performers and conductors who were often bigger draws than the individual films being screened (249). In addition, the pit orchestra musicians often commented on the films; in so doing, they "altered and disrupted the mainstream exhibition scenario," much to the pleasure of some members of the audience and to the displeasure of others, at times "flout[ing] black middle-class notions of 'proper' music and behavior" (250). Rather than following the "dominant style of white downtown theaters," the pit orchestra performances were "described as erupting into the spectators' consciousness, both visually and aurally, in 'discordant' moments of improvisatory performance unsubordinated to the narrative progression of the film. The exhibition context was imbued with a style of black musical performance that drew attention away from the screen, to the 'ranting, shimmying' musicians" (252, 253). The musicians sometimes commented musically and ironically on the action on-screen, "jazzing away" inappropriately on the song "Clap Hands, Here Comes Charlie" during a death scene (to cite one example) (254). Notes Carbine, "The discontinuity between a cinematic death scene and its musical 'accompaniment' suggests that Race orchestras might have gone beyond simply ignoring the narrative or the sheet music library to read films against the grain, undermining 'preferred readings' with satirical interpretations" (255).

Although the *Harlem* films are specifically modeled on the "singing cowboy" films popular in the 1930s, in which musical performance would not be unexpected, the willingness to include anachronistic music and dance also suggests the influence of these musical practices specific to segregated black theaters. In *Two-Gun Man from Harlem*, for example, what would have taken place separately from the feature film in the silent era movie houses—live performances by African American performers—is incorporated within the narrative via the inclusion of a nightclub scene (where we see performances by a solo percussionist and by a dancer). Such seemingly disruptive performances—the main story is set aside, sometimes for long periods of time, in favor of observing performers who are not part of the main plot—appear in black-audience films throughout the early sound era, perhaps a transposition of the exhibition practices of an earlier time carried over as a way of meeting audience expectations formed in the silent era. The *Harlem* films continue this tradition by including black sounds and other "specifically African-American practices" as part of the on-screen mise-en-scène, taking black musical performance out of the live theater and into the diegesis of the film. Other early sound era race films follow a similar pattern, frequently disrupting the narrative to include long scenes of black musical, dance, and theatrical performances. In the *Harlem* films, Cab Calloway references and other allusions to contemporary music and culture use dialogue to replicate a sense of the discontinuity of "inappropriate" signifying. All these elements of the *Harlem* films suggest the use of silent film era strategies for a similar purpose—to adapt a mainstream product to a black milieu.

★

In both the silent and sound eras, African American music has served as a specific method of reterritorialization, using sound in particular to alter received mainstream products, whether specific Hollywood-produced films shown in black silent era movie houses or received Hollywood genres with conventions and practices seemingly inhospitable to African American participation. The performance of a jazz band in a silent era theater and the introduction into a Western film of black performers jazzing away during a song about a "happy cowboy" create moments suggestive of what Josh Kun calls "audiotopia." Music, Kun argues, "functions like a possible utopia for the listener, . . . experienced not only as sound that goes into our ears and vibrates through our bones but as a space that we can enter into, encounter, move around in, inhabit, be safe in, learn from" (2). "We should be thinking of pieces of music," Kun continues, "as 'audiotopias,' small, momentary, lived utopias built, imagined, and sustained through sound, noise, and music" (21). Thinking of music as a "built place" requires "another adjustment, to think of music in terms of space and in terms of its spaces, the spaces that the music itself contains, the spaces that music fills up, the spaces that music helps us to imagine as listeners occupying our own real and imaginary spaces" (21).

That adjustment is perhaps easier to make when we think of Carbine's description of Black Belt silent era theater practices, in which "a performance context was layered over the film reception context," with African American music filling the real space of the theater and thus altering the way audiences would have experienced Hollywood films (248). "When we talk about music in America," Kun writes, "and music's role in shaping American identities and American meanings, we should be thinking of music in terms of the differences it contains, the differences it makes audible, not the unities or harmonies it can be used to fabricate" (21). Audiotopia is "a musical space of difference, where contradictions and conflicts do not cancel each other out but coexist and live through each other" (23). Audiotopias can thus be "understood as identificatory 'contact zones,' in that they are both sonic and social spaces where disparate identity-formations, cultures, *and* geographies historically kept and mapped separately are allowed to interact with each other" (23). The Black Belt silent film movie house physically realizes the idea of an audiotopia, a physical place where identity-formations and cultures "kept and mapped separately" are made to interact through specific performance and exhibition practices. Rather than trying to harmonize with mainstream American mass culture productions and the identities such products propagate, these silent film era exhibition practices provide a means of making difference "audible." We can see (and hear) that practice continuing in the use of musical performance in the *Harlem* films as well as in other early sound era black-audience films.

Although Western films would continue to include African American characters after the Jeffries series finished its run in 1940, the most successful mainstream motion picture featuring a black cowboy-hero—director Mel Brooks's *Blazing Saddles* (1974)—was not released until more than thirty years after Bob Blake rode off into the sunset for the last time. Although *Blazing Saddles* is generally cited as the one black cowboy film that everyone knows, it was part of a range of Westerns during this time period that featured African American actors in starring or supporting roles—Sidney Poitier in *Duel at Diablo* (1966), blaxploitation Westerns such as *The Legend of Nigger Charlie* (1972; starring Fred Williamson), and multiple European-made Westerns featuring blaxploitation film stars such as Williamson and Jim Brown, most notable among them *Take a Hard Ride* (1975).[7] One of the most significant films to precede *Blazing Saddles* was Poitier's directorial debut, *Buck and the Preacher* (1972), which Berry describes as having "the highest degree of significance since *Sergeant Rutledge* (1961) and the black westerns with 'the Bronze Buckaroo,' Herbert Jeffrey, in the late 1930s" (127–28). African American actors continued to be cast in the roles of sidekick, comic, and cook throughout the post–World War II era, but *Sergeant Rutledge, Buck and the Preacher*, and *Blazing Saddles* stand out as major studio films that feature African American characters, and *Buck and the Preacher* and *Blazing Saddles* share notable similarities with the *Harlem* Westerns.

Buck and the Preacher, with Poitier and Harry Belafonte in the two title roles, comes closest to the Harlem films in offering a predominantly black cast (with the exceptions being the roles of the Native American allies and the white villains). Buck is a wagon master leading groups of African American settlers to the west, negotiating passage across Apache territory and trying to avoid a group of "night riders" intent on preventing black western settlement by any means necessary. With director Mario Van Peebles's *Posse* (1993), set partly in the all-black town of Freemanville, *Buck and the Preacher* is the rare Western to feature groups of black settlers, a distinct contrast with the solitary black westerner of most film Westerns. Perhaps the most interesting character in the film is Belafonte's Preacher, a trickster figure in western garb, carrying a Bible but wearing guns and riding a horse. Preacher initially tags along with the settlers because he realizes that they have money (which he hopes to relieve them of), but once the group is attacked by the night riders, their money stolen, and their belongings burned, Preacher joins forces with Buck to recover the money and avenge the violence.

One of the film's standout scenes melds the comic portrayal of preachers in minstrelsy, the African American trickster tradition, and the genre Western. Buck and Preacher discover the night riders spending the stolen money in a brothel. Preacher enters the front room of the brothel and plays his preacherly role to the hilt, launching into an impromptu sermon on the evils of fornication. Preacher's performance exploits stereotypical beliefs about "funny" blacks. The night riders believe that Preacher is the object of a joke that he does not get. As in the *Harlem* films, Preacher's performance sets up a shift in the structure of the hostile joke, with him going from the object to the agent of humor, although the punch line of Buck and the Preacher's shared joke is particularly violent. While the group is laughing and clapping at the funny black preacher's performance, Buck steps in and opens up with both guns on the distracted riders. In this scene, we have a distinctive play on the structure of the minstrel gag. The black object of the joke, Preacher (who, the night riders believe, is engaged in "natural" behavior and does not realize that he is being funny), turns the joke around on the white spectators. In *Two-Gun Man from Harlem*, Herb Jeffries's trickster preacher, the Deacon, professes to preach the "gun gospel." Belafonte's Preacher takes that "gun gospel" a step further by keeping his gun hidden inside his hollowed-out Bible. When Buck enters the room, Preacher turns from a sermon against the evils of fornication to a demonstration of the "gun gospel," opening his Bible and then opening fire. Although the Jeffries films had not yet been found when *Buck and the Preacher* was produced, Belafonte's gun-toting preacher and trickster figure, a character very similar to the one Jeffries plays in *Two-Gun Man from Harlem*, suggests a concrete carryover from the earlier race film.

★

With a script cowritten by Richard Pryor (for which he won, with the other credited screenwriters, awards from the American Academy of Humor and the Writers Guild of America), *Blazing Saddles*, like the Bob Blake films, combines music and comedy within a loose Western plot. Although designed with a mainstream audience in mind, *Blazing Saddles* uses some of the same representational strategies as the Blake films and includes elements of authentic black humor. Although the influence is not direct, continuities between the films suggest at least that both the Blake series and *Blazing Saddles* were drawing at times from the same general sources of African American humor.[8] *Blazing Saddles* is often highly regarded for its originality in introducing a black cowboy in the Western plot and exploiting for humor the consequent surprises created by putting an African American character in an unexpected place. However, *Blazing Saddles* might more accurately be described as continuing a tradition of portrayals of the African American West, as creatively repeating and reinventing the elements and conventions of that tradition. Cleavon Little's Bart, with his Gucci saddlebags, is a cowboy-hero with a stylish difference. He is also a trickster figure gone western, continually outwitting rather than outshooting his opponents (he fires his gun only once): pretending to hold himself hostage to escape the ire of the citizens of Rock Ridge, who were not expecting an African American sheriff; inventing the exploding candy-gram to best the super-strong Mongo; and hatching the plan to build a false replica of Rock Ridge to fool Hedley Lamarr's gang of outlaws.

Unlike the Blake films, *Blazing Saddles* was produced for a mainstream audience rather than a specifically black audience, but, in contrast to the studio Westerns of the early sound era, *Blazing Saddles* also emerges in the context of a general mainstreaming of African American humor in the 1970s. If what Reid calls hybrid minstrelsy replaces white actors with African Americans but does so without changing the "inherently racist and tendentious nature" of the humor, *Blazing Saddles* reflects a shift in the representation of African American humor in mainstream cinema in two ways: by explicitly making white racism the object of the film's satire, and by self-reflectively commenting on minstrel humor in those moments when the film evokes that tradition (41). Both those shifts are evident in the film's opening sequence, which involves the white bosses of the railroad gang demanding that the African American workers provide entertainment by singing.

Railway foreman Lyle asks the black workers for a song. "When you was slaves," he comments, "you sang like birds." When the workers, angered by his less-than-polite language, start to move toward Lyle, Bart halts them; after a whispered consultation, he leads the group in Cole Porter's "I Get a Kick Out of You" in a cappella harmony, much to the disappointment of the white workers, who want something more entertainingly black. Pretending not to have heard of either of the songs Lyle suggests they sing, the workers watch with great amusement as Lyle and his fellow whites break into Stephen Foster's minstrel song "The Camptown Ladies." Feigned ignorance shifts the joke, as the white workers, in the guise of showing the black workers how, perform the song in a minstrel style (heavily emphasizing the dialect while dancing and gesturing extravagantly, although not literally in blackface) for the amusement of the black workers. This scene continues a practice of commenting satirically on minstrelsy by inverting the structures of the minstrel joke. Rather than on-screen whites enjoying the performance of the black object of the joke, the black workers function as audience surrogates, enjoying the ridiculous performance of the white workers, who do not realize that they are being funny. As the scene continues, Bart and Charlie further satirize minstrelsy by caricaturing the already caricatured performance of the white railway workers' "black" performance. As they head off on the handcar, they incorporate into their pumping action the exaggerated physical movements of the minstrel stage, performed in rhythm with the equally exaggerated rendering of "The Camptown Ladies" (giving the "doo dah" of the chorus an emphatic "doo *dar*"), their actions a parody not only of the performance of the white railway workers but of the entire tradition of blackface minstrelsy.

In one of *Blazing Saddles*'s most famous scenes, the introduction of Bart on horseback and in his sheriff's costume, the camera pans from his Gucci saddlebags up his body to show us his gun, sheriff's badge, and finally the cowboy hat on top of his head. That the black cowboy is introduced with a jazz soundtrack in the background is perhaps not a surprise, but, as the short scene continues, we realize that what we take to be nondiegetic music is actually coming from within the film narrative: The camera pulls back to reveal Count Basie and his orchestra surprisingly located on a bandstand set up in the middle of the desert. This is not a new joke but an amusing variation on a very old one. Count Basie's appearance in *Blazing Saddles* replays *Two-Gun Man from Harlem*'s anachronistic Cab Calloway joke, and the technique of inappropriate jazzing away originates in the practices of silent era segregated black theaters. The anachronistic appearance of Count Basie, the breaking of the illusion of the film by introducing black musical performance into the mainstream genre of the Western, and the introduction into a Western film of black performers jazzing away are not techniques that *Blazing Saddles* invents, but practices to which the film pays tribute and which it delightfully continues.

5

Oscar Micheaux, *The Exile*, and the Black Western Race Film

Although it might seem unusual to consider the centrality of South Dakota to African American history, two landmark events in the history of African American cinema are connected to the state. Writer and filmmaker Oscar Micheaux's *The Homesteader* (1919), the first feature-length silent film helmed by an African American director, is primarily set in South Dakota. Although interior filming took place elsewhere, Micheaux spent several days traveling around the state with his two stars for on-location filming. For the first African American–produced feature-length sound film, director Micheaux returned to the setting of South Dakota for *The Exile* (1931). Both films are based on Micheaux's experiences homesteading in South Dakota and are adapted from books he wrote about those experiences, *The Conquest* and *The Homesteader*. *The Exile* follows the books in the doubling of place (South Dakota and Chicago) as a representation of double-consciousness. This chapter examines how the place of South Dakota and the role of the frontier in Micheaux's storytelling evolves and changes over the years between the initial publication of *The Conquest* in 1913; the silent film version of *The Homesteader*; his earliest extant silent film, *The Symbol of the Unconquered* (1920); and Micheaux's return a decade or so after *Symbol* to the homesteading narrative as the source for *The Exile*.

This chapter examines a group of conventions common to "race film" Westerns, tracing the continuities and changes in those conventions from their origins in the silent era to their later evolution in the sound films of the 1930s and 1940s. Whereas Micheaux's earlier frontier stories are indeed stories of conquest and homesteading, the narrative emphasis in later race films shifts from the West to the East. Rather than East and West as completely opposing places, *The Exile* represents them as alternate frontier spaces, each one offering opportunity for the entrepreneur.

The vision of the frontier that begins to develop in *The Exile*—of the frontier as an abstract representation of black freedom and opportunity—provides a model for later race movies such as *Two-Gun Man from Harlem* (1938) and *The Girl in Room 20* (1946), which similarly imagine an American West that is more ideal than real and which similarly imagine both the rural West and the urban East as appealing frontier spaces.

In general, the American West and the history of African American film are intimately connected from the first films produced by independent African American filmmakers—Lincoln Motion Pictures's *The Realization of a Negro's Ambitions* (1916), Micheaux's silent features, and the films of Norman Studios, whose productions included *The Bull-Dogger* (1923), starring real-life rodeo hero Bill Pickett, and *Black Gold* (1928), set in the all-black town of Tatums, Oklahoma. The black-cast Westerns of the late 1930s and other black-cast films of the 1940s continue this trend. Jacqueline Najuma Stewart writes that early race films in general "reflect the fact that Black people had migrated to and settled in all corners of the country, broadly claiming America (not just the South or urban northern 'Black Belts') as their home" (*Migrating* 191). Like *Indianapolis Freeman* reports on the travels of black performers in all parts of the United States, the wide-ranging settings of race films not only reflect the fact of black migration but also provide a textual map of African American belonging, a visible claiming of space in the nation.

Unsurprisingly, many race films feature or allude to the Great Migration from the South to the North, but, as Stewart notes, "some also feature movements to and from the West, not surprising given that two of the most successful race film companies, the Micheaux Book and Film Company and the Lincoln Motion Picture Company, were founded by Black men from western states" (*Migrating* 191). Founded by a group led by actor Noble Johnson, Lincoln Motion Pictures preceded and influenced Micheaux's decision to go into the filmmaking business. *The Realization of a Negro's Ambitions* tells a story that Micheaux would no doubt have appreciated—a young black man, James Burton (played by Johnson), leaves behind his father's southern farm for the California oil fields. Initially denied a job because of race, he saves the life of a wealthy white man's daughter and earns a job leading an oil expedition for the man. When he realizes that the oil fields resemble the geography of his father's farm, he returns to the South and makes a fortune from the oil he discovers on the land. Starring an experienced film actor and telling an uplifting story of success, *Realization* earned both praise and box office returns. As Stewart notes, it also "featured a new setting for race films—the West" (*Migrating* 204). Burton's story "reflected the westward migration of thousands of other African Americans," and "since Lincoln's president and leading man, Noble Johnson, himself was born and raised in Colorado, he made films that exposed Black life west of the Mississippi to African American viewers in other parts of the country" (204). Later Lincoln films (none of which are extant) such as *The Trooper of Troop K* (1916) and *The Law of Nature* (1917) would continue this approach.

In addition to providing an "uplifting representation of the finer qualities of the Race" in the figure of Noble Johnson's James Burton, *The Realization of a Negro's Ambitions* also establishes a trope that is repeated throughout the race film era—the discovery of oil on the western frontier as the means for the black hero's success (Stewart, *Migrating* 204). In contrast to the necessity of years of hard (and uncinematic) work in the homesteading narrative, the discovery of oil provides a quick resolution to a story, which may account for part of its popularity. As the title of the Norman Studios' *Black Gold* suggests, the punning play on the word *black* and the suggestion that oil is, by association of color, the appropriate "gold" on which to found an African American fortune may have contributed to that popularity. The scenario may also have been a way of directly addressing the race film market in Texas/Oklahoma, an oil-producing part of the country that was also a lucrative market for race films (as it was for traveling black performers). In Micheaux Book and Film's heyday in the 1920s, the company established not only management offices in Chicago and Harlem but also "a southern outpost in Roanoke, Virginia, and a western branch in Beaumont, Texas," which allowed Micheaux to distribute to the network of segregated theaters in Texas and points further west (McGilligan 171). When Spencer Williams began directing films for Sack Amusements in the 1940s, the popularity of the oil discovery narrative would have been directly influenced by the Texas/Oklahoma audience, as many of those movies were filmed in and around Dallas and distributed regionally.

Following *The Homesteader* and completed in the same year as two other Micheaux films (*Within Our Gates* and *The Brute*), *The Symbol of the Unconquered* (1920) returns to the basic plot idea of *The Homesteader* but adds the twist of oil discovery to its conclusion. In this addition, Micheaux is no doubt as influenced by *The Realization of a Negro's Ambitions* as he is inspired by the film to embark on his own filmmaking career.[1] Although not the first story of the African American West to be filmed,

Symbol is the earliest extant film and thus holds a particularly important place in the tradition of black western cinema. *Symbol* is again the story of a black homesteader in South Dakota, Hugh Van Allen, who is, like Jean Baptiste, a gentlemanly, chivalrous, and hardworking young man who falls in love with (what seems to be) a white woman. In *Symbol*, however, we know that the love interest, Eve Mason, has African American ancestry from the beginning, when we see her at the bedside of her grandfather, clearly a black man, who bequeaths to her his claim to a homestead in the "Great Northwest." Information about Eve's racial identity is also conveyed to the audience by intertitles.

Eve, like Oscar Devereaux at the beginning of *The Conquest*, is a tenderfoot who arrives in Oristown, the same fictional name for Bonesteel, South Dakota, that Micheaux uses in the novel as the location of Devereaux's first attempt to purchase land through the lottery system. As much as the film is about Van Allen's defeat of the Ku Klux Klan and their attempt to steal his land, it is also about the transformation of Eve from someone who is quite literally a tenderfoot (she wears city shoes when trying to break soil for a garden) into a heroic western woman who dons a buckskin outfit, hops onto a horse, and rides to the rescue. Unlike the "Scottish woman" of *The Conquest* and *The Homesteader*, Eve is aware of her racial ancestry. The romantic dilemma is created because Hugh incorrectly assumes that she is white. Although there are characters similar to her in the novels, Eve is the first of Micheaux's strong women to take center stage. Stewart suggests that the changes Micheaux makes in the story of westward migration may result from the need to expand that narrative's "particular appeals to different segments of his audience," especially women (*Migrating* 223). Whatever the case, "Eve's determination to travel alone to a distant country makes her a uniquely strong and independent female character, and her bravery during the Klan attacks further distinguishes her from weaker, more dependent heroines found in other race films" and from characters such as Orlean in Micheaux's books (223). Whether Micheaux was responding to his audience or was merely developing his writing, we see stronger female characters and a far more dramatic and forceful commentary on racism and prejudice take place in his movement from novels to race films.

Also in contrast to Micheaux's early novels, the heroine is not the film's only major mixed-race character. The villain of the film is Driscoll, who, unlike the light-skinned Eve, chooses to pass as white. Like the reverend in the novels, Driscoll is both the hero's double and his opposite, but by re-creating this character type as a "white" man, Micheaux introduces a very different dynamic into the relationship. Unlike the various incarnations of the reverend, Driscoll does not allegorically represent the burden of unassimilated blackness. Rather, he is a far more complicated figure, operating more clearly as a mirror image of the hero (and vice versa). As Pearl Bowser and Louise Spence observe, "Driscoll is motivated by the same drives as the hero (indeed, as Micheaux himself)," even if he advances his interests "in unscrupulous ways," through "coercion and deception" and ultimately through antiblack violence (160). Like Devereaux and Baptiste, Driscoll falls in love with a white woman, but, unlike them, he proposes to her. The barrier between the lovers is not the hero's sense of race loyalty but the unexpected appearance of his mother (at the moment of Driscoll's marriage proposal, no less), whose dark features reveal the truth of Driscoll's racial ancestry (and put an end to his beloved's interest in his proposal). Driscoll goes west not only to escape limitations on black success but also to escape blackness itself, as westward migration enables his separation from his mother and from his black identity. Although Devereaux and Baptiste may wish to distance themselves from a "certain element" of African American society, a loyal connection to race remains central to their identities. Driscoll seeks a more complete erasure.

A key difference between *The Symbol of the Unconquered* and Micheaux's other western narratives is in the representation of double-consciousness, which is rendered psychologically rather than geographically. The film takes place entirely in one frontier setting, and there is none of the journeying back and forth between East and West that is central to the narratives of the novels and of Micheaux's first sound film, *The Exile*. As is frequently the case in African American fiction, especially narratives involving passing, the mixed-race characters in *Symbol* embody the dilemma of double-consciousness. Capable of assimilating not only culturally but physically, the mixed-race character concretely dramatizes the dilemma of choice. Furthermore, the mixed-race character who passes as white lives with the danger of being discovered. Although advertising for *Symbol* emphasizes the black-white conflict between Van Allen and "the insidious Ku Klux Klan," as Bowser and Spence observe, the presence of Driscoll as a member of the Klan and "his use of the same forces of intimidation that he would experience if his true racial identity were known" upset "the equilibrium of any clear-cut binary opposition" and make Driscoll a far more interesting and complex villain than the white vigilantes or the reverend of Micheaux's novels (160).

Micheaux's reverend characters can be seen as trickster figures, as their hypocrisy and their overindulgence in their appetites suggest, but in Micheaux's western narratives, Driscoll emerges as the most fully realized trickster figure. As Mel Watkins states, trickster tales "did not always idealize the trickster," who could "be mischievous, even arrogant and malicious" (73). We recognize Driscoll's use of deception, his passing as white, from his first appearance on the screen. "Although passing is not uncommon or automatically condemned by the Black community," Bowser and Spence write, "it is Driscoll's attitude of superiority, seeing Blacks as subhuman and taking pleasure in their misfortune, that is wicked—both a betrayal and a surrender" (165). Successful as a hotel owner, Driscoll uses that success to make life uncomfortable for African Americans, sending the dark-skinned traveling salesman, Abraham, out to the barn to sleep rather than renting him a room. In so doing, Driscoll also sets up his first trick. When Eve arrives, he first mistakes her for white, but after closer examination, he sends her to the hayloft for the night without letting her know that Abraham is already there. As a result, when she is awakened by a thunderstorm, she discovers Abraham and is so frightened by his unexpected (and grimacing) presence that she runs screaming out into the night and the rain. Observing from his bedroom window, Driscoll "takes sinister joy in her suffering" (Bowser and Spence 166). Her misery—made possible by her blackness, which allowed Driscoll to refuse her lodging in the hotel—underscores his sense of privileged whiteness. The mise-en-scène contributes to Driscoll's sense of triumphant whiteness: "Surrounded by an aura of shimmering whiteness (in white nightshirt and sheets, lit as if he were aglow), he thrashes his arms in triumph" (Bowser and Spence 166).

The scenario of Driscoll's triumph also plays out via the joking structure discussed in chapter 4. The window through which Driscoll watches the scene, made translucent by the rain, also suggests a movie screen—toward which Driscoll leans closer and closer as he watches the interesting scenario playing out before him almost as if he were watching a film. Eve's flight and Driscoll's role in setting up the conditions that cause it recall the structure of "tendentious" jokes, those that "make possible the satisfaction of an instinct (whether lustful or hostile)" (Freud 119–20). Driscoll is both the maker of the joke (or he has at least created the conditions that make the joke possible) and the viewer/listener who receives pleasure from the joke. Eve is the object of the joke's aggressiveness, the "'black' object of ridicule." Or, at least, Driscoll receives what transpires as a joke (and not as a cause for sympathy at her plight), and that reception makes Eve into an object of ridicule. This scene also plays on the minstrel joke that blacks have an excessive fear of ghosts or spirits. Seen in extreme close-up, the poorly lit face of Abraham "grimacing" as rain falls on him through the leaking roof distorts his features into a demonic mask. Eve's flight recalls a hundred such scenes of black characters fleeing from (seemingly) supernatural occurrences. Driscoll's success is twofold. He reminds Eve of her black inferiority by segregating her in the barn and then further degrades her by reducing her to a minstrel figure, a "black" object suffering discomfort and indignity for the sake of the pleasure of the "white" spectator.

Bowser and Spence observe that "what is so disturbing about Driscoll is his assumption of the posture of the oppressor *and* his terror of discovery. In Eve's pale face, he sees both his true identity and the possibility of being unmasked" (166). Westward migration makes possible Driscoll's erasure of race, but accompanying that erasure is "the terror of racial recognition," which haunts him (166). The excessiveness of his pleasure in the sight of a distraught Eve struggling in the storm might be explained as the result of his fear that he will become her, that he too might be or might become the black object rather than the white spectator. And, in fact, just such a reversal is in store for him.

The scene in *Symbol* that most effectively joins together the theme of double-consciousness with the conventions of both the Western and the trickster tale takes place in the Smith Brothers Saloon. An intertitle tells us that Driscoll has sold his hotel and established a new business, the Driscoll Land Company, which also involves a side business selling stolen horses. His first encounter with Van Allen is an attempt to sell him two such horses. As Van Allen goes off with the horses, Driscoll and the horse thief share a laugh at his expense. The black object of ridicule in this particular joke is Van Allen, who has been tricked by Driscoll, as Van Allen discovers when he is confronted by the owner of the horses. As the sequence plays out, this particular trickster will be outtricked, and his own joke turned on him.

We see Driscoll in the Smith Brothers Saloon regaling the bartender with the story of how he got the better of Van Allen: ". . . and I have sold him the most beautiful pair of old nags." He laughs expressively, not seeing Van Allen, who has entered the saloon and stands with hands on hips behind Driscoll. We cut to a shot of a mirror, which shows the two characters in its reflection, Van Allen in his white hat standing behind Driscoll in his black hat. As Driscoll lifts his shot glass and tosses back his head to drink, his eye catches the reflection in the mirror. Van Allen steps closer, and the two figures almost merge into one within the frame of the mirror. Of this shot, Bowser and Spence ask, "Does he see Van Allen as the horse-trade victim he has been mocking? Or is this that moment of racial recognition? Perhaps Driscoll sees his despised self, his own blackness, in Van Allen" (167). This shot recalls the earlier moment in the film when Driscoll sees his mother approaching and realizes that his attempt at passing has been compromised. That earlier moment of recognition is signaled by a close-up of Driscoll shot through a camera lens that has had the iris partially closed, creating a circular shading around his face that visually echoes the shot of Driscoll's face framed by the circular mirror.

The shot of Driscoll and Van Allen reflected in the mirror stands out as an expressive moment in a film that is otherwise shot realistically. The whole scene has a dreamlike quality to it, and, if we interpret it as we would a dream, this is clearly Driscoll's dream—or his nightmare. The mirror shot visually suggests Driscoll's double-consciousness, with Van Allen representing the repressed return of his "despised self," the black Other that he has (supposedly) left behind. As Van Allen steps closer and the figures merge into one another on the flat plane of the mirror, the only real visual difference between them is the color of their hats. And in choosing to wear a black cowboy hat, is Driscoll indicating his villainy (according to the codes of the Western) or unconsciously providing a clue to the truth of his identity?

As Van Allen confronts him, Driscoll tries to draw his pistol, but Van Allen grabs the other man's arm, and the only fired shots go into the air. With the bar patrons watching, the two fight.[2] In a scene that began with Driscoll telling a joke about fooling Van Allen, we have a shift in the joking structure. No longer in control of telling the joke, Driscoll has become part of the entertaining spectacle. The two men ultimately wind up wrestling on the sawdust floor. Their hats dislodged, their clothing covered in sawdust, it becomes difficult to tell one fighter from the other. Using one of the central conventions of the Western, the saloon fight, Micheaux stages the dilemma of double-consciousness, as this fight plays out as a battle between two parts of the same self: the man who remains loyal to the race, the man who rejects it; or, interpreted as Driscoll's dream, between the man who has rejected race and the "despised black self" that he has denied.

Micheaux frequently draws on minstrelsy's menu of coon figures for his comic characters. As Wallace writes, coon figures "always appear as ridiculously dressed, energetic clowns," their mismatched or loud costuming often signaling their difference from more realistically clothed figures (58). In *Within Our Gates*, a comic preacher, Old Ned, clearly derives from this tradition, a fact revealed when he receives a kick in the butt from one of the white characters amused by his antics. However, Wallace observes, "Micheaux's reinterpretation and historicization of the coon figure is also extremely noteworthy," as we have a moment where we see Old Ned regret his buffoonery: "One minute he is grinning and performing to the delight of his white benefactors; the next, as he shuts the door between himself and them, he is scowling for the viewer's benefit alone," an "extraordinary filmic moment" through which Micheaux reveals the pained self hidden by the minstrel mask (63–64). Micheaux's deployment of coon figures in his films is often complicated and layered. Such metacommentary on the coon figure (and other minstrel types) had long been taking place on the black stage (as discussed in chapter 1), and Micheaux continues that practice in his films.

The traveling salesman, Abraham, played by E. G. Tatum (who played a similar comic figure, albeit one with a tragic element, in *Within Our Gates*), is the only coon character in *Symbol*, but he plays an important role. His behavior toward Driscoll at the hotel is comically ingratiating. A short scene in which Abraham has a pantomimed argument with his mule also suggests his affinity with his comic predecessors in minstrelsy. However, like the comic figures in the *Harlem* films, the seemingly foolish Abraham (he does not seem to know that he will not get very far lecturing his mule) has a moment of reversal when he becomes an intentionally humorous character rather than a naive one. He enters the saloon as the fight is going on and quickly joins in with the cheering crowd. As the combatants stand, Van Allen begins landing a series of punches that knock Driscoll to the floor. Each time Driscoll hits the ground, Abraham starts counting down like a referee at a prize fight. His broad exaggerated gestures represent an intentional adoption of a comic persona, and the butt of this particular joke is not the coon character but the trickster Driscoll.

Hat in hand, Van Allen watches Abraham deliver a final count of eight to the floored Driscoll. Having settled his score, Van Allen leaves, and we see a disoriented Driscoll finally standing up and weaving around the room, to the amusement of the saloon's patrons. Angered at their laughter, Driscoll throws open the door, declaring that he will get his revenge. The amused Abraham, getting his own measure of revenge, pushes Driscoll through the door, kicking him in the butt (twice) to hurry his exit. Closing the door, he struts back into the saloon and up to the bar. The trickster Driscoll has been outtricked, and in a reversal of the earlier sequence in which the frightened Eve was the object of his ridicule, Driscoll has become the object of one of the most traditional of minstrel jokes, the comic kick in the butt. "To the spectators in the bar who are unaware of his racial identity," Bowser and Spence write, "this is a 'reversal' of the standard prank: it is a 'white' man, not the dark-skinned black, who is the butt of the joke and the object of ridicule" (168). For Driscoll, this is a reversal as well of his own racial expectations, the nightmare inversion of his earlier scenes with Abraham and Eve. Whether or not the spectators in the bar are aware of his racial identity, Driscoll has to recognize that he has had forced on him precisely the identity he has worked so hard to escape: the ridiculed black object of the joke whose humiliation amuses the white spectators.

That humiliation drives his desire for revenge against Van Allen. His subsequent failure to trick Van Allen out of his land results in Driscoll's determination to take the land by force with the help of white vigilantes. The footage of the final battle against the Ku Klux Klan has been lost, and the extant version of *Symbol* offers only an intertitle explaining that the Klan has been defeated. We then take up the story several months later, after "abundant oil fields" have been discovered on Van Allen's land.[3] Separated somehow during the fight, Van Allen and Eve have followed different paths to success, although they are reunited in the final sequence. Eve arrives at Hugh's office with a letter of introduction from the Committee for the Defense of the Colored Race, which reveals for the first time to Hugh the truth of Eve's racial heritage. The barrier between them removed, they declare their love for one another and indulge in a kiss, observed by Abraham, who has survived and prospered as well and who discreetly slips back out the door of the Van Allen Oil office when he sees the kiss. As J. Ronald Green writes, the final sequence "ties the project of racial uplift, and Micheaux's narrative structure, into a neat bundle," doing so in a more satisfying way than *The Homesteader* novel (*With a Crooked* 65). In contrast to the Scottish woman of *The Homesteader*, Eve is an active participant in the project of racial uplift, and a narrative and political balance exists in the coupling of the "good race man" with the "good race woman" (65). As Green observes, they form a "perfect couple who can now become an ambitious heterosexual economic and professional team that can realize the vision of uplift that informs *The Symbol of the Unconquered"* (65). The union also suggests a joining of East and West, with Eve representing what is presumably an eastern-based racial uplift organization (modeled as it is on the New York–based National Association for the Advancement of Colored People) and Hugh representing western entrepreneurship. The conclusion of *The Symbol of the Unconquered* finds a satisfying (and simultaneous) resolution to both the western and the racial uplift plots.

The dialogue between East and West, a fundamental element of the Western, is often played out in Micheaux's work as a concrete representation of double-consciousness, that internal conflict externalized in the geography of the narrative. In both *The Conquest* and *The Homesteader*, the protagonist extols the virtues of the West, but he continually finds himself drawn back East. He cannot assimilate so much into the dominant culture as to marry a white woman (the mysterious Scottish woman who is the love interest in both books as well as in *The Exile*). His desire to marry a black woman is an allegory for his continued loyalty to his race. Similarly, Devereaux's migration West into a predominantly white social context is, in a seeming paradox, an example of his race loyalty. In *The Conquest*, protagonist Oscar Devereaux sees his efforts and his success as representative, reflecting on the race as a whole and not just himself. He brings his sister and grandmother as well as his bride-to-be, Orlean McCraline, to South Dakota: "On October first, all three were ready to file on their claims, and Dakota's colored population would be increased by three, and four hundred and eighty acres of land would be added to the wealth of the colored race in the state" (199).

Through marriage to Orlean, he joins East and West by bringing part of the race to South Dakota, increasing both the population and "the wealth of the colored race in the state." However, his attempts to marry West and East, white frontier opportunity and black racial belonging, are fraught with difficulty and ultimately tragedy. Although *The Conquest* ends with separation of husband and wife, a rare Micheaux unhappy ending, *The Homesteader* adds a murder-suicide and the revelation that the Scottish woman is actually of mixed race; thus, the protagonist resolves his double-consciousness through marriage to a woman who shares both his race and the frontier values that he admires.

The Exile follows the books in the doubling of place and the conflict between East and West as a representation of double-consciousness, but whereas the majority of *The Conquest* takes place in South Dakota, the proportions are reversed in *The Exile*, with the South Dakota section accorded only twenty minutes or so of film time. In fact, the entire first half of the book, which details the hardship and struggle that eventually results in success for Devereaux's homesteading enterprise, is collapsed into a seven-word intertitle: "Somewhere in South Dakota, five years later." *The Exile* focuses instead during the South Dakota sequence on the romance between Baptiste and Agnes Stewart.

Even though the opening titles announce that the film is adapted from *The Conquest,* the lack of narrative space in the film devoted to the "conquest" of the land that is central to the book suggests just how much the movie departs from its source. The protagonist is named Jean Baptiste, the hero of *The Homesteader,* rather than *The Conquest's* Oscar Devereaux. Perhaps Micheaux's realization that he was breaking new ground with his first sound feature caused him to return to his first book rather than to *The Homesteader* as the announced source of the film. Micheaux had struggled to make the transition from silents to sound films, and his first two efforts, the part-talkies *Easy Street* (1930) and *A Daughter of the Congo* (1930) had been panned in large part because audiences were disappointed by films that had been advertised as having fully synchronized sound when in fact they did not. In contrast, "*The Exile* opened at the Lafayette in May 1931—to overflow crowds and triumphant notices. The 'first Negro all-talking picture' was completely ignored by the white press" but was championed by black newspapers, which "hailed the story, acting, musical sequences" and, as the *Pittsburgh Courier* stated, a "'portrayal of Negro life in a city that no one but a Negro, who has traveled and lived in cities could tell'" (McGilligan 256). As McGilligan writes in his biography of Micheaux, in a "career of switchback reversals, *The Exile* was the miracle comeback, a rebound for the ages" (256). "No other race-picture producer from the silent-film era," McGilligan continues, "broke through all the barriers and crossed over into the sound age. Micheaux was the first and only" (256).

As the *Courier's* praise of the film's "portrayal of Negro life in a city" suggests, *The Exile* differs as much from *The Homesteader* as from *The Conquest,* a fact announced in the first intertitle. While Micheaux's earlier frontier stories are indeed stories of conquest and homesteading, *The Exile* is "a story of Chicago," and the opening credits appear against drawings of the Chicago skyline. Rather than East and West as opposing places, *The Exile* represents them as alternate frontier spaces, both offering opportunity for the entrepreneur. The primary setting, "a mansion, somewhere on the south side," is established as a kind of urban frontier space.

Rather than Native Americans displaced by waves of white immigrants, *The Exile* depicts Chicago whites fleeing before a new group of colonists. The mansion has been abandoned by the heirs of white meat packers who "fled, frightened" before "a seemingly endless stream of Negroes, brought North to supply labor for the demands of war—and moving in this direction in quest of a place to live." The nonspecific "moving in this direction" seems deliberate, as directionality (west, north) is secondary to the quest for a better life, for frontier opportunity, whether that opportunity be rural or urban.[4]

As Stewart points out, "Although Micheaux frequently argued that the western frontier, not the city, was the ideal space where African Americans could succeed morally, financially, and socially and stake their most convincing claim to American citizenship, his filmmaking relied heavily on Black urban themes, audiences, and presses" (*Migrating* 225). Moreover, Micheaux loved cities, especially Chicago, and even though the South Dakota frontier remained an important symbol of possibility in his books and films, the closest he came to living in the state after the 1910s was Sioux City, Iowa. Although he visited family in Kansas and traveled west to distribute and promote films, the majority of his life from the mid-1910s onward was spent in urban environments. Both the need to tailor his films for his urban audiences and his increasingly urban life probably contributed to the shift in his filmmaking from South Dakota (where *The Symbol of the Unconquered* is exclusively set) to *The Exile* (the story of a successful homesteader who spends more time in Chicago than on the homestead).

As is the case with Micheaux's novels, the doubling of place in *The Exile* is echoed by the doubling of characters. The mansion on the South Side, the intertitle tells us, "is occupied now, however, by Edith Duval, a former maid, but since the war—and prosperity—an ambitious 'social leader.'" Edith, like Driscoll in *Symbol*, is "motivated by the same drives as the hero," and she shares Driscoll's willingness to engage in "unscrupulous" means to achieve those goals (Bowser and Spence 160). *The Exile* takes a number of Micheaux's concerns and character types and combines them in Edith. Like Eve Mason of *Symbol*, she is a strong female character, and like Driscoll and even like Micheaux's heroes, she is ambitious. Like the various reverends who populate Micheaux's stories, her appetite for vice contributes to her downfall, and although a "social leader," she is leading the race astray (according to the terms of Micheaux's preachment) rather than toward shared prosperity. Unlike Driscoll or the reverends, however, Edith is not a hypocrite. She states very clearly what she stands for and intends.

The doubling of Baptiste and Edith is suggested from the opening sequence, which cuts back and forth between the two characters as they dress for the evening. As Anna Siomopoulos observes, crosscutting between parallel scenes is a distinctive element of Micheaux's style, developed as early as *Within Our Gates* (1920) as a way of challenging D. W. Griffith's *The Birth of a Nation* "in the politics of its aesthetics" as well as in its content (111). Griffith's film, Siomopoulos writes, "uses crosscutting to present a very simple opposition between white virtue and black villainy; in contrast, [*Within Our Gates*] uses a complex editing pattern to present a larger social vision of many different, competing political positions within both white and African American society" (111). This complicated editing style, Siomopoulos continues, "works to constitute a spectator who is more politically critical than the spectator constructed by the classical Hollywood style of Griffith's film" (111–12). In *Within Our Gates*, Micheaux cuts between "five or six different locations and twice as many characters," demanding "an engaged and thoughtful spectator to discern conflicting and contradictory social and political claims" (112).

Although *The Exile* lacks the complexity of plot, location, and character found in *Within Our Gates*, the opening sequence's use of parallel editing suggests more than a simple opposition between Baptiste and Duval. Shot without dialogue, this silent opening sequence uses a variety of techniques to engage a "thoughtful" spectatorship, suggesting character qualities through both action and camera placement rather than spelling them out through dialogue or intertitles. There is little doubt that Driscoll is the villain of *Symbol*, but *The Exile* asks us to decide for ourselves—at least at the beginning of the film—which of the two characters will engage our identification and support.

We see the two characters in separate rooms, each dressing in front of a mirror. Although the matching of activities suggests an affinity between the two, performance and camera placement observe differences. Edith is seated at a dressing table, the camera behind her, so that we see both her and her image reflected in the table's mirror. The dividing of her image on-screen suggests duality, perhaps duplicity, and possibly self-involvement. (Throughout the scene, she gazes at her own image in the mirror.) The crosscutting between scenes establishes another possibility of doubling through editing—that as we are looking into these two rooms, we are in some ways viewing another split image, Baptiste and Duval, who mirror one another in their actions. That the camera is placed to Duval's left and to Baptiste's right reinforces the uncanny effect of mirroring, creating the illusion that we are cutting back and forth between one person and that person's reflection in the mirror, with right and left reversing with each cut. We do not know which is the "real person" and which the "mirror image."

In a sense, this sequence takes the brief shot of Driscoll and Van Allen in the barroom mirror and expands it into an extended meditation on Self and Other, on image and actuality, and on the difficulty of existential choices. The crosscutting between the two characters poses the question of which path to success is best for the black individual. Rather than between the racially denying self and the racially accepting self, as in *Symbol*, the duality here is between two African American ways of being in the world. That continuity is reinforced by the soundtrack. As Green observes, our first view of Edith is accompanied by "sweet jazz or incidental theater music" playing a brief theme that is repeated throughout the dressing room sequence, with strings initially dominating but other instruments taking up the melody as the sequence unfolds (*With a Crooked* 131). There are breaks throughout—the sweet jazz momentarily disrupted by a sudden drumroll or "a raucous hot-jazz break" (131). The breaks at times coincide with a cut from one room to the other, but at other times, the sweet jazz melody carries us from one space to the other without interruption, accompanying Edith's actions as much as Jean's. The music may suggest Edith's potential for villainy (as when a couple of bars of hot jazz accompany her shot of whiskey), but Baptiste also has moments when he is accompanied by hot jazz. For the most part, though, the same sweet jazz melody accompanies both characters. What could have been staged as the musical equivalent of crosscutting to suggest simple opposition (alternating segments of sweet jazz and hot jazz) instead creates a more complex pattern.

Baptiste stands rather than sits, and the top of his dresser holds an array of toiletries and other objects. Wearing a tuxedo, he matches Duval in her evening dress. Baptiste is thoughtful as he dresses, his eyes either unfocused in the distance or looking at the objects on the nightstand but rarely even glancing at his image in the mirror. Edith powders her face, pours a shot from a flask, sprays herself with perfume, fixes her hair. We eventually discover what is occupying Baptiste's mind. He picks up a telegram from the "Western Land & Townsite Co" informing him that he is the owner of the "finest land in the state of South Dakota—enough to make you a rich man in less than five years." Although in front of a mirror, neither he nor the camera looks into it. In contrast, Edith continually checks her appearance. This contrast in behavior suggests more than superficial vanity on Edith's part. As we discover, Edith puts her own interests above those of her race and is willing to exploit her fellows for her own gain. Her gaze at her own image in the mirror foreshadows her selfishness of motive, just as her solitary drinking from the flask suggests a tendency toward immoral behavior, although at this point in the narrative, these are only suggestions of character. The dramatic differences between Baptiste and Duval are revealed only after Baptiste's marriage proposal and her acceptance.

The mirroring of the two characters continues on the dance floor, as they move from their individual rooms to a meeting in the mansion's ballroom. The suggestion of potential discord comes from a conversation about the two taking place at a card game (presumably elsewhere in the mansion). As the proposal plays out, with Baptiste and Duval moving from the dance floor back to Edith's chambers, we cut back and forth between the couple and the quartet of card players. The parallel cutting here again raises a question and in so doing requires an engaged spectatorship. Do we trust Madge, the card-playing critic of Edith Duval? Or is Madge merely a gossip?

Jean pops the question, and Edith accepts. There is kissing on a couch. But Jean informs Edith that he has "plans" and that before they get married, he wants to be sure that she is willing to help him achieve his goals. Edith plays a similar role to Orlean McCraline in *The Conquest*, representing the race, the alternate choice to the Scottish woman who represents assimilation into the white world, a concrete representation of the protagonist's existential struggle between race loyalty and a desire for opportunity. However, Edith is no Orlean McCraline, not "an obedient girl" (216) noted for her timidity and submissiveness. Like Baptiste, Edith is an entrepreneur, aggressive in her pursuit of success. "I have some big plans of my own," Edith tells Baptiste; "There's good money in it."

Her frontier is that of the urban underworld, where she sees opportunity in operating "a social club" similar to one run by Frankie Dixon, which Baptiste dismisses as a "joint, a dive," built on bootlegging and gambling. "The whole mess," he asserts, "is against every principle I possess." Rather than admiring Frankie Dixon's success, Jean describes her as "the queen of the underworld. I loathe even the idea." Edith responds, "But she's making money. More money than any other woman I know."

"What is the difference," she asks, "if I get the money? After all, that is what counts." Edith and Jean clearly do not have the same ideas in their plans for the future.

When Baptiste protests, Edith chastises him, disdainfully referring to him as a "nice man" and a "goody man." "You need to buy yourself a little red toy balloon and float on up to heaven to get an angel for a wife," she tells him. "You're entirely too nice to be living in Chicago. You sissy. You sicken me. You are not like other men. You don't drink, and you don't stay out late at night. Never even asked me to kiss you. Just a sissy." Edith is openly disdainful of Baptiste's civilized manliness. Edith is the film's tough guy, and as love interest, antagonist, and double, she is a more interesting and complicated character than any of the female characters in the novels.

Dismissed as a "sissy" ("I'm a normal man in every way," he protests, "but I'll have nothing to do with any crooked underworld business"), Baptiste heads west to prove his manhood. As is the case in the novels, the hero's movements from East to West and West to East take place by train. However, rather than repeated sequences of Baptiste traveling back and forth between South Dakota and Chicago, we have one transitional section of moving trains. The repeated intercut scenes of trains traveling back and forth across the country, rapidly cutting from one shot to another of trains moving in various directions, gives concrete form to Baptiste's double-consciousness. Appearing in the narrative after a scene of dramatic conflict, the train sequence is more than just a transitional device; it is a vivid representation of the power of Baptiste's emotions. Although Baptiste is going only one direction—west to South Dakota— the trains on-screen come and go from every direction, right to left, left to right, from the upper right corner of the frame, from the lower right corner of the frame, sometimes moving toward the camera, sometimes moving away from it, suggesting in visual form his conflicting emotions.

An intertitle tells us that we are now "Somewhere in South Dakota, five years later," and after establishing inserts of cattle and of wheat being harvested, the film takes us to Baptiste's humble homestead. And at this point, *The Exile* becomes Baptiste's story, and we hear of Edith's adventures only via a letter from Baptiste's cousin: "She has turned that fine house into a joint. . . . I'm told that she's running a 'speak easy' in the basement and some games called 'skin' and 'black jack' upstairs. On Saturday night, she has the most awful dice game in Chicago. Sometimes they raid it and carry three or four loads to the police station. . . . [A]nd to think you might have married this awful person." This letter also succinctly establishes Baptiste's romantic difficulties: "I had a pretty girl all excited about you, but when she understood that she'd have to leave Chicago, she cried: 'What, marry an Exile (all the colored people call you 'The Exile') and live in the wilderness!' . . . The little fool! If you were not my cousin, I'd fly to So. Dak. [to] be your wife."

Baptiste does not respond to his cousin's broad hint and invite her to join him on the frontier. A new neighbor arrives, bringing a daughter. A romance soon develops, culminating within a few weeks in an on-screen cuddle and a kiss. "Oh, Jean," Agnes tells him, "You are magnificent." Baptiste responds, "Nothing can stop us from loving each other." However, the off-screen voice of Agnes's brother reminds Baptiste of his social situation, and he sends Agnes a letter: "We would be snubbed, insulted,—ostracized—and I love you too much to let you suffer all that. So I have decided to go away and try to put you out of my life. To remain near and do this—is impossible!" Trains rumble this way and that across the screen, and Baptiste returns to Chicago. These events are very much in keeping with those in *The Conquest*.

Through the parallel stories of Baptiste and Edith, Micheaux investigates two kinds of frontiers, two possible avenues to African American success. Consistent with the message of *The Conquest*, Micheaux condemns elements of African American life that he finds detrimental. However, his portrayal of the city is more ambiguous than that in *The Conquest* and *The Homesteader*. The differences between Edith Duval and Jean Baptiste likewise are not as pronounced as between Baptiste and Rev. McCarthy. Although the intertitles insist that Edith has made the wrong choices, the mise-en-scène consistently represents a Chicago lifestyle that is vastly more appealing than anything we see or hear in South Dakota. When Baptiste and Duval momentarily reconcile after his return to Chicago, he tells her, "I can't believe you would be willing to leave a place like this, with all its people, music . . . and settle in a land where the only music you'd be hearing after the sun went down would be that of yelping coyotes." With a soundtrack composed by Donald Heywood and performed by his band, the sound elements of *The Exile* reinforce that observation. If parallel editing in *Within Our Gates* demands engaged spectatorship, the contrasting messages suggested by the different elements of film form (mise-en-scène, plot, dialogue, music) in *The Exile* similarly demand an active spectator to sort out the conflicting messages.

In *The Homesteader*, Micheaux writes that Chicago is "the freest city in the world for the black man," although events in Chicago in the novel do not really address that sense of an urban frontier space (299). However, the Keystone Hotel, which Micheaux describes as "the oldest and most elite hostelry for Negroes in Chicago and the West," a "meeting place for men in nearly all walks of life," with a reputation for "wide open" experience (and upstairs gambling), is a model for the mansion of *The Exile* (299). Chicago nightlife in *The Homesteader* represents the degradation of Baptiste, where he is attracted by "ragtime music" into a hellish underworld of "various forms of vice," "the painted faces and the gorgeous eyes" of "familiar women" (348). After his sacrifice of the Scottish woman and in the midst of his troubled marriage to Orlean, Baptiste leaves South Dakota for Chicago. Seated at a bar, cocktail in hand, Baptiste "observed himself, all haggard and worn in the bar mirror" (348).

Although this scene provides a structural parallel for Baptiste's return to Chicago in *The Exile*, the contrast between the two is notable. In the film, Baptiste is hardly haggard and worn, and the implied seediness of *The Homesteader*'s bar scene is replaced by the lavishness of the mansion's dance floor and the sophistication, urbanity, and stylishness of the dancers, all suggestive symbols of uplift rather than vice. At the moment of Baptiste's return, the film sets his story aside to present a series of performances that he watches. McGilligan comments that "unlike most Hollywood directors, who were forever relegating musicians to the background of club scenes, diminishing their numbers by excerption, he showcased his performers' [*sic*] at length" (255). In what will become a hallmark of later race films, the plot of *The Exile* frequently takes a backseat to the filming of onstage performances. In addition to Heywood conducting his orchestra, "among the marvels in *The Exile* were Roland Holder, a buck-and-wing specialist, and Louise Cook, a sparkler from Connie's Inn, singing 'Make Hay While the Sun is Shining' while doing her shimmy and kootch" (253–54).

The stage is every bit as much a field of opportunity for African American success as the plains of South Dakota—and a far more attractive place to make hay while the sun is shining than in the hot fields of the plains. This long sequence devoted to displaying the skills of African American performers, full of sound and motion, marks a distinct contrast with the static scenes of South Dakota life, which consist mostly of actors sitting and talking. In the novels, such a contrast would suggest the superiority of South Dakota, but Micheaux's fondness for Chicago and his interest in African American performers and in the new technology that will bring the sound of those performers to his audience combine to create a far more appealing urban East than we see in Micheaux's novels. Who would choose to stay in the wheat fields, listening to coyotes yelping, after hearing Heywood and his band perform and after seeing Leonard Harper's scantily clad dancers—the Hot Chocolates—take the stage?

For that matter, Heywood's score, which juxtaposes jazz, spirituals, and orchestral music, suggests both continuity and disjunction, as we often cut back and forth between these different musical traditions, which do not often merge but rather jump from one to the other. When we first arrive in South Dakota, the soundtrack repeats the sweet jazz theme of the dressing room sequence, although without the hot jazz breaks. The repetition of the same melody behind the South Dakota scenes suggests a continuity between one frontier and another, in effect urbanizing the South Dakota frontier. The repetition also suggests that Micheaux well knew that his audience would much rather hear Heywood's jazz than yelping coyotes as an accompaniment to the South Dakota story. If the narrative attempts to maintain an opposition between East and West, the score consistently suggests continuity instead.

After Jean and Edith reunite and share a kiss, we cut back to the dance floor, where Heywood announces the song "Make Hay-Hay While the Sun Shines," the lyrics suggesting a parodic commentary (the sexual joke about making "hay-hay") on that impending marriage and wedding night. In a nod to the signifying practices of the Black Belt silent film theater orchestras, the introduction of a song that is both apt and comically inappropriate disrupts the story the film is telling to comment ironically on that story. The choice of this particular song also suggests a continuity in the film's rural and urban frontier ventures. Making hay-hay suggests making money as well as making love. Green comments that "Jean would rather be making literal South Dakota hay on his farm than euphemistic 'hay-hay' in the social clubs of Chicago," but farming is not the only route to success in *The Exile* (*With a Crooked* 117). Like Baptiste, the performers are also making hay while the sun shines (or, more likely, after the sun goes down), although they are working a different field of endeavor. The literal and euphemistic meanings of making hay may differ, but the decision to include this particular song in the film seems to draw our attention to the possible continuities between these two paths to success.

After this long sequence of music and dance, Duval appears in the ballroom, and, after a long conversation with Baptiste, the two decide to try marriage once again. However, the sins of the past catch up with Duval. After Baptiste leaves her, a former lover whom she has discarded comes to her chambers. Jango, a young man from Ethiopia whom Edith taught "to smoke those filthy reefers," decides that Edith will "never ruin another man" and kills her. Baptiste is accused of her murder, although he is exonerated when a witness appears. This dramatic climax is familiar, a reworking of *The Homesteader*'s concluding murder-suicide and Baptiste's eventual rescue from false accusation. As in *The Homesteader*, the Scottish woman makes her way to Chicago, where she reunites with Baptiste and reveals her hidden Ethiopian ancestry. In the final shot of the film, Jean and Agnes are on a train heading west, no longer exiled from Eden but returning to it. This train goes in one direction only, double-consciousness resolved as Baptiste and his new (and newly discovered as African American) bride ride off toward the sunset.

As the independently produced race film industry continued into the 1940s and 1950s, filmmakers followed Micheaux's lead in *The Exile*, although they went further than he did in collapsing the distinction between East and West, between the urban frontier of the city and the rural frontier of the West. More often than not, Harlem replaced Micheaux's Chicago as the space of alternate frontier opportunity in these later films. As Blake Allmendinger points out in *Imagining the African American West*, even the titles of such films as *Harlem on the Prairie* (1937) and *Harlem Rides the Range* (1939), collapse the distinction between East and West. *The Exile* prefigures these later films in suggesting a continuity between the rural West and the urban East as sites of African American freedom and opportunity.

Of the extant Herb Jeffries films, *Two-Gun Man from Harlem* suggests the greatest number of parallels to Micheaux's work. Cowboy and ranch foreman Bob Blake is falsely accused—by the owner's wife, who is covering for her lover, the real killer—of murdering the ranch's owner. Although she advises Bob to "get across the border" before he is arrested, Bob goes in the other direction, northeast. In the process, he also seems to leave behind the nineteenth century for the twentieth. As he moves from California to Chicago and finally to Harlem (with his arrival in both places announced on-screen by having the names of those cities appear in large letters superimposed over vibrant scenes of urban nightlife filled with automobiles and electric lights), he also leaves behind his horse. Paved roads suddenly appear, followed by a few cars, and, before we know it, we see him hitching a ride. The first thing he does after arriving in Harlem is go to a nightclub, where, with his cowboy hat and western drawl, he cuts quite a figure. As in *The Exile*, the scene in the nightclub provides the opportunity for a series of black performers to take center stage—a percussionist (Paul Blackman playing an upside-down washtub, cowbells, and a kazoo and tap-dancing as a "One Man Black Band"), a dancer (Dolores, played by Cotton Club dancer Rosalie Lincoln), and a vocal group (the Cats and the Fiddle, who also appear earlier in the film dressed in cowboy outfits as the Four Tones, backing up Bob on "I'm a Happy Cowboy").

The doubling of place borrows from *The Exile*, which similarly features both western (South Dakota) and eastern urban (Chicago) settings and which, like *Two-Gun Man from Harlem*, juxtaposes western frontier settings with scenes that posit the urban nightclub as a kind of frontier. The doubling of places—the western frontier of the film's opening, the urban frontier of its center—is paralleled by the doubling of characters. In the nightclub, Bob meets up with an underworld character known as the Deacon, also played by Herb Jeffries, dressed in black and sporting both a pair of glasses and impressive sideburns. The Deacon's girlfriend, the dancer, Dolores, has been flirting with Bob. When Blake and the Deacon confront each other, we could just as easily be in a western saloon. In this scene, as Allmendinger writes, "Harlem appears as an urban equivalent for the western frontier, a setting in which Blake and the Deacon are well matched as rivals. In turn, the frontier is a place where gangster's roam free" (*Imagining* 70).

As in *The Exile*, a character moves back and forth from one frontier to another, from West to East and back again. As in Micheaux's film, *Two-Gun Man from Harlem* features the doubling of characters, Bob and the Deacon. Whereas Baptiste moves back and forth from the white world of the frontier to the black world of the city, Bob Blake moves from one black world to another, as *Two-Gun Man* claims both the ranch and Harlem as African American space: Both settings are populated exclusively by African American characters. Thus, the doubling does not suggest double-consciousness. The doubling in the film also seems more self-consciously parodic and playful. Not only does Bob Blake appear in the speakeasy, but so do the Four Tones—in suits and ties rather than the cowboy outfits of *Two-Gun Man*'s opening scene, but nonetheless still singing in beautiful four-part harmony.[5] Have we traveled from the West to the East, or have we stepped through the looking glass into a mirror universe of doubles? In moving from the ranch (where nothing electrical or motorized is visible) to Harlem, have we also somehow jumped forward in time into the 1930s?

Inspired by his double, Blake disguises himself as the Deacon, returns west, and infiltrates the gang that is causing all the problems. That no one back at the ranch (except for Bill, the cook) recognizes that "the Deacon" is really Bob Blake with a change of clothing and a pair of glasses also contributes to the humor of the film. (Perhaps everyone is distracted by those sideburns.) When Bob returns to the ranch to solve the mystery of who really killed his employer, the film becomes an urban crime drama played out on the western frontier, with gangsters, contract killers, kidnappings, and movie gangster slang (the phrase *dirty rat* is used more than once). His six-shooter taken from him as evidence in the murder, Bob brings a pair of .45-caliber automatic pistols to the ranch, guns as out of place in a Western as Bob's cowboy hat is in the Harlem nightclub.

As Allmendinger notes, "In his dual roles as Blake and the Deacon, Jeffries combines aspects of the cowboy, the gangster, and the hard-boiled detective" and in so doing "injects the Western with a grittier, more profane, urban black sensibility" (*Imagining* 70). Repeated elements of *The Exile* (the same sweet jazz theme in both Chicago and South Dakota) suggest continuities between East and West, but *Two-Gun Man from Harlem* greatly expands that idea beyond anything in Micheaux's film. When bad guy Butch (Spencer Williams, again playing the *Harlem* heavy) comments on the Deacon's horsemanship—unusually good for a city slicker—Jeffries comments that he's an "Eleventh Avenue Cowboy," having learned his skills on horseback in the city, a much tougher place to ride a horse than out on the ranch.[6] When Butch has trouble striking a match, the Deacon helps by shooting a bullet that just scrapes the tip of the match and lights it. More than in any of the other films in the *Harlem* series, Jeffries in *Two-Gun Man* provides the most effective realization of the "Hoo-Doo cowboy," or, to use his phrase for the same concept, an "Eleventh Avenue Cowboy," combining as he does his western skills with his urban gangster disguise. Like the cowboy-hero, Bob, as Butch complains, "shoots too straight, and too fast, and with both hands," even as he uses a pair of pistols more appropriate for a 1930s gangster than a nineteenth-century cowboy. With his use of disguise and his clever wordplay that often leaves Butch confused, the Bob Blake story in *Two-Gun Man* is also the most extended version of a trickster tale in the *Harlem* series. In the other films, Jeffries may outtrick the trickster, but here he plays the trickster role himself.

In combining "aspects of the cowboy, the gangster, and the hard-boiled detective," *Two-Gun Man from Harlem* also brings together several of

Micheaux's favorite genres. Before Rudolf Fisher published *The Conjure-Man Dies* (1932), widely regarded as the first African American detective novel, Micheaux had already experimented with African American detectives. *Two-Gun Man* seems to signify on Micheaux's films in multiple ways. Elements of the film recall (among others) Micheaux's sound era gangster/detective films *Harlem after Midnight* (1932), *Murder in Harlem* (1935), and *Underworld* (1937). If the doubling in *Two-Gun Man* comments on a central element of many of Micheaux's films, it also seems to speak specifically to the silent film *Body and Soul* (1925). As in *Two-Gun Man*, we have a lead actor playing a double role in *Body and Soul*—Paul Robeson, who plays both the good guy, Sylvester, and the bad guy, the corrupt Isaiah Jenkins, who is not a deacon but a reverend. The Deacon's name in *Two-Gun Man* is explained in the film: "They say he was a preacher once, then killed a man and has been a killer ever since." This backstory seems to take up where Rev. Jenkins's story left off in *Body and Soul*. At the end of that film, his deception revealed to his congregation, Jenkins escapes into the woods, where he has a violent altercation with one of his pursuers. Leaving the man for dead, Jenkins disappears further into the woods and out of the film. Perhaps, *Two-Gun Man from Harlem* seems to suggest, he found his way to Harlem and continued with a life of crime. Or perhaps the parallels are coincidental; however, intentional or not, the preacher turned criminal in *Two-Gun Man* is a descendant of Robeson's criminal/trickster/preacher from *Body and Soul* as well of Micheaux's long line of dubious religious figures. *Two-Gun Man from Harlem*'s practice of double signifying on the conventions and tropes of both the genre Western and the race film (and, perhaps, specifically on Micheaux's films) makes it truly an African American Western and not simply a generic Western populated with black actors.

Two-Gun Man also sets the pattern for the next decade of Western-themed race films, especially those associated with Spencer Williams Jr., who transitions in the 1940s from *Harlem* heavy to writer and director (and sometimes leading man) of his own films. Working with producer and film distributor Alfred R. Sack, Williams oversaw the production of a dozen or so black-audience films from 1941 to 1947, including two religious-themed race film classics, *Go Down, Death!* (1944), and *The Blood of Jesus* (1941). Sack Amusements was a major distributor of black-cast films, and its location in Dallas provided an operational base for Williams, who filmed and/or set many on his 1940s films in and around the city and elsewhere in the Southwest.[7] For example, *Where's My Man To-Nite* (1943), also titled *Marching On,* written and directed by Williams, makes extensive use of location footage shot in and around Fort Huachuca, Arizona, a segregated training facility for black soldiers during World War II. Also in keeping with the practices of earlier race films, *Where's My Man To-Nite* joins western drama with eastern African American performance. Rather than going to Harlem, as is the case in *Two-Gun Man,* Harlem comes to Arizona via a stage show for the troops—a long performance sequence involving a jazz band and dancers. As in *The Exile* and *Two-Gun Man,* the plot and the western adventures taking place in the wild landscape around the base come to a halt as both the audience and the on-screen characters pause to watch the show.

In the opening titles of *Midnight Shadow* (1939, directed by George Randol) the setting is identified only as being in the "southern part of the country," although a more specifically western (Oklahoma, Texas) location is established as the film progresses. The film's plot recalls *The Symbol of the Unconquered.* We have an attempt to steal the deed to valuable land from an upstanding African American character, and as in *Symbol* and *The Realization of a Negro's Ambition,* the central trope of frontier opportunity is the discovery of oil. As the film progresses, the characters move across Oklahoma and Texas in search of the stolen deed and in an attempt to solve a murder and free the family friend falsely accused of the crime.

The film emphasizes not just the oil frontier but also the efficacy of black self-government. The film's southwestern setting is described as a place of "millions of black men and women in the most highly concentrated area of Negro population in America." "Here in certain communities, the like of which is found no where else in all the world," the opening intertitle sequence continues, "these people of darker hue have demonstrated their abilities in self-government by the orderly processes of law of which they are capable when unhampered by outside influences." The story that follows, although deeply involved with lawbreaking, ultimately demonstrates "the orderly processes of law" in an all-black community that stretches from Louisiana to Oklahoma. Those "orderly processes" are shown through the abilities of the black citizens and authority figures (a black police officer, the black president of the LA-TEX-OKLA Oil company) to restore the rule of law and the stolen deed to its rightful owner. Building on the history of such real all-black towns as Boley and Langston City, Oklahoma, *Midnight Shadow* continues the tradition of the *Harlem Westerns* by reimagining the American West as the African American

West, which emerges in the film as a self-contained and self-governing autonomous region.

Like *The Exile* and *Two-Gun Man from Harlem*, *The Girl in Room 20* (1946, directed by Spencer Williams) investigates the relationship between East and West. The film begins in the West (Prairieville, Texas) and follows an individual's journey to (and return from) Harlem. Closer in theme to Micheaux's "preachment," the film implicitly suggests that West is best, although, like *The Exile*, much of the film takes place elsewhere. Daisy, the protagonist of *The Girl in Room 20*, leaves Prairieville to pursue a singing career. Prairieville, according to the voice-over narration that begins the film, is "just a wide place in the road," but it is also a place "where people of several generations have lived and died without ever wanting to see, know, or hear about what went on in the outside world." *The Girl in Room 20* addresses the common Western theme of opposing East and West, but the film also develops the change in that theme begun in earlier sound era Western race films. Williams's films in general reimagine the West as African American space, so the journey in *The Girl in Room 20* (as in *Two-Gun Man from Harlem*) is from one black world to another. Daisy leaves her mother's home in Prairieville and ends up performing in "Mama's Place" in Harlem, the mirroring of one mother's place with another suggesting the way *The Girl in Room 20* undermines the distinctions between East and West. The film's nightclub setting similarly provides ample opportunity to showcase black performance. Although Daisy succeeds on this new frontier, she ultimately decides (after being shot by a jealous wife) to return to Prairieville, to set aside her desire for adventure on the urban frontier for the safety and security of the American West, which is not in this case a "strange white world" but Daisy's African American home.

The Girl in Room 20 and *Two-Gun Man from Harlem* offer an alternative vision to what Quintard Taylor calls the "stereotype of the black westerner as a solitary figure" (22). Although Micheaux's novels and *The Exile* repeat that myth, his silent *The Symbol of the Unconquered* departs from the myth by populating its frontier town with African American characters. Driscoll, although passing as white, is identified as being of African American descent; one of the horse thieves, described as a "half blood Indian" in the film, is played by an African American actor; Hugh Van Allen and Eve, of course, are identified as African American, as is the traveling salesman, Abraham; even Driscoll's African American mother shows up on the frontier, where she is taken in by the hospitable Eve. More so than

The Exile, Micheaux's 1920 silent film foreshadows the developments in later sound era race films by depicting a frontier town with a substantial African American population. In *Symbol*, Eve is the character we see migrate from the East (Alabama) to the West, from a black environment to a racially mixed one. Later films go further in having characters move from one black world to another. The difference between East and West is less prominently marked than in Micheaux's novels, in large part because each of these regions is claimed as African American space.

To a certain degree, *The Exile* suggests this development. Although the South Dakota of that film remains a "strange white world," the film moves toward collapsing the East/West opposition. Rather than populating the West with African American characters, *The Exile* alters the dynamic by exploring the eastern city as a possible frontier space. The idealization of the frontier in *The Exile* as an abstract representation of black freedom and opportunity provides a model for later race movie filmmakers, who similarly imagine an American West that is more ideal than real and who similarly imagine both the rural West and the urban East as appealing frontier spaces. The continuities between *Two-Gun Man from Harlem* and *The Exile*, which are repeated in, for example, Williams's race films into the 1940s, suggest that these African American Westerns constitute a coherent cinematic tradition. At the core of this tradition is Oscar Micheaux, whose films provide the call to which later filmmakers respond.

6

Sammy Davis Jr., Woody Strode, and the Black Westerner of the Civil Rights Era

"The Incident of the Buffalo Soldier," an episode of the popular long-running Western *Rawhide* that first aired on 6 January 1961, begins with Clint Eastwood's Rowdy Yates and fellow cowboy Jim Quince sitting by a campfire, talking—or, rather, with Quince nervously (they are heading into Kiowa country) talking and nervously taking offense at everything Yates says in reply while Yates tries to get Quince to shut up so he can sleep. Out of the darkness, an African American man, played by Woody Strode, steps out of the brush and into the light. Tall, athletic, and in the uniform of a member of the U.S. Army, he strides purposefully toward the fire, coffee cup in one hand, rifle in the other. For a moment, Yates and his partner are agog with wonder, not just at the sudden appearance of the man from the shadows but seemingly at the sudden and unexpected appearance of an African American man in the Western itself. "You're what the Indians call buffalo soldiers, ain't you?," Quince observes in a tone of wonder. An obliging Strode removes his cap to reveal a shaved head, commenting, "That's right, Mr. Quince. If I let my hair grow, it would be wiry and tight, just like buffalo hide." Throughout this campfire scene, Strode as Corporal Gabe Washington commands the attention of both cowboys and of the camera, which lingers on close-ups of Strode with only occasional cutaways to the staring Quince and Yates. Appearing unexpectedly in the unexpected place of the television Western, calling attention to his own difference by removing his cap and commenting matter-of-factly about his physical appearance, Strode introduces Washington as a specifically African American westerner, one who is at the center of the story that follows this opening scene, and one whose every move is watched as attentively by the camera as it is within the mise-en-scène by the other characters, particularly the fascinated Yates.

A year later, Sammy Davis Jr. made his first guest-star appearance on *The Rifleman*, in the episode "Two Ounces of Tin" (19 February 1962). Davis plays Tip Corey, a former member of the Buffalo Bill Wild West Show with expertise as a trick shooter. Drawing on Davis's quick-draw and fancy-shooting skills, Tip Corey whirls and twirls and holsters and unholsters his six-shooter at astounding speed, to the open-mouthed amazement of young Mark McCain (son of series hero Lucas McCain, the rifleman of the title, played by Chuck Conners). As is the case with *Rawhide*, we have a white series regular as the audience stand-in, registering the astonishment a viewer might experience in 1962 at the surprising appearance of an African American cowboy. However, Mark is amazed at Corey's skills, not at his race. When Mark first encounters Corey and his injured horse, the boy evinces no special surprise at the sudden appearance of a black man in North Fork, a town comprised almost exclusively of white characters. The real surprise of this episode is that no one in the town comments on or even seems to notice Tip Corey's race. In television and film Westerns of the 1960s and into the 1970s, these two moments establish the parameters for depicting the African American West, the dual strategies for representing the African American westerner on-screen— on the one hand, erasure, and on the other hand, the exact opposite, a narrative that explicitly draws our attention to race.

These two episodes of *Rawhide* and *The Rifleman* also establish another er pattern—the repeated casting of these two particular African American performers, Sammy Davis Jr. and Woody Strode, as the representatives of the African American West again and again throughout the decade. Other African American actors certainly appear in Western roles during the decade, but Strode and Davis stand out because of their repeated casting in a variety of Westerns and types of Westerns—television series, films, and, for Strode, several Italian- or other European-made Westerns (spaghetti Westerns) made by a combination of American, Italian, and other European actors and directors.[1] Davis's appearances in Westerns ranged from television series guest appearances on (among many others) *Zane Grey Theater* (1959), *Frontier Circus* (1962), *Lawman* ("Blue Boss and Willie Shay," 12 March 1961), and *The Wild Wild West* ("The Night of the Returning Dead," 14 October 1966) to a starring role in the made-for-television movie, *The Trackers* (1971) to film roles in *Sergeants 3* (1962), *Robin and the 7 Hoods* (1964) (which includes a musical number that displays Davis's trick-shooting skills), and *Gone with the West* (1975). A multifaceted singer and dancer, Davis also performed gun tricks on television variety shows of the era, demonstrating his spinning and fast-draw techniques in particular. Davis appeared in two episodes of *The Rifleman* in 1962, playing a different character in each episode. Although Strode's work in John Ford's film Westerns of the 1960s has received more critical attention, these two episodes of *The Rifleman* from 1962 featuring Davis are just as groundbreaking in their positive portrayal of a black westerner.

A former Olympic athlete, a college football star at UCLA, and one of the first African American athletes to play professional football (with the Los Angeles Rams), Strode began a career in television, film, and professional wrestling in the late 1940s. Throughout the 1960s, Strode appeared in multiple Westerns, alternating between playing "cowboy" and "Indian" roles. In his autobiography, *Goal Dust* (cowritten with Sam Young), Strode claims African and Native American (Creek/Cherokee and Blackfoot) ancestry, although he did not discover that he had "Indian blood" until college (2). "Because of my mixed background," Strode writes (and because of Hollywood's tendency to mix ethnicities at will), "I could play anyone. . . . I played natives in the old jungle pictures; I fought Tarzan to the death. They stuck a pigtail on me for *Genghis Khan*, and slanted my eyes and made me Chinese in *Seven Women*, and I could play all Indians. I never played myself, a Negro-Indian breed, until I did *The Professionals*" (5–6). Strode's appearances in four John Ford films established him as an actor recognized around the world. "My first Ford picture," Strode writes, "was *Sergeant Rutledge*, a major role for a black actor at that time. That one gave me dignity" (5). Other Ford films would follow, *Two Rode Together* (in a Native American role as Stone Calf), *The Man Who Shot Liberty Valance*, and as a wrestling warrior in *7 Women*. Strode also appeared in a number of Italian-made Westerns, including Sergio Leone's *Once upon a Time in the West*. With *Sergeant Rutledge* and *Liberty Valance*, Strode appeared in two of the most important revisionist Western films of the decade, and in *Once upon a Time in the West*, he played a role in a Western classic. Those films alone make Strode an important figure in Western film in general and a pioneer in the portrayal of the African American West. His status as an iconic black westerner is apparent as well in Mario Van Peebles's *Posse* (1993), a film that is (among other things) an extended homage to the spaghetti Western (particularly to Sergio Leone's films) and to the black West. Van Peebles cast the seventy-nine-year-old Strode as the Old Man/Storyteller whose narration frames the story and who introduces the audience to the history of the African American West.

Strode's film work is certainly important, but here, I emphasize primarily Strode's heretofore underexamined work in television Westerns, particularly his appearances on *Rawhide*.[2]

Although African American actors continually appeared in Westerns in minor roles as cooks and servants throughout the middle of the century, the late 1950s saw the beginnings of a more serious effort to represent the African American West on-screen and to incorporate the black cowboy into the Western mise-en-scène in more significant roles. Influential film Westerns such as Ford's *Sergeant Rutledge* and *The Man Who Shot Liberty Valance* no doubt contributed to this trend, but the appearances of Davis and Strode on *Rawhide* and *The Rifleman* may also account for the new attention to the black cowboy in the television Western of the 1960s and the 1970s. To provide just a few examples, long-running Western series such as *Have Gun, Will Travel, Death Valley Days, The Virginian, Bonanza, Gunsmoke, Daniel Boone,* and *Alias: Smith and Jones* aired episodes featuring African American guest stars.[3] The short-lived series *The Cowboys* featured an African American actor as a series regular—Moses Gunn as Jebediah Nightlinger (a role carried over from the 1972 John Wayne film of the same name, with Roscoe Lee Brown in the role of Jebediah).

Although the Western genre was popular in multiple mediums (novels, film, radio, television), the television Western (an underappreciated and often-dismissed form) is particularly important during the civil rights era, which coincides with the period when the Western genre was at the height of its popularity in the television form. The production of film Westerns, Richard Slotkin notes, declined sharply between 1955 and 1962; at the same time, that drop-off "was more than compensated by increases in prime-time television productions" (348). Western TV series rose from 4.7 percent of prime-time programming in 1955 to 24 percent in 1959, with that number fluctuating between 18 and 20 percent over the next decade (348). The popularity of Western films and TV shows picked up again after 1962 and remained high through 1972 before waning. As African American actors more generally were being incorporated into film and television roles during this era, it should not be surprising to see that black actors were often cast in roles in the most popular television genre of the 1960s.

The rise of the civil rights and Black Power movements also caused television programs of the period to take tentative steps toward exploring racial issues through Western stories and settings. As Slotkin observes,

"The Western and its informing mythology" have "offered a language and a set of conceptual structure rich in devices for defining the differences between competing races, classes, cultures, social orders, and moral codes" (350). After World War II, "the battles fought over the complex of issues and movements associated with the term 'civil rights' would emerge over the course of the next two decades as the most crucial and divisive concern of domestic politics" (350), although, Slotkin cautions, Western movies did not necessarily provide "American leaders with their marching orders" or offer "mere allegories of contemporary politics" (350). What we see, Slotkin argues, "is a pattern of reciprocal influence in which the preoccupations of politics shape the concerns and imagery of the movies, and in which movies in turn transmit their shapely formulations of those concerns back to political discourse" (350). The mythic space of the Western "should be thought of as a field for ideological play which is attractive precisely because a wide range of beliefs and agendas can be entertained there" (351). Belonging *in* the western and belonging *to* the nation are roughly equivalent in the mythic space provided by the genre. The Westerns of the era suggest contradictory positions on the possible outcomes of the civil rights movement, sometimes telling stories that suggest the relatively easy incorporation of African Americans into the Western genre and the American nation and at other times spinning out narratives that reveal the intransigence of prejudice and difficulty of fully incorporating black Americans into either the nation or the genre. In the wake of the assassinations of Martin Luther King Jr. and Malcolm X in the 1960s, a Western such as the *Alias: Smith and Jones* episode ("The Bounty Hunter") that ends with the series regulars (Smith and Jones, aka Kid Curry and Hannibal Hayes) unable to prevent the racist murder of the African American character at the center of the episode suggests a more pessimistic view of incorporating African Americans into the Western and into the nation as citizens with equal rights and protections. These Westerns of the 1960s and early 1970s explore "the range of possible and plausible resolutions" of the contemporary political issues raised by the civil rights movement as "shaped by the rules and expectations that inform the mythic landscape of the genre" (Slotkin 350–51).

This chapter outlines a framework of four categories for considering the African American presence in television and film Westerns: (1) the stereotyped black character, a figure rooted in the minstrel stage and indicative of the continuing influence of blackface minstrelsy in twentieth-century visual narrative; (2) the raceless westerner, an African American actor cast in a role in which no mention is made of race; (3) the opposite of the raceless westerner, the race representative, or the civil rights westerner, the African American character who is used explicitly to explore issues of racial equality and racial justice; (4) the post-soul or postracial westerner, an archetypal figure who is examined in more detail in chapters 7 and 8. Since my emphasis in this chapter is mainstream visual media, my categories do not include the more nuanced portrayals found in black-audience Westerns of the silent and early sound film eras. These categories provide a framework for discussion and are not absolute or mutually exclusive. Even the narrative of the raceless westerner, which often has the contradictory aims of incorporating African American actors into the genre Western and avoiding controversial racial commentary, can be read in terms of precisely the racial issues that it seeks to erase, reinscribing blackness via several techniques: through including an obvious black visual presence in the televisual narrative, through specific cues in the performance of the African American actor, or through verbal and visual cues that suggest an allegorical subtext.

Similar to the black-audience films of an earlier period, the development of "blaxploitation" films during the 1970s—which include several Westerns (or, to use Mikel Koven's phrase, "blaxploitation-Western crossover films") influenced by the movement—also fall somewhat outside of these categories or perhaps somewhere between the civil rights Western and the post-soul Western (139).[4] Particularly notable, however, are a number of Westerns starring Fred Williamson, including a couple of films in which his involvement included directing and screenwriting as well as acting. That involvement both in front of and behind the camera suggests the importance of considering the Williamson films of the 1970s as successors to an earlier era's black-audience films, and I conclude this chapter with a discussion of the Williamson Westerns.

The careful staging of the first appearance of the guest-starring African American actor is a feature of many television Westerns. *Rawhide* stages the appearance of Strode as a surprise, so that the startled responses of the white series regulars stand in for the (presumably) startled responses of the viewers. In *The Rifleman*, when Tip Corey first rides into North Fork, the townspeople react with concern and fear; as viewers, we initially are unsure whether that response is a racist reaction to the arrival of a black man in a white town or if some other reason exists. Only after the sheriff, Mikah, goes over to confront Corey do we realize that he is well known in North Fork and that he brings with him a reputation as a deadly gun for hire. Unaware of that reputation, Mark McCain's first sight of Corey elicits a different response. The always friendly Mark offers to help Corey with his injured horse. Only when Corey offers to demonstrate his Wild West show skills does Mark look at him with open-mouthed astonishment. Taking our cue from Mark, we as viewers are encouraged to stare in amazement at the character, but it is because of his amazing six-gun showmanship rather than his race.

In "The Most Amazing Man" (first aired on 26 November 1962), Davis plays Wade Randall, "the most amazing man I ever met" (as Mark McCain writes in an essay for a school assignment). Before we even see Randall, we are introduced to him through Mark's laudatory words, read aloud by Lucas. Randall's first appearance is carefully staged: Davis bounces cheerfully down the hotel stairs toward the lobby, pausing midway to pull his gun from the holster and give it a couple of spins before reholstering it. He comes down the rest of the flight of stairs and walks to the hotel counter, where he pulls a thin cigar from his pocket, spins it, tips his hat toward Mark and Lucas, and lights the cigar. Dressed in a fringed leather jacket, wearing a pair of white gloves, and with holsters and a belt covered in decorative metalwork, Randall is indeed an amazing sight, and while he stands out in North Fork as much for his dark skin as his stylish clothing, no one in North Fork comments on or even seems to notice his race. However, with Davis's emphasis on flashy and flamboyant individual style, he plays Randall as a cowboy with a difference, a Hoo-Doo cowboy who performs his difference from those around him even as the narrative overtly presents him as a raceless westerner.

In one of the early scenes in the episode, we see Randall sitting on an upturned barrel in front of the hotel, speaking to a crowd of North Fork's citizens. His is the only nonwhite face that we see. The crowd stares at Randall, his storytelling skills holding them enraptured, as he describes how he captured the entire Bolton gang single-handedly and brought them to justice by hitching them all "to a wagon like a team of horses" and making them pull him and themselves to the marshal twenty miles away. Although the self-described fastest gun in the West, Randall's particular talent is actually storytelling—his outrageously unlikely story of the capture of the Bolton gang connecting him to both African American and western tall-tale traditions. To punctuate the climactic event of his next story, his supposed killing of Red Morgan, Davis stands, pulls his gun, and spins it before pointing it as if to shoot. In an actual gunfight, the second or so the gun spends spinning would no doubt give any opponent a considerable advantage. Davis's repertoire of spinning moves, however, is part of his individual expressive style—an emphasis on style that suggests an African American identity that is cultural and performative rather than determined primarily by the phenotypes of race.

Randall arrives in North Fork with a reputation as gunfighter, which (as Lucas McCain suspects) is unearned and untrue, a product more of Randall's own mythmaking than actual fighting. Lovett, a friend of Morgan's, calls Randall out as a "liar and a murdering coward." Faced with the possibility of dying in the street in an actual gunfight, Randall's carefully constructed persona begins to fall apart. The episode originally aired several months after the release of *The Man Who Shot Liberty Valance* and borrows its plot from the film. In Ford's movie, eastern lawyer Ransom Stoddard (Jimmy Stewart) is the new arrival in the frontier town of Shinbone who hopes to replace the law of the gun with a civilized legal system. Bullied, beaten, and threatened by the outlaw, Liberty Valance (Lee Marvin), Stoddard discovers that the West still needs men like John Wayne's Tom Doniphon, a rough and uneducated rancher who prefers guns and fists to laws and statutes. In the film's climactic scene, Stoddard, finally angered to violence by Valance's murderous ways, meets him in the street for a showdown. To everyone's surprise, Valance ends up dead in the street. Credited with the killing of Valance, Stoddard is elected to office and thus begins a long and successful political career. Narrated by the older Stoddard, the episode unfolds to reveal the truth of what happened: the hidden Doniphon fired the shot that killed Valance, saving Stoddard's life and making him into a hero.

As Doniphon's companion, Pompey, Woody Strode plays a small but important role in the film. In some ways, *The Rifleman* episode revises Ford's film by taking the African American actor out of the sidekick role and into a part equivalent to Jimmy Stewart's Ranse Stoddard. Wade Randall's big talk draws fire. Rather than admit that he is living a lie, Randall goes out to face Lovett, preferring death in a gunfight to the ignominy of being revealed as a fake. As in *Liberty Valance*, Randall's reputation and life are saved by a hidden rifleman—in this case, Lucas McCain. "This is the West, Sir," newspaperman Dutton Peabody famously states after hearing Stoddard's story revealing the truth about the man who shot Liberty Valance. "When the legend becomes fact, print the legend." Lucas reveals a similar philosophy, devising a strategy that will protect both Randall's life and his self-constructed "legend." Before the two men can draw their guns, Randall stops the fight to proclaim, "My prowess with a gun is legendary. Mind if I demonstrate?" What follows is a display of trick shooting skills (with Randall shooting blanks and the hidden Lucas with his rifle doing the actual shooting) that frightens Lovett so completely that he abandons the gunfight and rides out of town. "Wade Randall," Randall comments, addressing himself to the watching crowd, "probably the most amazing marksman the West has ever known."[5]

The story of "The Most Amazing Man" could have been told with an actor of any race in the role of Wade Randall. Although the episode does not verbally raise the issue of race at any point in the narrative, the obvious visual presence of Davis, even if the citizens of North Fork do not notice or respond to it, still signifies race for the television viewer even as the actor plays the role of the raceless westerner. A visual black presence may alter our interpretation of a verbal text that seeks to erase (or neutralize) that presence and may suggest possible subtextual readings of the narrative.

After he is called out by Lovett, Randall reveals the truth about his identity to Lucas: "My name: It's Orly Fudd. I work for the railroad, but as a cook. They call me Cookie. Every time I heard that name, it pained me something terrible. They don't let cooks wear guns, Mr. McCain, but I bought me one." The idea that cooks are not allowed to have guns seems absurd, but that absurdity points to the transparency of the racial allegory, through which the episode addresses the contemporary issues that it cannot address directly. As an epithet, *Cookie* lacks the sting ("it pained me something terrible") that the racial slur it replaces surely would. That Randall is relegated to the role of cook also suggests an intertextual connection to the history of African Americans in Western films, where the dominant role has been that of the ranch or camp cook. Like Wade Randall himself, Davis steps outside the traditional African American role of servant to play an important part in the episode, the guest star whose character's story is at the center of the episode. Randall tells McCain that he "can't go back to being called Cookie." If we interpret the episode as a racial allegory, this is another story of erasure and double-consciousness. Randall would rather die than to return to that hated identity—to being defined by others, to having to see himself through the eyes of those others. Rather than accept an identity forced on him and associated with a "painful" name, Randall reconstructs himself as "the most amazing marksman the West has ever known." No longer Cookie, having erased that element of his identity, Randall nonetheless finds a way to assert his difference from those around him—that is, through displays of skill and style that figure his difference as positive traits rather than in terms of a hated word that also names his inferior status.

In his first appearance on *The Rifleman*, in the "Two Ounces of Tin" episode (19 February 1962), Davis again plays a raceless westerner. However, as with "The Most Amazing Man," the issue of race is raised subtextually and obliquely. Corey has vowed to kill the sheriff of North Fork, whomever that might be, as revenge against the actions of a former sheriff of the town. Racial injustice in the past is a key plot point, although the racial element is not underscored. The former sheriff refused to intervene to stop a group of drunk white men from assaulting an Indian woman. When Corey's father tried to stop them, he was killed by the gang. The sheriff neither prevented these deaths nor brought the killers to justice. "Two Ounces of Tin" could just as easily have been cast with a white actor playing Corey, but the decision to cast Davis in this part suggests a subtext that otherwise would not have been visible: Tip's vigilantism, his vow to see the badge of the sheriff of North Fork tossed in the dirt, is a response to a past injustice that is racial in nature. That we see him early in the episode visiting his father's unmarked grave—the grave of a heroic individual who, for the sake of justice, fought four "drunken trail hands" to protect an innocent woman from being sexually abused—further reinforces the subtextual idea that Corey's actions in the present have been very much shaped and directed by the racial injustices of the past.

Although the raceless westerner continues to be a strategy used to incorporate African Americans into the genre Western throughout the remainder of the twentieth century (and beyond), these episodes of *The Rifleman* stand out both in their suggestions of racial allegory in a scenario where race seemingly does not matter and in the willingness in both episodes to construct the African American cowboy as a complex individual character and, in the case of "Two Ounces of Tin," as a sympathetic villain. That complexity of character goes against the grain of the more usual portrayal of the raceless westerner. In his critique of the popular CBS miniseries *Lonesome Dove* (1989), Steve Fore observes that the series, despite its much praised "gritty realism" and supposedly revisionist take on the genre, continued to carry the same "ideological baggage" as other Westerns, especially in its portrayal of women and of minority characters, particularly the villainous "half-breed" Blue Duck and the representative minority good guy Deets, a black cowhand and scout played by Danny Glover (58). In contrast to Blue Duck, who is "portrayed as evil incarnate," Deets is his veritable opposite, "and here lies the 'problem' with

Deets—there's no 'there' there, no personality to speak of except for his unfailing kindness, sunny disposition, generosity, and competence" (59). "In a narrative environment," Fore continues, "full of prickly, rounded, strikingly individualized characters, Deets is distinctive only in his utter blandness" (59). He, of course, dies heroically—the stereotypical fate for the single African American character in Westerns.[6]

One of the problems with the *Lonesome Dove* miniseries is that it perpetuates the stereotype of the solitary black westerner and in so doing increases the weight of the burden of representation on the sole African American character, whose blandness results from the desire to create an African American westerner who is inoffensive. The raceless westerner strategy also seems to result from the same problem—a desire to include African Americans in the Western's ongoing narrative of national belonging, a controversial move that the Western's creators want to make without generating controversy or causing offense. In *The Professionals* (1966), Strode is cast as Jake Sharp, one of the four "professionals" hired by millionaire Joe Grant to retrieve his "kidnapped" wife (Maria, played by Claudia Cardinale) from Mexican bandit (or nationalist patriot, depending on your point of view) Jesus Raza (Jack Palance). The only moment that suggests anything unusual about having Jake in the group is when Grant asks Lee Marvin's Rico, "Any objections to working with a Negro?" Rico does not respond directly to the question, save for an irritated glance to the side (almost an eye roll) before answering, "What's the job?" From that point on, the group makes use of Jake's tracking skills and his expertise with a bow and arrow, particularly effective for killing more quietly than with a gun, and extremely useful, we discover, as a delivery system for sticks of dynamite.[7] In this case, the raceless westerner is a "raceless" westerner, his racial identity briefly observed and subsequently ignored.

Jake survives the movie, but otherwise his character is comparable to Glover's Deeks, mostly devoid of personality, seen rather than heard, extremely good at what he does, but not really characterized any further. The other "professionals"—Rico, Bill (Burt Lancaster), and Hans (Robert Ryan)—periodically disagree, argue, and have conflict with one another. Jake is mild-mannered to the point of obsequiousness, speaking politely on the rare occasions when he speaks at all. The raceless westerner can very easily become the emotionless westerner or the personality-less westerner.

The raceless westerner character type, or the African American westerner whose race is unremarkable, continues to appear beyond the 1960s, and these later versions of the raceless westerner are perhaps best exemplified by Morgan Freeman's role as Ned Logan in *Unforgiven* (1992; directed by and starring Clint Eastwood). Former guns for hire, the aging Logan and Will Munny (Eastwood) saddle up one more time to kill (for a bounty) two men who have cut up the face of a prostitute, Delilah (Anna Thomson). The money is raised by Delilah's fellow sex workers, since the town's sheriff, Little Bill Daggett (Gene Hackman), has done nothing to bring the men to justice (although he has offered to make sure that the woman's pimp gets compensation for the loss of her services). Although there is no reference to Ned Logan's race, no recognition within the diegesis that he is African American, he is not a colorless character. He is (or at least has been) a killer. He argues back and forth with the Schofield Kid (Jaimz Woolvett) throughout, and, in contrast to Munny, who abstains from receiving "advance payment" (in the form of sexual activity), both Ned and the Kid take advantage of the services offered by their employers.

Although Ned seems to have transcended the limitations American society placed on race in the late nineteenth century, the final actions of Little Bill seem intended to forcibly return race to the narrative and to force on Ned a racialized identity from which he has otherwise been freed. After Ned discovers that he has indeed aged and no longer has a taste for killing (he misses his target and shoots the man's horse but is unable to finish the job and shoot the downed man), he breaks up his partnership with the other two men and turns to go home. He is then captured by Little Bill, who tortures him to get information on Munny. Little Bill's method of torture—stringing up Ned, stripping him of his shirt, and repeatedly striking his back with a leather whip—seems designed not only to cause him pain but also to remind him of his place, which is as a slave to be whipped and not a free-ranging cowboy. The scene of torture also seems to comment on the character's genre placement—taking the African American Ned out of the Western and into the slave narrative (and the whipping scene that is a central convention of the genre), where he "belongs." Little Bill is the character who is most concerned in general with the representation of the West. His amusement with Beauchamp's novel painting English Bob (Richard Harris) as the "Duke of Death" (or as Bill amusingly mangles the name, the Duck of Death) provides another example of Bill correcting a Western text by also beating and humiliating the so-called hero of that text. The implications of Ned's whipping similarly suggest an intervention in a Western text—the film itself—that has dared to contradict Bill's vision of the way the West is and should be.

There are no African American cowboys in that vision of the Western text, and he corrects the text by whipping Ned as if he were a slave. After Ned's death, he displays the body like that of a lynching victim at the front of the saloon with a sign reading, "This is what happens to assassins around here," a message that similarly suggests (replace *assassins* with another noun) lynching.

Unforgiven returns race silently to the raceless westerner narrative in a particularly vivid and violent way, through the spectacle of whipping, through the visual display of the body that suggests the staging of a victim of a lynching. In a film that is already an extended commentary on the Western genre, Ned's story also seems to offer a metacommentary on the role of the black cowboy in Western films. In the end, Ned cannot escape from his predetermined role in the American narrative of race, a victim of violence who is tortured and lynched. Like many other solitary black westerners, he ends up dead. And by quietly suggesting Ned's fate as a commentary on racial injustice, *Unforgiven* transforms the story of a raceless westerner into a civil rights Western.

"The men of the United States Cavalry were more than soldiers," comments actor Dick Powell, the narrator of the western anthology series *Zane Grey Theater*, as part of his introduction to the episode "The Mission" (12 November 1959). Looking directly into the camera, he continues, "But these were not gods, but men, all kinds of men." After the camera cuts to a close-up of his face, he repeats those last four words with peculiar emphasis: "All . . . kinds . . . of . . . men." As we cut away from Powell to a long shot of eight African American men on horseback who ride toward and past the camera, we realize the importance of his emphasis. He is preparing us for the unexpected sight of these black men in the unexpected place of the television Western. Powell's emphasis also directs our interpretation of this sight and of the story that follows—that these are indeed men, deserving of respect and honor. Of all the members of the U.S. Cavalry, Powell continues, "One of the most respected units was the Tenth Cavalry, a group composed of all Negro soldiers. They even had their own standard to ride under. They called themselves the Buffalo Soldiers." With a motto of "Ready and Forward," Powell tells us, they were responsible for the "capture of Geronimo." Powell's introduction of the episode carefully frames the story so that we will see the actions of those eight men as representative, as part of a history of African American contribution to western expansion and to American nation building in general.

Central to that narrative of integration is casting the African American westerner in the role of the American hero as Indian fighter, falling back on the frontier narrative's fundamental white/Indian opposition, with the black cowboy proving that he belongs on the white side of that opposition by acting violently against American Indians (Slotkin 15). "Ain't but one way to bring in a Comanche," comments Davis's Corporal Smith, "and that ain't on a horse—it's across one." As Slotkin observes, in the "classic cavalry film Whites merge their differences to present a solid front to the enemy, and in later 'civil rights' variations [like *Sergeant Rutledge*] Blacks are integrated into the regimental society that opposes the demonized" Native Americans (377–78). In American mythology, Slotkin writes, the Indian war "provides a symbolic surrogate for a range of domestic social and political conflicts," and the role of African American cavalrymen in the Western (television and film) presents a "possible and plausible" solution to civil rights era social and political conflicts, suggesting the validity of African American demands for civil rights by demonstrating (in the field of myth) black belonging to the nation through shared violent action against a common enemy (13).[8]

"The Mission" seems to be the first African American–centered television Western. Other television Westerns certainly had included African American actors in minor roles, but "The Mission," starring Sammy Davis Jr., is remarkable in focusing entirely on African American troops. Powell is the only white character in the episode, and the only white actors are playing Native American characters.[9] Once Powell steps aside, we are completely within a story of the African American West. The plot involves a Comanche chief, Alou, who is being transported in secret to sign a treaty with the United States. Davis is Corporal Harper Smith, who must take over the unit when his sergeant (played by James Edwards) is killed in an attack by Apaches who are trying to prevent Alou from signing the treaty. The soldiers are ambushed and trapped, and they must decide whether to give up the chief and save their own lives or to die trying to complete their mission. As one of the Apaches tells Corporal Smith, "You are fools to die for a land that does not want you."

The episode directly addresses issues of racial justice, at least on the part of African Americans, and the Tenth Cavalry is presented as an important contributor to western and to American history as the episode celebrates the heroism of the black soldier. Even in "a land that does not want" them, the soldiers act heroically on behalf of the same people who treat them unjustly. Trapped and outnumbered, Smith agrees to the

Apache demands. He, however, trades clothing with Alou, and as he rides out alone and in disguise toward the Apache—and toward certain death when his ruse is discovered—his men escape with Alou and save both themselves and the treaty. "Men not brothers for what they are here," Alou tells Smith, touching his own face to indicate that "here" is skin color, "but what they feel here," placing his hand to his heart. Outsmarting the enemy, putting country before self, Smith demonstrates what is in his heart, and he is presented as an American hero, his self-sacrifice representative of African American contribution and belonging to the nation. The first televised African American Western is very much a civil rights Western.

Given the genre's long-standing interest in isolated forts and military outposts, and given the visual appeal of cavalry troops charging across the western plains or desert, it is not surprising to see the series Western turn to the Tenth Cavalry as a means of integrating African Americans into the western narrative and mise-en-scène. Following Davis in "The Mission," and probably more to the point, following his own cinematic portrayal of a buffalo soldier (in this case, with the Ninth Cavalry) in *Sergeant Rutledge*, Strode's guest-starring role in *Rawhide* puts him back in uniform, this time as Corporal Gabe Washington.[10] The episode's reference to Washington being demoted from sergeant is perhaps an intertexual nod to Strode's turn in the title role of *Sergeant Rutledge* and is not the episode's only evocation of that film.

In the opening scene of "The Incident of the Buffalo Soldier," Strode's Washington is friendly, forthright, and talkative. He crouches down at the fire to pour himself a cup of coffee while he chats with the still-standing Yates and Quince (who keeps his gun drawn throughout the scene). Washington removes a bullet from its shell with his teeth while keeping up a stream of conversation; he then pours the powder on the fire to signal his lieutenant that he has found Yates and comments, "This coffee ain't no better than army coffee, if you don't mind an opinion." As part of a general conversation about buffalo soldiers, Quince comments, "I've heard of you, but never seen you," in some ways speaking on behalf of the Western itself. And although Quince is speaking of buffalo soldiers in general, *you* could easily refer specifically to Gabe Washington, a type of a black character that the Western itself also has "never seen" or seen only too rarely: confident, opinionated, not the least bit accommodating, quick-tempered, assertive, not quite a hero but not quite a villain. Gabe is a complexly drawn character who enables Strode to show just how good he can be as an actor and performer when given a part that does not require him to be either meek and subordinate or overtly noble and self-sacrificing. Although Strode has several strong moments in *Sergeant Rutledge* (especially in the emotional scene where he is called to testify on his own behalf), the film emphasizes nobility and heroism of the African American soldier, whose stoic and controlled military bearing contributes to a stiffness in the portrayal (except in the action sequences) and a flatness in the character. Unlike Sergeant Rutledge, Strode's Gabe is not burdened with the necessity of demonstrating black heroism and nobility, and he plays Gabe with an appealing looseness and ease.

Gabe is by no means an inoffensively bland character. "Me and trouble," he comments to Yates, "we're old friends." During their exchange about buffalo soldiers, he tells Quince, "Buffalo soldiers? We can be drafted like any other idiot," to which the still nervously sensitive Quince responds, "Are you calling us idiots?" Of course, that is not what Gabe is suggesting, but he picks up on Quince's assertiveness and responds, "You want a fight, Mister, is that what you want to do?" The moment passes, but the opening scene establishes fairly quickly that Gabe is an individual who will stand up for himself, even against two white men. When Yates suggests that Gabe join the outfit as a cowboy when he musters out of the cavalry, he remains cheerfully contrary: "I wouldn't take this job if you begged." Yates responds, "You don't think much of us, do you?" Gabe replies, "I don't think much about your people at all. That plain enough for you?" Gabe Washington speaks much more plainly about post–Civil War (and perhaps contemporary civil rights) era racial relations than any other Woody Strode Western character does. The episode directly addresses some of key thematic concerns of the civil rights era about which the story of the raceless westerner is usually silent: distrust of white people, African American anger, and, as the episode eventually reveals, distrust of the American justice system.

Back at the fort, after helping Yates and Quince deliver the requisitioned cattle to the reservation Kiowa, Gabe relates the spectacle of the Kiowa's slaughter of the cattle (as if they were buffalo) in enthusiastic pantomime to an Indian man who begs at the fort. Although he treats the man disdainfully as a beggar, Gabe also steps forward to protect the man when another soldier, Corporal Lardface Jones, begins to abuse the man. Although the episode avoids the stereotype of the solitary black westerner by placing some of the action in the context of a group of African American cavalrymen, only Gabe and Lardface are developed as individual characters, and Lardface is a single-note character. He does not like Gabe (for reasons that are not explained) and serves as the antagonist who picks a fight with Gabe and ends up dead when he comes after Gabe with a knife. Although, as Yates, who observes the fight, comments, the death was clearly self-defense, Gabe does not trust Army justice and escapes (on Yates's horse) into the Black Hills.

The episode nonetheless has its silences and is particularly circumspect on the issue of slavery. Set four years after the Civil War, *Rawhide* frequently features plots that place the characters within the context of an antebellum society still affected by the war, even on the western plains seemingly untouched by the conflict. Gil Favor (played by Eric Fleming), who shares star billing with Clint Eastwood's Rowdy Yates, is a former Confederate officer, and the series in general builds on a subgenre of the Western that was popular during the middle of the century—that is, the Western centered on a southern character or characters. By the 1960s, however, Western creators were aware of the problematic elements of this subgenre and were working to find ways to continue to use its appealing elements (the figure of the former Confederate soldier, the romance of the Lost Cause) without repeating or professing its politics (particularly the subgenre's tacit support of slavery).

In "The Incident of the Slave Master," *Rawhide's* drivers are surprised when they encounter Victor Laurier (played by Peter Lorre) set up in a camp with his French chef and his African American servant, Jonah (played by Roy Glenn, who also played Corporal Lardface Jones in "The Incident of the Buffalo Soldier"), in a white dinner jacket, attending at Laurier's evening meal. As the episode unfolds, we discover that Laurier is a former Confederate officer, his mind broken by the defeat in the war, who has responded by continuing to hold captive a group of Union officers, even though the war ended four years earlier. Favor, also a former Confederate officer, pretends to be sympathetic to Laurier as a strategy for infiltrating his plantation. When Favor and one of his cowboys observe the forced labor taking place on the plantation, he comments with disgust, "Slaves all right. I'd like to go in there and tear that place apart." Although the slaves in this case are white, the disgust Favor expresses is not so much at the nature of the slaves as the nature of slavery itself— quite a transformation from Confederate officer to abolitionist angered by the idea of slavery. The "southern Western" of the civil rights era struggles to reconcile its love of the romance of the Lost Cause with the history of slavery that was part of that cause; having one of its main characters express his abhorrence of slavery is the strategy for achieving such a reconciliation.

In "The Incident of the Buffalo Soldier," *Rawhide* treads lightly around the issue of slavery, suggesting but not directly stating that slavery is the source of Gabe's anger even as the episode avoids clearly explaining even whether Gabe was enslaved before the war. Lieutenant Howard (Ray Montgomery), the white commanding officer, comments that Gabe is "hard as bitterroot most of the time," but when Yates asks if there is "any reason" for that hardness, Howard responds, "Who knows?" Yates joins with about a dozen black cavalrymen and Howard to search for the escaped Gabe. Separated from the troops, Yates goes off on his own, discovers Gabe, and tries to talk him into returning. Gabe says, "You won't get me there, I promise you. I don't like to be locked up, and I never liked to be punished, since I was a little boy." When Yates offers to testify on Gabe's behalf, he responds, "I don't trust nobody. I learned that a long time ago. . . . I didn't volunteer for the army, I got drafted. You ever been forced to do anything year in and year out that you hated? Like being ordered around." "I didn't volunteer for the army" confuses the issue. Is Gabe referring to southern enslavement when he complains about being forced to do something for years that he hated? Or to his time in the army? "Mr. Lincoln said it was going to be different," he tells Yates, "a whole new world. But it ain't that different, not the way I see it. Oh, I know most of my troubles are my own doing. I ain't no model citizen. I have as many faults as the next fellow. . . . Plus a temper when it goes off, somebody gets hurt, and sometimes me."[11]

"The Incident of the Buffalo Soldier" constitutes one of Strode's finest performances, a role that allows him to use his full intensity, to be prickly, and to play a character who is proud, bitter, and angry but nonetheless maintains a core humanity. The episode depends on Strode's ability to command the screen. His conversations with Yates are mostly one-sided, with Gabe doing most of the talking. After Gabe's escape attempt leaves Yates injured and unconscious, the episode becomes essentially a solo performance. Realizing that Yates is in danger of dying, Gabe repeats to himself, "Only one rule. Look out for yourself. Only one rule." He cannot follow that rule and returns to the injured Yates, giving up a chance at freedom to tend to him. Finally, when the men searching for him ride past and miss the signs that should point them to the injured Yates, Gabe reveals himself, sacrificing his own life to lead the troops to Yates.[12]

Both *Rawhide* and *The Rifleman* include complex portrayals of African American westerners but cautiously approach potentially controversial topics such as slavery, racial justice, and prejudice.[13] Later in the 1960s and into the early 1970s, Western series such as *Gunsmoke* on CBS ("The

Good Samaritans," 10 March 1969; "Jesse," 19 February 1973, featuring Brock Peters in the title role), NBC's *Bonanza* ("The Desperado," 7 February 1971, featuring Louis Gossett Jr.), and ABC's *Alias: Smith and Jones* ("The Bounty Hunter" in 1971, also guest starring Louis Gossett Jr.) make explicit the issue of racial injustice that remains a subtext in the Westerns from the early 1960s. All three of the episodes from the 1970s involve African American characters responding to or experiencing racially motivated violence. These television episodes respond to the American civil rights movement by relocating contemporary questions of justice and equality to Old West settings. To a large extent, *The Rifleman* and *Rawhide* episodes do so as well, but having appeared a decade earlier, they do so more cautiously.

The Tenth Cavalry makes another television appearance in "The Buffalo Soldiers" (22 November 1968), an episode of *The High Chaparral*, a series that focuses on the Cannon family and their ranch near Tucson, in the Arizona Territory of the 1870s. Guest starring Yaphet Kotto as Sergeant Major Creason and Robert Doqui as canny scout Corporal Larabee, "The Buffalo Soldiers" includes a large cast of African American actors as members of the Tenth Cavalry, and most of *The High Chaparral* regulars take on supporting roles for an episode that focuses on the guest stars. In the opening scene, Buck Cannon (Cameron Mitchell) takes on the audience surrogate role of astonished witness to the sudden appearance of African Americans in the West. Outnumbered at a watering hole by Apaches, the Cannons are saved when the Tenth Cavalry appears. As Sergeant Major Creason rides up to be introduced by the white Lieutenant Beckert (Charles Gray), Buck comments in awe, "I'll be danged! Them's buffalo soldiers!" Throughout the rest of the scene, he expresses his continued astonishment by repeating the phrase "Buffalo soldiers!" quietly to himself and shaking his head in amazement. By the end of the episode, his astonishment turns to friendship and sincere appreciation for the military skills the soldiers display in bringing law and order back to Tucson.

In the episode, strongman Pearsall has taken over Tucson, demanding protection money from business owners and subjecting anyone who fails to pay to tarring and feathering, an act taking place on the main street that is interrupted by the arrival of the Tenth Cavalry, the subsequent institution of martial law, and the requirement that all citizens relinquish their weapons. As the soldiers set up a system to collect the weapons, one of Pearsall's men objects: "The day I hand over my guns to a nig—." But he is interrupted by the sergeant major: "You'll do it. Right now." In contrast to the citizens of North Fork in *The Rifleman*, the white townspeople of Tucson are keenly aware of race. When Lieutenant Beckert is called back to the fort and leaves Creason in charge, the racial resentment in the town becomes even more pronounced. Pearsall swears that he and his men will "knock those tar babies back to the cotton patch," and he hires a group of gunmen and mercenaries to do so. Pearsall assumes that the cavalrymen are poor soldiers and that the army sent them to Tucson as an added insult to the town's citizens. However, the events of the episode demonstrate that the buffalo soldiers have been sent to Tucson because (in Creason's words) they are "the fightingest, shootingest outfit in the U.S. Army." With a display of precision horsemanship (as part of a spectacularly staged battle scene), the Tenth Cavalry splits, encircles, and essentially herds the outlaws like cattle back to the Tucson main street, where they are shut in, surrounded, and forced to disarm. The episode closes with a voice-over narration that hammers home the civil rights message of the story: "We must remember the historic and continuing contribution of the black American to our nation."[14] Although the opening sequence has the cavalry rescuing the Cannons from Apaches, the episode differs from other buffalo soldier Westerns by demonstrating the black Americans' "continuing contribution" to the nation by opposing them to a group of white outlaws.

If Sammy Davis Jr. and Woody Strode are the two African American performers who made the largest mark in Western roles in the 1960s, the 1970s arguably belonged to Fred "The Hammer" Williamson. Like Strode, Williamson was a former professional football player. He was featured in numerous blaxploitation films of the era as an action hero. His first Western role was the title character in the film *The Legend of Nigger Charlie* (1972), in which he leads a group of escaped slaves on a journey out West, a role he reprised in *The Soul of Nigger Charlie* (1973). Williamson also costarred with another former football player, Jim Brown, in *Take a Hard Ride* (1975). Although *Take a Hard Ride* is an entertaining Western and deserving of more critical attention, the most significant Westerns involving Williamson were *Boss Nigger* (1975) and *Adios Amigo* (1976). In varying roles as screenwriter, director, producer, and actor, Williamson exercised an unprecedented level of control over the cinematic representation of the African American West in making these two movies. The two films also revise the archetypes of the raceless westerner and the civil rights westerner, with *Boss Nigger* a high-octane version of the civil rights Western and *Adios Amigo* pushing the raceless westerner toward the category of the post-soul Western, moving beyond using the Western form as a vehicle for social protest without losing its connections to African American culture and history.

In *Boss Nigger*, Williamson plays a man known only as Boss. Boss and his partner/sidekick Amos (D'Urville Martin, who plays a similar role in the *Nigger Charlie* films) are bounty hunters in search of an outlaw, Jed Clayton. They wind up taking over as sheriff and deputy of a small town as part of their strategy for getting to Clayton. As Amos drolly comments to the town's white mayor, perplexed by the presence of African American bounty hunters in his town, "You all been hunting black folks for so long, we just wanted to see what it would be like to hunt white folks." The film begins with a conventional scene that inverts the Western's usual racial designations. Boss and Amos come across a group of white outlaws (rather than Native Americans) attacking a wagon carrying African American settlers. As the genre requires, they kill the outlaws and save the girl, Clara Mae (Carmen Hayworth), the daughter of the African American settler killed by the outlaws. From information provided by the outlaws, they discover that Clayton has taken over the nearby town ("protecting" it) because it lacks a sheriff. They drop Clara Mae off at a nearby village (or, rather, with the town's segregated Mexican American population) and ride on into town.

Their entry into the town comments on the surprising appearance convention of the black Western by exaggerating it to the extreme. The town folks gape with unconcealed astonishment and loathing. "I reckon people in this town ain't ever seen blacks before," comments Boss. One of the townspeople confirms this observation: "I've heard about these black devils before, but I ain't ever seen one," seemingly repeating Quince's comment about buffalo soldiers in *Rawhide* but making explicit the racism that is absent (or unstated) in that comment. In contrast to the television Westerns, in which the series regulars are accepting of and friendly to the African American strangers, Boss and Amos are greeted solely with opprobrium. "What are you niggers doing here?" the mayor asks, "and what do you want?" This civil rights Western comments explicitly throughout on white prejudice, and the racism that Boss and Amos encounter is one of the obstacles they must overcome to get their man.

Written by Williamson, *Boss Nigger* goes further than most African American Westerns in bringing together the trickster tale and the Western genre. African American animal tales as well as "Jack" tales (stories involving a slave named Jack, John, or Pompey who consistently outwits

Ol' Master) often "depict the triumph of physical weakness, hypocrisy, mischievousness, trickery, and cunning over brute strength and guileless-ness" (M. Watkins 72). As Mel Watkins writes, tales with Rabbit at the center celebrate "this weak but crafty animal's ability to consistently out-wit stronger, more powerful foes" (73). Boss and Amos enter a situation in which they are outnumbered by antagonistic foes, but they use wit and guile (backed up, in this case, by skillful gunplay, a Western addition to the African American trickster tale) to manipulate the mayor into hiring them as sheriff and deputy and ultimately to get their man. Williamson also plays the obsequious black when it serves his purpose to do so. When he enters the town's saloon, a man yells, "Hey, nigger, come here and shine my boots." Boss grins and shuffles his way over to the man's table—and shoots him in the foot. "Empty of pocket and on his wits as usual" (to bor-row W. C. Handy's phrase) is also a fair description of Amos, the smaller of the two bounty hunters and the one who talks his way out of trouble (and into money) more often than he uses his fists or guns. Wearing a sharp (if a bit dusty) double-breasted suit and matching hat, Amos is a black cowboy with a stylish difference. Playing on the notion of blue laws that dictate fines for unsocial behavior, Amos introduces a list of "black law" decrees: One imposes a fine for "calling someone nigger." In this par-ticular town, this is a moneymaking statute, and while Boss is tracking down the fugitive, Amos goes about relieving the townspeople of their money through fines for impolite action and language.

As a story of bounty hunters, *Boss Nigger* is one of several movie and television Westerns that cast the African American cowboy in that role. For example, an episode of the television series *Alias: Smith and Jones* fea-tures guest star Louis Gossett Jr. in the title role as "The Bounty Hunter." He captures Smith and Jones, recognizing them in fact as outlaws Kid Curry and Hannibal Hayes, and he comments to them (he is a talkative bounty hunter) on the appropriateness of that particular genre role for the African American westerner: "I'm a bounty hunter. A professional. Ain't much a black man can do these days. . . . Nobody will pay a black man more than room and board. And that's if you can get work." Even as a bounty hunter, Joe Sims finds barriers to success in this civil rights West-ern. Rather than taking Smith and Jones to the closest town, he has to go elsewhere because "the sheriff in Hartsville don't seem to like black folks too much. I don't figure he'd be too cooperating about that reward." When asked why he thinks the other town will be any different, he responds, "I don't. Just hoping, that's all." Groups of white men along the way refuse to acknowledge his authority, and as Kid Curry tells him, "You're in the wrong place, Joe. You're going to keep running into people that don't approve of you." In one instance, Joe is nearly lynched. Finally, he is stopped by a group of white men who take Curry and Hayes from him and tell him, "*You* don't go around arresting white people. . . . It's not your place." Appearing in the unexpected place of the Western, Joe continually encounters other characters who try to return him to the appropriate role in the American narrative of race—the object of white violence, not as the agent of law. *Boss Nigger* revises the civil rights Western by making its version of the American West into the place where the African American bounty hunter can repeatedly arrest white people. *Boss*'s bounty hunters also enact without restriction the genre's preferred mode of six-gun justice, killing the white outlaws when the action requires it.

Boss Nigger claims its place in a continuing tradition of black Westerns by revising conventional elements of those Westerns and by self-consciously commenting on specific Westerns within the tradition. In particular, Williamson quotes from and alludes to Woody Strode's earlier Western roles. Strode's character in *The Professional* is just that, a professional for hire; like the bounty hunter, he works outside the law but for the sake of justice. But Strode's brief appearance in Sergio Leone's *Once upon a Time in the West* is most significant for *Boss Nigger* and for later African American Westerns.

What Leone realizes that other western directors miss is Strode's potential as an icon of black Western masculine cool and discovers a visual strategy for depicting that iconic coolness. Appearing in the opening title sequence, Strode is one of three outlaws sent by Frank to meet (and kill) Charles Bronson's Harmonica. Strode is the first of the outlaws that we see on-screen as he steps into the railway station's ticket office. In one continuous shot that begins with a close-up of his boot pushing a door shut, the camera slowly pans up his body, taking thirteen seconds or so of screen time to move from the heel of his boot to the top of his black cowboy hat. The camera pauses briefly as it comes to his hand, his dark skin the first indication of his racial identity, zooms in slightly to travel the full length of his holstered gun, and then on up along his hips, waist, and chest before stopping at a close-up of his face as he stares intently and stoically at the station agent. Strode's initial appearance in *Once upon a Time in the West* imbues him with all the mythic grandeur of the Western hero—as if he is too large to fit on the screen and can only be revealed piece by piece.[15] Leone takes advantage of Strode's tall athletic build not by putting him into action—as Ford did, for example—but by slowing him down. In another shot, the camera essentially stops and stares at Strode as he stands motionless, framed in a doorway, fanning himself—using exaggeratedly slow movements—with his hat. Waiting on the arrival of the train, Strode stations himself beneath the "Cattle Corner" water tower, not even moving in response to dripping water. In contrast to the twitchy Jake Elam (annoyed by telegraph machines and buzzing flies), Strode is statuesque—and larger than life in Leone's close-ups—in his calm motionlessness, responding to the dripping water only by putting his hat on and remaining in place until enough water has collected on the brim for him to enjoy a drink before the train arrives and the action starts. Strode standing, legs apart, at the ready, beneath the tower as water drips seemingly unnoticed on his hat is one of the great images in Western film and is one of the two scenes from *Once upon a Time in the West* that Van Peebles's *Posse* includes in its closing montage of clips, part of that film's homage to Leone, the Italian Western in general, and Strode in particular.

Of particular importance to the tradition of the black Western is Strode's unusual weapon, a Winchester rifle with a shortened barrel and stock (a mare's leg pistol) that he wears holstered to his leg like a revolver. The modified Winchester is physically larger than the usual cowboy six-gun and packs a rifle's rather than a revolver's power. A bigger-than-life Western hero needs a similarly sized "pistol." Strode's connection to this particular type of weapon, which we later see him quietly loading and cocking and ultimately firing during the shootout with Harmonica, and the influence of his appearance in *Once upon a Time in the West* on later representations of the African American westerner, are made clear by repeated examples of black Western characters who are costumed with either a mare's leg pistol or a similar weapon, such as a shotgun with a similarly shortened barrel and stock modified for use as a handheld weapon. *Boss Nigger* references *Once upon a Time in the West* by having Boss carry the same weapon—a modified rifle that he wears in a holster on his thigh. And as with Strode, this large "pistol" seems fit to size for the large frame of the tall, athletic Williamson. *Boss Nigger* is the first of several Westerns to pay homage to Strode by adopting his *Once upon a Time in the West* pistol.

If *Boss Nigger* revises the civil rights Western, Williamson's next film, *Adios Amigo* (costarring Richard Pryor), which Williamson wrote, produced, and directed in addition to starring in, rewrites the story of the raceless westerner, freeing its African American characters from the burden of social protest to explore a different kind of Western story that draws even more heavily than *Boss Nigger* on African American cultural traditions by focusing on the trickster character and turning him loose in a Western setting.[16] The film does not abandon the issues that are central to the civil rights Western but rather shifts those issues to the edges of the story. Prejudice certainly exists, and the white characters in the film are aware of race. The plot starts when a wealthy white landowner hires a group of men to "clear that black off that piece of land and earn a hundred dollars." In keeping with the scenario of the civil rights Western, "that black"—Williamson's Big Ben—fights back against this injustice but is arrested for doing so. However, Ben's arrest is primarily an excuse for him to meet Richard Pryor's trickster character, Sam Spade (a name that offers another example of the film's satirical approach to racial issues), who robs the stagecoach that is transporting Ben to prison and thus frees him. Ben almost immediately returns the favor, saving Sam from banditos.

At this point, *Adios Amigo* becomes an extended trickster tale, with every good deed Big Ben does turned against him by the wily con man, Sam. Although Ben begins the film being set up as the avenging Western hero, robbed of his lands and falsely imprisoned, he primarily plays the role of dupe to Pryor's Sam, the larger, stronger Bear to Pryor's weaker, smaller (but smarter) Rabbit. When Sam comes upon a boxer and his promoter setting up fights with local challengers (and taking bets), he jumps right into gambling action and then arranges a challenge. "I was talking about my amigo," he tells the promoter, who mistakenly thinks Sam plans to fight; "he'll be along any minute." When the unsuspecting Ben arrives, he finds himself thrust into the ring and into a fight with a highly skilled and powerful boxer.

Throughout the rest of the film, Sam commits robbery, cheats at cards, sets up con games, enters Ben in contests without his knowledge, and leaves Ben holding the bag and taking the blame, the punch, the knife, or the bullet that belongs to Sam. Each time Sam slips out the door to leave Ben in trouble, he delivers his signature exit line, "Adiós, Amigo." When both Sam and Ben are arrested and sentenced to hard labor, Sam plays the obsequious black ("When I was on the plantation, I used to keep the master's place spotless") and ends up inside cleaning while Ben has to bust rocks outside in the heat. When trouble arises (or when Sam causes trouble), Sam comments, "That was the big fella out there. He's the troublemaker," and goes about his business. He robs the camp's safe and hides the money, and although he is caught, he makes a deal with his captors: "I'll go get the money, and if I don't come back, you can kill my amigo." This deal does not offer as much assurance to Ben as it does to the captors.

Appearing a few years after the miniseries *Lonesome Dove* aired, *The Adventures of Briscoe County, Jr.* (Fox, 1993) incorporates some of the developments exemplified by the Williamson films into the television Western. In creating the character of Lord Bowler (Julius Carry), another tall and athletic African American bounty hunter reminiscent of Williamson's Boss, *Briscoe County, Jr.* may even be alluding directly to *Boss Nigger*. In casting Carry as Lord Bowler, the series at least continues a practice of depicting the bounty hunter as a specifically African American Western character type. In general, *Briscoe County, Jr.* takes a different approach than most prior television Westerns, depicting an American West that revises the genre's usual marginalization of nonwhites in general and African Americans in particular. Rather than have a single character represent all of the black West, *Briscoe* includes African American actors in frequent and wide-ranging roles, major and minor, from heroes to victims to villains. In the two-part episode "High Treason" (13 and 20 May 1994), in addition to Lord Bowler (on trial for treason with cowboy-hero and fellow bounty hunter Briscoe County, Jr., played by Bruce Campbell), the sergeant at arms at the trial is played by African American actor Michael Jace; comic outlaw Pete Hutter's cellmate, Tiny, is played by the (not very tiny) African American actor (and professional wrestler the Harlem Warlord) Jaime Cardriche. Two members of Captain March's clandestine posse tracking down the escaped Briscoe and Bowler are African American. In the episode "Riverboat" (1 October 1993), the victim of riverboat gambler and crime lord Brett Bones, denim manufacturer and entrepreneur Wylie Turner, is played by African American actor Montae Russell. After Bones murders Turner's brother and business partner, Turner joins forces with Briscoe and Bowler to bring Bones to justice.

And the list goes on. No other television Western has been as inclusive of African American presence as *The Adventures of Briscoe County, Jr.* The science fictional elements of the series, such as its mysterious technologically advanced orb, which, among other things, enables Briscoe County, Jr. to travel through time in several episodes, opens up the Western genre to alternative possibilities. The American West of *Briscoe County* is similar to the one we know from American history and from the history of the Western genre, but it also differs from that received past. Taking place in the generic space between science fiction and the Western, *Briscoe*'s West seems not to have been party to the same history of racial injustice that marks American history—or perhaps the series reimagines the already highly fictionalized version of American history proposed by the Western to open the genre more fully to African American presence and participation. And in so doing, *Briscoe County* blazes a path for the visual narratives discussed in chapter 8—*The Book of Eli* and *Firefly*, both of which further expand the hybrid genre of Western sci-fi to incorporate black characters in their stories.

Bowler starts out as Briscoe's sidekick but ultimately becomes a costar as the series progresses. The African American Carry brings a black visual presence to the Western and a black colloquial voice to his readings of lines. As an actor, Carry also brought to the production a scholar's knowledge of the African American West, having researched what he describes as "the *real* black West" as part of a graduate school research project on Deadwood Dick (Shapiro 28). In particular, his research on "Bass Reeves, a deputy for the famous frontier judge Judge Parker," informed his portrayal of Lord Bowler (28). According to Carry, "When I saw how the character was written in the show, I realized there was a lot of Bass Reeves in Lord Bowler" (28). Irascible, irritable, and often angry (but with a "big heart"), Bowler is anything but bland, and like Briscoe County, his character is alternately heroic and comic (28). Although Bowler never encounters prejudice and no other character ever comments on his race, he is not a raceless westerner as such. He provides a distinctively African American presence in a Western scenario without the burden of racial representation carried by the civil rights westerner.

That sense of presence also results from multiple allusions to an African American history and culture that is a part of Bowler's character but that does not exclusively define him. In "High Treason," he sings a snatch of "Swing Low, Sweet Chariot" in the jail cell where he and Briscoe are awaiting execution. In "Hard Rock" (4 February 1994), he reveals to Briscoe for the first time that he served in the U.S. Army—specifically "the Tenth Cavalry," although he does not mention the phrase *buffalo soldiers* and notes only that he served "during the war" (which war is not specified). The reference to the Tenth Cavalry suggests that Bowler shares a history with other African American westerners, but that history is not the defining element of his character as it is in *Rawhide*'s "The Incident of the Buffalo Soldier" or *The High Chaparral*'s "The Buffalo Soldiers." Although *Briscoe County* seems to take place in an alternative universe that is similar to but not exactly our own, these allusions are significant gestures that draw Lord Bowler as a character who is specifically African American.

If *Briscoe* alludes to African American western history, the series is also keenly aware of genre history. "High Treason" combines two Woody Strode films, *Sergeant Rutledge* and *The Professionals*. Like *Sergeant Rutledge*, the episode is a courtroom drama, with both Bowler and County on trial (for treason rather than murder). The design of the courtroom setting and the staging of the trial scenes suggest *Sergeant Rutledge* as well, although there are no specific moments when Bowler evokes Strode's character. (In fact, Bowler is prone to outbursts in the courtroom not at all in keeping with Rutledge's stoic military bearing.) The episode also steals its primary plot line from *The Professionals*, though it shifts Bowler from Strode's supporting role to that of equal partner in their effort to save the "kidnapped" daughter from a Mexican bandit (or nationalist patriot, take your pick). As in *The Professionals*, they realize that the daughter is there by choice and reject the mission they have been assigned, resulting in the treason charge. The series is full of such borrowing and homages, especially to television and film Westerns of the 1960s and 1970s. However, the decision to combine allusions to these two specific films, which have little in common other than Strode, into one episode seems to be a strategy for acknowledging his influence on the character of Lord Bowler.

Bowler's portrayal also suggests the influence of the Williamson films. As a black bounty hunter who favors a gun similar to a mare's leg pistol as his weapon of choice, he specifically recalls Williamson's bounty hunter character from *Boss Nigger*. Bowler carries a double-barreled shotgun with shortened barrels and a modified stock that he fires like a pistol. Buck in *Buck and the Preacher* similarly carries a modified shotgun (or a pair of shotguns) rather than a rifle. Although different weapons, both the rifle and the shotgun have the same type of alterations, a shortening of the barrel and shortening and reshaping of the shoulder stock into a hand grip so that the weapon can be fired like a pistol. Bowler prefers to wear his version of the mare's leg in a holster on his back while carrying a more conventional pistol in a holster on his leg.

Elements of the episode "Riverboat" suggest Williamson's western trickster tale, *Adios Amigo*, with Briscoe taking on the trickster role in disguise as a gambler and coordinating an elaborate con to catch bad guy Brett Bones. Bowler takes on Williamson's Big Ben role from *Adios Amigo*, the straight man/dupe to Briscoe's trickster. Specifically, Briscoe reworks Sam Spade's boxing match scam with Bowler. He telegrams Bowler to join him on urgent business. Only when Bowler arrives does he reveal his plan to have Bowler go up against Bones's expert boxer. When Bowler hears what Briscoe has planned, his response is immediate: "Adiós, Amigo." Then he turns and heads for the door. When Bowler says "Adiós, Amigo," it is as if he is not just saying good-bye but telling us that he already knows this gag because he has seen it in the film from which it comes. Perhaps this is coincidental, but the combination of the boxing scam, a line of dialogue that seems to reference the title of the film that included a boxing scam, and the fact that the episode itself is an extended trickster tale suggests that the creators of *Briscoe County* are aware of the Williamson films. Coincidental or not, the episode places Bowler in a tradition of black Western trickster stories that was extended and revised by Williamson.

The civil rights westerner remains a popular type in contemporary Westerns that include African American characters. Versions of that type can be found in two of the most popular twenty-first-century television Westerns, HBO's *Deadwood* and AMC's *Hell on Wheels. Deadwood* includes several African American characters in recurring supporting roles as part of the town's multicultural mix of frontier settlers, miners, prospectors, con artists, and businessmen and -women: Franklyn Ajaye as Samuel Fields (referred to by the other characters as the Nigger general), Cleo King as Aunt Lou Marchbanks (George Hearst's cook and housekeeper), Richard Gant as Hostetler, and Omar Gooding as Aunt Lou's son, Odell. These characters continually navigate the racist attitudes and racial beliefs of Deadwood's townspeople, whether in the form of the servile masking of Aunt Lou with her employer Hearst (a masking that is revealed when we see her very different demeanor when playing cards) or of the behavior of Hostetler and Fields when a horse escapes from Hostetler's livery and accidentally kills a child, William Bullock. Even though they were not at fault, they immediately flee town, knowing that a lack of guilt is no barrier to a lynching.

Clearly influenced by *Deadwood, Hell on Wheels* is a revisionist Western that emphasizes the blood, mud, and dirt of frontier existence. The series takes place in the aftermath of the Civil War, and the ensemble cast is part of a society trying to put itself back together in the wake of that catastrophe. Railway entrepreneur Thomas Durant (Colm Meaney) suggests that the building of a transcontinental railway will help heal the wounds of that conflict: "The nation that nearly tore itself apart by North and South will be joined together by East and West." The nation, however, seems a long way from healing, and the war in many ways seems ongoing. Cullen Bohannon (Anson Mount) is the central character, a former Confederate soldier seeking vengeance against the Union soldiers who murdered his wife. Blasting occurs frequently, the explosions suggesting a battlefield. A black powder accident in "Jamais Je Ne T'Oublierai" (27 November 2011) creates a chaotic scene of explosions, wounded men, and survivors tending to the wounded. Sabotage to a track causes a train crash ("Derailed," 1 January 2012), and the scene of the aftermath of the crash—a makeshift hospital, twisting and smoking wreckage, injured men with missing limbs—recalls the ever-present catastrophe of the war beyond which the characters seem unable to move.

Hell on Wheels is the name of the railway encampment that travels along with the leading edge of the railway. As the railway moves forward, Hell on Wheels is continually pulling up stakes and moving forward as well—by its nature, always a frontier town. The unity of action required to build the railroad occasionally suggests the possibility of unification of the nation, but more often than not, both the work site and the Hell on Wheels camp become a frontier where different and competing ethnic groups (African American freedmen, low-paid Irish railway workers, German butchers, and so forth) clash with one another rather than joining together.

Elam Ferguson (Common) is the drama's central African American character, a member of a group of freedman, including his brother Psalms (though we do not learn that they are brothers until the end of season 2). In the episode "A New Birth of Freedom" (20 November 2011), Ferguson volunteers the black workers to take over the railway building work from a group of white workers who have been drafted for a rescue party: "We can do their work and our work." At the cut, breaking rocks and cutting away dirt to make a path before laying track, Psalms complains, "How come we got to do the white man's work? Because you think you is the white man." Ferguson responds, "This ain't for them. This is for us. The white man ain't going to give us nothing." Ferguson's actions in much of season 1 are in keeping with a civil rights agenda—proving to whites the worth of black workers, acting individually for the sake of proving the worth of the group, and continually asserting his rights as a free man. "We work as hard as them," Ferguson comments; "then why don't we get the same rewards?" When Psalms realizes that the specific "reward" is a visit to the camp brothel "to spend some hard-earned money, the same as" the white workers, he warns Elam, "You go in there, you coming out on the bad end of a rope." Psalms is ultimately proven right. Ferguson leaves the brothel without spending his money after he is rejected by one of the sex workers, Eva, who is threatened by an Irish immigrant, Mr. Tool. However, Eva visits him "off the books" later in the episode, and the two develop a relationship that, when discovered, nearly gets Ferguson lynched. (Only Bohannon's timely arrival saves him.)

Serial-oriented television shows such as *Deadwood* and *Hell on Wheels*, in which individual episodes are essentially chapters in a longer story arc, are sometimes difficult to analyze until the series is completed. In season 1 of *Hell on Wheels*, Elam Ferguson is very much a civil rights westerner, burdened by the necessity of taking actions "for us," of representing the race, someone who is angered by being denied his rights as a free man and whose life is endangered by his efforts to claim those rights. By the end of season 2, Ferguson has evolved from what was in some ways a one-note character (an angry black man demanding his rights) to a more complicated one, and Elam Ferguson has emerged as the costar of the series with Cullen Bohannon. And like former Confederate soldier and slave owner Bohannon, Ferguson has emerged as an ambivalent, sometimes contradictory, individual—a hero of sorts, but a flawed one. Having been taught how to shoot a gun by Bohannon in the aftermath of the attempted lynching, Ferguson proves himself an adept gunman by the end of season 1, and railway owner Durant gives him an under-the-table position that takes advantage of his skills with a gun.

As a killer for hire, Ferguson both does Durant's dirty work and acts as a kind of vigilante for justice—killing a man who murdered a prostitute when it becomes clear that the man will not be charged or prosecuted for that crime. The position with Durant earns him money but forces him to sacrifice his romance with Eva, who wants to settle down; Ferguson, in contrast, wants to explore his newfound "freedom" as a high wage earner. His status gives him access to public spaces denied the other black workers (though he is tolerated but not welcomed) but causes a rift with Psalms and the other freedmen, leaving him isolated in the camp. He often spends his evenings alone in the Irish-owned bar, the only black customer, part of the public space but not part of the crowd. In "The Railroad Job" (12 September 2012), from season 2, Elam recognizes a visitor to town as one of the former Confederate soldiers who has been robbing trains, and he warns Durant that something is wrong. He then goes about preparing to defend the camp from the robbers. His heroism saves the camp, and the robbers end up dead, but Ferguson's reward is to be kicked out of the saloon by the white workers whom he enlisted to defend the camp. They see themselves as the heroic defenders and conveniently forget Ferguson's major role. That rejection, however, results in Ferguson's reconciliation with Psalms and his fellow freedmen.

Elam and Psalms negotiate their lives within the limitations placed on them, pressing for freedoms when they can and finding ways to make lives for themselves. Aided by Common's complex and nuanced portrayal, *Hell on Wheels* makes a serious effort to incorporate African American characters into the Western plot in a way that does not ignore social conditions that limit possibilities for black freedom in the nineteenth century but that also do not let those limitations totally define the characters.

7

Looking at the Big Picture

Percival Everett's Western Fiction

T he African American characters in Percival Everett's short stories and novels set in the contemporary American West seem to have achieved what earlier generations of black westerners have sought but seldom found—an existence not defined or limited by American narratives of race. As Madison Smartt Bell observes about Everett's first Western novel, *Walk Me to the Distance* (1985), "Its narrator is a black man in a landscape where there aren't any others . . . and because his color isn't a consuming subject for him the reader doesn't hear much about it either; in *Walk Me to the Distance*, race is not an issue" (vii–viii). In fact, the reader hears so little on the subject that the text contains no explicit references to David Larsen's race, no textual indication that he is either white or black, and the primary implicit indication is the extratextual jacket photograph of the African American Everett. David's central marker of identity is that of Vietnam veteran, one who, "though certainly affected by his tour," did not "come home emotionally or mentally scarred" but rather "returned as unremarkable as he had been when he left" (3). His parents dead, his sister an antiwar activist, David leaves his home in Georgia to head west soon after his tour of duty ends, and, by accident— he shoots a hole in his car's radiator while firing his pistol at jackrabbits along the roadside—he is stranded in Slut's Hole, Wyoming, where he remains and finds a home. The primary outsiders in the book are the tourists whom David encounters while working at a rest stop on Interstate 90: "He smiled with a confidence, a comfort, a knowledge that he belonged to this big, beautiful place and they didn't" (80). If David is a black man, then race is indeed "not an issue" in determining who does or does not belong in this landscape, who is or is not accepted by this community.

In Everett's early short fiction set in the West, his protagonists are similarly either not identified by race or identified only briefly in passing. In the story "A Good Home for *Hachita*," the only reference to protagonist Evan Keeler's race is the narrator's comment that the desire of Keeler's estranged wife "to be liberal had certainly supported a more favorable portrayal of her father" to their daughter, "lest her hatred of him be construed as racially rooted" (18). In "Esteban," we know that border agent Cole Dixson is African American only because his partner refers to him as the "black black sheep" of the family (65). Issues of racial, ethnic, cultural, and sexual difference are nonetheless addressed in these stories, but not necessarily through the experiences of the African American protagonists. Dixson is an agent of the dominant culture, his difference from white America made irrelevant in the Mexican American community by his job: "Cole glanced about the room. Mothers looked away from his uniform. He knew some of them were illegals and they knew he knew" (66). Searching the desert for Esteban, a lost boy, Cole is bitten by a rattlesnake and suffers a broken leg. Dying, Cole finds the boy but needs him to go for help. "Am I a white man?," he asks (73). When the boy shakes his head, Cole responds, "You can trust me," but the boy does not, and the story ends with Cole losing consciousness as he realizes that the boy, like the mothers at the clinic, sees only Cole's uniform, which is a more important marker of identity than the color of his body (73).

Although there may not be any black men in the Wyoming landscape of *Walk Me to the Distance*, there are Others, individuals whose difference from the norm makes them as remarkable as David is unremarkable. He settles in with Chloë Sixbury ("She's got a wooden leg. She hates for people to look at it.") and her son, Patrick, a mentally impaired adult man ("He's an idiot. Don't say nothing.") whom David soon discovers having sex with a sheep (6). In contrast to the Otherness and visible difference of these white characters, David is unremarkable. If race is not an issue in the novel, the question of difference from the norm that is often a central concern of African American literature remains, but the primary character through which Otherness is figured and explored is not the (presumably, possibly, maybe) African American protagonist. *Walk Me to the Distance* is in many ways paradigmatic of Everett's western fiction, and through his consistent use of disabled characters and metaphors of disability (physical or mental), he both explores and deflects the issue of race. The inclusion of a disabled character (or a wounded or disabled animal) signals a racial subtext that otherwise might pass as unremarkable. Race in Everett's work is placed under erasure, but in a different way than what we have previously seen. If earlier African American writers used erasure as a strategy for adapting unfriendly cultural narratives to articulate their own experiences, Everett does so intentionally to interrogate blackness and, more particularly, to trouble the textual practices used to represent African American identity in twentieth-century writing.

★

Everett is a prolific writer with "a conspicuously heterogeneous *oeuvre*" notable for an "extraordinary diversity of styles and genres" that ranges from the "exuberant humor and linguistic play of *God's Country* [1994], *Glyph* [1999], and *Grand Canyon, Inc.* [2001]" to the "spare, transparent narration" and "straightforward, minimally self-conscious prose" of *Walk Me to the Distance* and *Cutting Lisa* (1986) (Russett 363). His work is not easily assimilable to critical attempts to categorize, to evaluate, or to unify it as a whole. Even though it is a small subset of that corpus, his straightforward and realistic contemporary western fiction is diverse enough to make critical generalizations difficult. Nonetheless, a noticeable difference exists between Everett's earliest fiction set in the American West and the western writing he has published since *God's Country*, a parody of the genre Western set in the nineteenth century that pointedly foregrounds the issue of race. These more recent stories are often developmental narratives that trace the evolution of a character for whom race "isn't a consuming subject" into someone who becomes deeply (if reluctantly) committed to issues of racial, social, and/or environmental justice. Everett's short fiction, particularly the collection *Big Picture* (1996), has received less critical attention than his novels but is also important. Not only are Everett's short stories masterfully crafted, but they also reflect the thematic concerns of his novels, and an examination of those stories demonstrates how he has varied and developed those themes over his career.

Finally, Everett's later stories in particular place the American West at the thematic center of the narratives. In his discussion of *God's Country* and *Watershed* (1996), Leland Krauth points out that the two novels reveal something about "Everett's engagement with the West—the West of fiction as well as actuality" (314). In *God's Country*, Everett "cheerfully demolishes [the] most cherished features" of the genre Western while also "recuperat[ing] it, infusing into its clichés some gritty realities and exploiting its abiding mythic power" (321). In Everett's fiction, the West—whether the Old West of the genre Western or the new West

of contemporary realistic regional writing—is a complex and even ambivalent place, sometimes suffering from the same social, political, and
environmental problems as the rest of the country, at other times offering
a haven from those problems. Of his Wyoming home, John Hunt in the
novel *Wounded* (2005) comments, "This is America. I've run into bigotry
here" (52). Having erased the difference between the West and the rest of
the country, John then reintroduces it: "Of course, the only place anybody
ever called me nigger to my face was in Cambridge, Mass." (52). The idea
that the American West is an exceptional place, fundamentally different
from the rest of the country, is one of the oldest and most repeated tropes
of western writing, and it is typical of Everett's fiction that he repeats *and*
critiques that trope, his characters cynically realistic about western racial
relations but also idealistically hopeful that the West is indeed (or could
become) such a haven.

Not merely incidental or marginal to the plots and characters, the
setting in Everett's fiction comments on the West itself, often from perspectives that are alternately idealist and realist. A commitment to social
justice often coincides with or is preceded by an allegiance to place, particularly to the unspoiled (but threatened) beauty of the western landscape. If the inclusion of a disabled character signals a racial subtext in
Everett's fiction, the presence of "wounded" or damaged western landscapes suggests the imbrication of racial and environmental issues. While
such damaged landscapes counter idealistic representations of unspoiled
western nature, they also suggest a complex reworking of the mythology
of western exceptionalism, as Everett's characters often seek to repair or
preserve the exceptional places that they simultaneously doubt can exist.

While I focus here on Everett's representation of the American West,
it is also important to place his work within the context of what theorists of African American culture call the "post-soul aesthetic," a term
used to describe the distinctive features of literature, art, and music produced by many contemporary black artists. If African American writers
coming of age in the era of the civil rights and Black Power movements
explored such topics as the problems of segregation or worked to articulate a distinctive "black aesthetic" and sense of identity, contemporary
African American writers may explore the possibilities and problems of
desegregation and may focus their work on "cultural mulattos," individuals who have been "educated by a multi-racial mix of cultures" (Ellis 235).
Responding to such elements of contemporary black experience as desegregation, economic and geographic mobility, and globalization, post-soul

artists address the "fractures and fissures" that accompany such periods of political and social flux and work to depict the fluid and multiple black identities that have subsequently emerged (Neal 6).

In his fiction set in the contemporary American West, Everett consistently depicts individuals whose lives reflect post-soul African American experience, especially in their efforts to establish a sense of identity in a desegregated world. In novels such as *Walk Me to the Distance, Watershed,* and *Wounded* and in the short fiction collected in *The Weather and Women Treat Me Fair* (1987), *Big Picture* (1996), and *Damned If I Do* (2004), Everett creates characters who appear to have successfully integrated into either predominantly white or multicultural western communities. Although in some stories "race is not an issue," others directly address the question of racial identity. As Margaret Russett observes, "The integrity of Everett's project consists in maintaining an unrelenting assault on constricting fictions of identity . . . while insisting on their real and unevenly distributed effects" (366). Especially in his later western fiction, Everett explores how individuals respond to the "real" effects of cultural identity scripts, how they negotiate the resultant and often conflicting demands of multiple identifications—westerner, black, husband, son, artist, cowboy, rodeo performer. His characters sometimes find workable metaphors of selfhood in a western landscape that is also "fractured and fissured" (Neal 6). In the story "Wash," protagonist Lucien Bradley observes that "He was like the space between the walls of the [Rio Grande] gorge, being from a black father and a white mother. . . . The gorge was a vastness that couldn't be ignored, but really couldn't be defined" (95). The American West as Lucien experiences it, with its landscapes that invite identification but do not offer definition and with its absence of black communities, provides a particularly appropriate setting for a post-soul interrogation of black identity. The walls of the gorge are as concrete as black people and white people, but what if one's sense of self falls in the space between these concrete defining categories? Even if a vast space of possible identities exists between these two positions, how does one establish a definable and stable sense of self in the face of such vastness?

Mark Anthony Neal suggests that while an earlier generation of writers addressed the problems of segregation, the works of post-soul writers and artists attempt to "liberate contemporary interpretations of that experience from sensibilities that were formalized and institutionalized during earlier social paradigms," particularly fixed or essentialist notions of "blackness" and of individual identity (3). Post-soul artists and texts, writes Bertram Ashe, "trouble blackness, they worry blackness; they stir it up, touch it, feel it out, and hold it up for examination in ways that depart significantly from previous—and necessary—preoccupations with struggling for political freedom, or with an attempt to establish and sustain a coherent black identity" (614). Everett's work is certainly part of this liberation, and his protagonists are often of the generation after the civil rights era, but if his writing troubles notions of a "coherent black identity," his characters also remain troubled by earlier events even as they think of themselves as beyond them, in part because they continue to encounter white people whose sensibilities have not been liberated.

In the story "Alluvial Deposits," hydrologist Robert Hawks (also the protagonist of the novel *Watershed*) travels to the small town of Dotson, Utah, where he observes, "For reasons too familiar and too tiresome to discuss, I was a great source of interest as I idled at the town's only traffic signal" (41–42). Although Robert does not reveal why he is such a source of interest ("too tiresome to discuss"), the elderly white woman whose permission he needs to cross her land makes it clear when she slams her door in his face "and managed to squeeze the word *nigger* through the last, skinniest gap" (42). In *Assumption* (2011), a collection of three novellas set in New Mexico and linked by the character of deputy sheriff Ogden Walker, a similar scene plays out when Walker investigates a report of shots being fired at the house of a Mrs. Bickers. Walker "sensed that the old woman didn't like him because he was black, but that was probably true for half of the white residents of the county" (6). As the story progresses, Mrs. Bickers is discovered to have been involved with a hate group known as the Great White Hope, and as the bodies pile up in rural New Mexico, Walker is drawn further into the investigation. Two FBI agents appear, searching for a missing undercover agent who had infiltrated the group. When Walker becomes a person of interest to them, he dryly observes, "Leave it to the FBI, though. They lose a man investigating the fucking KKK and they hunt down the only black man in a five-hundred-mile radius" (78).

As is frequently the case in African American fiction, mixed-race characters in Everett's work are often used to explore double-consciousness. Ogden Walker's father had "moved to New Mexico from Maryland because there were fewer people and so, necessarily, fewer white people. He hated white people, but not enough to refrain from marrying one, Ogden's mother" (13). The mixed-race Ogden comes to believe that "his father hated half of him" (13). His father (deceased when the story begins) "would never have approved of his son's job with the sheriff's office" and "would have made it clear that he believed Ogden to somehow be a traitor" (13). "A traitor to what would have remained forever unclear," Everett writes, "but it would have been tinged with the language of race and social indignation" (13). From his father's perspective, Ogden's job as a deputy would be a rejection of his blackness, a declaration of allegiance to the white world and to the uniform associated with the oppression of black people. However, Ogden rejects not so much blackness as his father's concept of black identity. Ogden's double-consciousness does not involve a tension between white and black as much as between his own post-soul sense of blackness and his father's sense of what it means to be black (something "forever unclear," according to Ogden, but "tinged with the language of race and social indignation"). Double-consciousness in Everett's work is often played out in the relationship between son and father (or son and grandfather) and is representative of a generational divide in African American society more than of the classic Du Boisian sense of a twoness that emphasizes the division between black America and white America. Those black and white divisions remain present in Everett's work, but that is not the duality he is most interested in exploring.

In "Wash," Lucien "grew up confused by his father's belief in simple and precise answers; one answer in particular, that one can move away and live without the world. Now, Lucien understood all too well why his father moved to the high desert. It was a matter of leaving the world and its problems with his race behind. So he left black people and hopefully white people as well, but 'of course there was no escaping them'" (98). Lucien's father "once told him while they were chopping wood in the backyard that being angry was a part of life. His father had worked up a good sweat and stopped to lean on the axe. 'White people don't understand'" (104). Lucien, the son of a black man and a white woman who grew up "protected" from the world, both does and does not understand: "His father had been right, and he couldn't explain it because he didn't know. His father left him with only a vague understanding of his anger, a vague awareness and respect for it" (105). Like the vastness of the Rio Grande gorge, his father's anger cannot be ignored, but for Lucius, that anger remains as abstract and undefined as the space between the walls of the gorge. A post-soul child, Lucien realizes that identity, black and white, is a fiction, but he also recognizes through the lessons imparted by his father that such fictions have real effects, although he must accept on faith his father's views, which have been shaped by his civil rights era experiences.

In *Watershed*, Robert Hawks, whose father and grandfather were actively involved in the civil rights movement, has distanced himself from that past history: "I considered how I had done so much to remove all things political from my life. . . . I did not know or associate with many black people. . . . I didn't believe in god, I didn't believe in race, and I especially didn't believe in America" (152, 153). As William Handley observes, "Being a true believer in *Watershed* . . . represents the opposite of the disinterested scientist that Robert aims to be, for whom not caring means not to believe in things one cannot observe or read to mean just what they mean" (311). His antipathy to faith and his intentional disconnection from others (or his repression of such connections) becomes impossible to maintain as the novel progresses. Robert is driven both by circumstances and by his "desire to know more" (153). The violence against blacks that he observed as a child is uncannily replayed before his adult eyes through his observations of the developing conflict between agents of the federal government and Plata Indians.

Robert is an integrated individual, an unremarkable presence in the community around Plata Mountain, and his separation from black culture has in part represented a response to the violence of the civil rights era. Through his reluctant involvement in an American Indian radical group, however, he finds himself returned to the issues and activism of his father's generation. Robert's "emergence from this political and moral coma" is, as Krauth notes, "the center of the novel," even though his evolution from "self-protective apathy to dangerous commitment" is slow (324–25). The growth of his involvement with the Plata Indians is paralleled by the increasing narrative space given over to his memories of the traumas his family members experienced because of their civil rights activism. Everett suggests in *Watershed* that neither the post-soul generation African American nor the first-generation black westerner has as much transcended the sensibilities of an earlier generation as repressed them. Only through returning to those past traumas, like Robert, and only through a "dangerous commitment" to activism can the post-soul generation truly move beyond the sensibilities—and the social and political inequities that inform those sensibilities—of an earlier time and place. If apathy and noncommitment are self-protective stances, so is distancing oneself from the issue of race. If the evolution from apathy to commitment is an important thematic concern in Everett's novels, the first step in that evolution for many of Everett's characters is to acknowledge (or discover) the real effect fictions of race play in their lives.

The characters who make such "dangerous commitments" to social issues also commit themselves to specifically western places. If identity through place is as fictional a construct as identity through race, Everett's characters nonetheless sometimes find an empowering sense of self through faith (even if troubled) in that particular identity script. Robert Hawks doubts until looking back over his maps and records, where he discovers an abnormally low volume of water passing through Dog Creek. When he hikes onto the mountain, he finds that "there, in the middle of nowhere on Dog Creek, was a dam, a real honest-to-goodness poured-concrete dam" (167). This alteration in the Plata Mountain watershed diverts the drainage of Dog Creek (and the leakage from illegally stored biochemical agents that pollute it) onto the Plata Creek Indian Reservation and away from the lake that provides water for non-Indians. After helping to bring supplies to a group of Indian activists holed up in a cabin and surrounded by FBI agents, Robert further commits himself by voluntarily sneaking past the armed guards to deliver a roll of film showing the ecological damage caused by the illegal storage facility. Despite the danger, Robert insists on carrying out the mission: "I know this mountain. I know this mountain better than anybody. They can't keep up with me" (196). That the government cares more for its weaponry than for the land or the people damaged by the storage of those weapons indicates the intertwining of racial and environmental issues. Robert's sense of identification with a particular western place ("I know this mountain better than anybody") enables his commitment to racial justice. Although Robert is haunted by the traumas experienced in another place (the American South), Everett's placement of this story in the American West suggests a tentative faith in the idea of western exceptionalism—maybe at this time and in this place, justice will be achieved. Such a possibility rests on Robert's willingness to claim this western place as home and to protect this place from those who seek to damage it.

Like Robert Hawks in *Watershed* and John Hunt in *Wounded*, the characters in Everett's later short fiction (particularly *Big Picture*) start with a strong sense of belonging to a western community and with a solid sense of identity (hydrologist, artist, horse trainer) that becomes troubled as the story progresses. The western landscape poses for Lucien the question of identity that is his central struggle, but other characters find in the West a place for establishing a strong sense of self. Standing on a ridge overlooking Wyoming's Red Desert, "red in the midday light, just like its name implied, stretching out forever," John Hunt comments, "I know this is my life and this is my place" (134). Hunt's belief that "it's okay to love something bigger than yourself without fearing it" is, as his friend, David comments, "almost religious" (134). That belief that the unchanging ("stretching out forever") beauty of the western landscape will always anchor his sense of identity, his sense of belonging to this world, becomes unmoored as the novel progresses and as events steadily push John toward a crisis of faith.

Everett's stories often turn on an encounter with a fractured Other (a mute handyman, a one-legged cowboy, an impoverished elderly woman, or a strangely behaving or damaged animal, such as the three-legged coyote in *Wounded*). These encounters with the otherness of disability, deformity, or poverty result in or foreshadow moments of existential crisis, disintegration, and fragmentation during which the character becomes aware of the illusory nature of both his sense of wholeness and his sense of successful integration and belonging. The distress and unease these characters experience at various moments in the stories, which in many ways is an unconscious rather than fully conscious response, might be better described in terms of what Freud calls the experience of "the uncanny," which is a quality of feeling associated with the sublime, similarly called forth by an encounter with "circumstances and . . . objects" outside the self but evoking "feelings of repulsion and distress" rather than "feelings of a positive nature" (930). The uncanny (*unheimlich*, which literally translates from German as "unhomely") belongs to "that class of the frightening" associated not with something new and horrible but with "what is known of old and long familiar" (930). The peculiar experience of the uncanny comes from the way in which what is familiar is made suddenly strange, the way in which the homely suddenly appears unhomely. "For this uncanny," Freud writes, "is in reality nothing new or alien, but something which is familiar and old-established in the mind and which has become alienated from it only through the process of repression" (944).

What "is known of old and long familiar" for many of Everett's characters is an identity forged in the civil rights era and earlier, an existence shaped by experience in a segregated world that seems far away from the homes and identities they have established in the American West. The central dramatic event, or the catalyst for that event, involves a moment when the homely becomes unhomely, when the familiar becomes strange, and that uncanny experience usually precedes a moment when the racialized identity that the protagonist has left behind, transcended, or repressed or that has simply become only one part of the protagonist's sense of self returns to centrality. Concurrently, the American West that has become home for so many of Everett's characters becomes instead an unhomely place.

In the story "Turned Out" (from *Big Picture*), rodeo performer Lawrence Miller draws a particularly ferocious bull and comments, "Strike you funny that I'm the only black man here and I draw the monster?" (25). His friend, Kemp, as if considering this point for the first time, responds, "That ever get you down? I mean, being the only black person somewhere? I never been the only white person, except when I was alone" (25). In response, "Lawrence shook his head, smiling," and then "both nodded hello to a couple of passing men," moving fairly quickly in this exchange from an awareness of racial difference to a return to their usual sense of solidarity, nodding together in greeting to the other men (25). The references to race evoked by "the monster" pass as well. As readers of Westerns, we suspect early in the story that Lawrence's sense of dread as he awaits his time to ride the bull is merely a prelude to his eventual triumph—that Lawrence, after much travail, will emerge victorious, defeating both the monster that is the bull and the monster of racist attitudes through his heroic and manly performance in the ring. But what we expect to occur does not, and the familiar experience of bull riding merges into the uncanny when the monster steps out of the gate and does nothing, becomes "dead in space" (30). After several seconds, "Lawrence kicked the bull in the sides. Nothing. He felt empty, hollow. There he was a black man, still, forever and always, as good as naked in front of everybody" (30). If Lawrence has experienced identity in the West as multiple and fluid, the odd behavior of the bull, its visible difference from the norm, returns to him a sense of his own visible difference and returns him to an identity that he experiences as fixed and essentialized, "a black man, still, forever and always."

As the bull remains motionless, Lawrence "had time to pick out faces in the crowd, to nod to the familiar ones, but they were too terrified to notice" (30). No joking comment, no friendly nod acknowledging familiarity, restores his former sense of ease. The lack of recognition reinforces Lawrence's sense of Otherness, as he has become part of the strange spectacle, a monstrosity of sorts himself. Wordplay here reinforces the sense of connection between the animal and the rider, especially the word *still*, used to describe them both. As Lawrence is "a black man, still, forever and always," the bull is also "so still" (29). Each usage plays on a different meaning of the word, motionless to describe the bull, an indication of continuance when describing Lawrence: still, always, continually. But each usage contains elements of the other meaning. Lawrence is also motionless, "a black man, still," and the bull remains motionless, "dead in space" and "dead still," the meaning of still in the case of the bull depending on whether we read *dead* as a noun ("still dead in space," a description of continuance) or as an intensifying adjective ("*very* still") (29–30). As the incident stretches on, Everett writes, "He was still in the ring and the animal was still motionless" (31). In this case, *still* is used in both senses to describe each; Lawrence is motionless in the ring and continues to be in the ring, and the bull continues to be motionless, as indicated by the playful redundancy of "still motionless," another way of saying "still still." The scene also takes place in the dead stillness of silence, and with another redundancy, the crowd in the stands is described as "still silent" (31). All have been made still at this point in the story, frozen in a state of continuing motionlessness and silence, *still* still and still *still*. If the bull is described in terms that echo descriptions of Lawrence, the bull also uncannily doubles the crowd: "The bull's face was scary to see, blank, his eyes glazed over" (31). Here and later in the story, the blank gaze of the bull mirrors the white characters' continuing glazed fascination with the spectacle Lawrence offers.

Even after Lawrence has jumped off the bull and the animal has finally trotted out of the ring, there is no return to the status quo, as what Lawrence has experienced previously as an unmarked difference has become a marked visible difference for the others around him: "'Everybody's saying it's the damnedest thing they ever saw,' Fussey said, his eyes locked on Lawrence. His pupils were covered with the shine of a few beers" (33). Out of the ring, Lawrence finds himself uncannily returned to it, as this white cowboy has suddenly become the double of the bull, with his pupils "covered with the shine of a few beers" mirroring the bull's "blank" and "glazed over" eyes. In the form of Fussey, Lawrence is confronted with the conjoined gazes of both the white spectators and the strangely behaving bull, and he responds, "Are you going to eat me or something? . . . I mean, stop looking at me like that" (33). Others in the bar "were staring at him. All were aware of him. As always" (34). Outside the ring, Lawrence still experiences the same sensation as inside it, as much an object of curiosity as the bull that transformed him into the spectacle that he has always been.

The uncanny, Freud writes, "is in reality nothing new or alien" (944). What is "familiar and old-established" in the minds of the characters in this story, black and white, is the history of American racial relations and conflicts, and though the characters at times seem to have transcended (or maybe just repressed) those attitudes about race, the oddly behaving bull serves as a catalyst for the return to preset roles in the American drama about race (944). Rather than fluid and multiple identities, everyone, observers and observed, has been locked into essentialized positions by his strange event. That the still and silent bull doubles "the onlookers in the stand [who] made no noise," that the bull's glazed eyes double the "shine" of Fussey's eyes, that the bull is also in a sense Lawrence's double, points to the complex imbrication of the participants in this drama (30). As a result, each participant becomes somewhat monstrous in the eyes of the other. Lawrence becomes, like the bull, a spectacular curiosity, part of "the damnedest thing they ever saw"; the white spectators become like the bull, their faces "scary to see" and their "eyes glazed over," as naked as Lawrence feels in their revelation of fear and hunger. All have become, "still, forever and always," black and white.

In other stories in *Big Picture*, a disabled character's perceptible difference serves as a metaphor for the visible difference of race; even when the protagonist's race goes unmentioned in a story, the presence of the disabled character alerts us to the racial subtext of the narrative. Disability, Lennard J. Davis observes, "is a disruption in the visual, auditory, or perceptual field as it relates to the power of the gaze" (2402). Although Davis does not draw an explicit connection between the disruption in the "perceptual field" occasioned by disability to the similarly disruptive potential of racial difference, other theorists of disability studies have argued for consideration of disability in terms of contemporary understandings of ethnicity. Within the perceptual field of the dominant culture, observes Rosemarie Garland Thomson, "those bodies deemed inferior become spectacles of otherness while the unmarked are sheltered in the neutral space of normalcy" (*Extraordinary* 8). Continues Thomson, "No firm distinction exists between primarily formal disabilities and racial physical features considered atypical by dominant, white standards" (14). As an example of American culture's fascination with spectacles of Otherness and of the lack of distinction made between forms of difference, Thomson points to the "freak shows" popular in America well into the twentieth century. As part of the freak show, "a nondisabled person of color billed as the 'Fiji Cannibal' was equivalent to a physically disabled, Euro-American called the 'Legless Wonder'" (63).

As Thomson points out in *Staring: How We Look* (2009), Frantz Fanon in *Black Skin, White Masks* identifies "staring as a tool of domination" in a racist society—especially "the kind of staring that 'fixes' a person in gender, race, disability, class, or sexuality systems" (42, 43). However, in describing his resistance to the racist stare that fixes "his identity as Black," Fanon "recruits disability as the true mark of physical inadequacy from which he wishes to differentiate racial marking" (Thomson, *Staring* 42). According to Thomson, at this moment in *Black Skin, White Masks*, a "'crippled veteran' tells Fanon's brother to 'resign' himself to his color, just as the veteran himself" has become resigned to his disability (42). This comparison, Thomson continues, "outrages Fanon, who claims that racial difference does not make one inferior, but disability does" (42). Rather than similarly recruiting disability as a foil against which one's own normalcy can be better seen, Everett consistently refuses such abled/disabled, superior/inferior oppositions in his portrayal of characters with disabilities.

In *Big Picture*'s penultimate story, "Squeeze," the disabled figure is a white man, "Jubal Dixon, the cook, a short, one-legged man," whose disability makes him as much a target for the story's antagonist, Lucius Carter, as protagonist Jake Winston's blackness makes him a target (126). Through remarks that are, in spirit, racial slurs (referring to Jubal as "Hoppy," for example), Lucius expresses indirectly the racial hatred that he lacks the courage to address directly to Jake (129). In contrast to some of the other protagonists in the book, Jake is not particularly unsettled by Jubal's disability or is at least no more bothered by Jubal's missing leg than Jubal is bothered by Jake's racial difference. As Thomson observes, disability is "not so much a property of bodies as a product of cultural rules about what bodies should be or do" (*Extraordinary* 6). The cultural rules that define a one-legged man as disabled do not determine Jake's perception of Jubal, and throughout the story, the narrative shows Jubal adroitly negotiating the world around him, surprising Jake by "vault[ing] up the carpeted steps to the second-floor landing with his crutch swinging close to his leg" or by using the crutch as a cue in a pool game (127).

What gives Jake a serious case of the willies, however, is Jubal's missing teeth—more specifically, the set of false teeth that replaces them. Jake "wasn't sure what he was seeing at first. He did a double take. [Jubal] had his dentures out of his face and in his lap and was polishing them with his handkerchief. Winston didn't say anything, just kept his eyes forward on the road" ("Squeeze" 127). Disability and, just as important, the perception of what constitutes disability depend on subjective response rather than the properties of individual bodies themselves. For Jake, the disruption in the "perceptual field" (he "wasn't sure what he was seeing") is not the "obvious" disability of a missing limb but the unexpected appearance of a prosthetic device—false teeth. Although we might expect that a story about a black cowboy will revolve around his difference, the primary narrative (and comic) concern of "Squeeze" is how Jake negotiates and comes to terms with the newly discovered and disorienting Otherness of Jubal's dentures.

In *Watershed*, the catalyst for the return of the past is the uncanny figure of someone whose visible difference from the norm recalls to the protagonist his own sense of difference: Louise Yellow Calf, an Indian woman "the size of a child," whose "little bones" feel "unreal in [his] grasp" when Robert shakes her hand (9–10). Shortly after this first encounter with Louise, Robert recalls a hunting trip with his grandfather, who turns to the eight-year-old boy and tells him, "When you're older . . . the police will stop you and search you and, if they don't shoot you, they'll take you in and say you look like another 'nigger.' They may not use that word, but that's what they'll mean. It's happened to me. It's happened to your father. It will happen to you" (14). Other than one earlier reference to his grandmother as "a member of the AME Church," this is the first moment in the text in which Robert is directly identified by race, and it is the first time that we realize that racial conflict has been a formative part of his past (3). The return of that memory occurs after he meets Louise and gives her a ride, and immediately after he sits down to eat, "thinking all the while about that little woman Louise out there someplace in the cold" (13). Because of her size, Louise may remind Robert of the child he once was, for her presence in the narrative almost always takes him back to his own childhood, and she is in many ways both his opposite and double. Consistently identified throughout the story by race, gender, and size ("a midget Indian woman"), the narrative (primarily through the comments of other characters within the story) marks her difference in a way that contrasts with Robert's unremarkableness, his ability to pass as any other member of the community as long as he remains politically neutral (51). Robert passes, but Louise does not; Louise is committed, but Robert avoids commitment—until his continuing involvement with Louise leads him to act in support of the Plata Indians' cause.

In "Cerulean," only a hospital orderly's reference to protagonist Michael Lawson as "brother man" hints at his racial identity, although he is more clearly designated as African American in later stories (19). The disabled figure is a mute man, presumably homeless, who appears with a broken-down lawnmower and offers to mow Michael's lawn and then uncannily returns every day thereafter to do the same. Worried by the man's mowing the lawn in a heavy wool shirt in oppressive heat, Michael loans him "a light blue" University of North Carolina T-shirt (2). He takes the man's soaked wool shirt, drapes it over a railing, and goes to wash his hands. After finishing the lawn, "the man then handed Michael the sweaty, light blue T-shirt. Michael took it, and his fingers touched the slick, salty water from the man's body," a contact that leads him once more to the sink and "lathering up his hands" (4). The disturbance of identity put in motion by the disabled character produces symptomatic behavior, obsessive hand washing, as if Michael's own skin has been—or could be—physically contaminated by contact with the mute man's Otherness and impoverishment.

Lennard Davis suggests that the response of the physically abled person when confronted with disability is akin to the "feelings of repulsion associated with the uncanny," in part because the familiar experiences recalled are our own forgotten or repressed memories of the body of infancy and childhood, a body incapable of "normal" human actions, an experience of "disability" that is "common to all humans" (2412, 2411). Drawing on the Lacanian concept of the mirror stage, Davis points out that "the most primitive, the earliest experience of the body is actually of the fragmented body," of a body in "pieces" that only gains coherence through the infant's observation of its own image in a mirror (2409). The child recognizes (or misrecognizes) a "unified image [of] his or her self," an image of wholeness, ability, and control (2410). According to Lacan, this "unified image" contrasts with "the turbulent movements that the subject feels are animating him" and the child's actual "motor incapacity and nursling dependence" (Davis 1286). The child's identification with the image in the mirror "is really the donning of an identity, an 'armor' against the chaotic or fragmentary body" (2410). Davis goes on to suggest that in the encounter with disability, the able-bodied person sees in the mirror of the other's body not the illusion of wholeness that he expects but rather the uncanny and unsettling "true self of [our own repressed] fragmented body" (2410). In this encounter, "the disabled body causes a kind of hallucination of the mirror phase gone wrong. The subject looks at the disabled body and has a moment of cognitive dissonance, or should we say a moment of cognitive resonance with the earlier state of fragmentation" (2410). One reason that an encounter with disability in Everett's fiction can be so unsettling for his characters is that the disabled Other returns an image of visible difference, of a body "deemed inferior," an image of Self that produces a moment of "cognitive dissonance," or rather, "cognitive resonance" with an earlier image of racialized identity—"They'll take you in and say you look like another 'nigger'"—that the character has presumably escaped or transcended.

So disturbing is the encounter with the mute man for Michael in "Cerulean" that even such a neutral object as a T-shirt becomes uncannily marked by association. After a shower, "He slid open the closet door and there, sitting on top of a stack of sweaters and pullovers was the light blue UNC T-shirt. He stared at it" (7). Even though the shirt has been freshly laundered, "He touched it, thinking about how it had been on the body of that man. He was ashamed that he was afraid to put it on. . . . He looked at himself in the mirror and noticed how old he was getting" (7). Michael is uncannily disturbed by the shirt and by the man who wore it, both acting as mirrors that return to Michael an image "gone wrong," so much so that he must reassure himself of his own identity by looking into an actual mirror, which also returns an image that differs from his own internal image of self; however, the difference he sees in the mirror is age, not color. As a painter, Michael is obsessed with color, particularly blues and yellows, but he indicates no conscious awareness of himself as "colored." His observation in the mirror seems either a misrecognition or a displacement of the source of the anxiety produced by his encounter with the mute man.

The uncanny figure of the mute, perspiring yardman alters Michael's experience of his own home, which indeed becomes an unhomely place that strangely evokes the yardman. He and his wife, Gail, are disturbed by a squealing clothes dryer that echoes the "rhythmic squeak" of a wheel on the yardman's beat-up lawnmower ("Cerulean" 1). In working on the dryer to eliminate the sound, Michael sweats so profusely that he soaks through his clothing, becoming so visibly different from himself and so much like the perspiring yardman that Gail thinks he "look[s] sick" (9). More washing restores him to himself, but as soon as he showers off his sense of difference, the yardman uncannily returns to mow "the already mowed lawn," a strange action that makes unhomely again the home that Michael has worked so hard to restore to normalcy (10). Worried about the strange sense of connection he feels with the man, Michael asks, "How old do you think that guy is?" (11). When Gail guesses sixty, Michael responds, "I'd bet he's our age," even if he looks older; as a further indication of Michael's growing identification with the man, he then observes, "Of course, I feel sixty" (11).

As the story progresses, the source of the uncanny shifts from the yardman to the six-by-eight-foot painting on which Michael begins to work: "He began to cry as he put blues on his palette: cerulean, cobalt—hue and color, pthalo, and indigo" (13). The blue of the painting reflects Michael's own feeling of the blues, which he expresses visually rather than musically. Michael's blues is a one-note performance, as he is "able to apply only one shade, cerulean," from his palette (13–14). The choice of shade suggests that the painting is both an abstract self-portrait of Michael and a portrait of the yardman, as it is the color of the shirt that connects the two men. Michael's obsessive painting also mirrors the yardman's obsessive lawn mowing, which becomes a kind of artistry as well: "Michael looked at the lawn, which had been cut day after day, and saw that nothing made it look any different. But something was better about it. He tried to see where the man left off in the middle of the job, but there was nothing there, just grass the same height and green-turning-to-brown color everywhere" (16). The description of lawn mowing and of the lawn with its monotone "green-turning-to-brown color," reoccurs in the descriptions of Michael painting: "He took a brush and put more cerulean onto the canvas. The added paint didn't change the blue on the canvas, didn't make it darker or more blue, but he continued to apply it: the same color over the same color" (17–18). As additional cuttings of the lawn do not make "it look any different," added paint does not "change the blue on the canvas," but that lack of visible change fails to stop either man from repeatedly working on his canvas.

If we interpret the painting as a self-portrait, Michael paints a picture of a man whose identity is abstractly rendered through one distinctive feature: color. That color, however, is blue rather than black, a displacement, perhaps, of the source of Michael's identity trouble. His encounter with the yardman's difference begins a process of disintegration and fragmentation that ends with Michael's hospitalization after he nearly kills himself by ingesting the blue paint, but he cannot seem to bring to consciousness the reason for his disturbance. In contrast to "Turned Out," where Lawrence recognizes that a return to a racialized identity is the cause of his sense of disturbance (and who thus is able to confront and to move beyond the experience of "cognitive dissonance" by the end of the story), Michael's story in "Cerulean" ends ambivalently, the disturbance of identity unresolved, his sanity in question, and his marriage on the rocks.

In "Squeeze," Jubal's dentures, which Jake repeatedly encounters out of context and out of Jubal's mouth, give back an image of a body in pieces that disturbs Jake's equilibrium (Davis 2409). That Jubal's disability produces a "moment of cognitive resonance" that returns to Jake his own sense of fragmentation and difference is indicated by the excessiveness of his response, described at various times as "stone-chilled" and "confused, dizzy"; at one point he "nearly fainted, actually swayed" (130–33). After an encounter with Lucius in a bar ends with Jubal drunkenly swinging a crutch at the man and then passing out, Jake takes the unconscious man back to their hotel room, where he begins to choke because of his dentures: "A cowboy touched a lot of things, [Jake] thought, blood, dung, placenta, but here he was, stone-chilled by the prospect of reaching in and pulling out the man's dentures. But he did it . . . and ran into the bathroom and washed his hands for a considerable time, nearly disappearing one of those little wafers of hotel soap" (130). Here, as in other stories, the fact that the protagonist's feeling of "revulsion and distress" takes place in a bathroom—the one room where an encounter with a mirror is inevitable—suggests that the key to the disturbance is not some specific quality of the other but the subject's suddenly troubled self-image. As in the story "Cerulean," repeated and vigorous hand-washings follow contact with the other, as if that Otherness may be contagious, which in a sense it is; the other's physical difference threatens the protagonist's sense of anonymity and integration, as an affiliation with another makes visible the protagonist's own difference. Jubal, goaded in the bar by Lucius's comments, makes a spectacle of himself and draws Jake into the center of attention of white gazes. Carrying the passed-out man over his shoulder, Jake walks "past a clump of tourists who probably thought this was a neat piece of local color, or maybe they thought the dusty black cowboy was taking the one-legged, unconscious, old man upstairs to have his way with him" (130). Jake, a cowboy at the beginning of the story, has become a black cowboy by the middle, "a neat piece of local color" in more than one way, an object of white attention, his own difference made more visible by association with the spectacle of his friend.

When Jake imagines himself as "a neat piece of local color," he feels himself "local" as well as "color[ed]." The characters in Everett's fiction who resolve dissonance remain "local" and find the solution to the crisis of identity in precisely the western places where those crises were initiated. Michael's story, conversely, is one of continual displacement, especially when he seeks unsuccessfully to moor his identity not in the western landscape but in the cerulean sky above.

A recurring character in the stories collected in *Big Picture*, Michael continues to find himself in uncanny situations, particularly in "Dicotyles Tajacu," which begins as he burns his paintings and drives north and ends with him again driving north, avoiding rather than confronting his troubles, moving across the western landscape rather than finding a place within it. Beset by headaches and abandoned by Gail, Michael attempts to erase every marker of identity, "no longer a husband, no longer a lover, and he no longer resided in that house in Denver" (66). The uncanny Other in the story that is figured as Michael's double is a bedraggled and ancient mounted head of a javelina (*Dicotyles tajacu*) that he discovers in a roadside diner. "Unsatisfied, agitated, desolate in heart and entrails, sick with pain," Michael makes the stuffed head "an object of that sickness" and refuses to leave the diner until the cook sells him the head (62). Punningly reflecting Michael's identity crisis and loss of self, the javelina is missing an eye. As "he imagined the pain when the wind blew through an empty socket to the exposed nerves," Michael's description of the "dead for twenty-five years, but still breathing" animal represents his own emptiness as well as his physical and emotional pain (64, 66).

If the revelation of Michael's racial identity is deferred and only obliquely referenced in "Cerulean," race is brought directly to the forefront in "Dicotyles Tajacu" when an acquaintance, Harley, spots Michael in Laramie: "I saw the truck and I said, hey, that looks familiar, then I saw this black guy getting in it and I said, hey, that must be, and it is" (67). Michael seems more conscious of his racial identity and more aware of a history of racial violence that is coextensive with western history. As he turns onto a Laramie street, he observes the spot "where in 1913 or so a black man had been lynched on a pole that was still standing. . . . The man had been dragged out of jail by citizens who were chastised the next day by the editor of the town paper for being such poor shots. . . . Michael always looked at the pole as he drove by" (68). Later, visiting Harley and his wife, Michael goes to the bathroom and finds himself in a too-bright room that was "white everywhere, white fixtures, white walls, white tile, white bidet, white towels, and even the soap in the white dish was white" (71). This unhomely space, "the bathroom of monochrome torture" with its "white light" that he can "still see and feel" while sitting in the dining room, uncannily figures his social situation in the West (74, 76). Deeply disturbed, he "was truly afraid of what the light in that room would do to him. He would open the door, flip the switch, and his brain would rupture" (77). The undercurrent of racial tension at the dinner party and the reminder of past racial violence he observes on the way to the party might be contributing to his unease, but Michael blames the room itself rather than the "whiteness" that surrounds him everywhere else. Whatever discomfort he may feel as a black man in a predominantly white society remains below consciousness but is expressed through physical symptoms (headaches, dizziness) and sensations.

The brightly lit bathroom also recalls the opening of Ralph Ellison's *Invisible Man* and the narrator's "hole in the basement" where "there are exactly 1,369 lights," a place *"full* of light" where Invisible Man "hibernates" (7, 6). Ellison's Invisible Man loves light "because I *am* invisible. Light confirms my reality, gives birth to my form" (6). Through light, "I've illuminated the blackness of my invisibility," states Ellison's protagonist (13). Michael hates the light, perhaps for the same reason—it confirms an invisibility and illuminates a blackness that he does not yet fully acknowledge. The allusion to Ellison's novel provides another indication of the racial subtext to Michael's identity crisis, and reading this story in conjunction with Ellison's makes explicit what Everett's story only implies. Ellison's narrator observes, "I am invisible, understand, simply because people refuse to see me. . . . They see only my surroundings, themselves, or figments of their imagination" (3). Rather than seeing Invisible Man in terms of his unique individuality, people see him only in terms of his blackness. When Harley first sees Michael, he sees "this black guy," not a fellow artist. As Invisible Man is seduced by a white woman who sees not him but "primitive" vitality and hears not his words but the "tom-toms beating" in his voice, Michael (to his dismay) is beset by a guest at the party, Edwina, whose "sneaked glances" and "smacking" lips indicate her hunger and desire (Ellison 413; Everett, "Dicotyles" 75). She is so intent on seducing him that "she licked her lips even when she wasn't licking her lips" (77). Edwina recalls the white spectators of "Turned Out," and Lawrence's comment to Fussey, "Are you going to eat me or something? . . . I mean stop looking at me like that," voices what Michael seems to be thinking but does not speak aloud (33).

Taking literally Ellison's invisibility trope, Everett presents a character who spends the last part of the story studiously avoiding artificial light of any sort and wandering invisibly through the dark house. Like Invisible Man, who "walk[s] softly so as not to awaken the sleeping ones," Michael desperately tries to avoid Edwina (who crawls naked through the house searching for him) and just as desperately tries to find a place other than "the bathroom of monochrome torture" to empty his bladder (Ellison 5; Everett, "Dicotyles" 76). That the light Michael avoids is in part the light of self-illumination is indicated by the excessiveness of his fears and responses, by the disorientation he experiences, by the way the physical effects of exposure to light center on parts of the body associated with consciousness and selfhood—his head, his brain, his eyes. When he sneaks through the darkness into the master bedroom's bath and turns on the light, "Pain detonated in his head like a blasting cap and the heat of it ripped through his eyes. This room turned out to be just as bright white as the other one. He was reeling and losing his balance" (79). The physical symptoms here replicate those of other characters in *Big Picture* who experience disorienting moments of psychological disintegration, but Michael "cover[s] his eyes with his hands," empties his bladder, and retreats back into darkness and invisibility, hiding in the tub with the lights off (79). Michael avoids multiple confrontations here—with the white bathroom, with the white woman who stalks him, with the other characters in the house, and with himself. The story ends with him finally rushing from the house to his truck and back to "the head of the *Dicotyles tajacu*," wishing "it were alive . . . so that he could let it go" (82). But "the head was only a head," and the bathroom was only a bathroom, and Michael drives on into the night, consciously steering away from whatever revelation might be derived from either of those uncanny "heads" (82).

Everett's novel, *Wounded*, reiterates, clarifies, yet complicates several of the themes and motifs found in the short fiction. As in several of Everett's other western stories, we have an African American character who has achieved a degree of equality and success for himself but who comes to recognize the inequalities experienced by others. In a short story that prefigures the concerns of *Wounded*, "Cry about a Nickel," Joe Cooper finds a job taking care of horses at an Oregon farm, where he discovers that the owner's son, Charlie, is being persecuted (particularly by his father) because he is gay. In contrast to *Wounded*'s John Hunt, who moves from an apathetic response to a hate crime—the murder of a gay man—to an active commitment to avenging that death and another, Joe is unable to do anything, and the story ends with him moving on and leaving Charlie's situation unchanged. The protagonists (Joe Cooper, Cole Dixson) in the stories collected in *The Weather and Women Treat Me Fair* (1987) seem stymied by the injustices they observe and are unable or unwilling to create alliances across boundaries of racial, ethnic, or other forms of difference. If Everett is interested in reinventing as well as parodying Western conventions and myths, a key element in that reinvention is a renewed commitment to place. Joe Cooper is just passing through, but John Hunt is firmly grounded in a western place, and the threat he experiences is not just to his own sense of identity but to his vision of the West and his allegiance to a unique and beautiful western landscape.

As John Hunt rides his horse out toward Wyoming's Red Desert, he observes, "It was dramatic land, dry, remote, wild. It was why I loved the West. I had no affection necessarily for the history of the people and certainly none for the mythic West, the West that never existed. It was the land for me. And maybe what the land did to some who lived on it" (*Wounded* 45). In this meditation, Hunt both dismisses ("never existed") and then reasserts the idea of the "mythic West" by suggesting that some quality of the land itself can do something to the people who live there. But if, as Frederick Jackson Turner suggested, the unique qualities of the natural West and the special conditions experienced on the western frontier can transform people and societies, people can also transform that landscape, damage and wound it. Although Hunt distinguishes his love of place from his lack of affection for people, the narrative of *Wounded* suggests that he must commit himself to saving (or avenging) both, as the hate crimes perpetrated by a group of white supremacists wound both the land that Hunt loves and the people that he comes to love.

As Hunt rides along the edge of the Red Desert, he sees "something odd. On the red soil, the black was out of place" (*Wounded* 45). The "black" that is out of place here is not the African American man riding through the desert but the actions of the neo-Nazis, who have blackened the landscape by pouring gasoline into a coyote's den: "The entrance was blackened from the fire. The coyote had run a hundred yards aflame and whoever had struck the match had followed along in the truck, watching. I felt sick. I was confused, near tears, angry" (45). Through the burning of the coyote's lair, the western landscape is reconfigured as a site that recalls southern lynchings; the attack on the coyote is a hate crime perpetrated against the natural West that mirrors in its cruelty the earlier murder of a gay man. Later in the novel, Hunt investigates cattle killings on the land of Daniel White Buffalo, who is targeted because he is an American Indian. In addition to killing his cattle, the perpetrators leave a more explicit message: "Written in snow, in red, in cow's blood, were the words *Red Nigger*" (111). As a disabled character signals racial subtext in Everett's fiction, so does the wounded landscape, especially when that landscape is altered to articulate racist ideology.

But has nature been altered here? Or does the natural element of this scene (the snow) uncannily reveal a truth about the social context? In Hunt's description, the message is not written *on* snow but *in* snow, and perhaps the snow itself is as important to the message as the words. As hatred of difference becomes more apparent in this community, so does the color white become a more visible presence in the narrative. The first visit by David (the gay man whom Hunt befriends) to Hunt's ranch is marked by an unusually early snowfall. Blanketing snow continues to fall for much of the remainder of the novel so that the Wyoming landscape uncannily reminds us (on a much larger scale) of "the bathroom of monochrome torture" from "Dicotyles Tajacu." Although the weather is always realistically described, the continual snowstorms coincide with the increasing threat created by the neo-Nazis, and the blanketing snow suggests as well that the attitudes made explicit by the small group of supremacists may be more widespread than Hunt wishes to admit.

As the title of the novel suggests, almost every one of the characters we encounter is (or will be) wounded in some way—physically, psychologically, or emotionally—and each character (animal as well as human) represents varying levels of disability: Uncle Gus's limp, Hunt's emotional distance (a form of disability caused by the trauma of his wife's death). The coyote pup rescued from the blackened remains of its den has a fire-damaged leg that Hunt amputates. Although the affiliation with an Other that makes visible the protagonist's own difference is Hunt's friendship with the openly gay David (who is able-bodied but emotionally wounded), this three-legged coyote serves as the primary disabled character through whom race is both displaced and addressed. Late in the novel, Hunt observes the coyote walking through the snow alongside his dog, Zoe: "Zoe made two continuous tracks, punctuated by deep impressions of her feet. The coyote left a similar pattern, but wherever she stopped, there was a place of undisturbed or barely disturbed snow under her left forepaw. . . . [T]hat gap, that space, that break in her track fascinated me because it was only there briefly and only while she was still there. Once she moved on, her rear foot stamped its impression where her front one had been" (185). The coyote passes as normal, the sign of her difference—which is, in fact, the visible absence of a sign—erased by her own movement. As other critics have observed and as the title of Everett's most famous novel, *Erasure* (2001) suggests, Everett is a canny practitioner of literary racial *sous rature* and a playful commentator on the relationship between race and representation. In the allegory of the three-legged coyote, race (or, more accurately, difference) is erased, ironically, by inscription—by the marking of the unmarked snow.

After overhearing a homophobic remark from a man he counts as a friend, Hunt feels "as if the whole world was upside-down," and he comments to Gus, "I'm that three-legged coyote. . . . I can't recognize my own tracks until I stop moving" (188). If the mirror stage creates the illusion of a unified image of self, Hunt's moment of cognitive dissonance, of seeing the world he thinks he knows inverted, reversed, "upside-down," reveals to him not his unity with that world but his difference from it. That moment of dissonance is followed by a moment of cognitive resonance, as he realizes why he was so fascinated by the uncanny movement of the coyote in the snow. What he sees for the first time is the break, the gap, that has been concealed by the movement of what appears to be everyday normal behavior. Hunt's comment also returns us to the story of Lawrence, "still motionless" in the ring ("Turned Out" 188). "Only while [the coyote is] still there" can identity be fixed (*Wounded* 185). That moment of fixity and stillness, however, is also its own type of erasure, as the complexity of individual identity is reduced to the still image of the stereotype—of the single trait (blackness, three-legged-ness) isolated from the whole and elevated to the category of *the* identifying marker. Through the lack of a mark in the snow, Hunt recognizes his own invisibility, seeing for the first time the sign of difference that is not there.

A complex, subtle, and beautiful novel, *Wounded* is difficult to address briefly, as even its most concrete descriptions resonate with and reflect the emotions and psychologies of its characters. The novel also comments on *Watershed*, as suggested by the similarities in the names of the two protagonists, Hawks and Hunt, both of whom are "hunters" of a sort—reluctant detectives who solve the mystery at the center of each novel and reluctant seekers of self-knowledge. In *Watershed*, Hawks begins as a disinterested observer but eventually comes to have faith in a cause; *Wounded*'s Hunt is a true believer who finds his faith shattered at the end of the novel. The unsettling question for Hunt is whether the neo-Nazis represent a new force threatening to change the West he loves or whether he has been misreading the natural and political landscapes all along. Are the neo-Nazis an aberration or part of a larger conspiracy that also includes the white ranchers and townspeople whom he considers friends? Has this landscape always been marked by signs of hatred of difference? Is his observation that "on the red soil, the black was out of place" a moment when Hunt unconsciously articulates a true vision of how others see him? Or is he accurate in his interpretation that the actions of those who have altered the natural meaning of this landscape to reflect their own political ideology are out of place?

If Everett employs a post-soul aesthetic in his interrogation of black identity, his characters also seem in search of a post-soul ethics to replace the no-longer-viable identity politics embraced by an earlier generation. Everett clearly embraces humor, irony, and skepticism as part of his aesthetic, and, as Krauth observes, "equally evident is his deep feeling for ethical—even compassionate—action" (326). Nowhere is that commitment to an exploration of the ethics of action more apparent than in Everett's western fiction. Such an ethics also involves a commitment to place, to environmental as well as social justice, and Everett's stories ask if place can be as foundational for a politics of ethical action as race is for identity politics. The cynically realistic Hawks of *Watershed* becomes a reluctant believer by combining his commitment to racial justice with his allegiance to a particular place, but *Wounded* ends with the idealistic Hunt's loss of faith. As Elvis Monday comments in the novel's last line of dialogue, "This is the frontier, cowboy. . . . Everyplace is the frontier" (207). In the context of the violent actions that precede this comment, Hunt can no longer confidently reply, "I know this is my life and this is my place" (134). The homely West has become unhomely, no longer the transformative Turnerian frontier but a combat zone where different groups of people stand in conflict with each other; it is no longer an exceptional place: "Everyplace is the frontier." Is the West exceptional? Can a commitment to place replace or supplement an identity-based politics? Whereas *Watershed* suggests yes, *Wounded* suggests (at best) only a qualified maybe. Taken together, the two novels represent different ways of responding to this dilemma, suggesting that the answers to those questions remain open.

8

The Post-Soul Cowboy on the
Science Fiction Frontier

A
s we move on through the twenty-first century, developments
in the Western genre, particularly in the hybrid genre of the science fiction Western, have opened a new space for imagining and
performing an African American West. Rather than the traditional Old
West settings of *Deadwood* or *Hell on Wheels* or the contemporary West
of Percival Everett's novels, these hybrid Westerns feature settings that
are futuristic and/or postapocalyptic. Film and television Westerns with
science fiction elements such as Joss Whedon's *Firefly* (2002) and *Serenity* (2005) and the Hughes Brothers' postapocalyptic Western film *The
Book of Eli* (2010) are unusual as Westerns in the emphasis they place on
casting African American actors in a variety of roles, in starring roles,
as members of the primary cast, as villains, as supporting characters. By
freeing the genre from the (already highly fictionalized) historical setting
of the American West, these hybrid narratives move beyond the racial
mythologies that have long operated within the Western. Freed as well
from long-standing expectations about African American roles (comic
relief, sidekick) in Westerns, these narratives experiment with different
strategies for performing the role of the black westerner. *Firefly* also includes African American women in heroic roles. Zoë in *Firefly* represents
the most significant developments in the Hoo-Doo cowgirl since Eve in
her buckskin dress rode off to fight the Ku Klux Klan in Oscar Micheaux's
The Symbol of the Unconquered. Nearly a century later, we finally have a
Western brave enough to put a weapon in the hands of an African American woman.

The characters of African descent in these hybrid Westerns gesture
toward an identity that is not quite after race but that nonetheless moves
beyond earlier ways of conceptualizing African American identity. Like
the raceless westerner, the post-soul westerner transcends the socially

imposed limitations of race, is judged by his or her character rather than color. Unlike the character in the civil rights Western, the post-soul westerner is not burdened by the allegorical necessity of representing the cause of racial justice. Unlike the raceless westerner, blackness is still an important part of his or her identity, but being black is understood as something more than being a victim of white oppression or representing a problem of injustice waiting to be solved. Everett's characters often begin as post-soul westerners but become progressively entangled in precisely the racial issues that they hope to have transcended. The science fiction settings of these hybrid Westerns, however, make possible an imagined frontier where identity is not constrained by contemporary politics or by the necessity of directly reflecting the sociopolitical reality of a particular historical era.

The Western genre, Neil Campbell observes in "Post-Western Cinema," has survived well into the twenty-first century, and despite a constant chorus of voices declaring the form to be dead, buried, and long ago read its last rites, the Western is constantly being "resuscitated," Campbell argues, surviving by "traveling across generic boundaries, poaching and borrowing from many different earlier traditions, whilst contributing to the innovation of the genre" (409–10). Rather than dying out and fading away, the Western as a genre is notable for its continued "reinvention and survivance (its 'living on' in new or altered forms)," even if we do not always initially recognize those new forms as Westerns (409). The Western "has in fact shown a remarkable 'impurity', over-spilling its boundaries," involved in "'a sort of participation without belonging—a taking part in without being part of'" (410).[1] Rather than seeing generic transformation as a falsification or degradation of the Western form, Campbell praises the "impurity" of new Western forms as evidence of "the genre's capacity to respond to a changing social, economic, and cultural landscape and *still* be a" Western (411). Participating without belonging, the post-Western establishes a critical distance from the genre, enabling it to be both a Western and a commentary on the Western form.

The central element of the post-Western, Campbell argues, is the "deliberate jarring of expectations," often accomplished through the juxtaposition of seemingly clashing elements—from "*Lonely are the Brave*'s horse on the highway to *Down in the Valley*'s use of the San Fernando Valley" (413). *The Big Lebowski* (1998), for example, begins with "a reassuring cliché of 'west-ness,'" a tumbleweed tumbling across a desert landscape (413). However, as "we literally follow the tumbleweed's reassuring path it takes us suddenly beyond our expectations, over a ridge, and into a less familiar landscape, looking down onto Los Angeles' neon sprawl" (413). The science fiction Western goes a step further by juxtaposing Western tropes with the unfamiliar landscape of a futuristic frontier or by juxtaposing the rural nineteenth-century iconography of the Western with the new technology of the future, as is the case with the image of the spaceship *Serenity* flying over a herd of horses in the opening credits of *Firefly*. The folksy ballad that accompanies the credits, played mostly over scenes of sci-fi technological advancement—of *Serenity* soaring through space—creates another contrast. And for viewers who recognize the voice of blues singer Sonny Rhodes, the central placement of an African American voice ushering us into this series that melds two genres—science fiction, Western—that have traditionally not been hospitable fields for African American participation likewise "takes us suddenly beyond our expectations."

The "inherent strange familiarity" created by such juxtapositions, Campbell argues, jars the viewer "into a space of reflection, a critical dialogue with the form, its assumptions and histories," moving us "to think differently and better" about not only the history and assumptions of the genre itself but also about the historical realities that Westerns mirror back to us (414, 413). We do not have to look far to find such "deliberate jarring of expectations" in Westerns that feature African American actors and characters. Herb Jeffries's *Harlem* series provides example after example—from the tap-dancing cowboy in *The Bronze Buckaroo* to the Deacon and his .45-caliber automatic pistols in *Two-Gun Man from Harlem*. The supposed incompatibility of the film Western's sheriff and an African American man playing that role is presented in *Blazing Saddles* for both humor and pointed satire. Think of the citizens of Mel Brooks's western town confronting the "strange familiarity" of Cleavon Little's Bart riding into town for the first time. Those moments indeed move us "into a space of reflection, a critical dialogue with the form, its assumptions and histories," self-reflexively commenting on the whitewashing of history in the genre Western that has contributed to making it an "unexpected place" to see an African American character.

Albert and Allen Hughes, African American brothers who codirect their films under the credited name the Hughes Brothers, began their careers as independent filmmakers focused on depicting contemporary African American urban life, offering gritty and violent crime dramas such as *Menace II Society* (1993) and *Dead Presidents* (1995). Although a later film, *From Hell* (2001; a Jack the Ripper film), departs from the specifically African American subject matter of their earliest work, their 2010 collaboration, *The Book of Eli*, combines the mainstream elements of the later film with the African American focus of the earlier films. In particular, *The Book of Eli* again places an African American actor, Denzel Washington, in the lead role. *The Book of Eli* takes place in a postapocalyptic America, "thirty winters" after a catastrophe that has pretty much destroyed the world, leaving a blasted landscape of crumbling buildings and roads and small groups of survivors barely hanging on to life. The causes of the catastrophe are obliquely described. We know that there was a war and that there was a flash that "tore open the sky," presumably a nuclear detonation that drove anyone who survived that initial blast underground for a year. The basic plot of the film is that Eli is in possession of the only surviving Bible.[2] After the war, all the Bibles were burned (because, some say, the Bibles were the cause of the whole conflict). His quest is to carry the Bible west, and, when the film begins, he has been doing so for nearly thirty years, although he is finally nearing his destination.

Taking place in the science fictional world of the future, *The Book of Eli* evokes the Western genre in multiple ways. Much of the film was shot in New Mexico, and it makes extensive use of that western desert landscape. Whenever anyone asks Eli where he is going, he simply replies, "West." When someone asks him who he is, he replies, "I'm nobody," a line referencing both Terrence Hill's character in *My Name Is Nobody* (1973) and Clint Eastwood's Man without a Name from director Sergio Leone's *Dollars* trilogy—and references as well Eastwood's own *High Plains Drifter* (1973), a film that *Eli* particularly evokes, especially in its envisioning of the American West as a kind of hell rather than the promising new frontier of most Westerns. In its depiction of a war-torn landscape with blasted out buildings, *Eli* visually alludes to Leone's *The Good, the Bad, and the Ugly* (1966), which takes place against the backdrop of the American Civil War. These explicit references to earlier films signal the filmmakers' awareness of their film as participating in the genre Western even as the postapocalyptic setting takes us beyond the usual nineteenth-century time period.

From the film's earliest moments, *Eli* suggests that we are both in a Western and beyond the form. One of the first images that we see onscreen is a revolver, but this particular handgun is on the ground, covered in dirt and grime, its cylinder open, its chambers empty. As the camera pans past the gun, we see the outstretched hand of a dead man, perhaps a gunfighter who lost his last gunfight, his weapon flying from his hand as he died. As the camera continues to pan along the man's decaying body, we finally get our first view of a camouflaged Eli, waiting with a drawn bow and arrow—his target, a feral cat that has come to feed on the body but instead ends up as Eli's dinner. If the scene suggests the death of the Western through its display of the decaying corpse of a gunfighter, the revelation of the hidden Eli at the end of the long pan suggests the resurrection of the Western hero in different form. This scene also plays specifically on the opening sequence of Sergio Leone's *Once upon a Time in the West*, which similarly begins with an "almost speechless sequence" of waiting "that echoes familiar Westerns like *High Noon* (with the gang awaiting the arrival of their leader)" (Campbell, *Rhizomatic* 121). Rather than waiting for a train, Eli is waiting for a cat, and the gunfight that is preceded by the waiting in *Once upon a Time in the West* is already long past. The heroic gunfighter-versus-gunfighter battles of the Western, this opening suggests, have been replaced by a battle for survival that sometimes involves the very nonheroic hunting of animals such as cats. What has carried over from *Once upon a Time in the West* is the black cowboy, played by Woody Strode in Leone's film. One of the first cowboys we see in *Once upon a Time*, Strode is introduced with a long pan that moves from his boot to his holstered gun and then moves slowly up his body to his hand (the first indication of his race) and then to his face, a camera movement that is echoed by Eli's opening sequence, which starts with a gun, moves to a hand, and then reveals the rest of the body (its race unclear). The black cowboy in *Eli* is revealed only when the camera continues to move past the dead body to the waiting figure in camouflage. In contrast to *Once upon a Time*, this black cowboy is not dead by the time the opening credits come to an end. If Denzel Washington's presence in the film recalls both the actual history of the African American West and the cinematic history of the black cowboy, Eli's continuing survival certainly takes the black cowboy far beyond his stereotypical role in the Western, which is to disappear completely from the plot, to recede into the background, or to experience an early death.

As we eventually learn, Washington's grizzled survivor is as dangerous to humans as he is to cats, and if his fighting skills with a gun and machete are drawn as much from martial arts films as from Westerns, the shattered world through which he moves is, as Campbell observes of *Once upon a Time in the West*, "both familiar (as iconically 'western') and unfamiliar (stretched and distorted) at the same time" (*Rhizomatic* 121). The film references the mise-en-scène of John Ford's Westerns shot in Monument Valley. But rather than a sublime natural landscape, the wreckage of civilization visually echoes those Monument Valley landscapes: towering bridges, partially destroyed, shot from below and dominating the skyline; abandoned cooling towers of a decaying power plant echoing the shape of rock formations in Monument Valley. We see other elements that are familiar to the iconography of the Western: a lonely homestead with a dilapidated single windmill, for example. Eli's path takes him through a newly established town, a frontier community constructed on the wreckage of a formerly abandoned and nearly destroyed city. Although a barely legible sign may read "J. Crew," the facades are clearly modeled after the town sets of classic Westerns. Likewise, the town's saloon, although located inside what used to be a movie theater, with its dust-covered interior and scattered tables of equally dust-covered patrons drinking and flirting with the "saloon girls," suggests the classic Western saloon. From the moment Eli walks through the doors and goes up to the bar (for a refill of his water bottle, since water has become more precious than alcohol), we know that a barroom fight is the inevitable outcome. And before Eli leaves town, there is a likewise equally inevitable shootout on the main street. In the cracked mirror of *The Book of Eli*, we see a distorted vision of both our own contemporary moment (or the wrecked remains of that moment) and the familiar settings of the genre Western—the strange familiarity doubled by their being joined together in the postapocalyptic mise-en-scène.

In addition to destroying both infrastructure and the social fabric, the catastrophe of the war has (seemingly) destroyed the inequalities of the earlier social formation. Race no longer seems to be the dominant marker of difference.[3] No one remarks on the fact that Eli is black. The roving gangs he encounters, the various hijackers, and the gang that runs the frontier town are predominantly but not exclusively white (the cast includes actors of Asian, African, Latino, and Native American descent). A white male power structure still exists in the form of Gary Oldman's Carnegie, the man who rules this particular frontier town and who sends out his various henchmen in search of books, a rarity in this world. Eli's most significant difference is his age, since the flash and its aftermath have killed off most of the people from "before." And, like Carnegie, Eli is one of the few literate people left alive.

Although racial injustice is not an issue in this postapocalyptic culture, *The Book of Eli* is an African American Western not only because of the presence of Washington. Signifiers of African American culture appear throughout the film. Like the rest of society, African American culture has been torn apart, but it still exists in fragments that are as significant as the allusions to science fiction films, such as posters of *A Boy and His Dog* and *A Clockwork Orange*. For example, we see at one point a 1970s pinup poster of a black woman with an afro. One of the publications that Carnegie's men scavenges for him is an issue of *O: The Oprah Magazine*. Still surviving after the apocalypse is the image of Oprah Winfrey, which smiles back at us from the cover of the magazine. Most important, African American music has survived. Eli possesses what might be the last surviving MP3 player, and he listens ritually to Al Green's version of "How Can You Mend a Broken Heart?" George and Martha, the cannibalistic couple encountered by Eli and Solara, entertain them by playing Anita Ward's "Ring My Bell" on an old record player. These gestures, these references to African American cultural contributions and the continuing survival, or survivance, of black culture even in a fractured world are part of what makes *The Book of Eli* a post-soul Western.

One of the film's most important and most moving scenes consists of nothing more than a man listening to music. Eli takes shelter in an abandoned house, where he finds its most recent occupant dead, hanging from the rafters of an interior room. The dead man, apparently a suicide, ironically suggests safety—that Eli can take refuge here without worrying about a returning or hidden owner. After a dinner of freshly killed cat, Eli takes out his grime-covered MP3 player (with a screen warning of a low battery), puts in his earbuds, and listens to "How Can You Mend a Broken Heart?" The choice of song signifies in multiple ways, adding a sense of melancholy to the visual imagery of the solitary Eli, his only companion a mouse (with whom he ironically shares a bit of roasted cat), and suggesting the loneliness partially hidden by Eli's stoic demeanor. The lyrics of the song, placed in this postapocalyptic context, signify something larger than a failed romance and point to Eli's larger dilemma: How can one man mend an entire broken world?

The way this scene of listening is staged encourages the spectator's identification with Eli. Although we initially hear the music from an outside perspective, filtered and distorted as if being played through someone else's earbuds, the sound switches from diegetic to nondiegetic, and suddenly we are within the space of Eli's head, hearing the music as he hears it, as a sound that goes directly into our ears. As Eli goes through the nightly ritual of preparing for sleep—sharpening his machete, cleaning his gun, washing himself with a single sanitary wipe from a Colonel Sanders restaurant—we watch him do so as the song continues, with Green's voice rising and swelling to fill the space of the theater and seemingly the space of the abandoned house. We have a few external noises, the scrape of the whetstone against the machete, the tearing of paper as he opens the wipe, but those rhythmic noises merge with the rhythm of the song, fusing the two together. Although he only temporarily inhabits this space, Eli transforms it into home by playing music. The abandoned house filled with sound becomes the physical realization of the psychological experience of audiotopia. In a sense, every time Eli listens to this song, he creates a home space to inhabit, a friendly and familiar place, no matter what actual space he physically inhabits. Recalling earlier black films, this is also a moment when the story comes to a halt to showcase African American performance. For two minutes of screen time, both our hero and his story rest while he and we listen to Al Green, a utopian moment in a dystopian postapocalyptic landscape made possible by the total immersion into the sounds of black musical performance.

Although "How Can You Mend a Broken Heart?" is not a blues song as such (although the blues are definitely part of its genealogy), this is certainly a blues moment in the film, suggestive of what Graham Lock calls "Blutopia," which Kun explains as "a musical utopia that is 'tinged with the blues, an African-American visionary future stained with memories,' a musical utopia that envisions an alternate future without relinquishing the black past" (24). As Lock explains, "it is the refusal to forget its history that distinguishes Blutopia from other utopian futures" (3). In *The Book of Eli*, the black past comes to us most powerfully through Green's voice, which is not only a singular voice from a lost and destroyed world but representative of the survival of an entire musical tradition, as Green's performance of this song is situated solidly in an African American musical history that includes spirituals, gospel music, blues, and soul.

Kun observes that audiotopia is "a musical space of difference, where contradictions and conflicts do not cancel each other out but coexist and live through each other" (23). As a song written by a white songwriter (Barry Gibb) and performed by a black singer, "How Can You Mend a Broken Heart?" also exemplifies at the micro level what is taking place in the larger narrative, which is a white generic text that is in the process of being transformed by the African American performance of that text.[4] We have Western story directed by an African American directorial team and an identifiably Western hero performed by an African American actor. Washington's presence and performance suggest possible meanings and significations that would not exist had a white actor been cast in the role.⁵ Similarly, in realizing the written script in visual and auditory form, the Hughes Brothers make choices—the sounds of Al Green and Anita Ward, the visual allusions to African American print culture—that alter that script and ensure that the black past is represented and remembered in this American future. Although the film does not, like the civil rights Westerns of the 1960s, directly address issues of racial justice, it also does not forget the black past but incorporates that past into its vision of the future.

Although *Eli* does not explicitly comment on the black past of slavery in America, the film nonetheless carries reminders of that central trauma of African American history by drawing on elements of the slave narrative in telling its story. If nothing else, Eli's determined journey across America recalls earlier quests for the promised land of freedom from slavery, even if freedom is not Eli's specific goal. The most significant way that the film incorporates African American cultural tradition into its narrative is through what Henry Louis Gates Jr. calls the trope of the talking book, which first appears in James Albert Ukawsaw Gronniosaw's 1770 slave narrative. After observing his master praying over the Bible, the enslaved Gronniosaw places his ear to the book and, hearing no voices, concludes that the book refuses to speak to him because he is black. That variations of this scene subsequently appear in later slave narratives demonstrates that "even the earliest writers of the Anglo-African tradition read each other's texts and grounded these texts in what soon became a tradition" (Gates 131). The repetition of the trope signifies the establishment of a convention that is central to African American literature, one that reveals "the curious tension between the black vernacular and the literate white text, between the spoken and the written word, between the oral and the printed forms of literary discourse" (131). Both *Firefly* and *The Book of Eli* allude to this convention, but *The Book of Eli* represents the most extensive reconfiguring of this trope, making it an integral element of the film's remapping of the Western.

At the center of the movie is the Bible, the same book that in the slave narrative introduces the destabilizing influence of written culture to African identity. *Eli* plays with the tension between the oral text and the printed word, moving among tropes of speaking, listening, hearing, and writing and ultimately undermining the opposition between the oral text and printed word. Eli's nightly ritual involves both listening to music and reading the Bible (although not simultaneously), a dual practice that fuses—or at least juxtaposes—a black voice with the written word. Both of those rituals are important to sustaining Eli's mission. Eli's story also reverses the "figure of the Talking Book that fails to speak" to Gronniosaw (Gates 132). Gronniosaw observes that when his master reads, he moves his lips as if in conversation, inspiring Gronniosaw to open the book and wait for it to speak. When it does not, he moves his ear closer to the book to catch any snatches of voice that might come from it. According to Gates, "Gronniosaw can speak to the text only if the text first speaks to him," but "the text does not, not even in the faintest whisper" (137). As Gates describes the scene, "The book had no voice for Gronniosaw; it simply refused to speak to him, or with him. For Gronniosaw, the book—or, perhaps I should say, the very concept of 'book'—constituted a silent primary text, a text, however, in which the black man found no echo of his own voice" (136).

After Eli leaves the frontier town, he is followed by Solara, the daughter of the woman whom Carnegie is keeping as his "wife." Solara in a sense becomes Eli's disciple, and as he recites passages from the Bible to her, he also tells her the story of his relationship with the book he carries: "One day I heard a voice. I could hear it as clear as I'm talking to you. It led me to the place where I found this book, buried under some rubble. The voice told me to carry the book out West. I know what I heard. I know what I hear." In this version of the story of the talking book, the book not only speaks to the black figure, it speaks first. *Eli* takes the trope even further as Eli does more than gain mastery over the written word (the demonstration of such mastery being the signal achievement of the slave narrative's author). The book of the film's title refers, of course, to the book that Eli carries, but we eventually realize that the title refers to the character himself, as, finally, he *is* the book.

Chased by Carnegie and his henchmen, Eli is shot and left for dead, the book taken from him. Solara is taken captive, but she escapes and returns to try to save Eli, only to discover that his body is missing. She eventually finds him, still moving west, limping along the highway. Although Carnegie has the artifact, Eli still possesses the book, which he has committed to memory. When Eli and Solara finally reach the edge of the continent, they arrive at a colony on Alcatraz Island, which has become a repository for the world's remaining books. "We're going to teach people about the world they lost," Lombardi, the island's governor, tells them.[6] "Write down everything I say," Eli responds, "exactly as I say it." Not only does the book speak, but it speaks in Eli's voice. More than finding an echo of his own voice in the text, he becomes it, not just a black man to whom the book speaks but himself a talking black book. In a series of scenes that quietly allude to the earliest origins of African American writing, the "as told to" narratives of former slaves who recited their life stories to literate white writers, the dying Eli "reads" the Bible out loud to Lombardi, who transcribes his narration. The final images of the film evoke this key moment in the history of African American writing: a scene of a black speaker and white amanuensis. Although the words he speaks are not his own, they nonetheless tell the story of his life—of the thirty years of wandering through the wilderness and reading and committing to memory this text.

Eli transforms the written word into a spoken performance as he narrates for transcription the Bible from start to finish, a process that completely undermines the opposition between "the spoken and the written word, between the oral and the printed forms of literary discourse." In a final twist, we discover that Eli is blind and that his Bible has survived because it is written in braille, which Eli—but few other people—can read. With this particular version of the written word, the African American man is almost the only person alive who is literate in the form. At the end of the film, the positions of literate white master and illiterate black slave delineated in Gronniosaw's narrative are also inverted. The book will not speak to the white Carnegie, the film's villain. Although he touches the pages it with his fingers—a gesture that recalls Gronniosaw laying his face against the pages of his master's book—the book still refuses to give him the knowledge he seeks. The book speaks only to Eli, and he in turn becomes the voice of the book itself, enabling this primary text of Western culture to reenter history via a black voice. At the end of the film, Eli combines in his person two distinctively different narrative histories, as he is both the cowboy-hero of the Western and the talking book of the slave narrative.

Eli's journey west ends with the completion of his quest and finally his death. At the end of the film, Solara, his disciple and apprentice, becomes the gunfighter who takes his place. With Eli's machete and pistol strapped to her back and with his MP3 player plugged into her ears, Solara walks off alone into the—well, not the sunset, since she is as far west as she can go—sunrise, the visual imagery (if not the direction) returning us to the Western genre and to the traditional ending of the hero silhouetted against the sun.

★

Explicitly conceived as a "space Western," Joss Whedon's short-lived television series, *Firefly*, takes great pleasure in mixing and combining science fiction and Western tropes.[7] The *Firefly* series replaces the western frontier with the frontier of space but retains many elements of the genre Western, including train robberies and cattle rustling. As Fred Erisman writes, *Firefly* draws not only on the history of the Western genre but also on "a single Western classic, John Ford's *Stagecoach* (1939), to shape its structure and its nature" and as a source of character archetypes (249). Although they are traveling on a spaceship rather than a stagecoach, we have a similarly disparate set of travelers, with Malcolm Reynolds (Nathan Fillion) filling in for John Wayne's outlaw hero the Ringo Kid; *Serenity* pilot Wash (Alan Tudyk) for *Stagecoach*'s "serio-comic driver," Buck; Simon Tam (on the run with his sister, River, whom he has rescued from captivity, though at the hands of not "savages" but civilized authorities, the Alliance) for the doctor's role; Shepherd Book (Ron Glass) for Ford's Reverend Peacock; and, "in an especially telling reversal, the prostitute Dallas becomes Inara Serra (Morena Baccarin), a licensed and respected Companion . . . whose presence aboard the ship gives it" respectability rather than the air of notoriety and scandal Dallas brings to the stagecoach (Erisman 251). Several characters have "no direct counterparts"—ship engineer Kaylee (Jewel Staite), "muscleman" Jayne Cobb (Adam Baldwin), and, most important, *Serenity* first officer and former Independent forces sergeant under Captain Mal Reynolds (also her superior on *Serenity*), Zoë Washburne, played by Gina Torres, an American actress of Afro-Cuban descent (251). If Zoë has no counterpart in *Stagecoach*, it is because black women in general have no counterpart in *Stagecoach* or in almost any other Western. We might, however, trace her character's ancestry to other John Ford Westerns and to Woody Strode, one of the most familiar faces of the black cowboy in the 1960s.

Black characters are incorporated into *Firefly* in much the same way as in *Briscoe County, Jr.*, most notably with continuing characters Shepherd Book and Zoë Washburne but also by casting African American actors in major and minor guest roles, as in the episode "Objects in Space," with Richard Brooks as bounty hunter Jubal Early, a casting choice that may suggest a connection to such earlier black bounty hunters in Western television and film as Louis Gossett Jr. in *Alias: Smith and Jones*, Julius Carry's Lord Bowler, and Fred Williamson's Boss. In the Whedonverse, African American actors play a variety of roles on the continuum from "big damn heroes" (to quote Zoë) to villains. By including a variety of black characters played by talented and experienced African American actors, the series opens up a space for a character such as Early: a complex antagonist ably performed by an African American actor who, unburdened by the need to present a "positive image," creates in "Objects in Space" one of the most memorable and original villains in either the Western or the science fiction genre.

The contemporary multicultural and progressive politics that *Firefly* brings to the Western genre, however, conflicts with the conservative (often racist) politics that inform its closest generic precursors, "southern Westerns." In these Westerns, the cowboy-hero is often a former Confederate soldier and southerner—Yancy in *Cimarron*, Gil Favor in *Rawhide*. Deeply invested in the romance of the Lost Cause (and with some of the visual iconography of the Confederacy), *Firefly* wants to celebrate the former Confederate cowboy-hero of mid-twentieth-century Westerns and at the same time move beyond the politics associated with the Confederacy. Several moments throughout the series indicate that Whedon is aware of the ethical question of how to appropriate elements of these earlier Westerns without repeating their problematic politics. Most obviously, there is the decision to cast African American actors in major and supporting roles. The presence of black characters among the Independent troops visually asserts that this rebellion was not fought for the same reasons as the American Civil War. Also, references to slavery crop up with some frequency, sometimes as odd asides that seem to have little to do with the main plot. The purpose of those references seems to be to establish Mal's difference from the Confederate cowboys of earlier Westerns. In "Shindig," the opening fight scene is sparked by Mal's disdain for the group of slave traders with whom he is playing pool: "They earned [the money Mal steals from them] with the sweat of their slave-trading brows." Other episodes suggest a reversal of the historical Confederate and Union positions on slavery, with the Union/Alliance practicing a kind of enslavement of its subject citizens (if not actually supporting slavery as such) and the Confederates/Browncoats opposing any imposition on individual freedom. Mal's antipathy to slavery is further established later in "Shindig," when he comments to Inara, "You think following the rules will buy you a nice life, even if the rules make you a slave." In "Our Mrs. Reynolds," Zoë caustically comments to Mal, "Are you enjoying your own nubile little slave girl?" She seems to have chosen a comment that she knows will cut deeply: accusing Mal of being a slaveholder. The frequency of references to slavery indicates *Firefly*'s efforts to distance itself from the politics of earlier southern Westerns even as it appropriates the romantic appeal of the Lost Cause. As noted in chapter 6, *Firefly* is not the only Western series to have a troubled relationship with the genre's affection for the former Confederate cowboy-hero. If *Firefly* struggles to reconcile its love of the Lost Cause with the history of slavery that was part of that cause, it also follows its precursors in adapting a similar (not completely satisfactory) strategy for doing so—having one of its main characters express his abhorrence of slavery.

The central conflict in *Firefly*, as it often is in the Western, pits "civilization" against "savagery." As Richard Slotkin writes in *Gunfighter Nation: The Myth of the Frontier in Twentieth-Century America*, "The moral landscape of the Frontier Myth is divided by significant borders, of which the wilderness/civilization, Indian/White border is the most basic" (14). "Although the Indian and the Wilderness are the settler's enemy," Slotkin continues, "they also provide him with a new consciousness through which he will transform the world" (14). The myth's heroes "must therefore be 'men (or women) who know Indians'—characters whose experiences, sympathies, and even allegiances fall on both sides of the Frontier" (14). The heroes in *Firefly* are similarly located in the space between civilization and savagery. *Serenity* physically moves them between these positions, between the civilized and Alliance-affiliated core planets and the outer border planets on the edge of deep space, which are more primitive in their environments and sometimes only partially colonized, with frontier settlements that mix futuristic and nineteenth-century technologies—travel by horse and hovercraft existing side by side, for example. As in *Hell on Wheels*, the *Firefly* universe is a postbellum society still feeling the effects of a recently ended civil war, with, in *Firefly*'s case, the defeated rebels (the Independents) now under the control of an authoritative Alliance that is civilized to the point of totalitarianism. As is often the case in the frontier myth, civilization in *Firefly* is "corrupt," overcivilized, a place of "false values" that need to be "purged" if there is to be any hope that "a new, purified social contract [will be] enacted" (Slotkin 14).

Serenity itself serves as an in-between or third space for its travelers, providing a physical location for temporary and occasional utopian moments in the larger dystopian universe where the action takes place.[8] Individual characters aboard the ship represent different positions on a continuum between savagery and civilization, with the most civilized being the educated Shepherd Book and the highly educated Companion Inara (who in terms of conventional morality should be his opposite, but that is not the case in *Firefly*), and with Mal, Zoë, and Jayne, the former soldiers and mercenaries at the other end of the scale, associated as they are with violence and lawlessness. Within this third space, conflict and difference do not disappear (or are not erased by the homogenizing culture of the Alliance), and the creative tension that develops within the extended family of the crew ultimately suggests the possibility of an alternate form of civilization to what the Alliance offers.

The extremes of civilization and savagery that frame the *Serenity* crew are represented on the one side by the Alliance and on the other by the Reavers, a group of "nomadic, cannibal-scavengers" who, as Stanley C. Pelkey II observes, fulfill the "thematic and narrative functions of film Indians" (217). The Reavers "occupy the same conceptual space in the main characters' understanding of their social universe on the frontier as American Indians occupied in the minds of most white characters in countless Westerns" (217). As a savage threat, the Reavers may occupy the same "conceptual space" as the Hollywood Indian, but they are clearly established as differing significantly from American Indians. They are not indigenous to this region of space, nor are they a racially or ethnically specific group. They do, however, provide the frontier myth's representation of savagery in the *Firefly* universe. Although several episodes of *Firefly* use explicitly Western themes and Western mise-en-scènes ("Train Job" and "Heart of Gold," for example), in other episodes, *Firefly* maintains its sense of belonging to the Western by exploring the themes of the genre (such as its meditation on civilization and savagery) in more general ways without using concrete Western motifs (trains, desert landscapes, cattle, and so forth)—for example, through the presence of the Reavers.

In "Bushwhacked," the conflict between civilization and savagery is played out when *Serenity*'s crew is caught between a group of Reavers and an Alliance ship, both of which represent a danger to the crew. The core plot of "Bushwhacked" is identifiably Western: a group of settlers travels beyond civilization to set up a border colony and is attacked and massacred. The *Serenity* crew discovers the massacre when they board what they assume is a derelict ship on an illegal salvage mission. When the massacre is discovered, Jayne comments, "Reavers ain't men." He begins a conversation among the crew about the relationship between civilization and savagery and whether it is possible to go so far into savagery that one will not be able to come back. Shepherd Book says, "They are [men]. Too long removed from civilization perhaps." Mal answers, "Jayne's right. Reavers ain't men. They forgot how to be. They're just nothing. They got out to the edge of the galaxy, to that place of nothing, and that's what they became." The commentary on the Reavers also reflects the situation of the *Serenity* crew. How far to the edge of civilization can they go before reaching that "place of nothing"?

As the crew debates how to respond to their discovery of the massacre, Shepherd Book wants to return to the derelict to pray for the slaughtered humans: "How we treat our dead is part of what makes us different from those that did the slaughtering." Shepherd Book represents the values of civilization and morality, and the primary voicing of enduring human moral and ethical values in the episode issues from the body of a black man, inverting the frontier myth's more usual association of whiteness with civilization and any other race with savagery. This does not mean, however, that Book is a bland "positive" image of future blackness. If the members of the crew represent various qualities associated with either civilization or savagery, individual characters often suggest the same continuum within themselves. The civilized Book, we learn, may have a less-than-civilized past, and he consistently finds his values being tested and modified by life on the frontier. At the end of "Serenity, Parts 1 and 2," Book seeks out Inara, whose sexual openness is seemingly at odds with his vow of celibacy; however, he is searching for spiritual rather than physical solace. Book tells her, "I've been out of the abbey two days. I've beaten a lawman senseless. I've fallen in with criminals. I've watched the captain shoot a man I swore to protect. And I'm not even sure if I think he was wrong." In one of the series' many reversals and inversions of expectations, the prostitute hears the preacher's confession and sympathizes with his moral and spiritual dilemma.

Also, in casting African American Ron Glass as Shepherd Book, *Firefly*'s creators consciously or unconsciously, knowingly or unknowingly, evoke the central trope of black literary tradition: the talking book. Shepherd is quite literally a talking Book. Unlike the enslaved Gronniosaw, puzzled by the unfamiliar technology of printing, Shepherd has mastered the text that represents for Gronniosaw the justification for his enslavement. To master the book, in the slave narrative tradition, is to claim one's full humanity in a context that denies it. Shepherd is the crew's most eloquent speaker, the embodiment of literacy and civilization, the only member of the crew we see carrying or reading from a printed book. As is the case with Eli in *The Book of Eli*, this Book's dialogue often suggests an undermining of the difference between the oral and the written. "Book," he tells Kaylee in "Serenity, Part 1," "I'm called Book," and his only destination, he continues, is to "maybe bring the word to thems that need it told." Book both brings the (printed) word and speaks it.

Although Book is a character whose speech is touched with the same "border" colloquialisms and sentence constructions ("thems that need it told") shared by the whole crew, he emerges as the most literate character, the one who most frequently shares quotations from books—Sun Yu's writings on war and torture as well as the Bible. In "Heart of Gold," two of the sex workers ask Book to lead a prayer meeting for them, revealing that the last shepherd to pass through took out his payment in "trade" and then "only read the one passage." At the end of the episode, we see Book presiding over the burial of Nandi, his Bible held to his chest, presumably having read more than one passage. The religious service with Book at its center is an example of civilization imported to the frontier. Book, the most eloquent speaker in the series, the most prominent figure of literacy on the uncivilized frontier, brings the Word to those who need it throughout the series.

In a chapter of the anthology *Investigating* Firefly *and* Serenity, Laura L. Beadling points out *Firefly*'s "complex negotiations of gender and sexuality" (54). The female characters in the series are "complexly gendered," representative of "the most diverse, powerful, and interesting female characters on television" (55). In general, women have not fared well in Westerns. As Kerry Fine observes in her discussion of two television shows set in the contemporary American West, *In Plain Sight* and *Sons of Anarchy*, "Traditional depictions of heroic power in western literature and film suggest that heroic power is inherently masculine, a 'natural' attribute of men" (153). "In creating female characters who wield heroic power," *In Plain Sight* and *Sons of Anarchy* (as well as *Firefly*) call into question "the masculine nature of heroism" and redefine the "socially constructed terms of who is permitted to exercise that power" (153). Drawing on the work of developmental psychologist Kaj Björkqvist and his analysis of different types of aggression, Fine notes the distinction between "expressive aggression" (which is impulsive, emotional, and marked especially by anger but also encompasses self-defense) and "instrumental aggression," which is more calculated (155). These types of aggression have also been culturally gendered, with "expressive aggression" more "associated with feminine gender norms" (155). Instrumental aggression is "most explicitly linked with the masculine" and is often described as "cool"—that is, "formulated with forethought and carried out purposefully" (155). Because instrumental aggression is proactive (rather than reactive, as in the case of defensive action), "it fits neatly into the active/passive gender binary, solidifying its association with the masculine" (155). In *Firefly*, Mal uses instrumental aggression, but so does Zoë and other women the crew encounters, most explicitly Nandi, who owns a collection of guns that impresses Mal and that she uses to protect her business enterprise, an unlicensed brothel, when attacked.

In *Firefly*, the gendering of instrumental aggression is reversed in the portrayal of the two primary African American characters. Shepherd Book, who follows a peaceful path, is the more traditionally feminine of the two characters, his moments of violence usually defensive or constrained in some way (using a water cannon to defend Nandi's brothel from attackers, for example). Even when he uses instrumental aggression, as when he takes part in the operation to rescue the captain from Niska, he avoids killing but observes that the Bible "is somewhat fuzzier on the subject of kneecaps" ("War Stories"). In the cinematic African American West, black men are sometimes allowed to use instrumental violence (or, as is the case with Pompey in *The Man Who Shot Liberty Valance*, to threaten to use it), but an African American woman with a gun is indeed a rarity. In a nearly century-old tradition of African American western visual narratives, Zoë Washburne pretty much stands alone as a black woman who uses instrumental aggression.[9] In the portrayal of this character, creator Joss Whedon and actress Gina Torres have few female precursors on whom to build, so the characters played by Woody Strode become particularly important to consider as models. If Shepherd Book's connection to African American tradition is via the trope of the talking book, Zoë's connection is specific to the African American West and is revealed to us through a series of allusions to earlier African American performers.

While there are stereotypical elements to Strode's Pompey, the character departs in a number of ways from prior African American characters in mainstream Westerns. His placement in the kitchen of Hallie's restaurant suggests a stereotypical role—he is not even a cook, just kitchen help. And as an indication of the effectiveness of his performance, Pompey, the 6'5" Strode manages to make Pompey the most unobtrusive figure in most of his scenes, a sharp contrast to later film and television Westerns that emphasize Strode's dominating physical visual presence. In *Liberty Valance*, he is a sidekick of sorts to John Wayne's Tom Doniphon, but, unlike the hero/sidekick pairing of Wayne with Blue Washington in *Haunted Gold*, the story allows some ambiguity in portraying the relationship between Wayne and Strode. At times, Pompey seems to be Tom's servant or hired hand, but they share a living space on Tom's ranch, and the film suggests that the two men may be partners in that enterprise. Pompey's public displays of subservience may be an act—masking—for the sake of appearances to hide a more egalitarian friendship between the two men. When action is necessary, Pompey certainly drops any hint of subservience, saving Tom from a fire and providing him with the rifle he uses to kill Valance in the final confrontation. In contrast to most mainstream Westerns that have cast African Americans in subservient sidekick roles, *Liberty Valance* suggests a difference between Pompey's public persona and his private one.

Early in the film, Liberty Valance severely beats and whips Ranse Stoddard. When Valance discovers Ranse waiting tables in Hallie's restaurant, he takes the opportunity to cause more mischief, tripping Ranse as he walks past with a tray of food. Tom protects Ranse, standing between Ranse and Valance and his two men, with everyone except Ranse holding a gun. Valance comments, "Three against one," to which Tom replies, "My boy, Pompey. Kitchen door." Valance turns to look behind him, and the camera pans to show Pompey, rifle in the crook of his arm, framed by the kitchen doorway, face resolute, ready to fire. The simple sequence—the hero confronts a group of villains who appear to have him outnumbered and outpositioned but is saved when an ally (whom the hero expects but the audience does not) appears—is a common one in Westerns. In *Liberty Valance*, the surprise is not just the appearance of an ally with a gun but the fact that the armed man is Pompey, the subordinate black kitchen helper. Pompey doubles the surprise by appearing in both the unexpected place of the kitchen doorway (Valance clearly does not expect any trouble from the "womanly" kitchen help) and in the unexpected role of gun-toting Western hero, sights trained on the villains (particularly since the villains are white).

We see variations of this scene throughout *Firefly*. Although this conventional sequence is not original to *Liberty Valance*, the two are connected by the surprising appearance of the black individual with a gun—with Zoë as the hidden black presence backing up Mal's play. In "Train Job," Mal goes to an Alliance bar on Unification Day, basically to pick a fight. "Tell me that to my face," he tells the Alliance patriot who is muttering insulting words about the Independents. When the man does so, Mal comments, "I just wanted you to turn around so she could get behind you." A surprise to both the audience and the Alliance patriot,

Zoë suddenly appears and pops him in the head with the stock of her gun. Not only does Zoë use instrumental violence, she also, like many male Western heroes, gets involved in completely gratuitous violence—joining the barroom brawl with great relish (and success). In "Safe," a hidden Zoë fires a rifle to protect Mal and Jayne during a gunfight resulting from a cattle deal gone wrong. Stepping out into a clear area in a grove of trees, the framing even recalls the similar moment in *Liberty Valance*, replicating the frame-within-a-frame composition. At the beginning of "Our Mrs. Reynolds," where Mal (disguised as a woman) and Jayne pretend to be settlers on a horse-drawn barge to lure outlaws, the editing suggests the reveal of Pompey in the *Liberty Valance* sequence—a quick cut to Zoë, hidden at the back of the barge and leaning out, rifle draped over one arm. She then shoots the outlaw who has a bead on Mal. Of course, in the *Firefly* universe, a black man or woman holding a gun on a white man is not necessarily a cause for surprise (as it would have been in 1962, when *Liberty Valance* premiered), and Zoë goes much further than Pompey ever does by firing at and killing bad guys. Jayne and Zoë sometimes switch places, with Jayne taking the role of hidden backup and Zoë accompanying Mal as one of the "big damn heroes" at the forefront of the action rather than behind the scenes. The positioning of Zoë and Jayne depends on situational strategy rather than the contingencies of racial or gender politics.

Like Strode, Torres is a physically striking presence. At 5'10", Torres, especially when wearing combat boots, is as tall as (or taller) than anyone else on-screen. Zoë's husband, Wash, often trails behind her when she enters a scene, his sometimes stoop-shouldered stance making him seem diminutive compared to her. The episode "War Stories," which plays on Wash's occasional masculine insecurity, best illustrates Zoë's use of instrumental violence in the series. With both the captain and Wash captured by Niska, Zoë takes over command, putting together and delivering ransom money to retrieve the men and aggressively interrupting Niska with a sharp "Him!," indicating Wash, when Niska attempts to force her to choose which of the two men to save. When she returns to *Serenity*, she tells the crew, "We're going to get the captain. You let me lead. Cover my back." "If it moves," she tells them, "shoot it." Armed with multiple weapons, including pistols, a rifle, and grenades, Zoë leads the group to the captain, killing at least half a dozen of Niska's men in the process. "Formulated with forethought and carried out purposefully," the raid demonstrates instrumental violence.

If scenes involving Zoë sometimes recall Pompey's scenes in *Liberty Valance*, the series also uses props to further draw out the connection between Zoë and other Western characters Strode played. Like Strode's gunfighter at the beginning of *Once upon a Time in the West* and other black westerners in TV and film, Zoë's weapon of choice is a mare's leg pistol (a rifle with the barrel and stock shortened) holstered to her leg. The connection between Zoë and Lord Bowler is particularly close because *Firefly* uses two of the same prop guns as *Briscoe County, Jr.*—Bowler's modified shotgun and the mare's leg pistol used by Sheena Easton when she guest starred as another bounty hunter. Although Eli's primary weapon in *The Book of Eli* is a machete, he also follows Lord Bowler in carrying a similarly modified shotgun on his back. Zoë's weapons in *Firefly* suggest a direct link to the specific history of the portrayal of the black cowboy in the film and television Western. The repeated use of this particular type of weapon for black cowboys suggests film and television artists' awareness of that history and has resulted in the development of a weapons convention specific to the tradition of the African American Western, a tradition that seems to have originated with Strode's performance in *Once upon a Time in the West*.

American racial formations, destroyed perhaps with everything else on "Earth that was" in the distant past, do not seem to operate in the *Firefly* universe. Or, more accurately, since this universe does not exist but was created by people who are very much part of the "Earth that is," the imagined universe of *Firefly* suggests a possible future that has moved beyond current social formulations, even as that future mirrors back to us (and cannot help but do so) a distorted reflection of the current historical moment that produced it. At the very least, *Firefly*'s universe suggests that race—specifically, whether one's ancestry is European or African— and gender do not predetermine one's place on the civilization/savagery continuum.[10] There are no African Americans in *Firefly*'s world because there is no Africa and no America. However, *Firefly*'s black frontiersmen and frontierswomen are not raceless westerners as such, as the series suggests a continued connection and belonging to "Earth that was," to the "talking book" of the slave narrative. *Firefly* also demonstrates its connection to the specific history of the "genre that was," the Western, and the series uses allusions to specific portrayals of the African American West in television and film to suggest an affiliation with the history of the black westerner in film. Through *Firefly*, Whedon has created not only an entertaining television series but also a genre history that includes elements of the genre, such as African American cowboys, that have been forgotten by most academic studies of the Western.

Conclusion

The D Is Silent

Accompanied by both praise and criticism, *Django Unchained* (2012), director Quentin Tarantino's twin homage to the blaxploitation film and the spaghetti Western, opened strongly on Christmas Day and will likely become the most profitable and popular story of the African American West since *Blazing Saddles*. Even though the film has a historical setting in the nineteenth-century past, in style and approach it is very much what Neil Campbell calls a post-Western—particularly in its self-reflective "poaching and borrowing" from Westerns and from other film genres ("Post-Western" 409). As is the case with *The Big Lebowski*'s opening sequence of a tumbleweed tumbling toward contemporary Los Angeles, *Django Unchained* similarly uses its first scene deliberately to jar our expectations (413). The film opens with reassuring clichés of "west-ness": the sight of men on horseback moving through a desert landscape, the splashy bold red letters of the title sequence (an homage to the spaghetti Western).[1] What takes us beyond the expectations suggested by these conventions is the unexpected presence of a coffle of enslaved black men, their movements restricted by their chains. Placed within a typical Western mise-en-scène (men on horseback, a desert landscape), we have the atypical presence of slavery—men in chains, their backs visibly scarred from whippings.

The opening scene of *Django Unchained* provides in quick visual form a microcosm of the film's genre innovation—its "poaching and borrowing" from two seemingly incompatible sources, the genre Western and the story of slavery. As an explicit commentary on the American institution of slavery, *Django Unchained* is very much a civil rights Western or perhaps a civil rights post-Western. Its political philosophy is drawn from the civil rights and Black Power movements of the 1960s and 1970s (or, rather, those movements as refracted through the lens of the blaxploitation film and as interpreted through Tarantino's unique filmmaking and writing sensibilities), and its aesthetic philosophy is distinctively post-Western in its "deliberate jarring of expectations," its explicit drawing of attention to its own acts of "poaching and borrowing" from other films (413, 409).

Among the enslaved men in the coffle is Django (played by Jamie Foxx). Django is rescued/purchased by bounty hunter King Schultz (Christoph Waltz), who realizes that Django can identify three wanted men. When Django aides Schultz in killing the three men (and collecting the bounty on them), Schultz offers to buy Django's freedom and take him on as a partner. The first half of the film is the story of that partnership. In the second half of the film, Schultz and Django infiltrate the Mississippi plantation of Calvin Candie (Leonardo DiCaprio) to free Django's wife, Broomhilda (Kerry Washington). The expected showdown (or, rather, showdowns, with each one progressively more over the top—more bodies, more blood, more explosive violence—than its predecessor) occurs, and the film ends as a Western should, with the captive released, the hero triumphant, and the villain defeated.

Django Unchained draws on multiple sources, including Sergio Leone's *Dollars* trilogy, especially *For a Few Dollars More* (with its plot involving two rival bounty hunters, Clint Eastwood and Lee Van Cleef, who become partners). The immediate predecessor is director Sergio Corbucci's *Django* (1966), from which *Unchained* gets its title character's name and theme song (and a cameo by original *Django* actor Franco Nero) and which perhaps inspires the appearance in *Unchained* of a proto–Ku Klux Klan group of hood-wearing vigilantes (though in the first movie, the hoods are red). *Unchained* was influenced in general by the violent blaxploitation and blaxploitation-related films of the 1970s, but the most specific film of that era referenced by *Unchained* is *The Legend of Nigger Charlie*, which starred Fred Williamson (but did not include his involvement as a director or screenwriter). *The Legend of Nigger Charlie* follows a narrative path out of the South and into the West, out of shackles and onto horseback. Its climactic battles and showdowns take place in identifiably western settings such as the frontier saloon. *Django Unchained* revises *The Legend of Nigger Charlie* by reversing that trajectory, beginning in the West and traveling back to the South.

That *Django Unchained* effectively conjoins a story of slavery with a Western plot of rescue from captivity, vengeance, and regeneration through violence suggests the surprising affinity between the distinctively American genres of the slave narrative and the Western. African American writers have long been aware of those affinities and have experimented extensively with combining the two forms, but *Django Unchained* represents an unusual willingness to engage in such experimentation in a mainstream big budget film—a major studio release opening on Christmas Day. In contrast to most other mainstream visual narratives that depict the African American West, *Django Unchained* places the Western in the unexpected place of the world of southern slavery, rather than (or in addition to) placing an African American character in the unexpected place of the Western.[2] Because of that unexpected juxtaposition, *Django Unchained* has the potential to move us "into a space of reflection, a critical dialogue with the form, its assumptions and histories," particularly in terms of the twentieth-century Western's romance with the southern cowboy-hero, the former Confederate soldier set loose on the western frontier (Campbell, "Post-Western" 414). In *Unchained*, the southerner remains the villain, without the redemption of a sudden change of heart about slavery that we see with countless other southern cowboy-heroes. The slavery plot also suggests *Django Unchained*'s affinity with the civil rights Western, as the film's explicit depiction of the realities of slavery serves as a protest against the whitewashing of that history in both the southern Western and American cultural memory in general.

In his discussion of blaxploitation films, Mikel J. Koven observes "a distinct difference between the images of African-Americans when directed by white filmmakers and when directed by black filmmakers" (14). "This is not to say," Koven comments, "that black filmmakers never pandered to white stereotypes, nor that white filmmakers are necessarily insensitive to black representation," but "certain differences" nonetheless appear (10–11). One difference between *Django Unchained* and other narratives of the African American West is the film's relationship to both African American tradition in general and the African American Western specifically. Although *Django Unchained* has clear connections to earlier African American Westerns, those connections seem to have developed logically from the situation of placing an African American character in a Western plot rather than from any extensive awareness of that tradition by writer-director Tarantino, who seems completely unaware that such a tradition exists and who, if we take him at his word (not always a wise thing to do with filmmakers or writers), believes that he has invented the African American Western (which he calls a "new, virgin-snow kind of genre") with *Unchained* (McGrath). Most of the narratives I have examined here (even television series involving white writers and directors such as *Briscoe County* and *Firefly*) have suggested some sensitivity not only to the specific history of the representation of the African American

West but also more generally to African American cultural and literary tradition. *Django Unchained* does not. To borrow Koven's comment on Jim Brown's *Take a Hard Ride*, "this is not to say the film isn't a cracker of a spaghetti western," but it is to draw a distinction between Tarantino's African American Western and the other narratives examined in this book (141). For example, another generic hybrid of blaxploitation and spaghetti Western, Mario Van Peebles's *Posse*, contains multiple references and allusions to the African American West, particularly in its closing montage, which combines historical photographs (including images of Nat Love) and clips from earlier Westerns featuring African American actors. Such references are absent from *Unchained*.

Although some moments in *Django Unchained* do suggest allusions to 1970s African American Westerns, those moments are relatively few (especially in comparison to the multiple allusions to spaghetti Westerns), and most involve references to one film, *The Legend of Nigger Charlie*.[3] That as vociferous a film buff as Tarantino seems mostly unaware of prior civil rights Westerns says much about the sad state of general knowledge about the African American West. That lack of awareness has been replicated in much of the popular and critical response to the film. Multiple *Blazing Saddles/Django Unchained* mashups have appeared on YouTube, but nothing thus far has appeared combining, for example, *Unchained* and *Posse*, *Unchained* and *Buck and the Preacher*, or *Unchained* and *Sergeant Rutledge*.

The critical response (in the form of film reviews) to *Django Unchained* has followed a similar path, emphasizing the novelty of Tarantino's approach. Reviewing the film for the *New York Times*, A. O. Scott writes, "But in placing his story of righteous payback in the Old South rather than the Wild West, and in making its agent a black former slave, Mr. Tarantino exposes and defies an ancient taboo. With the brief and fascinating exception of the blaxploitation movies and a few other works of radical or renegade art, vengeance in the American imagination has been the virtually exclusive prerogative of white men. More than that, the sanctification and romanticization of revenge have been central to the ideology of white supremacy. . . . The idea that regenerative violence could be visited by black against white instead of the reverse—that a man like Django could fill out the contours of the hunter—has been almost literally unthinkable." Rather than being "literally unthinkable," this idea has been thought again and again in African American literature and film, even if this tradition of the African American Western and of African American adaptation of the myth of regenerative violence remains invisible or perhaps, like the *D* in Django's name, silent. Even more accurately, it is a tradition that has been vocal but unheard because we have not been listening. Many of the elements Tarantino introduces in his version of the black Western have been there before, including the bounty hunter as a specifically African American Western archetype.[4] Likewise, we have seen the representation of the Ku Klux Klan (or its stand-in white vigilante groups) again and again in frontier narratives as the "savage" enemy that civilized African Americans must defeat. The inversion of the frontier myth's racial categorization of savagery and civilization and the reversal of the trope of regenerative violence have been staples of the African American Western from at least as early as Pauline Hopkins's novel, *Winona: A Tale of Negro Life in the South and the Southwest*, and such inversions have been repeated elements of films from Micheaux's *The Symbol of the Unconquered* in 1920 to *Buck and the Preacher* in 1972. Ishmael Reed's *Yellow-Back Radio Brokedown*, Pearl Cleage's *Flyin' West*, Percival Everett's *Wounded*, and David Anthony Durham's *Gabriel's Story*, along with many other literary examples, have thought the unthinkable by imagining their African American protagonists as the agents rather than the objects of regenerative violence.[5]

The joining of the frontier narrative to the slave narrative is at least as old as John Marrant's *A Narrative of the Lord's Wonderful Dealings with John Marrant, a Black* (1785).[6] The explicit joining of a commentary on slavery with Western tropes to make a southern Western is perhaps most fully realized in *Winona*, which, like *Django Unchained*, sets its story against the backdrop of the Civil War. For that matter, the 1960s television series *Daniel Boone* joins slave narrative and frontier narrative in multiple episodes involving fugitive slaves making their way to freedom, often with Boone's assistance. In the episode "Mother Cooper" (which originally aired on 5 February 1970), *Daniel Boone* even offers a plot similar to *Django Unchained*, only the escaped slave returns south to free his mother rather than his wife. In "Mother Cooper," Daniel Boone (Fess Parker) plays the King Schultz role to Gabe Cooper's Django, accompanying him on a journey out of Kentucky to a plantation on the other side of the Cumberland Gap. There, Gabe (Rosey Grier) finds his dying mother (played by singer Ethel Waters), and he and Daniel help her achieve her final wish—to die on free land. In contrast to *Django Unchained*, which centers on the masculine story of rescue and revenge, *Daniel Boone* shifts the narrative focus to the "captive," to Rachael (Mother Cooper), after the male rescuers have arrived at the plantation. Rachael's realization of the desire to be on free land, and not the masculine narrative of rescue, drives the second part of the episode. At no point does *Django Unchained* similarly shift its point of view from the male protagonists to Broomhilda.

Although his devotion to his wife, Broomhilda, suggests a connection to family and home that has not been completely severed, the first half of *Django* follows what Quintard Taylor has called the "stereotype of the black westerner as a solitary figure loosened from moorings of family, home, and community" (22). Even when Django goes to rescue his wife, the story remains focused on his individual actions, and even if Django acts in defense of an African American home life, the film gives little sense that Django acts on behalf of or in concert with an African American community. With the exception of Stephen (Samuel L. Jackson), who emerges as Django's antagonist rather than an ally, the other enslaved men and women primarily watch the action from the sidelines (or serve as a means of depicting the brutality of slavery—as victims of white violence). In contrast to the Fred Williamson Westerns (including both *Nigger Charlie* films), which emphasize not only the Williamson character's individual heroism but also his leadership role in bringing together a multiracial group of people to oppose the villains, *Django Unchained* primarily celebrates individual violence and vengeance. Although far above these earlier films in terms of production values (and budget), *Django Unchained* is arguably not as innovative or as politically charged in its imagining of an African American western as the Williamson films, a possibility that has escaped most reviewers of *Django*, who seem unaware of the prior existence of African American Western narratives.

Without a critical awareness of the genre of the African American Western in which *Django Unchained* participates, it is difficult to see what the film accomplishes and what it does not accomplish. Using a research tool no more arcane than the Internet Movie Database (IMDb.com), it is absurdly easy to locate dozens of examples of Westerns featuring African American actors and characters. Following Tarantino's lead (his claim of striking out into virgin territory with *Django*), early reviews of the film suggest a too ready willingness to attribute to a white screenwriter and director a generic innovation that African American writers and filmmakers have been creatively inventing and reinventing for centuries. Both African American participation in the history of settling the American West and African American participation in the genres of the Western and the frontier narrative have been ongoing, yet in terms of both actual history and genre history, we seem continually to forget that participation.

Moreover, we seem so certain that the African American westerner does not exist that we fail even to make a cursory search for that presence.

At the 2012 Western Literature Association conference, Kalenda Eaton made a similar observation as part of a panel discussion on the African American West. Eaton's presentation, "I Wish They All Could Be Calafía Girls: Black Women and California's Cultural Mythology," examined contemporary writing about California by African American women (especially Octavia Butler's *Kindred*, another combination of slave and frontier narratives that adds science fiction to the mix). Eaton placed her analysis in the context of Garci Rodríguez de Montalvo's *Las Sergas de Esplandián* (1492–1506), and specifically that text's story of the black Queen Calafía. Eaton argues that *Las Sergas de Esplandián* is "a foundational text within Black diasporic and literary studies" and that Queen Calafía (whose name and kingdom, the Island of California, provide the state with its name) is a foundational figure for African American women's writing about California: an "independent, powerful, single, and willful image introduced" in Rodríguez de Montalvo's epic whose model is observable in contemporary fiction. However, as Eaton notes, "While even preliminary research uncovers Calafía's role of inspirational 'mother,' from which California receives its name and legacy, yet her presence (literary or otherwise) is largely unknown." As is the case with many figures related to the African American West who are similarly hidden in plain sight, Calafía is silent only because we are not listening, invisible only because we fail to see her even when we look right at her. Those black western presences remain unknown in contemporary cultural memory.

As Taylor observes, despite recent interest in acknowledging and documenting the history of the black West, "we still know woefully little about large areas of the African American past in this region" (23). In his introduction to *Jennie Carter: A Black Journalist of the Early West*, Eric Gardner notes that "Carter's life and work call on us to begin to reexamine just what the 'literary West' and the 'black West' might mean" (xxviii). Such a reexamination hinges on an expanded notion of the literary that goes beyond traditional genres. Developing an accurate picture of the African American West requires us to acknowledge the intellectual and aesthetic value of multiple types of documents and narratives, both on the page and on the screen. "If we are to have a fuller sense of black women, black literature, and the black West," Gardner continues, "we need to use the archive more and to build that archive into something much more widely accessible" (xxxi). *Hoo-Doo Cowboys and Bronze Buckaroos* sketches out a framework of what types of materials might comprise such an expanded archive of the African American West. Among others whose scholarship often focuses on the African American West, Gardner's work on nineteenth-century black-audience periodicals, Eaton's work on Calafía, Blake Allmendinger's *Imagining the African American West* (especially the chapters on California writers and on women writers), and Emily Lutenski's work on Harlem Renaissance writers in the regional context of the Mexico-U.S. borderlands suggest further ways of building that archive, especially in terms of black women's western experiences and representations of African American western women. As that archive is expanded and made more accessible, as scholars continue to develop conceptual frameworks for understanding the material collected in that archive, we will begin to have a fuller picture of how the African American West has been experienced, imagined, and performed.

Notes

INTRODUCTION

1. To these works written by individual critics, we might add anthologies such as *African Americans on the Great Plains: An Anthology* (2009), edited and with an introduction by Bruce A. Glasrud and Charles A. Braithwaite, and *The Harlem Renaissance in the American West* (2012), edited by Glasrud and Cary D. Wintz, which include a mix of history, biography, and literary criticism. In addition, Daniel Moos's *Outside America: Race, Ethnicity, and the Role of the American West in National Belonging* (2005) includes important chapters on Oscar Micheaux's South Dakota memoirs and novels (and provides one of the most comprehensive overviews available of Micheaux's entire literary output) and on African American "self-published" Western narratives (including discussions of the work of Micheaux, Nat Love, Thomas Detter, and Robert Ball Anderson). Anthologies of primary texts such as Gardner's *Jennie Carter: A Black Journalist of the Early West* (2007) and Cynthia Davis and Verner D. Mitchell's *Western Echoes of the Harlem Renaissance: The Life and Writings of Anita Scott Coleman* (2008) also contain useful critical overviews of the lives and works of those particular African American western writers.

2. For an anthology of Coleman's fiction, nonfiction, and poetry, see her *Western Echoes of the Harlem Renaissance*.

3. The field of Oscar Micheaux criticism, especially criticism related to his films, has developed significantly. Recent work such as Bowser and Spence's *Writing Himself into History* and Patrick McGilligan's biography of Micheaux have recognized and effectively explained the complexity of the racial portrayals in both his films and his novels.

4. For a discussion of the visual imagery, including a series of pen-and-ink drawings, that illustrates *The Life and Adventures of Nat Love*, see Speirs.

CHAPTER 1

1. As Abbott and Seroff write in *Ragged but Right*, "*The Freeman* is a truly remarkable document of black professional stage activity, far-reaching, insightful, and uniquely representative of the thoughts and opinions of black musicians and performers. By the end of the nineteenth century, it had become a clearinghouse for black entertainment news" (4).

2. In *On the Real Side*, Mel Watkins relates a story that illustrates how minstrel expectations played out in real life:: "On at least two occasions, groups of white men [in Mississippi] detained [Watkins's father] and insisted that he dance for them. In one

instance, his hesitation prompted them to draw their pistols and fire at his feet. When I first heard this story, I associated it only with those Western movies in which villains amused themselves by terrorizing some innocent *white* victim while firing at his feet and yelling, 'Dance!' [Watkins's father's ordeal] reflects how deeply and pervasively minstrelsy's stereotype of the happy-go-lucky, dancing black Sambo had influenced Americans" (102). Watkins's telling of the story and his recognition of the distinctively Western movie element of it suggest that the incident also reveals a particularly unfortunate combination of two popular culture forms in the perpetrators' minds.

3. As Mel Watkins points out, minstrelsy endured long past the end of the nineteenth century: "According to Joseph Boskin, 'every city, town, and rural community had amateur minstrel groups' at the turn of the century. Citing the distribution of minstrel songs and scripts by the federal government as late as World War II . . . and even isolated performances by local amateur groups in small towns as late as 1970, Boskin contends that minstrelsy persisted until at least midcentury" (99).

4. African American performers also entered into popular culture representations of the American West through traveling Wild West shows. As Christine Bold notes, the participation of the African American Ninth and Tenth Cavalry in the Spanish-American War, especially the famous Theodore Roosevelt–led battles in Cuba, was restaged as part of the Buffalo Bill's Wild West Show in 1899. "It was in this context," Bold writes, "that black veterans performed themselves, bivouacking in Cuba and then storming San Juan Hill. While the African-Americans were not exactly stars of the event, the program did draw attention to them through its illustrations and its text" (290). However, as black participation in the famous battle was increasingly expunged from contemporary accounts, "All mention of black soldiers disappeared" from Wild West Show reenactments after 1902 (291). Black performers nonetheless remained part of various Wild West shows, increasingly so by 1910 as black musical performance grew in popularity. Rather than appearing in the central spectacles, however, black performers were relegated to the sideshow tents (as was the case with circuses). "Out of sight and seemingly invisible to historians," Abbott and Seroff note in *Ragged but Right*, black performers were hard at work in a variety of Wild West shows and were very visible to the readers of the *Indianapolis Freeman*, which "published reports from black bands and minstrels in the sideshows of the original Buffalo Bill Wild West Show, Miller's 101 Ranch Shows, Kit Carson's Buffalo Ranch Show, Young Buffalo's Show, Circle D Wild West, and Old Buffalo Wild West Show, among others" (183). For a more complete overview of African American performers in traveling Wild West shows, see Abbott and Seroff 183–200.

5. Mark Berresford summarizes Lowery's importance to early twentieth-century black music: "Of the many black circus and concert bands working in the early years of the century, that of cornet virtuoso Perry George Lowery (1870–1942) was the best known and the most highly regarded. The Lowery band's repertoire, in common with other circus sideshow bands, ran the whole gamut of orchestral music, circus overtures, operatic arias, marches, concert arrangements of popular tunes of the day, and orchestral ragtime. Lowery, who was the first African American graduate of the Boston Conservatory of Music, was a friend of Scott Joplin, and from relatively early in Joplin's career championed his compositions" (29).

6. In a study of western newspapers of the late nineteenth and early twentieth centuries, Gayle K. Berardi and Thomas W. Segady observe that the reportage in those papers "tended to be highly selective, reflecting racial and ethnic biases within the rapidly growing towns" (225). Western newspapers rarely reported on the activities of African American citizens; when such stories appeared, they emphasized "negative characteristics" (fighting, drinking, and so forth), especially violent crime (226). In this regard, both the Greenwood County, Kansas, and Meagher County, Montana, newspapers seem to have been quite exceptional in their interest in the everyday activities of their black residents and in the lack of negative stereotyping in their reporting.

7. We see a similar strategy taking place in Kansas. As Clifford Edward Watkins writes, in July 1895, Lowery and his stepbrother, E. O. Green, on break from their touring duties with the Nashville Students, appeared "at a benefit concert for the Eureka community band: 'The proceeds of the concert will be applied toward the purchase of instruments and uniforms'" (24).

8. Early in the twentieth century, antiblack laws began to catch up with the black residents of western states. By 1910, Montana in particular had started to become a much less inviting place for African Americans. As western territories applied for statehood, they often adapted state constitutions that included some of the same restrictive laws against black participation in civic life (such as grandfather laws restricting voting rights) that were common in other states. The 1910 census recorded the high point of African American residency in Montana, with the state's black population rapidly declining thereafter.

9. The opening of public space to black participation in performance did not necessarily extend to other areas of the public sphere, nor did that participation necessarily extend equally to all African American citizens. The Lowerys maintained a cemetery on their land in part to provide a burial place for the local black community, which was excluded from the segregated Reece Cemetery (C. E. Watkins 8). Although Mary Lowery, P. G.'s stepmother, was apparently buried in Reece, full participation in the rights of citizenship was the exception rather than the rule, as the cemetery "was generally reserved for whites" (9). The antislavery egalitarianism of Greenwood County also eroded in the twentieth century, giving way before the rise of active racist organizations in the county and to a wave of antiblack sentiment throughout the American West (6).

10. For Houston A. Baker Jr., the manipulation of the minstrel mask is an essential component of modernist African American literature and culture: "The mastery of the minstrel mask by blacks . . . constitutes a primary move in Afro-American discursive modernism" (quoted in Grandt 134).

11. As Abbott and Seroff note in *Ragged but Right*, "The comedian-producers of the big shows weaned mainstream audiences away from the crude character delineations of nineteenth-century minstrelsy and conditioned them to appreciate verisimilitude in black comedy representations. 'Natural expression' in racial caricature became the cutting edge of black comedy. Still in blackface makeup, black comedians dared to bring forth modern, recognizable characters who spoke directly to black audiences, creating a revolutionary dynamic that became a cornerstone of twentieth-century African American minstrelsy and vaudeville" (81).

12. According to Sotiropoulos, the coon song craze began in 1896 with the publication of Ernest Hogan's "All Coons Look Alike to Me" and Ben Harney's "Mister Johnson Turn Me Loose" (89). The vast majority of coon songs "used some amount of dialect, syncopation, and reference to black stereotype," and they initially were popular with both black and white audiences, with the terms *coon song* and *ragtime* used interchangeably at the turn of the century (90). By 1910, the dominance of white-authored coon songs and white racists' adoption of the word *coon* as a pejorative had turned most of the African American audience away from the genre. However, "by the end of the first decade of the twentieth century well over six hundred 'coon' songs had been produced, selling in the millions of copies" (90). For a description of the differences between white-authored and black-authored coon songs, see Sotiropoulos 89–105.

13. In addition to incidents of racism, minstrel and sideshow travel was a decidedly dangerous business. The *Indianapolis Freeman* frequently reports on various mishaps such as train accidents, windstorms causing havoc with canvas tents, fires, and other types of misadventure. Lowery trombonist Earl Granstaff reported to the *Freeman* that when the Hagenbeck-Wallace Circus played Lowery's hometown in 1914, a mishap nearly ended Lowery's life and career: "The parade had just left the lot, and for some reason or other, it stopped, leaving the back wheels of our band wagon on a short bridge. The bridge gave way so quick that it threw P. G. who was sitting on the right part, out over the side of the wagon and down into the creek, a distance of 20 feet, on his head and shoulders. We picked him up almost unconscious and he was hurried to the nearest doctor in an automobile" (quoted in Abbott and Seroff 198).

14. Whitney also demonstrates his mastery of classical rhetoric, employing the three Aristotelian appeals in his argument: ethos (credibility as well as an appeal to shared values: "fairplay"); pathos (emotion, in this case, humor); logos (the appeal to reason).

15. The "something told me" phrase pops up in *Father of the Blues* as it does in *Born to Be*. However, in Handy's work, the phrase seems to imply only "my intuition told me." In *Born to Be*, the phrase is more significant in part as a result of sheer repetition and in part because of incidents when the information that is imparted by "something" to Gordon seems to come from outside his own knowledge base. There are also incidents when the aid he receives seems to take the form of supernatural possession or at least is described in ways that recall voodoo possession—he is mounted by a spirit. At one point, Gordon gets a job for the U.S. government returning a mental patient to his home in the West Indies. After their arrival in Barbados, authorities "locked me up, and the crazy man, too" (153). After getting himself and his charge out of prison, Gordon has further trouble trying to secure the man's finances, and after writing a letter in support of the man's cause, Gordon finds himself in danger of being arrested for practicing law without a license. The solicitor "asked me where I had been and if they still burned my kind in Mississippi: he said he could well understand the reason why" (157). Gordon notes, "I was handicapped. I didn't want to let him know my real speed by cussing . . . and cussing words were my best way of expressing myself, verbs and adjectives" (157). However, "right out of a clear sky phrases came to me that got [the hotel manager] laughing," and before long, the three are drinking beer and smoking cigars together (157). Again, in a moment of danger, Gordon seems to be

aided by a supernatural force that, in this case, speaks through Gordon with phrases that come not from Gordon's own mind but from "a clear sky."

16. Legends associated with Elegba have migrated with various groups of African people. The deity Eshu is his equivalent among the Yoruba. In Haitian culture, he is known as Papa Legba.

17. The "commentator" here may be Whitney, referring to himself in the report in third person, as Whitney was frequently the correspondent for the Smart Set.

18. Gardner locates his *Unexpected Places* in a group of similar scholarly projects that he labels "the 'new regionalism' in nineteenth-century African American studies," an approach to African American literature that is as attentive to the local as to the national, that moves beyond the focus in African American studies on single-author books to look more broadly at the available archive of literary material (especially periodical writing), and that emphasizes looking for places beyond the expected urban centers where black writing has flourished (12). *Unexpected Places* "emphasizes placing African American culture and literature more complexly, with more awareness of the ways in which specific locations shaped enactions of African American-ness" (13).

19. My analysis of "The St. Louis Blues" focuses on the lyrics. The musical elements of the composition, however, similarly draw on and combine multiple influences. As Jürgen E. Grandt points out in *Shaping Words to Fit the Soul*, the song's "embellishments included the middle section in what Handy calls a tango rhythm, for which he drew on a more recent sojourn to Cuba. Mapping what Paul Gilroy almost a century later would influentially dub 'the Black Atlantic,' the classically trained Hardy avers that '[a]ltogether, I aimed to use all that is characteristic of the Negro from Africa to Alabama' in 'St. Louis Blues'" (79). My interpretation of the song suggests that we extend our understanding of Handy's mapping beyond the east coast of "the Black Atlantic" and follow the path the song sketches out of "Alabama" and into the continent's interior.

20. Popular from its publication in 1914, "The St. Louis Blues" was "the best selling song in any medium by 1930" (Gussow 75).

21. Both "The St. Louis Blues" and "The Memphis Blues" circulated widely in the American West through performances by minstrel troupes and sideshow bands (see Abbott and Seroff, especially 188–90). Because of the popularity of "The St. Louis Blues," the song was also frequently featured by the sideshow bands traveling with the Wild West Shows. Some Americans' first experience of "The St. Louis Blues" would have been as part of a traveling Wild West show.

22. Gardner continues, "Brown's *Narrative* contributed to making black St. Louis a deeply unexpected place for stories of and by African American residents" (*Unexpected* 27). This chapter of Gardner's book complicates that vision of St. Louis by looking at other contemporaneous accounts, including John Berry Meachum's *An Address to All the Colored Citizens of the United States*, which suggests "a story of a St. Louis that offered select free blacks . . . opportunities deeply tied to black unity, religious-industrial education, and especially western expansionism" (27).

23. Notes Painter, "In the end, only the refusal of riverboats to stop for Exodusters and their slow starvation on the banks of the Mississippi broke the movement's momentum" (196).

CHAPTER 2

1. Between 1913 and 1947, Micheaux published seven books, including *The Conquest: The Story of a Negro Pioneer* (1913), *The Homesteader* (1917), *The Wind from Nowhere* (1944), and *The Masquerade: An Historical Novel* (1947). Over roughly the same span, Micheaux produced and directed around forty films, beginning with his first silent movie in 1919, *The Homesteader* (based on his novel). Micheaux's film work has garnered more critical study than his books. See, for example, J. Ronald Green's *Straight Lick: The Cinema of Oscar Micheaux* (2000); Pearl Bowser and Louise Spence's *Writing Himself into History: Oscar Micheaux, His Silent Films, and His Audiences* (2000); Jane M. Gaines's *Fire and Desire: Mixed-Race Movies in the Silent Era* (2001); Pearl Bowser, Jane Gaines, and Charles Musser's *Oscar Micheaux and His Circle: African-American Filmmaking and Race Cinema of the Silent Era* (2001), an anthology of essays; and Gerald R. Butters Jr.'s *Black Manhood on the Silent Screen* (2002). For a discussion of Micheaux's novels, see Jayna Brown's "Black Patriarch on the Prairie: National Identity and Black Manhood in the Early Novels of Oscar Micheaux." For a thorough discussion of all Micheaux's novels, see Dan Moos, "Reclaiming the Frontier: Oscar Micheaux as Black Turnerian," which is particularly useful for an extended discussion of one of Micheaux's final novels, *The Wind from Nowhere*.

2. As an example of the white supremacist ideology of the Western, Barbara Will notes the "xenophobic and racist views put forth" in an 1895 essay, "The Evolution of the Cow-Puncher," by Owen Wister, author of the popular and influential Western, *The Virginian* (1902) (309). For Will, the essay explicitly states the racial philosophies that underlie the Western genre. Quoting from the essay, Will argues that Wister "glorifies the triumph of the racially pure, 'untamed Saxon' cowboy" over the "'encroaching alien vermin, that turn our cities to Babels and our citizenship to a hybrid farce'" (309). For Wister, the East is the place of hybridity, a racially mixed "Babel" that horrifies the pure Anglo-Saxon who fantasizes an American West where the white cowboy naturally rises to the top and triumphs over all others.

3. Although I refer primarily to the general tendencies of the Western, I occasionally refer to Owen Wister's *The Virginian* as a specific example for comparison. I have chosen to use *The Virginian* for several reasons, including that it falls roughly within the same time period as Micheaux's novel. Also, *The Virginian* is widely regarded as a foundational text in establishing the genre's conventions. Finally, Micheaux was apparently familiar enough with the book to make a comparison with *The Homesteader* potentially revelatory in examining the way he revised this source material (Bowser and Spence 9).

4. Minor characters in the novel make occasional jokes about the hero's "French name," referring to him as John the Baptist or as St. Jean Baptiste. The choice of name also points to the history of African American participation in westward expansion, to Jean Baptiste Point du Sable, the pioneer settler (originally from Haiti) who established the first permanent settlement in what is now Chicago.

5. Of the students (including himself) studying at Hampton Institute, Washington comments, "The great and prevailing idea that seemed to take possession of every one was to prepare himself to lift up the people at his home. No one seemed to think of himself" (36). Although Washington encourages individual success in *Up from Slavery*, he, like

Micheaux, emphasizes that individual actions contribute to the collective good of "lift[ing] up the people at his home."

6. In his philosophical position on "the race question," Micheaux is by no means an anomaly among African American writers of this period. In fact Micheaux's uplift plot has much in common with the black women writers (such as Frances Watkins Harper, Pauline Hopkins, and Amelia E. Johnson) of the post-Reconstruction period (1877–1915) that Claudia Tate discusses in *Domestic Allegories of Political Desire* (1992). These women, Tate states, "repeatedly wrote novels about the moral development, spiritual maturation, professional aspirations, and economic advancement of and of course social justice for black Americans," goals that were frequently inscribed "within the familiar marriage plot of nineteenth-century white women's sentimental fiction" (11). As in *The Homesteader*, the "successful marriage" in these works symbolizes not only individual fulfillment but also the possibility of "society's reform" (11).

7. A comparable example from *Up from Slavery* involves Washington's decision to teach the trade of brick making at Tuskegee Institute. Washington comments, "The individual who can do something that the world wants done will, in the end, make his way regardless of his race. One man may go into a community prepared to supply the people there with an analysis of Greek sentences. The community may not at that time be prepared for, or feel the need of, Greek analysis, but it may feel its need of bricks and houses and wagons" (91).

8. Such behaviors relate to environment and disposition and are not innate racial traits, according to Micheaux's philosophies. He provides examples of white characters who also have "undependable habits" (*Homesteader* 161). He likewise includes African American characters who embody the qualities he admires. For the most part, these characters are peripheral to the central plot, which focuses on Baptiste's efforts to reform "the average colored man" and woman (107).

9. For a discussion of twoness in Micheaux's films, see Green. Green argues that Micheaux's films have a "non-assimilative style" that reflects rather than glosses over "the turmoil of [the] struggle" of double-consciousness (49). Twoness in Micheaux's films is symbolized by the tension created by the desire both to emulate Hollywood films (with their high production values) and to reject the "glossy illusionism" of those films in favor of what Green calls an "aesthetics of moderation," a rougher but intentionally less spectacular style of filmmaking (48, 29).

10. See especially Bederman's discussions of African American prize fighter Jack Johnson (1–10, 20–23, 41–42) and of Ida B. Wells's antilynching campaign (45–78).

11. Both McCarthy and McCraline are based on Micheaux's father-in-law, N. J. McCracken, an elder in the African Methodist Church. For a discussion of the relationship between events in Micheaux's life and his re-creation of those events in his artistic work, see VanEpps-Taylor; McGilligan.

12. As Bowser and Spence note, in the various incarnations of his biographical legend, "there are contradictory, even multiple, Micheauxes" (39). Baptiste's refusal to flatter McCarthy and "make him think he's a king" contrasts sharply with Micheaux's actions (210). According to Bowser and Spence, "To survive in business, Micheaux drew upon all his considerable resourcefulness. He acted shrewdly, often with guile and not infrequently

with subterfuge" (17). To "outwit his foes" (such as white-dominated censor boards), he used "calculated flattery and psychological trickery" (17). Baptiste's condemnation of such tactics may reveal him as an idealized version of his author, or Baptiste's unwillingness to resort to "calculated flattery" might be interpreted as a character flaw. Orlean, distraught and emotionally fragile in wake of the death of her firstborn child, is left alone with her father, who continually works to poison her opinion of her husband. The pressure of being pulled in opposite directions by husband and father causes her condition to worsen. Jean Baptiste "could have settled matters . . . by sacrificing principle" (261). But although "he could have sentimentally appeased his father-in-law," Micheaux writes, "Jean Baptiste at no time sacrificed his manhood for any cause"—not even for the sake of his wife's emotional and physical health (262).

13. Although Micheaux writes the novel in third person and occasionally switches among different narrative perspectives, much of the book is filtered through Baptiste's consciousness as we see events from his point of view. Baptiste's perspective presents the reader with a distorted view of the events surrounding his marriage. Those events might be interpreted in terms of a delayed working through of Baptiste's Oedipal conflict, with Orlean substituting for the desired mother and McCarthy for the forbidding father. Baptiste's unnatural desire for his mother is displaced onto the relationship between Orlean and the reverend, which the novel clearly represents as emotionally incestuous. The submerged sexual nature of that relationship is implied by the murder-suicide, in which Orlean stabs the reverend's in his bed before killing herself. For further discussion of Micheaux and Oedipal conflict, see Green, especially 15–17.

CHAPTER 3

1. Rose Gordon's unpublished writings are in the Emmanuel Taylor Gordon Family Papers, 1882–1980 (Manuscript Collection 150), Montana Historical Society Archives, Helena.

2. In their discussion of Anita Scott Coleman's writing in her *Western Echoes of the Harlem Renaissance*, Cynthia Davis and Verner D. Mitchell observe the importance of the concept of home not only in Coleman's western writing but in the work of African American women writers in general: "The home space functions as a refuge from injustice, misunderstanding, and discrimination in the work of number of black women writers" (4). In Coleman's writing, "home is not a restrictive space or a domestic prison for women, or even an escape from racist reality, but a site of agency for the African American family. Home thus functions as both a response to and a goal of migration and diaspora" (5).

3. "Herein lie buried many things which if read with patience may show the strange meaning of being black here in the dawning of the Twentieth Century," writes Du Bois; "This meaning is not without interest to you, Gentle Reader; for the problem of the Twentieth-Century is the problem of the color-line" (1).

4. For a brief overview of Gordon's life, see Sherfy.

5. Gordon Papers, Box 9, Folder 5.

6. Letter, 15 March 1951, Gordon Papers, Box 7, Folder 11.

CHAPTER 4

1. The films discussed here represent a sampling of Westerns that include black characters. For a discussion of a broader range of films, see Loy, especially 184–96. Particularly informative is Loy's discussion of African American actor Fred "Snowflake" Toones, who appeared with such stars as Gene Autry and John Wayne in many of Republic Picture's serial Westerns. Loy also provides a listing of Westerns (with brief synopses) from 1930 to 1955 that included African American actors in their casts.

2. I follow Jeffries's later practice of using Herb Jeffries, the version of his name he used during his singing career, rather than his given name, Herbert Jeffrey, which appears on the film credits. Explaining this name change, Jeffries commented, "My original name that was used on the series of western films was Herbert Jeffrey. Later on, when I went with Duke Ellington's band, I had a record that was relatively successful and somebody spelled my name wrong on it. They spelled it Jeffries . . . and abbreviated my first name to Herb. I thought it was more euphonious than Herbert Jeffrey, and since I wasn't making motion pictures any longer, I decided to leave that name alone. Besides, there was six or seven hundred thousand records that had been sold, and we couldn't call 'em back, so I just said it doesn't matter. I continued to use Herb Jeffries" (Berry 46).

3. For a discussion of Buell's role in musical Westerns of the 1930s, including the production of his "now-cult classic *The Terror of Tiny Town*" (1938), see Miller 65.

4. Jeffries re-recorded some of the songs performed in the films for his album, *The Bronze Buckaroo Rides Again*.

5. *Harlem on the Prairie* premiered in New York on Broadway at the Rialto Theater. Jeffries commented, "We thought it would only be distributed in the black theaters, but with the help of Gene Autry we found a distributer down in Dallas, Texas, Saks Amusement [*sic*], and we were able to get the film total distribution, not only in the black theaters, but in white theaters as well" (Berry 48).

6. In *Two-Gun Man from Harlem*, the Four Tones are actually played by the group the Cats and the Fiddle. The song was re-recorded for later films by Jeffries and the Four Tones.

7. Other examples include *The Legend of Nigger Charley* (1972), starring Williamson, and *100 Rifles* (1969), starring Brown, Raquel Welch, and Burt Reynolds (filmed in Spain).

8. Mel Watkins suggests that Pryor was "perhaps influenced by Ishmael Reed's 'Hoodoo Western' *Yellow Back Radio Brokedown*" to begin a "script for a cowboy movie, which he called *Black Stranger*. That script led to Pryor's later efforts as a cowriter with Mel Brooks and others on *Blazing Saddles*" (540).

CHAPTER 5

1. For a discussion of Micheaux's complex relationship with George and Noble Johnson, see McGilligan 112–24.

2. Unlike Baptiste in *The Homesteader*, Van Allen does not go to the law to settle his issues with Driscoll; rather, Van Allen follows "Western" fashion and opts for a man-to-man fight, abandoning, at least for the moment, the civilized manliness that Devereaux

and Baptiste struggle to maintain in *The Conquest* and *The Homesteader*, respectively. For a more detailed discussion of gender roles in *The Symbol of the Unconquered*, see Johnson 93–97.

3. The intertitle also explains that as a result of this discovery, "enormous plumes of smoke now obscure the sky," and the film features a long shot of the landscape dominated by just such a cloud of smoke. As Green observes, "The shot of the black cloud over a rural town and otherwise pristine landscape is disturbing to the viewer in today's era of ecological awareness," although in 1920, when *Symbol* was filmed, this image would have been intended by the filmmaker and received by the audience as "a sign of progress, of American economic leadership, and of uplift for Micheaux's entrepreneurial hero and his race" (*With a Crooked* 64).

4. The music played over this opening sequence of explanatory titles is a vocal song, a spiritual performed by Donald Heywood's choir. Green identifies the song as a particular type of spiritual, a jubilee song. Jubilee spirituals "reflected a fusion of earthly and spiritual emancipation in the culture of slavery, the equating of the North with heaven, of the North Star with the star of Bethlehem, of the Ohio River with Jordan" (*With a Crooked* 122). The language of the jubilee song was widely applicable. We can see elements of the jubilee spiritual in the language used by the Exodusters to describe their journey to the "promised land" of Kansas. Micheaux's jubilee spiritual layered over the intertitle story of migration to Chicago in the context of a story based on his homesteading novels suggests a connection between these various migrations.

5. More accurately, in this scene, the Cats and the Fiddle appear as themselves rather than adopting the guise of the Four Tones, as at the beginning of the film.

6. The Deacon's invocation of the Eleventh Avenue Cowboys—"I used to ride down Eleventh Avenue in front of the train, waving the lantern"— references an actual Manhattan practice. According to the *Forgotten New York* web site, diesel and steam railroads "rumbled down the centers of a number of Manhattan avenues well into the" twentieth century. On West Street, "mounted cowboys held off traffic with a red flag" until 1934.

7. Sack Amusements also served as the distributor for the *Harlem* film series. Most of the films from the 1940s discussed in this chapter are part of the G. William Jones Film and Video Collection at Southern Methodist University. Neglected for many years, prints of the films were acquired in 1983 by SMU from storage in a warehouse in Tyler, Texas. Several of those films were made available in digitally restored editions through *The Tyler, Texas Black Film Collection* (2004) DVD box set. For more information on the interesting story of the "transformation of these objects from a pile of neglected canisters to the prized archival collection at Southern Methodist University" see Stewart, "Discovering" 147.

CHAPTER 6

1. Of particular note are actors James Edwards, Brock Peters, and Ossie Davis, all three of whom appeared with some regularity in film and television Westerns of the period. Edwards had one of the earliest African American TV Western roles as Batt in three 1960

"Texas John Slaughter" episodes of *Walt Disney's Wonderful World of Color* that starred Thomas Tryon as the title character. Sidney Poitier appeared in several film Westerns, including *Duel at Diablo* (1966), in which his character was a "raceless westerner," a supplier of horses for the U.S. Cavalry who ends up joining the soldiers on a disastrous mission, and *Buck and the Preacher* (1972), which Poitier also directed.

2. In addition to appearing in two episodes of *Rawhide* (playing different characters in each), Strode also guest starred in an episode of *Daniel Boone*, "Goliath" (29 September 1966), in which he played the title character, a slave whose wrestling skills (taking advantage of Strode's professional wrestling experience for the climactic wrestling match) not only win the day but also earn him his freedom. Set specifically in frontier Kentucky (but filmed in California), *Daniel Boone* evokes a more general notion of the frontier than it does any particular place. The series is also notable for frequently including the stories of fugitive and former slaves in its plots, with Boone often aiding fugitives in their quests for freedom.

3. This chapter does not attempt to provide a comprehensive overview of all African American roles in television and film Westerns of the 1960s and 1970s. Collecting and cataloging the archive of the African American West in this era of television and cinema is a task that still needs to be done, but it is too big a topic for this chapter. Rather, I emphasize here close readings of select group of representative texts.

4. Koven suggests that these films, even those made during the blaxploitation era (roughly 1970–74, according to Koven), might be best considered "blaxploitation-by-association" rather than as "part of the Blaxploitation genre/movement" (142, 141). For example, Koven describes the Italian-made *Take a Hard Ride* (1975), which features blaxploitation stars Jim Brown, Fred Williamson, and Jim Kelly, as "very much a late-period spaghetti western and not a Blaxploitation film at all," which is not to say, he observes, that "the film isn't a cracker of a spaghetti western" (141). Italian-made Westerns of the 1960s and 1970s frequently featured (or included) African American actors, including Strode. Neil Campbell suggests that Sergio Leone frequently cast his films with an eye toward "using different nationalities" to give the films "immediate multicultural impact," sometimes "deliberately miscasting actors whose ethnicity conflicts with their role" (*Rhizomatic* 141). By "deliberately going against the grain" and "jumbling ethnicities," Leone demonstrates "the actual (but often hidden) multiculturalism of the West" (141). The presence of African American actors in Italian-made Westerns is another possible area of investigation for the continuing documentation of the African American West in cinema.

5. Coincidentally or not, the outcome of this story has parallels in African American folklore (and it is certainly possible that the screenwriter of the episode, knowing that Davis would be in the cast, drew on black folktales in writing the script). In one example of this type of story, in which an outmatched combatant tricks his opponent into abandoning the contest because he believes the trickster has superior skills, one master bets another that his slave "will whip the one you got, or else take his nerve so he won't fight" (Courlander 434). The trickster slave digs up a tree, replants it in a hole at the contest site, and puts "some leaves around to make it look like the tree growed there" (435). He tells his master to tie him to the tree, as if he is so fierce that that is the only way to control him. The trickster eventually displays his "strength" by pulling up the (rootless) tree. Like Lovett in

The Rifleman, the opponent is so frightened by the display of "superior" strength and skill that he runs off before the contest takes place.

6. For example, Isaiah in *Cimarron,* Davis in *The Rifleman,* Strode in *Rawhide,* Gossett in *Alias: Smith and Jones,* Freeman in *Unforgiven.* Mario Van Peebles's film, *Posse,* cleverly evokes the "stereotype of the single black westerner" by inverting it—with Stephen Baldwin's Jimmy Teeters as the single *white* member of the "posse." True to (inverted) type, he also dies heroically before the end of the film.

7. As Strode observes in his autobiography, director and screenwriter "Richard Brooks uses an opening scene to explain the Negro side" of the character, but "the movie doesn't make mention of my Indian side. Richard Brooks just stuck a bow in my hand" (Strode and Young 225).

8. This convention is reversed in *Buck and the Preacher* (1972), directed by Sidney Poitier. Chased by a posse after a bank robbery, Buck and Preacher are saved by a tribe of Indians, who arrive just in time to prevent the posse from overtaking the two "outlaws."

9. In addition to Davis and James Edwards, other credited actors include Felix Nelson and Roy Glenn. Both Edwards and Glenn appear frequently in television series throughout the 1950s and 1960s, including small parts in several Westerns.

10. The theme song played over the opening credits for *Sergeant Rutledge* is "Captain Buffalo," which is about a model African American soldier. It refers to "top soldier" Rutledge as well as making clear the connection between the troops in the film and the buffalo soldiers of history—although the term *buffalo soldier* is not mentioned until later in the film.

11. Gabe's comments here echo those of Braxton Rutledge in *Sergeant Rutledge*: "It was all right for Mr. Lincoln to say we were free, but that ain't so. Not yet. Maybe someday, but not yet."

12. Strode subsequently returns to *Rawhide* in "The Incident of the Boomerang" (24 March 1961), playing the role of Binnaburra, a goateed and boomerang-slinging scout traveling with an Australian ranch owner who wants to take a herd of American cattle back to Australia. (He plans to drive them to the coast and load them on a ship.) Binnaburra is something of a muddled character: He bears scarification marks on his forehead, has an astonishing ability to take out enemies with his boomerang, and is named for an Australian place; he also speaks Australian slang with an American accent, has an American scout's knowledge of western geography and climate, and is played by a mixed-race Native American and African American. Is he an Australian Aborigine? An American given an Australian nickname by his employer? This ambiguity means that "The Incident of the Boomerang" does not fit quite neatly into the category of African American Western. Nonetheless, both "Boomerang" and "The Buffalo Soldier" allow Strode to play fierce characters, to shed the meekness and accommodating demeanor of the characters he plays in *Liberty Valance* and *The Professionals.*

13. Later television series will also be more explicit in addressing the issue of slavery. Several episodes of *Daniel Boone* from the late 1960s feature stories of fugitive slaves traveling through Boone's frontier Kentucky on their way north to freedom. In the episode "Onantha" (3 November 1966), Daniel and Mingo come across Onantha (Lila Perry), a

child separated from her parents, who are part of a group of fugitive slaves making their way to Canada. Daniel helps her catch up with the group, ultimately forging an alliance with the fugitives and helping them fend off a pair of slave hunters and escape. When one of the slave hunters argues that "in a civilized spot, my argument would prevail," Daniel responds, "We're a long way from civilization here." *Daniel Boone* repeatedly suggests that racism in general and slavery in particular are products of a corrupt civilization, and the value of the frontier as it is imagined in *Daniel Boone* is that it is indeed "a long way" from that civilization. In "My Name Is Rawls" (7 October 1965), Rawls (Rafer Johnson) is stealing furs to earn money for passage back to Africa. Although determined to stop the thefts, Daniel finds an alternate means for Rawls to seek his freedom, both stopping the problem with the furs and addressing the problem of injustice. "Onantha" and "My Name Is Rawls" are just two of many *Daniel Boone* episodes that address the issue of slavery.

14. The episode also makes particularly effective use of music. The arrival of the buffalo soldiers in Tucson is heralded by the sound of "The Camptown Races," with lyrics altered ("We bet our money on the buffalo") and adapted as a marching song. At a Sunday morning service led by Sergeant Major Creason, the episode comes to a pause while the soldiers sing the spiritual "Ain't Gonna Study War No More." When the soldiers leave town, law and order restored and their mission accomplished, they sing a variant of the "Sweet Thing"/"The Crawdad Hole" song, with lyrics again adapted for marching/riding soldiers.

15. *Posse* again suggests the iconic importance of Strode and of this shot in particular by including it in a montage of clips played during the film's closing title sequence.

16. Mikel Koven notes in *Blaxploitation Films* that "there is very little to recommend" *Adios Amigo*, although he acknowledges that "part of the problem may have been the viewing conditions under which I watched it: the DVD copy I bought was a dreadful pan-and-scan copy that didn't seem to be panning or scanning on anything in particular. Furthermore, the images themselves were so dark that it was often impossible to actually ascertain what was happening in the scene" (140). In my opinion, *Adios Amigo* is a good film in dire need of a better DVD transfer. Several different companies have made the film available on DVD, and, while there are better-quality DVDs than the one Koven viewed, none of them are particularly good. It is possible, however, to find copies of the film that at least have visible images throughout.

CHAPTER 8

1. Campbell quotes here from Jacques Derrida's "The Law of Genre." In the full quotation, Campbell argues that the post-Western exhibits "'a principle of contamination, a law of impurity, a parasitical economy . . . a sort of participation without belonging—a taking part in without being part of, without having membership in a set'" (quoted in Campbell, "Post-Western" 410).

2. The first suggestion of a name for the character occurs when he unzips his backpack to reveal a "Hello My Name Is" sticker with the name *Eli* written in. Whether the name Eli refers specifically to this person or is the name of someone else who had possession of the

backpack along the way is not clear. At the end of the film, after his death, the single word *Eli* is carved on his tombstone.

3. Gender, however, remains a marker of difference in *Eli*'s world. Solara ultimately escapes her gendered destiny as prostitute, victim, bait, or kept woman (the primary female roles in the film) and emerges as a machete-wielding heroine, but she is the exception.

4. Although written by Barry Gibb, "How Can You Mend a Broken Heart?," like most American popular music, also has roots in African American music, with, among other qualities, the repeated questions of its chorus suggesting the lyrical structure of a blues song.

5. Although Washington is one of Hollywood's most popular actors and has been featured in a variety of roles, he has also carefully chosen a number of signature roles that directly draw on African American history, from his Civil War soldier in *Glory* (1989) to his Oscar-nominated performance in the lead role in Spike Lee's *Malcolm X* (1992). Many filmgoers will bring the memory of those roles to the theater with them, and the knowledge of those earlier performances will provide part of the context for interpreting the character the actor plays in a given film, even when, and maybe especially when, an actor performs against type, as Washington does in playing the villain, a rogue cop, in *Training Day*, for which he received the Best Actor Oscar in 2001.

6. Lombardi is played by Malcolm McDowell in an uncredited role. McDowell's casting constitutes another knowing allusion to the history of one of *Eli*'s generic forerunners, *A Clockwork Orange*, one of the most famous dystopian future films and one in which McDowell plays the lead role.

7. When *Firefly* originally appeared on Fox, the network aired the episodes out of the intended order. When the series was released on DVD, Whedon returned them to their original sequence. The DVD also includes several episodes that never aired, so I do not include information about the original air dates, especially as most viewers of *Firefly* have watched it on DVD rather than through broadcast.

8. In *The Rhizomatic West*, Campbell defines third space as involving the "ability to think 'between' opposites simultaneously" and moving "between established parameters and binary oppositions" as a "means of rethinking space in a transdisciplinary manner" that "rejects the either/or perspective and recognizes instead a both/and logic that encourages new combinations alongside the mixing and hybridizing of thought and idea" (21, 25, 58–59). I thank Neil Campbell for the association of the interior space of the ship *Serenity* with the idea of third space. The idea for this section of the chapter originated with a panel discussion of *Firefly* that I cosponsored with Campbell at the 2008 Western Literature Association Conference. As a prelude to the panel, we used an online blog, Firefly and Western Literature. Several of the points raised in this chapter were first formed via that online discussion or during the conversation at the conference.

9. To the best of my knowledge, the only other instance when black women in a Western use guns are in *Posse*, when two characters help defend the town of Freemanville. Even in *Posse*, where one of the women is played by blaxploitation star Pam Grier, these are brief inset shots taking place away from the main action.

10. In a review of Rhonda Wilcox and Tanya Cochran's edited volume, *Investigating* Firefly *and* Serenity: *Science Fiction on the Frontier*, Corey Dethier observes that "while

some of the essays do touch on the problematics of the show," the contributions "could have gone much further than they did regarding legitimate concerns with tokenism and racial stereotypes" (219). Here, I emphasize what the series does well rather than what it does poorly, especially as I am viewing those characters in the context of a genre, the Western, that has portrayed black westerners poorly more often than that it has done so well. One problematic element of the series is that while it casts actors of African descent in a variety of nonstereotyped roles, suggesting that African people have survived the destruction of "Earth that was," African culture has not similarly survived, and there are very few indications of specifically African cultural elements in a mise-en-scène that is often used to suggest a multicultural mixture of global traditions, with the greatest emphasis on Asian influences. As Stanley C. Pelkey II writes, the *Firefly* universe suggests a fusion of "American and Chinese political systems and cultures," but it is puzzling that African cultures are not included in this mix, especially because individuals of African descent continue to exist in this universe and feature more prominently than do individuals of Asian descent in the series' stories (211). As Pelkey continues, the use of music as well as "the sets, costumes, props, and other visual elements in *Firefly* help to establish this blending of Eastern and Western cultures" (211). However, while "on the surface this is admirable," Pelkey examines how the music in particular "ironically perpetuat[es] stereotypical Western representation of Asian exoticism," using musical cues that generally suggest Asianness or the exotic for Western listeners but that are not actually drawn from Asian musical sources (211). Although "we hear and see representations of Chinese language, and we see many other elements of traditional Chinese culture," the lack of Chinese (or any other Asian group) characters, the lack of authentic Chinese music, and the reliance on generic musical signifiers of Asianness further efface "the real presence of Chinese people (not to mention those of Middle Eastern and Indian descent) and their culture in the series" (212).

CONCLUSION

1. The opening sequence is also an homage specifically to director Sergio Corbucci's *Django* (1966), one of the primary influences on *Django Unchained*. Both the red letters of the titles and the "Django" theme song that plays over the title sequence come directly from Corbucci's film.

2. Another precursor text to *Django Unchained* is *Skin Game* (1971), starring James Garner and Louis Gossett Jr., a film that similarly sets a black and white pair of con artists in the context of slavery. The "game" in *Skin Game* is that Garner's character repeatedly sells Gossett's character (and then helps him escape) to various marks across Missouri and Kansas. The *Skin Game* plot also has its source in Sergio Leone's *The Good, the Bad, and the Ugly*, where one character continually turns another into the sheriff's office for the bounty and then, at the last moment, saves him from hanging.

3. The "one hundred rifles" gathered by the marshal outside the saloon where Django and Schultz have taken refuge may be a reference to the title of a Jim Brown film, *100 Rifles*; similarly, the astonished response of the townspeople when Django and Schultz ride into a

Texas town (they have never seen, Django explains to Schultz, a black man on horseback) suggests dozens of similar scenes in African American Westerns, although the reference is probably specifically to *The Legend of Nigger Charlie*, as Shultz and Django's commandeering of the saloon when the bartender refuses to serve Django certainly is. Although related in a general way to the trickster tale, *Django Unchained*'s undercover infiltration of "Candie Land" is predominantly that of the con game or caper genre, and the emphasis is on role playing ("Stay in character," Schultz advises) rather than on "the spontaneous wit and verbal dexterity" that Mel Watkins sees as the central element of African American trickster tradition. However, Scott Reynolds Nelson suggests that *Django Unchained* draws on the "bad nigger" archetype of African American folklore (especially as that archetype was rendered cinematically through blaxploitation films) and thus might be connected to African American tradition through that archetype rather than through the trickster.

4. Again, this characterization seems to have developed from Tarantino's adaptation of the bounty hunter stories from Sergio Leone's films rather than from any specific awareness of how that character type has developed in African American Westerns.

5. In *Wounded*, for example, John Hunt comes to the conclusion that "Sometimes things were just simple. . . . The people you expect to do the bad thing did the bad thing. I believed the rednecks had done something to David and I was going to find out. Maybe I should called the sheriff, but I didn't know whom I could trust" (199). The novel ends with a showdown and a burst of violence.

6. For a discussion of Marrant's conjoining of the slave narrative with the frontier narrative of Indian captivity, see Johnson 31–45.

Bibliography

7 Women. Dir. John Ford. Perf. Anne Bancroft, Sue Lyon, Margaret Leighton, Woody Strode. MGM, 1966.

100 Rifles. Dir. Tom Gries. Perf. Jim Brown, Raquel Welch, Burt Reynolds. Twentieth Century Fox, 1969.

Abbott, Lynn, and Doug Seroff. *Ragged but Right: Black Traveling Shows, "Coon Songs," and the Dark Pathway to Blues and Jazz.* Jackson: University Press of Mississippi, 2007.

Adios Amigo. Dir. and writer Fred Williamson. Perf. Fred Williamson, Richard Pryor. Po' Boy Productions, 1976.

The Adventures of Briscoe County, Jr. Perf. Bruce Campbell, Julius Carry. Fox, 1993.

Allmendinger, Blake. "African Americans and the Popular West." *Updating the Literary West.* Ed. Dan Flores. Fort Worth: Western Literature Association, in association with Texas Christian University Press, 1997. 916–20.

———. "Deadwood Dick: The Black Cowboy as Cultural Timber." *Journal of American Culture* 16.4 (Winter 1993): 79–89.

———. *Imagining the African American West.* Lincoln: University of Nebraska Press, 2005.

———. *Ten Most Wanted: The New Western Literature.* New York: Routledge, 1998.

Ammons, Elizabeth. "Afterword: *Winona*, Bakhtin, and Hopkins in the Twenty-First Century." *The Unruly Voice.* Ed. John Cullen Gruesser. Urbana: University of Illinois Press, 1996. 211–19.

Anderson, Robert Ball. *From Slavery to Affluence: Memoirs of Robert Anderson, Ex-Slave.* 1927. Steamboat Springs, CO: Steamboat Pilot, 1988.

Ashe, Bertram D. "Theorizing the Post-Soul Aesthetic: An Introduction." *African American Review* 41.4 (Winter 2007): 609–23.

Baker, Houston A., Jr. *Blues, Ideology, and Afro-American Literature: A Vernacular Theory.* Chicago: University of Chicago Press, 1984.

———. *Long Black Song: Essays in Black American Literature and Culture.* Charlottesville: University Press of Virginia, 1972.

Beadling, Laura L. "The Threat of the 'Good Wife': Feminism, Postfeminism, and Third-Wave Feminism in *Firefly*." *Investigating Firefly and Serenity: Science Fiction on the Frontier.* Ed. Rhonda V. Wilcox and Tanya R. Cochran. London: Tauris, 2008. 53–62.

Beckwourth, James P. *The Life and Adventures of James P. Beckwourth as Told to Thomas D. Bonner.* Lincoln: University of Nebraska Press, 1972.

Bederman, Gail. *Manliness and Civilization: A Cultural History of Gender and Race in the United States, 1880–1917.* Chicago: University of Chicago Press, 1995.

Bell, Madison Smartt. Introduction. *God's Country.* Boston: Beacon, 2003. vii–ix.

Berardi, Gayle K., and Thomas W. Segady. "The Development of African American Newspapers in the American West, 1880–1914." *African Americans on the Western Frontier.* Ed. Monroe Lee Billington and Roger D. Hardaway. Niwot: University Press of Colorado, 1998. 217–30.

Berresford, Mark. *That's Got 'Em!: The Life and Music of Wilbur C. Sweatman.* Jackson: University Press of Mississippi, 2010.

Berry, S. Torriano. *The 50 Most Influential Black Films.* New York: Citadel, 2001.

The Big Lebowski. Dir. Joel Coen. Perf. Jeff Bridges, John Goodman. Polygram, 1998.

Black Gold. Perf. Lawrence Criner, Katherine Boyd. Norman Film Manufacturing, 1928.

Blazing Saddles. Dir. Mel Brooks. Perf. Cleavon Little. Warner Bros., 1974. DVD.

The Blood of Jesus. Dir. Spencer Williams. Perf. Spencer Williams, Cathryn Caviness. Amegro Films, 1941.

"Blue Boss and Willie Shay." *Lawman.* Perf. John Russell, Peter Brown, Sammy Davis Jr. ABC. 12 March 1961.

Body and Soul. Dir. Oscar Micheaux. Perf. Paul Robeson, Julia Theresa Russell, Mercedes Gilbert. Micheaux Film, 1925.

Bold, Christine. "Where Did the Black Rough Riders Go?" *Canadian Review of American Studies* 39.3 (2009): 273–97.

The Book of Eli. Dir. Hughes Brothers. Perf. Denzel Washington. Alcon Entertainment, 2010.

Boss Nigger. Dir. Jack Arnold. Writer Fred Williamson. Perf. Fred Williamson, D'Urville Martin. Dimension Pictures, 1975.

"The Bounty Hunter." *Alias: Smith and Jones.* Perf. Pete Duel, Ben Murphy, Louis Gossett Jr. ABC. 9 December 1971.

Bowser, Pearl, Jane Gaines, and Charles Musser, eds. *Oscar Micheaux and His Circle: African-American Filmmaking and Race Cinema of the Silent Era.* Bloomington: Indiana University Press, 2001.

Bowser, Pearl, and Louise Spence. *Writing Himself into History: Oscar Micheaux, His Silent Films, and His Audiences.* New Brunswick, NJ: Rutgers University Press, 2000.

Braxton, Joanne M. *Black Women Writing Autobiography: A Tradition within a Tradition.* Philadelphia: Temple University Press, 1989.

The Bronze Buckaroo. Dir. Richard C. Kahn. Perf. Herb Jeffries (credited as Herbert Jeffrey), Spencer Williams, Clarence Brooks, F. E. Miller, Lucius Brooks, the Four Tones. Original Music by Lew Porter. 1938. Videocassette. Timeless Video, 1993.

Brown, Jayna. "Black Patriarch on the Prairie: National Identity and Black Manhood in the Early Novels of Oscar Micheaux." *Oscar Micheaux and His Circle: African-American Filmmaking and Race Cinema of the Silent Era.* Ed. Pearl Bowser, Jane Gaines, and Charles Musser. Bloomington: Indiana University Press, 2001. 132–46.

Brown, William Wells. *Narrative.* 1847. *From Fugitive Slave to Free Man: The Autobiographies of William Wells Brown.* Ed. William L. Andrews. Columbia: University of Missouri Press, 2003.

Bruce, H. C. *The New Man: Twenty-Nine Years a Slave, Twenty-Nine Years a Free Man.* 1895. Lincoln: University of Nebraska Press, 1996.

The Brute. Dir. Oscar Micheaux. Perf. Evelyn Preer, Sam Langford. Micheaux Film, 1920.

Buck and the Preacher. Dir. Sidney Poitier. Perf. Sidney Poitier, Harry Belafonte. Columbia Pictures, 1972.

"The Buffalo Soldiers." *The High Chaparral*. Perf. Yaphet Kotto, Robert Doqui. NBC. 22 November 1968.

The Bull-Dogger. Perf. Bill Pickett, Anita Bush. Norman Film, 1923.

Burton, Art. *Black Gun, Silver Star: The Life and Legend of Frontier Marshal Bass Reeves*. Lincoln: University of Nebraska Press, 2007.

Butler, Octavia E. *Kindred*. New York: Doubleday, 1979.

Butters, Gerald R., Jr. *Black Manhood on the Silent Screen*. Lawrence: University Press of Kansas, 2002.

Campbell, Neil. "Post-Western Cinema." *A Companion to the Literature and Culture of the American West*. Ed. Nicolas S. Witschi. West Sussex: Blackwell, 2011. 409–24.

———. *The Rhizomatic West: Representing the American West in a Transnational, Global, Media Age*. Lincoln: University of Nebraska Press, 2008.

Cantor, Paul A. "'Order out of the Mud': *Deadwood* and the State of Nature." *The Philosophy of the Western*. Ed. Jennifer L. McMahon and B. Steve Csaki. Lexington: University Press of Kentucky, 2010. 113–38.

Cantwell, Robert. *When We Were Good: The Folk Revival*. Cambridge: Harvard University Press, 1996.

Carbine, Mary. "'The Finest outside the Loop': Motion Picture Exhibition in Chicago's Black Metropolis, 1905–1928." *Silent Film*. Ed. Richard Abel. New Brunswick, NJ: Rutgers University Press, 1996. 234–62.

"A Century of Greenwood County, KS History, 1875." 1997 [1968]. http://www.skyways.org/ genweb/greenwoo/century/1875.shtml.

Cimarron. Dir. Wes Ruggles. Perf. Richard Dix, Irene Dunne, Eugene Jackson. 1930. Videocassette. Warner Video, 2000.

Cleage, Pearl. *Flyin' West and Other Plays*. New York: Theatre Communications Group, 1999.

"Coals of Fire." *Frontier Circus*. Perf. Sammy Davis Jr. CBS. 4 January 1962.

Coleman, Anita Scott. *Western Echoes of the Harlem Renaissance: The Life and Writings of Anita Scott Coleman*. Ed. Cynthia Davis and Verner D. Mitchell. Norman: University of Oklahoma Press, 2008.

Courlander, Harold. *A Treasury of Afro-American Folklore*. New York: Marlowe, 1976.

The Cowboys. Dir. Mark Rydell. Perf. John Wayne, Roscoe Lee Browne. Warner Bros., 1972.

The Cowboys. Perf. Moses Gunn, Diana Douglas, Jim Davis. ABC, 1974.

Cripps, Thomas. "The Films of Spencer Williams." *Black American Literature Forum* 12.4 (Winter 1978): 128–34.

Daniel Boone. NBC. 1964–70.

A Daughter of the Congo. Dir. Oscar Micheaux. Perf. Joe Byrd, Katherine Noisette. Micheaux Film, 1930.

Davis, Lennard J. *Enforcing Normalcy: Disability, Deafness, and the Body*. 1995. *The Norton Anthology of Theory and Criticism*. Ed. Vincent B. Leitch. New York: Norton, 2001. 2400–2421.

Dead Presidents. Dir. Hughes Brothers. Perf. Larenz Tate, Keith David. Caravan, 1995.

Deadwood. HBO. 2004–6.

Dempsey, Mary A. "The Bronze Buckaroo Rides Again." *American Visions* 12.4 (August–September 1997): 23–25.

Derrida, Jacques. "The Law of Genre." *Critical Inquiry* 7.1 (Autumn 1980): 55–81.

"The Desperado." *Bonanza.* Perf. Louis Gossett Jr. NBC. 7 February 1971.

Destry Rides Again. Dir. George Marshall. Perf. Marlene Dietrich, James Stewart, Lillian Yarbo. 1939. Videocassette. MCA Home Video, 1987.

Dethier, Corey. Review. *Investigating* Firefly *and* Serenity: Science Fiction on the Frontier. Ed. Rhonda V. Wilcox and Tonya R. Cochran. *Western American Literature* 47.2 (Summer 2012): 218–19.

Detter, Thomas. *Nellie Brown; or, The Jealous Wife, with Other Sketches.* 1871. Lincoln: University of Nebraska Press, 1996.

Django. Dir. Sergio Corbucci. Perf. Franco Nero. B. R. C. Produzione, 1966.

Django Unchained. Dir. Quentin Tarantino. Perf. Jamie Foxx, Christoph Waltz, Leonardo DiCaprio, Kerry Washington. Columbia Pictures, 2012.

Drums along the Mohawk. Dir. John Ford. Perf. Claudette Colbert, Henry Fonda, Beulah Hall Jones. 1939. Videocassette. Key Video, 1988.

Du Bois, W. E. B.. *The Souls of Black Folk.* 1903. New York: Penguin, 1989.

Duel at Diablo. Dir. Ralph Nelson. Perf. Sidney Poitier. Cherokee Productions, 1966.

Durham, David Anthony. *Gabriel's Story.* 2001. New York: Anchor, 2002.

Early, Gerald. Introduction. *Lure and Loathing: Essays on Race, Identity, and the Ambivalence of Assimilation.* Ed. Gerald Early. New York: Penguin, 1993. xi–xxiv.

Easy Street. Dir. Oscar Micheaux. Perf. Lorenzo Tucker, Willor Lee Guilford. Micheaux Film, 1930.

Eaton, Kalenda. "I Wish They All Could Be Calafía Girls: Black Women and California's Cultural Mythology." Western Literature Association Conference, 7–10 November 2012.

Ellis, Trey. "The New Black Aesthetic." *Callaloo* 12.1 (Winter 1989): 233–43.

Ellison, Ralph. *Invisible Man.* 1952. New York: Vintage, 1995.

Erisman, Fred. "*Stagecoach* in Space: The Legacy of *Firefly.*" *Extrapolation* 47.2 (Summer 2006): 249–58.

Everett, Percival. "Alluvial Deposits." *Damned If I Do.* St. Paul, MN: Graywolf, 2004. 39–59.

———. *Assumption.* St. Paul, MN: Graywolf, 2011.

———. *Big Picture.* St. Paul, MN: Graywolf, 1996.

———. "Cerulean." *Big Picture.* St. Paul, MN: Graywolf, 1996. 1–24.

———. "Cry about a Nickel." *The Weather and Women Treat Me Fair.* Little Rock, AR: August House, 1987. 37–45.

———. *Cutting Lisa.* Baton Rouge: Louisiana State University Press, 1986.

———. *Damned If I Do.* St. Paul, MN: Graywolf, 2004.

———. "Dicotyles Tajacu." *Big Picture.* St. Paul, MN: Graywolf, 1996. 57–82.

———. *Erasure: A Novel.* Hanover: University Press of New Hampshire, 2001.

———. "Esteban." *The Weather and Women Treat Me Fair.* Little Rock, AR: August House, 1987. 64–73.

———. *Glyph*. St. Paul, MN: Graywolf, 1999.

———. *God's Country*. 1994. Boston: Beacon, 2003.

———. "A Good Home for *Hachita*." *The Weather and Women Treat Me Fair*. Little Rock, AR: August House, 1987. 16–26.

———. *Grand Canyon, Inc.* San Francisco: Versus, 2001.

———. "Squeeze." *Big Picture*. St. Paul, MN: Graywolf, 1996. 125–38.

———. "Turned Out." *Big Picture*. St. Paul, MN: Graywolf, 1996. 25–36.

———. *Walk Me to the Distance*. New York: Ticknor and Fields, 1985.

———. "Wash." *Big Picture*. St. Paul, MN: Graywolf, 1996. 93–110.

———. *Watershed*. 1996. Boston: Beacon, 2003.

———. *The Weather and Women Treat Me Fair*. Little Rock, AR: August House, 1987.

———. *Wounded*. St. Paul, MN: Graywolf, 2005.

The Exile. Dir. Oscar Micheaux. Perf. Eunice Brooks, Stanleigh Morrell. Micheaux Film, 1931.

Fine, Kerry. "She Hits Like a Man, but She Kisses Like a Girl: TV Heroines, Femininity, Violence, and Intimacy." *Western American Literature* 47.2 (Summer 2012): 153–73.

Firefly. Perf. Nathan Fillion, Gina Torres, Ron Glass. Creator and Executive Producer Joss Whedon. Fox. 2002–3.

Fisher, Rudolph. *The Conjure-Man Dies: A Mystery Tale of Dark Harlem*. 1932. Ann Arbor: University of Michigan Press, 1992.

A Fistful of Dollars. Dir. Sergio Leone. Perf. Clint Eastwood. Constantin Film, 1964.

Flamming, Douglas. *African Americans in the West*. Santa Barbara, CA: ABC-CLIO, 2009.

Fletcher, Tom. *100 Years of the Negro in Show Business*. 1954. New York: Da Capo, 1984.

Flipper, Henry O. *Black Frontiersman: The Memoirs of Henry O. Flipper, First Black Graduate of West Point*. 1916. Ed. Theodore D. Harris. Fort Worth: Texas Christian University Press, 1997.

For a Few Dollars More. Dir. Sergio Leone. Perf. Clint Eastwood, Lee Van Cleef. Constantin Film, 1965.

Fore, Steve. "'The Same Old Others: The Western, *Lonesome Dove*, and the Lingering Difficulty of Difference." *Velvet Light Trap* 27 (Spring 1991): 49–62.

Forgotten New York. "Manhattan's Steam Railroad." 2012. http://forgotten-ny.com/1999/08/manhattans-steam-railroad/.

Freud, Sigmund. *Jokes and Their Relation to the Unconscious*. 1905. Trans. James Strachey. New York: Norton, 1989.

———. "The 'Uncanny.'" 1919. *The Norton Anthology of Theory and Criticism*. 929–52.

From Hell. Dir. Hughes Brothers. Perf. Johnny Depp. Heather Graham. Twentieth Century Fox, 2001.

Gaines, Jane M. *Fire and Desire: Mixed-Race Movies in the Silent Era*. Chicago: University of Chicago Press, 2001.

Gaines, Kevin. "Assimilationist Minstrelsy as Racial Uplift Ideology: James D. Corrothers's Literary Quest for Black Leadership." *American Quarterly* 45.3 (September 1993): 341–69.

Gardner, Eric. Introduction. *Jennie Carter: A Black Journalist of the Early West*. Ed. Eric Gardner. Jackson: University Press of Mississippi, 2007. vii–xxxiii.

———. *Unexpected Places: Relocating Nineteenth-Century African American Literature.* Jackson: University Press of Mississippi, 2009.

Gates, Henry Louis, Jr. *The Signifying Monkey.* New York: Oxford University Press, 1988.

Gibbs, Mifflin Wistar. *Shadow and Light.* 1902. Lincoln: University of Nebraska Press, 1995.

Girl in Room 20. Dir. Spencer Williams. Perf. July Jones, Geraldine Brock. United Films, 1946. DVD. *Tyler, Texas Black Film Collection.*

Glasrud, Bruce A., and Charles A. Braithwaite, eds. *African Americans on the Great Plains: An Anthology.* Lincoln: University of Nebraska Press, 2009.

Glasrud, Bruce A., and Laurie Champion, eds. *The African American West: A Century of Short Stories.* Niwot: University Press of Colorado, 2000.

Glasrud, Bruce A., and Michael Searles, eds. *Buffalo Soldiers in the West: A Black Soldiers Anthology.* College Station: Texas A & M University Press, 2007.

Glasrud, Bruce A., and Cary D. Wintz, eds. *The Harlem Renaissance in the American West: The New Negro's Western Experience.* New York: Routledge, 2012.

Go Down, Death! Dir. Spencer Williams. Perf. Spencer Williams, Myra Hemmings. Harlemwood Studios, 1944.

Gone with the West. Dir. Bernard Gerard. Perf. James Caan, Stefanie Powers, Sammy Davis Jr. Cougar Productions, 1975.

The Good, the Bad, and the Ugly. Dir. Sergio Leone. Perf. Eli Wallach, Clint Eastwood, Lee Van Cleef. Constantin Film, 1966.

"The Good Samaritans." *Gunsmoke.* CBS. 10 March 1969.

Gordon, Emmanuel Taylor, Family Papers, 1882–1980. Manuscript Collection 150. Montana Historical Society Archives, Helena.

Gordon, Rose. "Gone Are the Days." Emmanuel Taylor Gordon Family Papers, 1882–1980. Manuscript Collection 150. Montana Historical Society Archives, Helena. Box 11, Folder 2.

———. "My Mother Was a Slave." *Meagher County News,* 25 May 1955.

———. Scrapbook. Emmanuel Taylor Gordon Family Papers, 1882–1980. Manuscript Collection 150. Montana Historical Society Archives, Helena. Box 13, Folder 7.

Gordon, Taylor. *Born to Be.* 1929. Lincoln: University of Nebraska Press, 1995.

Grandt, Jürgen E. *Shaping Words to Fit the Soul: The Southern Ritual Grounds of Afro-Modernism.* Columbus: Ohio State University Press, 2009.

Green, J. Ronald. *Straight Lick: The Cinema of Oscar Micheaux.* Bloomington: Indiana University Press, 2000.

———. *With a Crooked Stick—The Films of Oscar Micheaux.* Bloomington: Indiana University Press, 2004.

Griggs, Sutton E. *Imperium in Imperio.* 1899. New York: Arno, 1969.

Gronniosaw, James Albert Ukawsaw. *A Narrative of the Most Remarkable Particulars in the Life of James Albert Ukawsaw Gronniosaw, an African Prince, Written by Himself.* 1770. *Black Atlantic Writers of the Eighteenth Century.* Ed. Adam Potkay and Sandra Burr. New York: St. Martin's, 1995. 23–66.

Gussow, Adam. *Seems Like Murder Here: Southern Violence and the Blues Tradition.* Chicago: University of Chicago Press, 2002.

Handley, William R. "Detecting the Real Fictions of History in *Watershed*." *Callaloo* 28.2 (Spring 2005): 305–12.

Handy, W. C., ed. *Blues: An Anthology*. 1926. Bedford, MA: Applewood, 2001.

———. *Father of the Blues*. 1941. Ed. Arna Bontemps. New York: Da Capo, 1991.

Harlem after Midnight. Dir. Oscar Micheaux. Perf. Lorenzo Tucker, Dorothy Van Engle. Micheaux Film, 1932.

Harlem on the Prairie. Dir. Sam Newfield. Perf. Herbert Jeffries, Mantan Moreland, Flournoy E. Miller, Spencer Williams. Associated Features, 1938.

Harlem Rides the Range. Dir. Richard C. Kahn. Perf. Herb Jeffries (Herbert Jeffrey), Spencer Williams, Clarence Brooks, F. E. Miller, Lucius Brooks. 1939. Videocassette. Timeless Video, 1994.

Haunted Gold. Dir. Mack V. Wright. Perf. John Wayne, Sheila Terry, Blue Washington. 1933. Videocassette. MGM/UA Home Video, 1994.

Hell on Wheels. Perf. Common, Anson Mount. AMC. 2011–.

Hemenway, Robert. Introduction. *Born to Be*. Taylor Gordon. 1929. Seattle: University of Washington Press, 1975.

Higgins, Therese E. *Religiosity, Cosmology, and Folklore: The African Influence in the Novels of Toni Morrison*. New York: Routledge, 2001.

High Plains Drifter. Dir. Clint Eastwood. Perf. Clint Eastwood, Verna Bloom. Universal, 1973.

Himes, Chester. *If He Hollers Let Him Go*. 1945. New York: Thunder's Mouth, 1986.

The Homesteader. Dir. Oscar Micheaux. Perf. Evelyn Preer, Charles Lucas. Micheaux Book and Film, 1920.

Hopkins, Pauline. *Winona: A Tale of Negro Life in the South and the Southwest*. 1902. Hopkins, *The Magazine Novels of Pauline Hopkins*. New York: Oxford University Press, 1988. 285–437.

"The Incident of the Boomerang." *Rawhide*. Perf. Woody Strode, Clint Eastwood. CBS. 24 March 1961.

"The Incident of the Buffalo Soldier." *Rawhide*. Perf. Woody Strode, Clint Eastwood, Roy Glenn. CBS. 6 January 1961.

"The Incident of the Slave Master." *Rawhide*. Perf. Eric Fleming, Peter Lorre, Roy Glenn. CBS. 11 November 1960.

"Jesse." *Gunsmoke*. Perf. Brock Peters. CBS. 19 February 1973.

Jesse James. Dir. Henry King. Perf. Tyrone Power, Henry Fonda, Ernest Whitman. 1939. Videocassette. Twentieth Century Fox Home Entertainment, 1967.

Jeffries, Herb. *The Bronze Buckaroo Rides Again*. CD. Warner Bros. Records, 1995.

Jiles, Pauline. *The Color of Lightning*. New York: Morrow, 2009.

Johnson, Michael K. *Black Masculinity and the Frontier Myth in American Literature*. Norman: University of Oklahoma Press, 2002.

Katz, William Loren. *The Black West*. 1987. New York: Touchstone, 1996.

Kolodny, Annette. *The Lay of the Land: Metaphor as Experience and History in American Life and Letters*. Chapel Hill: University of North Carolina Press, 1975.

Koven, Mikel J. *Blaxploitation Films*. Harpenden: Kamera, 2010.

Krauth, Leland. "Undoing and Redoing the Western." *Callaloo* 28.2 (Spring 2005): 313–27.

Kun, Josh. *Audiotopia: Music, Race, and America*. Berkeley: University of California Press, 2005.

Lape, Noreen Groover. *West of the Border: The Multicultural Literature of the Western American Frontiers*. Athens: Ohio University Press, 2000.

The Law of Nature. Perf. Noble Johnson, Clarence Brooks. Lincoln Motion Picture, 1917.

Leab, Daniel J. *From Sambo to Superspade: The Black Experience in Motion Pictures*. Boston: Houghton Mifflin, 1975.

The Legend of Nigger Charlie. Dir. Martin Goldman. Perf. Fred Williamson, D'Urville Martin. Paramount, 1972.

Lerner, Neil. "Music, Race, and Paradoxes of Representation: Jubal Early's Musical Motif of Barbarism in 'Objects in Space.'" *Investigating* Firefly *and* Serenity: *Science Fiction on the Frontier*. Ed. Rhonda V. Wilcox and Tanya R. Cochran. London: Tauris, 2008. 183–90.

Lewis, Nathaniel, ed. *Unsettling the Literary West: Authenticity and Authorship*. Lincoln: University of Nebraska Press, 2003.

Leyda, Julia. "Black-Audience Westerns and the Politics of Cultural Identification in the 1930s." *Cinema Journal* 42.1 (Fall 2002): 46–70.

Lock, Graham. *Blutopia*. Durham, NC: Duke University Press, 1999.

Lonesome Dove. CBS. 1989.

Love, Nat. *The Life and Adventures of Nat Love, Better Known in the Cattle Country as "Deadwood Dick."* 1907. Lincoln: University of Nebraska Press, 1995.

Loy, R. Philip. *Westerns and American Culture, 1930–1955*. Jefferson, NC: McFarland, 2001.

Lutenski, Emily. *Beyond Harlem: New Negro Cartographies of the American West*. Lawrence: University Press of Kansas, forthcoming.

Man of the Frontier. Dir. B. Reeves Eason. Perf. Gene Autry, Smiley Burnette, Eugene Jackson. 1936. DVD. Alpha Video, 2002.

The Man Who Shot Liberty Valance. Dir. John Ford. Perf. Jimmy Stewart, John Wayne, Lee Marvin, Woody Strode. Paramount, 1962.

Marrant, John. *A Narrative of the Lord's Wonderful Dealings with John Marrant, a Black*. 1785. *Black Atlantic Writers of the Eighteenth Century*. Ed. Adam Potkay and Sandra Burr. New York: St. Martin's, 1995. 67–105.

Marvin, Thomas F. "Children of Legba: Musicians at the Crossroads in Ralph Ellison's *Invisible Man*." *American Literature* 68.3 (September 1996): 587–608.

McGilligan, Patrick. *Oscar Micheaux: The Great and Only*. New York: Harper Perennial, 2008.

McGrath, Charles. "The Visionaries: How Quentin Tarantino Concocted a Genre of His Own." *New York Times,* 19 December 2012.

Meachum, John Berry. *An Address to All the Colored Citizens of the United States*. Philadelphia: King and Baird, 1846.

Menace II Society. Dir. Hughes Brothers. Tyrin Turner, Larenz Tate. New Line Cinema, 1993.

Micheaux, Oscar. *The Conquest: The Story of a Negro Pioneer*. 1913. Lincoln: University of Nebraska Press, 1994.

——. *The Homesteader.* 1917. Lincoln: University of Nebraska Press, 1994.

——. *The Masquerade: An Historical Novel.* New York: Book Supply, 1947.

——. *The Wind from Nowhere.* New York: Book Supply, 1944.

Miller, Cynthia J. "Tradition, Parody, and Adaptation: Jed Buell's Unconventional West." *Hollywood's West: The American Frontier in Film, Television, and History.* Ed. Peter C. Rollins and John E. O'Connor. Lexington: University Press of Kentucky, 2005. 65–80.

"The Mission." *Zane Grey Theater.* Perf. Sammy Davis Jr. CBS. 12 November 1959.

Mitchell, Lee Clark. *Westerns: Making the Man in Fiction and Film.* Chicago: University of Chicago Press, 1996.

Moos, Dan. *Outside America: Race, Ethnicity, and the Role of the American West in National Belonging.* Lebanon, NH: University Press of New England, 2005.

——. "Reclaiming the Frontier: Oscar Micheaux as Black Turnerian." *African American Review* 36.3 (Autumn 2002): 357–81.

Morrison, Toni. *Paradise.* New York: Knopf, 1998.

"The Most Amazing Man." *The Rifleman.* Perf. Chuck Conners, Sammy Davis Jr. ABC. 26 November 1962.

"Mother Cooper." *Daniel Boone.* Perf. Fess Parker, Rosey Grier, Ethel Waters. NBC. 5 February 1970.

Murder in Harlem (original title: *Lem Hawkins' Confessions*). Dir. Oscar Micheaux. Perf. Andrew Bishop, Dorothy Van Engle, Clarence Brooks. Micheaux Film, 1935. DVD. *Tyler, Texas Black Film Collection.*

My Name Is Nobody. Dir. Tonino Valerii. Perf. Terence Hill, Henry Fonda. Rafran Cinematografica, 1973.

Neal, Mark Anthony. *Soul Babies: Black Culture and the Post-Soul Aesthetic.* New York: Routledge, 2002.

Nelson, Scott Reynolds. "*Django* Untangled: The Legend of the Bad Black Man." *Chronicle of Higher Education* 11 January 2013.

"The Night of the Returning Dead." *The Wild Wild West.* Perf. Robert Conrad, Ross Martin, Sammy Davis Jr. CBS. 14 October 1966.

Once upon a Time in the West. Dir. Sergio Leone. Perf. Claudia Cardinale, Henry Fonda, Charles Bronson, Jack Elam, Woody Strode. Paramount, 1968.

Painter, Nell Irvin. *Exodusters: Black Migration to Kansas after Reconstruction.* 1976. New York: Norton, 1986.

Pelkey, Stanley C., II. "Still Flyin'?: Conventions, Reversals, and Musical Meaning in *Firefly.*" *Buffy, Ballads, and Bad Guys Who Sing: Music in the Worlds of Joss Whedon.* Ed. Kendra Preston Leonard. Toronto: Scarecrow, 2011. 209–42.

Posse. Dir. Mario Van Peebles. Perf. Mario Van Peebles, Charles Lane, Woody Strode. Polygram, 1993.

The Professionals. Dir. Richard Brooks. Perf. Burt Lancaster, Robert Ryan, Lee Marvin, Woody Strode, Claudia Cardinale. Columbia Pictures, 1966.

The Realization of a Negro's Ambitions. Perf. Noble Johnson, Clarence Brooks. Lincoln Motion Picture, 1916.

Reed, Ishmael. *Yellow Back Radio Broke-Down.* 1969. McLean, IL: Dalkey Archive, 2000.

Reid, Mark. *Redefining Black Film*. Berkeley: University of California Press, 1993.

The Return of Frank James. Dir. Fritz Lang. Perf. Henry Fonda, Jackie Cooper, Ernest Whitman. 1940. Videocassette. Twentieth Century Fox Home Entertainment, 1968.

Riders of the Black Hills. Dir. George Sherman. Perf. Robert Livingston, Ray "Crash" Corrigan, Max Terhune, Fred "Snowflake" Toones. 1938. Videocassette. Republic Pictures Home Video.

Riley, Glenda. "African American Women in Western History: Past and Prospect." *African American Women Confront the West, 1600–2000*. Ed. Quintard Taylor and Shirley Ann Wilson Moore. Norman: University of Oklahoma Press, 2003. 22–27.

Riley, Peggy. "Women of the Great Falls African Methodist Episcopal Church, 1870–1910." *African American Women Confront the West, 1600–2000*. Ed. Quintard Taylor and Shirley Ann Wilson Moore. Norman: University of Oklahoma Press, 2003. 122–39.

Robin and the 7 Hoods. Dir. Gordon Douglas. Perf. Frank Sinatra, Dean Martin, Sammy Davis Jr. P-C Productions, 1964.

Rodríguez de Montalvo, Garci. *Sergas de Esplandián*. 1496–1510. Madrid: Editorial Castalia, 2003.

Russett, Margaret. "Race under *Erasure*." *Callaloo* 28.2 (Spring 2005): 358–68.

Scheckel, Susan. "Home on the Train: Race and Mobility in the *Life and Adventures of Nat Love*." *American Literature* 74.2 (June 2002): 219–50.

Scott, A. O. "The Black, the White and the Angry." *New York Times* 24 December 2012.

Serenity. Dir. Joss Whedon. Perf. Nathan Fillion, Gina Torres, Ron Glass. Universal Pictures, 2005.

Sergeant Rutledge. Dir. John Ford. Perf. Woody Strode. Warner Bros., 1961.

Sergeants 3. Dir. John Sturges. Perf. Frank Sinatra, Dean Martin, Sammy Davis Jr. Essex Productions, 1962.

Shapiro, Mark. "Bounty Hunter." *Starlog* 204 (July 1994): 27–30.

Sherfy, Marcella. "Rose Beatris Gordon." *African American National Biography*. Ed. Henry Louis Gates Jr. and Evelyn Brooks Higginbotham. Oxford: Oxford University Press, 2008. 3:556–58.

Siomopoulos, Anna. "The Birth of a Black Cinema: Race, Reception, and Oscar Micheaux's *Within Our Gates*." *The Moving Image* 6.1 (Fall 2006): 111–18.

Skin Game. Dir. Paul Bogart. Perf. James Garner, Louis Gossett Jr. Cherokee Productions, 1971.

Slotkin, Richard. *Gunfighter Nation: The Myth of the Frontier in Twentieth-Century America*. New York: Harper Perennial, 1993.

Sotiropoulos, Karen. *Staging Race: Black Performers in Turn of the Century America*. Cambridge: Harvard University Press, 2006.

The Soul of Nigger Charlie. Dir. Larry G. Spangler. Perf. Fred Williamson, D'Urville Martin. Paramount, 1973.

Speirs, Kenneth. "Writing Self (Effacingly): E-Race-D Presences in *The Life and Adventures of Nat Love*." *Western American Literature* 40.3 (Fall 2005): 301–20.

Stagecoach. Dir. John Ford. Perf. Claire Trevor, John Wayne, Andy Devine. Walter Wanger Productions, 1939.

Stanfield, Peter. *Hollywood, Westerns, and the 1930s: The Lost Trail.* Exeter: University of Exeter Press, 2001.

Stewart, Jacqueline Najuma. "Discovering Black Film History: Tracing the Tyler, Texas Black Film Collection." *Film History* 23.2 (June 2011): 147–73.

————. *Migrating to the Movies: Cinema and Black Urban Modernity.* Berkeley: University of California Press, 2005.

Strode, Woody, and Sam Young. *Goal Dust.* New York: Madison Books, 1990.

The Symbol of the Unconquered. Dir. Oscar Micheaux. Perf. Iris Hall, Walker Thompson, Lawrence Chenault. Micheaux Book and FIlm, 1920.

Take a Hard Ride. Perf. Jim Brown, Fred Williamson. Bernsen-Ludwig-Bercovici Productions, 1975.

Tate, Claudia. *Domestic Allegories of Political Desire: The Black Heroine's Text at the Turn of the Century.* New York: Oxford University Press, 1992.

Taylor, Quintard. *In Search of the Racial Frontier: African Americans in the American West, 1528–1990.* New York: Norton, 1998.

Taylor, Quintard, and Shirley Ann Wilson Moore, eds. *African American Women Confront the West, 1600–2000.* Norman: University of Oklahoma Press, 2003.

"Texas John Slaughter: Apache Friendship." *Walt Disney's Wonderful World of Color.* Perf. Tom Tryon, Gene Evans, James Edwards. ABC. 19 February 1960.

"Texas John Slaughter: Geronimo's Revenge." *Walt Disney's Wonderful World of Color.* Perf. Tom Tryon, Betty Lynn, James Edwards. ABC. 4 March 1960.

"Texas John Slaughter: Kentucky Gunslick." *Walt Disney's Wonderful World of Color.* Perf. Tom Tryon, Darryl Hickman, James Edwards. ABC. 26 February 1960.

Thompson, Era Bell. *Africa: Land of My Fathers.* New York: Doubleday, 1954.

————. *American Daughter.* 1946. St. Paul: Minnesota Historical Society Press, 1986.

Thomson, Rosemarie Garland. *Extraordinary Bodies: Figuring Physical Disability in American Culture and Literature.* New York: Columbia University Press, 1997.

————. *Staring: How We Look.* Oxford: Oxford University Press, 2009.

Tompkins, Jane. *West of Everything: The Inner Life of Westerns.* New York: Oxford University Press, 1992.

The Trackers. Dir. Earl Bellamy. Perf. Sammy Davis Jr., Ernest Borgnine. ABC. 14 December 1971.

Trooper of Troop K. Perf. Noble Johnson, Beulah Hall. Lincoln Motion Picture, 1916.

Two-Gun Man from Harlem. Dir. Richard C. Kahn. Perf. Herb Jeffries (Herbert Jeffrey), Clarence Brooks, Margaret Whitten, Mantan Moreland, Spencer Williams, the Four Tones. Original Music by Herb Jeffries (Herbert Jeffrey). 1938. Videocassette. Timeless Video, 1993.

"Two Ounces of Tin." *The Rifleman.* Perf. Chuck Conners, Sammy Davis Jr. ABC. 19 February 1962.

Two Rode Together. Dir. John Ford. Perf. James Stewart, Richard Widmark, Woody Strode. Columbia Pictures, 1961.

Tyler, Texas Black Film Collection. G. William Jones Film and Video Collection/Hamon Arts Library at Southern Methodist University, 2004. Three-disk DVD set.

Underworld. Dir. Oscar Micheaux. Perf. Oscar Polk, Ethel Moses. Micheaux Pictures, 1937.

Unforgiven. Dir. Clint Eastwood. Perf. Clint Eastwood, Morgan Freeman, Gene Hackman. Warner Bros., 1992.

VanEpps-Taylor, Betti Carol. *Oscar Micheaux, a Biography: Dakota Homesteader, Author, Pioneer Film Maker.* Rapid City, SD: Dakota Press, 1999.

Wallace, Michele. "Oscar Micheaux's *Within Our Gates:* The Possibilities for Alternative Visions." *Oscar Micheaux and His Circle: African-American Filmmaking and Race Cinema of the Silent Era.* Ed. Ed. Pearl Bowser, Jane Gaines, and Charles Musser. Bloomington: Indiana University Press, 2001. 54–66.

Washington, Booker T. *Up from Slavery.* 1901. Ed. William L. Andrews. Oxford: Oxford University Press, 1995.

Watkins, Clifford Edward. *Showman: The Life and Music of Perry George Lowery.* Jackson: University of Mississippi Press, 2003.

Watkins, Mel. *On the Real Side: A History of African American Comedy from Slavery to Chris Rock.* New York: Simon and Schuster, 1994.

Where's My Man To-Nite. Dir. Spencer Williams. Perf. Emmet Jackson, George T. Sutton. Bourgeois-Jenkins Pictures, 1943. DVD. *Tyler, Texas Black Film Collection.*

Whitaker, Matthew C. *Race Work: The Rise of Civil Rights in the Urban West.* Lincoln: University of Nebraska Press, 2005.

Whitney, Salem Tutt. "Seen and Heard while Passing." *Indianapolis Freeman* 20 March 1915.

Wilcox, Rhonda V., and Tanya R. Cochran, eds. *Investigating* Firefly *and* Serenity: *Science Fiction on the Frontier.* London: Tauris, 2008.

Wild Horse. Dir. Richard Thorpe and Sidney Algier. Perf. Hoot Gibson, Alberta Vaughn, Stepin Fetchit. 1931. Videocassette. Hollywood Select Video, 1995.

Will, Barbara. "The Nervous Origins of the American Western." *American Literature* 70.2 (June 1998): 293–316.

Wister, Owen. *The Virginian: A Horseman of the Plains.* 1902. Lincoln: University of Nebraska Press, 1992.

Within Our Gates. Dir. Oscar Micheaux. Perf. Evelyn Preer, William Starks, E. G. Tatum, Lawrence Chenault. Micheaux Book and Film, 1920.

Young, Joseph A. *Black Novelist as White Racist: The Myth of Black Inferiority in the Novels of Oscar Micheaux.* Westport, CT: Greenwood, 1989.

Index